Editor: Ellen J. Hawes

Continuity Editor: Kevin Kulp

Graphic Design, Layout, and Prepress: Don Rosso

Cover Artist: Ken Kelly

Interior Artists: Scott Drouin, Andrew Hale, Jeremy Mohler, John O'Connor, Scott Purdy, Jim Zubkavich

Additional Playtest and Design: Matt Beall, Matt (Eridanis) Bogen, Craig (Upper_Krust) Cochrane, Greg (dinkeldog) Dinkelman, Brannon (Ashy) Hollingsworth, Kevin (Piratecat) Kulp, Brian Lasater, Keith (pogre) Pogue, John (jonrog) Rogers, Eric Tam, Steve "Conan" Trustrum, Alex (Plane Sailing) White.

Open Gaming Content

This product is produced under the terms of the Open Gaming License v1.0a and the d20 System License v5.0. A copy of the Open Gaming License may be found at the end of this book. Open Content consists of rules-related text only.

All game mechanics within this work are designated Open Content. Publishers who wish to use only a portion of the Open Content contained within this work are encouraged to contact Bad Axe Games (support@badaxegames.com) to obtain an abbreviated copyright notice specific to the Chapter or the Open Content they wish to reuse.

Designation of Product Identity

The following items are hereby designated as Product Identity:

1. The name "Bad Axe Games" as well as all identifying marks of Bad Axe Games, LLC., including but not limited to the Bad Axe Games logo, the CORE logo, and the phrase "Games With Grit;"
2. The product name "Grim Tales" except for its use within Section 15 of the Open Game License;
3. All artwork, illustration, trade dress, and graphic design including any text contained within such artwork, illustration or graphic design;
4. The text and language used to describe the game mechanics in Chapter Five, Eight, Nine, Ten, Eleven, and Twelve;
5. The Fight or Flight metagame found in Chapter Ten: Horror and Insanity.

Copyright and Trademark Notice

The Core Mechanic Explanatory Notice

This product uses the CORE MECHANIC task resolution method:

. Roll a d20.
. Add any relevant modifiers.
. Compare the result to a target number to determine success or failure.

The CORE logo is a trademark of Bad Axe Games, LLC.

This product requires the use of a Roleplaying Game Core Book published by Wizards of the Coast, Inc.

The *Dungeons & Dragons, Third Edition* Core Books, and/or the *d20 Modern Roleplaying Game*, published by Wizards of the Coast, Inc., are recommended for this purpose.

BA03201: GRIM TALES, First Printing. ISBN: 0-9720416-9-9. Copyright 2004, Bad Axe Games, LLC. www.badaxegames.com

TABLE OF CONTENTS

Introduction

What is Grim Tales?

Is Grim Tales a campaign setting?

No. Grim Tales is a rulebook, designed to allow experienced GMs to run exciting, low-magic, high-adventure campaigns from any genre, but particularly "pulp"-style fantasy and sci-fi genres. Grim Tales provides the rules you need to play in the worlds of your favorite books, movies, comic books, computer games, and so on.

Is Grim Tales a stand-alone rulebook?

Grim Tales is designed for experienced GMs and players who are already familiar with the d20 System rules; thus, this product requires the use of a core rulebook published by Wizards of the Coast. In particular, we recommend the *d20 Modern Roleplaying Game*, which you will find a useful and complete reference for weapons, equipment, monsters, spells, combat resolution, and so forth. Even if you intend to run a swords-and-sorcery style game in an archaic era, the *d20 Modern Roleplaying Game* remains your best resource. If you already own the *Dungeons and Dragons* Players' Handbook, the DMG, and/or the MM, you will find them a useful resource as well.

Because Grim Tales is built upon the foundations of the d20 System, you can use material from nearly any d20-compatible source: equipment, spells, monsters, feats, and so on. Some chapters herein also explain how to "import" your favorite material from other sources.

How is Grim Tales Different?

Grim Tales is different from most d20 campaigns, even the games presented in the official rulebooks, primarily because it is low-magic. There are fewer magic spells and magic items to bolster the heroes, who nevertheless must contend with all-new threats and challenges. Horrific encounters can cause even an experienced group of adventurers to break and flee. Low-level creatures that are laughably ineffective in high-fantasy games become deadly threats to characters without magic weapons, armor, or healing. The lowliest demon becomes a force to contend with when there are no holy weapons to bypass its damage reduction...

Of course, magic is not totally non-existent. Many of the threats the heroes will face wield dark and terrible magic, and many supernatural creatures still stalk the shadows. The primary difference between Grim Tales and high fantasy games is that magic is not an everyday tool; indeed, it is more likely to be feared, shunned, or viewed with great suspicion. Magic is the tool of the enemy; the heroes may use magic, but it is usually at a terrible price.

GM's Playground

Most importantly, Grim Tales allows the GM to get "under the hood" of his campaign and tweak the rules to his liking. Within this book you will find rules to customize classes, skills, feats, and talents; to tinker with the lethality of combat in your campaign; to add campaign components *a la carte* such as spellcasting, horror, firearms, cyberware, vehicles, and so on; rules for using and converting monsters from other d20 sources, as well as for creating your own monsters from scratch; and rules for designing balanced encounters, engaging adventures, epic campaigns, and awarding experience accordingly.

Threat Levels

Many of the options presented in this book are presented in varying threat levels.

☠ One skull means the variant is the most forgiving, slanted in the PCs favor, for campaigns with heroic action and piles of dead bad guys.

☠☠ Two skulls is a moderate threat level; the standard for most games.

☠☠☠ Three skulls is a high threat level, slanted in favor of the rat-bastard GM and likely to end in a pile of dead good guys.

Characters

Characters in Grim Tales are unlike the characters in most roleplaying games; they are among the most self-reliant heroes you will find in any game system. The core character classes, feats, talents, and skills combine to create a great deal of flexibility in character design. Rather than pushing characters into preconceived roles or "classes" within each campaign, you can create a character that more closely matches your heroic vision.

The six core classes of Grim Tales are defined in broad terms by the ability score upon which the class primarily relies: the Strong hero (Strength), the Fast hero (Dexterity), the Tough hero (Constitution), the Smart hero (Intelligence), the Dedicated hero (Wisdom), and the Charismatic hero (Charisma).

If you want to play a "fighter," for example, your first inclination might be to play a Strong hero. But what if you want to play a rapier-and-pistol wielding swashbuckler? Easy enough: add a few levels of Fast hero. By combining the core classes with the proper feats and talents, you can play nearly any character you can imagine, in any era.

Ability Scores

The six ability scores are Strength, Dexterity, Constitution, Intelligence, Wisdom, and Charisma. Your GM will advise you on how to generate and assign these ability scores. As a point of reference, "ordinaries"– that is, the vast cast of non-heroic supporting characters who populate the game world– have a standard score array of 15, 14, 13, 12, 10, and 8, assigned across the six abilities. Your GM will advise you how to generate ability scores and the degree to which your hero exceeds the "ordinary" ability score array, if any.

Grim Tales features rules that use the six ability scores in new and important ways. Players are advised to consider carefully when assigning ability scores.

Strength

Strength is the most important attribute, because it determines your bonuses to hit and damage in combat, and governs how much equipment your hero can carry. In addition, if the campaign allows spellcasting, a high Strength will allow a character to cast more spells before succumbing to physical exhaustion.

Dexterity

This ability score is perhaps the most unchanged from standard d20 rules. Dexterity is the most important attribute because it improves your character's ranged attack rolls, initiative, and armor class. Because most Grim Tales campaigns are very low magic, magical armor and other protective devices are hard to come by. Every ounce of armor class your character can scrape out is very important, and Dexterity's importance is similarly increased.

Constitution

Constitution is the most important attribute because it keeps your character alive. In addition to improving your character's hit points, the single most important change to Constitution is to the Massive Damage Threshold. Any attack that exceeds your character's Massive Damage Threshold is potentially a deadly strike, regardless of hit points. A character with many hit points but a low Con score is often more vulnerable than a character with fewer hit points but a respectable Con.

Intelligence

Intelligence is the most important attribute because it governs how many skill points you have to spend. Because Grim Tales is a low-magic campaign, you will find your characters relying more on their skills than on their equipment. A high Int score will give your character more skill points to spend on those all-important skills.

Wisdom

Wisdom is the most important attribute because it strengthens your character's willpower. When magic does crop up in Grim Tales, it is more often in the hands of the enemy. Wisdom is extremely important in fending off magical and mental attacks, in addition to increasing your character's chances of surviving a horrific encounter.

Charisma

Charisma is the most important attribute for a hero in a Grim Tales campaign, because it allows your character to talk his way out of dangerous conflicts. A high Charisma score also allows your character to stand fast and strike true against the horrific and the supernatural.

Action Points

Action points are a game mechanic that differentiates heroes from ordinary characters: by spending action points, you can activate heroic abilities, improve the results of your die rolls, strike critical hits, and more.

A character can spend an action point to do one of these things:

Improve a d20 Roll

You can spend an action point to improve a single d20 roll used to make an attack, a skill check, an ability check, a level check, or a saving throw.

When a character spends 1 action point to improve a d20 roll, add 1d6 to the d20 roll to help meet or exceed the target number. A character can declare the use of 1 action point to alter a d20 roll after the roll is made—but only before the GM reveals the result of that roll (whether the roll succeeded or failed). A character can't use an action point on a skill check or ability check when he or she is taking 10 or taking 20, it may only be used to improve a random roll.

Activate a Heroic Ability

You can activate a feat, a class talent or class feature for which the expenditure of 1 action point is required. When a character spends 1 action point to use a class feature, he or she gains the benefit of the feature but doesn't roll an action die. In this case, the action point is not a bonus to a d20 roll, it is merely spent to activate the ability.

Make a Heroic Strike

You can spend an action point to "strike true" against an opponent with damage reduction. (See Chapter Six: Combat.)

Improve Your Defense

You may spend an action point at any time to improve your AC by the amount rolled on the action die. This bonus lasts until the start of your next turn. You may not spend an action point in this way if your AC has already been increased by spending an action point.

Confirm a Critical Hit

You must spend an action point to turn an attack into a critical hit.

If your attack roll is a natural 20, you score an automatic hit, and the attack may be also be a critical threat. If the result of your attack roll would ordinarily hit the target (despite being an automatic hit), then you may spend an action point to turn the strike into a critical hit.

Generally, a critical hit does x2 damage when you roll a natural 20 (a critical threat). Note that some weapons and some abilities allow you to improve your threat range (19-20, 18-20, or better) or to increase your critical multiplier (x3, x4, etc.).

If you do not have an action point to spend, or if you *require* an automatic hit to strike the target— the total of your roll plus all bonuses still does not equal or exceed the target's AC— you cannot strike a critical hit.

Confirm a Critical Success with a Skill

You can spend an action point to turn a skill check into a critical success. The results of a critical success are better than a "normal" success; see the Chapter Two: Skills for details.

Healing After Combat

Immediately after any combat, you may spend one action point to heal a number of hit points equal to the amount rolled on the die. You must rest for 1 minute in order to regain hit points.

Variant: Action Point Dice By Character Level

In this variant, the type of action die rolled increases as you gain character levels.

Character Level	Action Point Die Rolled
1st-5th	1d4
6th-10th	1d6
11th-15th	1d8
16th-20th	1d10

Variant: "Exploding" Action Dice

In this variant, each time the action die rolls a maximum result (for example, a 4 on a d4, a 6 on a d6, etc.) you may roll the die again, adding the second result to the previous result. There is no limit to how high the action die total can go: as long as you keep rolling the maximum result, you can keep adding the result.

Spending Multiple Action Points

You may spend more than one action point in a round, but never more than one action point for any single purpose. For example, you could spend an action point to activate an ability, and another action point to improve a die roll, but you could not spend two action points to improve the same die roll or to activate the same ability twice in a round.

Replenishing Action Points

You begin play with a number of action points equal to 5 + one-half your character level (round down). Thus, 1st level characters begin play with only 5 action points.

Your GM decides how often your supply of action points replenishes, according to the desired threat level of the campaign:

☠ Each Game Session: In this variant, designed to keep the action flowing (and the characters alive) your action points replenish at the beginning of each session of play.

☠☠ Each Character Level: In this variant, your action points replenish only when you gain a level. Each time you gain a level, your action points "reset" to 5 + one-half your new character level.

In either of these first two variants, if you have more action points already (because you have gained action points during play— see below) you may keep the higher total.

☠☠☠ Never Replenish: In this grim variant, your action points never replenish. They represent the finite amount of luck that your hero can rely on. The only way to gain action points in this variant is to have them awarded to you by the GM.

Gaining Action Points During Play

There are a number of ways you can actually gain action points during play. The GM does not have action points to spend; instead, he "spends" action points by awarding them to the players. Most of the time, action points are gained as a "consolation prize" when the GM inflicts some calamity upon your character, usually as a result of a bad roll on your part or a stroke of luck on your enemies' behalf.

Activate a Critical Failure with a Skill: At his discretion, the GM may award you 1 action point in order to activate a critical failure for a skill check (see Chapter Two: Skills).

Activate a Critical Hit: At his discretion, the GM may award you 1 action point to activate a critical threat scored against your character.

Activate a Critical Miss: When you make an attack roll and get a natural 1 (the d20 actually shows 1) your attack automatically misses. In addition, this is a threat for a critical miss.

If your attack roll would normally hit (despite rolling a 1) the attack simply misses. The GM may not activate a critical miss.

However, if your attack roll is a 1 and would normally have resulted in a miss despite being an automatic miss, at his discretion, the GM may award you 1 action point and activate a critical miss.

The GM is free to determine the effect of a critical miss as he sees fit. Some common examples include dropping your weapon, being *stunned* for a round, striking another adjacent target by mistake, or even striking yourself. There is no limit to the depravity of the GM in these situations, so take what comfort you can from your extra action point.

Heroic Rewards: At the end of a session of play, your GM may award you an action point if your character was played particularly characterfully or heroically.

The GM may rarely, and at his discretion, award your character an action point *during play* for particularly heroic actions performed at the dramatically appropriate time. Remember that all characters are expected to be heroic; it would be rare indeed to find a character so heroic as to earn more than one action point during play.

Tasty Snacks: The GM may award you an action point before play begins if you show up for your gaming session with tasty snacks to share with the group.

Allegiances

A character may have up to three allegiances, listed in order from most important to least important. These allegiances are indications of what the character values in life, and may encompass people, organizations, or ideals. A character may have no allegiances (being either a free spirit or a lone wolf) or may change allegiances as he or she goes through life.

If the character acts in a way that is detrimental to his or her allegiance, the GM may choose to strip the character of that allegiance (and all its benefits) and assign an allegiance more suitable to those actions.

A hero's allegiance can take the form of loyalty to a person, to an organization, to a belief system, to a nation, or to an ethical (law/chaos) or moral (good/evil) philosophy. In general, a character can discard an allegiance at any time, but may only gain a new allegiance after attaining a new level.

With the GM's permission, the character gains a +2 circumstance bonus on Charisma-based skill checks when dealing with someone of the same allegiance— as long as the character has had some interaction with the other character to discover the connections and bring the bonus into play.

Backgrounds

While your character class is the path your character follows in her heroic journey, your background defines what your character did *before* she became a hero.

The backgrounds listed below are not specific to any particular genre; rather, they are broadly-defined background roles that can exist in nearly any place or time. Your GM will advise you of the genre in which his campaign is set; however, you can feel confident in choosing any of the backgrounds below.

Your background gives you 3 or more skills which form the basis of your core skill list (see Chapter Two: Skills).

Academic

Academics include librarians, archaeologists, scholars, professors, teachers, and other education professionals.

- Craft (any academic related)
- Knowledge (any two of your choice)
- Research

Agitator

Agitators include demagogues, politicians, street preachers, demonstrators, and other rabble-rousers.

- Bluff
- Diplomacy
- Perform (any one)

Athlete

Athletes include amateur athletes of Olympic quality and professional athletes of all types, including gymnasts, weight trainers, wrestlers, boxers, martial artists, swimmers, skaters, and those who engage in any type of competitive sport.

Choose three of the following:

- Balance
- Climb
- Drive
- Jump
- Ride
- Swim
- Tumble

Bureaucrat

This category includes all those who keep the wheels of society moving— or grinding to a halt, depending on which side of the desk you're standing.

- Diplomacy
- Forgery
- Intimidate
- Knowledge (law)

Criminal

This background includes con artists, burglars, crime family soldiers, gang members, and career criminals.

Choose three of the following:

- Bluff
- Disable Device
- Disguise
- Escape Artist
- Forgery
- Hide
- Intimidate
- Move Silently
- Sleight of Hand

Diplomat

Diplomats, negotiators, advisors, messengers, and even tribal wise men fall under this category.

- Diplomacy
- Gather Information
- Sense Motive

Entertainer

This category covers a wide range of backgrounds, from artists to circus performers, from street to stage. The entertainer has a creative inclination and generally makes his living from the goodwill of the audience.

Choose three of the following to specialize in a field of entertainment:

- Bluff
- Craft (any entertainment related)
- Concentration
- Disguise
- Handle Animal
- Perform (any two)
- Ride
- Tumble

Entrepreneur

Entrepreneurs have an abundance of confidence and a knack for putting together business plans, gathering resources, and getting a new venture off the ground.

- Appraise
- Gather Information
- Knowledge (finances)
- Research

Explorer

The explorer is driven to seek out new experiences in new vistas, and though they are often paid for their service, it is the thrill of discovery that drives them.

- Spot
- Survival
- Use Rope

Gentry

Members of the gentry usually get their wealth from family holdings and trust funds. The typical gentry has no job, few responsibilities, and at least one driving passion that occupies his or her day. That passion might be a charity or philanthropic foundation, an ideal or cause worth fighting for, or a lust for living a fun and carefree existence.

- Bluff
- Diplomacy
- Knowledge (etiquette)
- Craft, Drive, Perform, or Ride (any one)

Healer

Healers include those of any era whose background shows a focus on the healing arts. This may also include holy men, counselors, and psychiatrists whose goal is to heal the spirit and the mind as well as the body.

- Craft (herbal, medical, or pharmaceutical)
- Diplomacy
- Heal
- Knowledge (herbalism, medicine, etc.)

Investigator

There are a number of jobs that fit within this category, including law enforcement, interrogators and inquisitors, spies, and others who use their skills to gather evidence and analyze clues.

- Gather Information
- Knowledge (any applicable field, e.g. forensics)
- Research
- Search

Laborer

This includes factory workers, service jobs, construction, and others that are not considered to be desk jobs.

Choose three of the following:

- Appraise
- Craft (any one)
- Drive (any one)
- Handle Animal
- Intimidate

Merchant
The motto of the merchant is "buy low, sell high." Those from this background have a knack for determining the true value of an item or commodity— and convincing others to pay double. • Appraise • Bluff • Diplomacy • Sense Motive

Religious
Ordained clergy of all persuasions, as well as theological scholars and experts on religious studies fall within this category. • Concentration • Knowledge (religion) • Sense Motive

Rural
Farm workers, hunters, and others who make a living in rural communities fall under this category. Choose three of the following: • Drive (ground vehicle) • Handle Animal • Knowledge (farming) • Knowledge (nature) • Listen • Spot • Survival

Military
Military covers anyone with a background of military service, whether it be ground forces, navy, or air force. • Climb • Jump • Spot • Survival

Underprivileged
The category covers those with no job and no prospects. The underprivileged live on the fringes and subsist on the leavings of society. • Hide • Search • Sleight of Hand • Spot

Reputation

Reputation is used to determine whether an NPC recognizes a character. Those who recognize the hero are more likely to help the hero or do what he or she asks, provided the reputation has a positive connotation to the character who recognizes the hero. A high Reputation bonus also makes it difficult for the hero to mask his or her identity.

Most of the time, a hero doesn't decide to use his or her reputation. The GM decides when a hero's reputation can be relevant to a scene or encounter. At the moment it becomes relevant, the GM makes a Reputation check for an NPC who might be influenced in some fashion due to the hero's fame or notoriety, as detailed below.

Fame and Infamy

Most characters with a high Reputation bonus (+4 or higher) are considered well known within their profession or social circle. Whether this has a positive or negative connotation depends on the point of view of the person who recognizes the hero.

When an NPC has a positive opinion of a hero's reputation, the hero is considered to be *famous*. Fame, when recognized, provides a bonus to certain Charisma-based skill checks.

When an NPC has a negative opinion of a hero's reputation, the hero is considered to be *infamous*. (Also, at the GM's option, a hero might be considered infamous in certain situations due to events that have transpired in the campaign.) Infamy, when recognized, provides a penalty to certain Charisma-based skill checks.

Using the Reputation Bonus

Whenever the GM decides that a character's reputation can be a factor in an encounter, the GM makes a Reputation check (DC 25) for the NPC involved. A Reputation check is 1d20 + the hero's Reputation bonus + the NPC's Intelligence modifier. (Some Knowledge skill modifiers might apply instead of the Intelligence modifier, if the hero would be well known in the field covered by the Knowledge skill.) Modifiers to the Reputation check depend on the hero and the NPC in question, as shown below. Note that if the NPC has no possible way of recognizing a hero, then the Reputation check automatically fails.

If the NPC succeeds at the Reputation check, he or she recognizes the hero (for good or ill). This provides a +4 bonus or a –4 penalty on Bluff, Diplomacy, Gather Information, Intimidate, and Perform checks for the duration of the encounter.

Situation	Reputation Check Modifier
The hero is famous, known far and wide with either a positive or negative connotation	+10
NPC is part of the hero's professional or social circle	+5
The hero has some small amount of fame or notoriety	+2

The GM must decide that a character's fame or infamy can come into play in a given situation to make a Reputation check. An NPC who doesn't know (or at least know of) the hero can't be influenced by his or her reputation.

Character Classes

There are six core classes in Grim Tales, each tied to the single ability score that most clearly defines the class: The Strong Hero, the Fast Hero, the Tough Hero, the Smart Hero, the Dedicated Hero, and the Charismatic Hero. Each of the core classes is described in the following pages.

Multi-Classing

There is no penalty for multi-classing. Generally speaking, the abilities of a multiclass character are the sum of the abilities provided by each of the character's classes, except as noted below:

Stacking Features

Hit points, base attack bonus (BAB), saving throws, Defense bonus, and Reputation from different classes all stack. Find the value accorded to each individual class level and simply add them together.

Skills

Skill maximum ranks are determined by character level. Core skills are limited to character level + 3, and non-core skills are limited to one-half (character level +3). When a multiclass character gains a level, he gains skill points to spend according to the new class.

Class Features

The character gets all class features (talents, bonus feats, or other special abilities) of all classes for the levels he or she possesses in each class.

Character Level

"Character level" is a character's total number of levels from all classes combined. It is used to determine when feats and ability score increases are gained. "Class level" is the character's level in a particular class. For a hero whose levels are all in the same class, character level and class level are the same.

Experience Points

As characters accumulate experience points (XP), they advance in level. The amount of experience points required to advance to the next level is equal to the character's current level x 1000 XP, +1 experience point.

The GM can increase this target (to slow down character advancement) or reduce it (to speed up character advancement).

Feats

A character receives a new feat every three character levels, regardless of individual class level. Taking one level in a new class does not entitle a character to the two feats that a beginning 1st-level character receives.

Ability Score Increases

A character increases one ability score by +1 every four character levels.

Character Level	Feats	Ability Increase	XP Total
1	2 feats		0-1000
2			1001-3000
3	+1 feat		3001-6000
4		+1 increase	6001-10,000
5			10,001-15,000
6	+1 feat		15,001-21,000
7			21,001-28,000
8		+1 increase	28,001-36,000
9	+1 feat		36,001-45,000
10			45,001-55,000
11			55,001-66,000
12	+1 feat	+1 increase	66,001-78,000
13			78,001-90,000
14			91,001-105,000
15	+1 feat		105,001-120,000
16		+1 increase	120,001-136,000
17			136,001-153,000
18	+1 feat		153,001-171,000
19			171,001-190,000
20		+1 increase	190,001–210,000

Using Classes from Other Sources

You may wish to add a class, prestige class, or advanced class from another source. If your GM permits this, you gain the features of the new class as you would with any other multiclass. However, you may spend skill points from such a new class only on the skills granted to that class; any skill not listed as a class skill for such outside classes, even if they are otherwise a core skill for a Grim Tales character, are considered non-core when spending skill points granted by the outside class. The flexibility of the core skills within Grim Tales is applicable only to the core classes.

The Strong Hero

Ability: Strength

There is little uncertainty about the Strong Hero's preferred problem solving method. If the issue cannot be resolved quickly, quietly and civilly, then the fastest solution is to simply bash the problem into non-existence. Knowing that his impressive Strength is his best quality, the Strong Hero focuses on issues that have a straightforward and outright physical solution. To him, combat is commonplace, labor is a love, and anything physical is a pleasure. The Strong Hero is not always a mindless brute, however, as he knows that occasionally he must wear the silken glove over his iron fist. Despite any appointed aplomb, a deep seated part of his psyche aches for the sound of things breaking and the comfortable feeling of matter doing precisely what his body tells it to.

Examples of Strong Heroes

Archaic: Sword-wielding warriors, brutish ogres, and mighty dragon-slayers.

Modern: Prizefighters, bodyguards, soldiers, street thugs, punks, steel workers, coal miners.

Apocalyptic: Cyborgs, most mutants, gang leaders, mercenaries, and heavy weapons experts.

Starting Features

A 1st level character who chooses Strong Hero as a starting class receives the following starting features:

> ***Hit Points***: 8
> ***Skill Points***: (3 + Int modifier) x4
> ***Feats***: The 1st level Hero can choose any two feats.
> ***Bonus Starting Feats***: In addition to two starting feats, the Strong hero gains Armor Proficiency (all), Martial Weapon Proficiency (all)*, Shield Proficiency, and Simple Weapons Proficiency.

* If the campaign uses Firearms, you may substitute Personal Firearms Proficiency instead of Martial Weapon Proficiency (all).

A character who chooses Strong Hero as a multiclass does not receive these starting features.

Strong Hero Advancement

Strong Heroes advancing beyond first level receive the following features as normal:

> ***Hit Die***: 1d8
> ***Skill Points Each Additional Level***: 3 + Int modifier.

Class Features

Talents

At 1st level and every odd-numbered level thereafter, (3rd, 5th, 7th, 9th, etc.) the Strong hero may choose a talent from the following basic talents. As long as the hero qualifies for all prerequisites, he or she can select freely from any talents. No talent can be selected more than once unless expressly indicated.

Basic Talents

Extreme Effort, Ignore Hardness, Melee Smash.

Advanced Talents

A character with at least 3 Strong class levels may also choose Advanced Talents available to Strong heroes, including those from the following list:

> Living Weapon, Weapon Specialization (Greater Weapon Specialization, Improved Critical)

Bonus Feats

At 2nd level and every even-numbered level thereafter, (4th, 6th, 8th, 10th, etc.) the Strong hero gains a bonus feat. The bonus feat must be chosen from the following list:

> Blind-Fight, Brawl (Improved Brawl, Knockout Punch), Combat Reflexes, (Whirlwind Attack), Improved Shield Bash, Improved Unarmed Strike (Improved Grapple), Mounted Combat (Ride-By Attack), Power Attack (Cleave, Great Cleave, Improved Bull Rush, Improved Sunder), Skill Familiarity (any Strength-based skill), Skill Focus (any Strength-based skill), Weapon Focus (Greater Weapon Focus).

Table 1-1: The Strong Hero

Level	BAB	Fort	Ref	Will	Class Features	Defense	Reputation
1	+1	+1	+0	+0	Strong Talent	+1	+0
2	+2	+2	+0	+0	Strong bonus Feat	+2	+0
3	+3	+2	+1	+1	Strong Talent	+2	+0
4	+4	+2	+1	+1	Strong bonus Feat	+3	+0
5	+5	+3	+1	+1	Strong Talent	+3	+1
6	+6/+1	+3	+2	+2	Strong bonus Feat	+3	+1
7	+7/+2	+4	+2	+2	Strong Talent	+4	+1
8	+8/+3	+4	+2	+2	Strong bonus Feat	+4	+1
9	+9/+4	+4	+3	+3	Strong Talent	+5	+2
10	+10/+5	+5	+3	+3	Strong bonus Feat	+5	+2
11	+11/+6/+1	+5	+3	+3	Strong Talent	+5	+2
12	+12/+7/+2	+6	+4	+4	Strong bonus Feat	+6	+2
13	+13/+8/+3	+6	+4	+4	Strong Talent	+6	+3
14	+14/+9/+4	+6	+4	+4	Strong bonus Feat	+7	+3
15	+15/+10/+5	+7	+5	+5	Strong Talent	+7	+3
16	+16/+11/+6/+1	+7	+5	+5	Strong bonus Feat	+7	+3
17	+17/+12/+7/+2	+8	+5	+5	Strong Talent	+8	+4
18	+18/+13/+8/+3	+8	+6	+6	Strong bonus Feat	+8	+4
19	+19/+14/+9/+4	+8	+6	+6	Strong Talent	+9	+4
20	+20/+15/+10/+5	+9	+6	+6	Strong bonus Feat	+9	+4

The Fast Hero

Ability: Dexterity

Speed, precision, and adaptability are the keys to the Fast Hero's existence. Because her physical and mental flexibility are the only things that have kept her alive so far, the Fast Hero depends on her Dexterity to get her out of the tight pinches in which she often finds herself. Whether it is wriggling out of some tightly bound ropes, slipping hidden from one shadow to the next, or deftly palming a sought-after item for "safe-keeping," the Fast Hero knows that her well honed and practiced skills will see her through. While she might not always be physically the fastest wolf in the pack, the Fast Hero might possess lightning-quick reflexes, the natural poise and balance of a ballerina, or the quick hands of a five-finger discount specialist.

Examples of Fast Heroes

Archaic: Crafty rogues, fleet-of-foot swashbucklers, and nimble cutpurses.

Modern: Street magicians, gymnasts, and most martial artists.

Apocalyptic: Street urchins/rats, scavengers, and gutter-runners.

Starting Features

A 1st level character who chooses Fast Hero as a starting class receives the following starting features:

> ***Hit Points***: 8
> ***Skill Points:*** (5 + Int modifier) x4
> ***Feats***: The 1st level Hero can choose any two feats.
> ***Bonus Starting Feats***: In addition to two starting feats, the Fast hero gains Armor Proficiency (light) and Simple Weapons Proficiency.

A character who chooses Fast Hero as a multiclass does not receive these starting features.

Fast Hero Advancement

Fast Heroes advancing beyond first level receive the following features as normal:

> ***Hit Die***: 1d8
> ***Skill Points Each Additional Level***: 5 + Int modifier.

Class Features

Talents

At 1st level and every odd-numbered level thereafter, (3rd, 5th, 7th, 9th, etc.) the Fast hero may choose a talent from the following basic talents. As long as the hero qualifies for all prerequisites, he or she can select freely from any talents. No talent can be selected more than once unless expressly indicated.

Basic Talents

> Evasion (Opportunist, Uncanny Dodge, Defensive Roll, Improved Uncanny Dodge); Increased Speed.

Advanced Talents

A character with at least 3 Fast class levels may also choose Advanced Talents available to Fast heroes, including those from the following list:

> Deflect Arrows (Snatch Arrows, Deflect Bullets); Improved Evasion (Heightened Reflexes); Flurry of Blows (Improved Flurry of Blows, Advanced Flurry of Blows, Greater Flurry of Blows); Improved Reaction; (Trap Sense).

Bonus Feats

At 2nd level and every even-numbered level thereafter, (4th, 6th, 8th, 10th, etc.) the Fast hero gains a bonus feat. The bonus feat must be chosen from the following list:

> Combat Expertise (Improved Disarm), Combat Reflexes, Defensive Expertise (Combat Throw, Elusive Target, Unbalance Opponent), Dodge (Agile Riposte, Mobility, Shot on the Run, Sidestep, Back Off), Lightning Reflexes, Point Blank Shot, Quick Draw, Run, Skill Familiarity (any Dexterity-based skill), Skill Focus (any Dexterity-based skill), Two Weapon Fighting (Two Weapon Defense), Weapon Finesse

Table 1-2: The Fast Hero

Level	BAB	Fort	Ref	Will	Class Features	Defense	Reputation
1	+0	+0	+1	+0	Fast Talent	+3	+0
2	+1	+0	+2	+0	Fast bonus Feat	+4	+0
3	+2	+1	+2	+1	Fast Talent	+4	+1
4	+3	+1	+2	+1	Fast bonus Feat	+5	+1
5	+3	+1	+3	+1	Fast Talent	+5	+1
6	+4	+2	+3	+2	Fast bonus Feat	+6	+2
7	+5	+2	+4	+2	Fast Talent	+6	+2
8	+6/+1	+2	+4	+2	Fast bonus Feat	+7	+2
9	+6/+1	+3	+4	+3	Fast Talent	+7	+3
10	+7/+2	+3	+5	+3	Fast bonus Feat	+8	+3
11	+8/+3	+3	+5	+3	Fast Talent	+8	+3
12	+9/+4	+4	+6	+4	Fast bonus Feat	+9	+4
13	+9/+4	+4	+6	+4	Fast Talent	+9	+4
14	+10/+5	+4	+6	+4	Fast bonus Feat	+10	+4
15	+11/+6/+1	+5	+7	+5	Fast Talent	+10	+5
16	+12/+7/+2	+5	+7	+5	Fast bonus Feat	+11	+5
17	+12/+7/+2	+5	+8	+5	Fast Talent	+11	+5
18	+13/+8/+3	+6	+8	+6	Fast bonus Feat	+12	+6
19	+14/+9/+4	+6	+8	+6	Fast Talent	+12	+6
20	+15/+10/+5	+6	+9	+6	Fast bonus Feat	+13	+6

The Tough Hero

Ability: Constitution

The Tough Hero trusts that his indomitable nature will never fail him and answers each challenged presented to him thusly. He does not hesitate to attempt new feats which might give others pause or perform particularly dangerous actions which might lead to extensive bodily injury. The Tough Hero wades into the thick of the battle, endures onslaughts of pain that would send most men spiraling into unconsciousness, and drives himself onward despite horrific wounds or injuries. The Tough Hero knows that he can rely on his resilient nature to protect him from infections, diseases and other toxins that would slay normal men; he can eat nearly anything regardless of its state and remain unaffected. Further, environmental hazards do little to deter him as he merely slogs through the worst of it all, enduring whatever life throws at him.

Examples of Tough Heroes

Archaic: Grim survivalists, lean, weathered rangers, and wasteland-dwelling barbarians.

Modern: Olympic/Triathlon athletes, Airborne rangers, Navy seals, and survival experts.

Apocalyptic: Post-nuke nomads, solitary bounty hunters, and most benevolent leaders.

Starting Features

A 1st level character who chooses Tough Hero as a starting class receives the following starting features:

> ***Hit Points***: 10
> ***Skill Points***: (3 + Int modifier) x4
> ***Feats***: The 1st level Hero can choose any two feats.
> ***Bonus Starting Feats***: In addition to two starting feats, the Tough hero gains Armor Proficiency (light and medium), Martial Weapon Proficiency (any one)*, Shield Proficiency, and Simple Weapons Proficiency.
>
> * If the campaign uses Firearms, you may substitute Martial Weapon Proficiency (any one) for Personal Firearms Proficiency.

A character who chooses Tough Hero as a multiclass does not receive these starting features.

Tough Hero Advancement

Tough Heroes advancing beyond first level receive the following features as normal:

> ***Hit Die***: 1d10
> ***Skill Points Each Additional Level***: 3 + Int modifier.

Class Features

Talents

At 1st level and every odd-numbered level thereafter, (3rd, 5th, 7th, 9th, etc.) the Tough hero may choose a talent from the following basic talents. As long as the hero qualifies for all prerequisites, he or she can select freely from any talents. No talent can be selected more than once unless expressly indicated.

Basic Talents

> Energy Resistance; Remain Conscious; Robust (Stamina); Second Wind.

Advanced Talents

A character with at least 3 Tough class levels may also choose Advanced Talents available to Tough heroes, including those from the following list:

> Damage Reduction; Harm's Way (Protective Strike, Protective Bonus), Improved Energy Resistance; Rage (Tireless Rage, Mighty Rage); (Stay in the Game); (Improved Second Wind).

Bonus Feats

At 2nd level and every even-numbered level thereafter, (4th, 6th, 8th, 10th, etc.) the Tough hero gains a bonus feat. The bonus feat must be chosen from the following list:

> Alertness, Brawl (Improved Brawl, Knockout Punch, Streetfighting, Improved Feint), Endurance (Die Hard), Frightful Presence, Great Fortitude, Improved Damage Threshold, Power Attack (Cleave, Improved Bull Rush, Improved Sunder, Skill Familiarity (any Constitution-based skill), Skill Focus (any Constitution-based skill), Toughness

Table 1-3: The Tough Hero

Level	BAB	Fort	Ref	Will	Class Features	Defense	Reputation
1	+0	+1	+0	+0	Tough Talent	+1	+0
2	+1	+2	+0	+0	Tough bonus Feat	+2	+0
3	+2	+2	+1	+1	Tough Talent	+2	+1
4	+3	+2	+1	+1	Tough bonus Feat	+3	+1
5	+3	+3	+1	+1	Tough Talent	+3	+1
6	+4	+3	+2	+2	Tough bonus Feat	+3	+2
7	+5	+4	+2	+2	Tough Talent	+4	+2
8	+6/+1	+4	+2	+2	Tough bonus Feat	+4	+2
9	+6/+1	+4	+3	+3	Tough Talent	+5	+3
10	+7/+2	+5	+3	+3	Tough bonus Feat	+5	+3
11	+8/+3	+5	+3	+3	Tough Talent	+5	+3
12	+9/+4	+6	+4	+4	Tough bonus Feat	+6	+4
13	+9/+4	+6	+4	+4	Tough Talent	+6	+4
14	+10/+5	+6	+4	+4	Tough bonus Feat	+7	+4
15	+11/+6/+1	+7	+5	+5	Tough Talent	+7	+5
16	+12/+7/+2	+7	+5	+5	Tough bonus Feat	+7	+5
17	+12/+7/+2	+8	+5	+5	Tough Talent	+8	+5
18	+13/+8/+3	+8	+6	+6	Tough bonus Feat	+8	+6
19	+14/+9/+4	+8	+6	+6	Tough Talent	+9	+6
20	+15/+10/+5	+9	+6	+6	Tough bonus Feat	+9	+6

The Smart Hero

Ability: Intelligence

Because her lifestyle often involves danger and intrigue, the Smart Hero realizes her true strength and protection derive from her intellect and her ability to combine, process, and interpret information quickly and accurately. She further understands that only her mental abilities stand between her and the less desirable aspects of this life, so she continually hones her mind to a razor's edge. The Smart Hero has an unquenchable thirst for knowledge and a hunger to learn new things, often traveling to places she never imagined and seeing things she never before believed possible. With each new acquisition of knowledge, she yearns for even more information. The types of knowledge she acquires matter little: the newest and most cutting edge hold the same captivating effect as the ancient scraps of forgotten lore.

Examples of Smart Heroes

Archaic: Wizards, monks, sages, archivists, clockwork tinkerers, and alchemists.

Modern: Nobel-prize winners, computer gurus, and theoretical physicists.

Apocalyptic: Code-crackers, mutative geneticists, and interpretive archeologists.

Starting Features

A 1st level character who chooses Smart Hero as a starting class receives the following starting features:

> ***Hit Points***: 6
> ***Skill Points***: (9 + Int modifier) x4
> ***Feats***: The 1st level Hero can choose any two feats.
> ***Bonus Starting Feats***: In addition to two starting feats, the Smart hero gains Simple Weapons Proficiency.
> ***Core Skills***: A starting Smart Hero may choose any three additional Intelligence-based skills as core skills.

A character who chooses Smart Hero as a multiclass does not receive these starting features.

Smart Hero Advancement

Smart Heroes advancing beyond first level receive the following features as normal:

> ***Hit Die***: 1d6
> ***Skill Points Each Additional Level***: 9 + Int modifier.

Class Features

Talents

At 1st level and every odd-numbered level thereafter, (3rd, 5th, 7th, 9th, etc.) the Smart hero may choose a talent from the following basic talents. As long as the hero qualifies for all prerequisites, he or she can select freely from any talents. No talent can be selected more than once unless expressly indicated.

Basic Talents

> Linguist, Savant.

Advanced Talents

A character with at least 3 Smart class levels may also choose Advanced Talents available to Smart heroes, including those from the following list:

> Exploit Weakness (Sneak Attack); Favored Enemy; Magical Adept (Improved Caster Level, Master Eldritch Flow); Obscure Knowledge; Plan; Trapfinding; Trick.

Bonus Feats

At 2nd level and every even-numbered level thereafter, (4th, 6th, 8th, 10th, etc.) the Smart hero gains a bonus feat. The bonus feat must be chosen from the following list:

> Alertness, Blind-Fight, Combat Expertise (Improved Disarm, Improved Trip), (Elusive Target), Dodge (Agile Riposte), Far Shot, (Improved Feint), Iron Will, Lightning Reflexes, (Precise Shot), Skill Familiarity (any Intelligence-based skill), Skill Focus (any Intelligence-based skill), Surgery, Weapon Focus, Windfall

Table 1-4: The Smart Hero

Level	BAB	Fort	Ref	Will	Class Features	Defense	Reputation
1	+0	+0	+0	+1	Smart Talent	+0	+1
2	+1	+0	+0	+2	Smart bonus Feat	+1	+1
3	+1	+1	+1	+2	Smart Talent	+1	+1
4	+2	+1	+1	+2	Smart bonus Feat	+1	+2
5	+2	+1	+1	+3	Smart Talent	+2	+2
6	+3	+2	+2	+3	Smart bonus Feat	+2	+2
7	+3	+2	+2	+4	Smart Talent	+2	+3
8	+4	+2	+2	+4	Smart bonus Feat	+3	+3
9	+4	+3	+3	+4	Smart Talent	+3	+3
10	+5	+3	+3	+5	Smart bonus Feat	+3	+4
11	+5	+3	+3	+5	Smart Talent	+4	+4
12	+6/+1	+4	+4	+6	Smart bonus Feat	+4	+4
13	+6/+1	+4	+4	+6	Smart Talent	+4	+5
14	+7/+2	+4	+4	+6	Smart bonus Feat	+5	+5
15	+7/+2	+5	+5	+7	Smart Talent	+5	+5
16	+8/+3	+5	+5	+7	Smart bonus Feat	+5	+6
17	+8/+3	+5	+5	+8	Smart Talent	+6	+6
18	+9/+4	+6	+6	+8	Smart bonus Feat	+6	+6
19	+9/+4	+6	+6	+8	Smart Talent	+6	+7
20	+10/+5	+6	+6	+9	Smart bonus Feat	+7	+7

The Dedicated Hero

Ability: Wisdom

The Dedicated Hero is able to always fall back on one inalienable aspect of her personality: her uncanny Wisdom. She is able to, no matter the circumstances, always ground herself firmly in the ideals and morals that she has always deeply felt. Sometimes, these principles act as a guide during times of trouble arise; other times they act as a jump-start to her soul, propelling her forward to affect a situation when it seems that no one else will take up the cry. The Dedicated Hero, being one of the precious few with a strong moral or ethical foundation, often finds herself at the center of a great movement and occasionally, a martyr. This fact does little to distract her, however, as she knows without doubt that she must follow her convictions to the end, regardless of what that end might be.

Examples of Dedicated Heroes

Archaic: Priests, prophets, knights, and templars.

Modern: Priests, prophets, civil rights leaders, and humanitarians.

Apocalyptic: Prophets, seers, defenders of the downtrodden, and founders of new religions.

Starting Features

A 1st level character who chooses Dedicated hero as a starting class receives the following starting features:

Hit Points: 6
Skill Points: (5 + Int modifier) x4
Feats: The 1st level Hero can choose any two feats.
Bonus Starting Feats: In addition to two starting feats, the Dedicated hero gains Armor Proficiency (light and medium), Shield Proficiency, and Simple Weapons Proficiency.

A character who chooses Dedicated Hero as a multiclass does not receive these starting features.

Dedicated Hero Advancement

Dedicated Heroes advancing beyond first level receive the following features as normal:

Hit Die: 1d6
Skill Points Each Additional Level: 5 + Int modifier.

Class Features

Talents

At 1st level and every odd-numbered level thereafter, (3rd, 5th, 7th, 9th, etc.) the Dedicated hero may choose a talent from the following basic talents. As long as the hero qualifies for all prerequisites, he or she can select freely from any talents. No talent can be selected more than once unless expressly indicated.

Basic Talents

Empathy (Improved Aid Another, Intuition); Healing Knack (Healing Touch); Insight (Aware, Faith).

Advanced Talents

A character with at least 3 Dedicated class levels may also choose Advanced Talents available to Dedicated heroes, including those from the following list:

Aura of Grace (Aura of Courage, Aura of Health); Improved Intuition; Favored Enemy; (Cool Under Pressure); Harm's Way (Protective Strike, Protective Bonus), Living Weapon, Magical Adept (Improved Caster Level, Master Eldritch Flow); Minor Medical Miracle (Major Medical Miracle), Smite; Turn Undead (Destroy Undead, Banish Outsiders); Zen Defense, Zen Focus (Zen Strike).

Bonus Feats

At 2nd level and every even-numbered level thereafter, (4th, 6th, 8th, 10th, etc.) the Dedicated hero gains a bonus feat. The bonus feat must be chosen from the following list:

Alertness, Blind-Fight, Endurance (Die Hard), Far Shot (Improved Aim), Frightful Presence, Great Fortitude, Improved Damage Threshold, Iron Will, Mounted Combat (Spirited Charge), Skill Familiarity (any Wisdom-based skill), Skill Focus (any Wisdom-based skill), Skill Supremacy, (Stunning Fist), Toughness, Track, Weapon Focus (Greater Weapon Focus)

Table 1-5: The Dedicated Hero

Level	BAB	Fort	Ref	Will	Class Features	Defense	Reputation
1	+0	+1	+0	+1	Dedicated Talent	+1	+1
2	+1	+2	+0	+2	Dedicated bonus Feat	+2	+1
3	+2	+2	+1	+2	Dedicated Talent	+2	+1
4	+3	+2	+1	+2	Dedicated bonus Feat	+3	+2
5	+3	+3	+1	+3	Dedicated Talent	+3	+2
6	+4	+3	+2	+3	Dedicated bonus Feat	+3	+2
7	+5	+4	+2	+4	Dedicated Talent	+4	+3
8	+6/+1	+4	+2	+4	Dedicated bonus Feat	+4	+3
9	+6/+1	+4	+3	+4	Dedicated Talent	+5	+3
10	+7/+2	+5	+3	+5	Dedicated bonus Feat	+5	+4
11	+8/+3	+5	+3	+5	Dedicated Talent	+5	+4
12	+9/+4	+6	+4	+6	Dedicated bonus Feat	+6	+4
13	+9/+4	+6	+4	+6	Dedicated Talent	+6	+5
14	+10/+5	+6	+4	+6	Dedicated bonus Feat	+7	+5
15	+11/+6/+1	+7	+5	+7	Dedicated Talent	+7	+5
16	+12/+7/+2	+7	+5	+7	Dedicated bonus Feat	+7	+6
17	+12/+7/+2	+8	+5	+8	Dedicated Talent	+8	+6
18	+13/+8/+3	+8	+6	+8	Dedicated bonus Feat	+8	+6
19	+14/+9/+4	+8	+6	+8	Dedicated Talent	+9	+7
20	+15/+10/+5	+9	+6	+9	Dedicated bonus Feat	+9	+7

The Charismatic Hero

Ability: Charisma

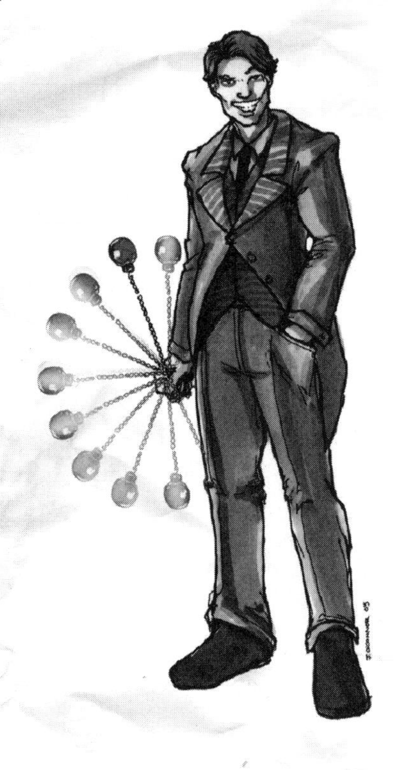

The Charismatic Hero knows that he possesses not only the raw material but also the refined and finished product that is required to survive in any situation. He relies solely upon his Charisma and its sweet fruit time and time again. Using his silver tongue, subtle hints and innuendo, as well as his very being, the Charismatic Hero takes seemingly small and insignificant things-- a smile here, a compliment and a nod there-- and, before anyone is conscious of what has happened, he is completely in charge of the entire situation. The Charismatic Hero either uses these potent gifts to further himself (even to the point of selling his skills to the highest bidder) or to further his purpose, which could range from a world-spanning political movement to merely eking out a morsel of food and a safe home for his family.

Examples of Charismatic Heroes

Archaic: Lore-steeped bards, influential rulers, crafty merchants.

Modern: Double agents, politicians, celebrities, and salesmen of all varieties.

Apocalyptic: Ladies of the night, shifty con artists, rambling gamblers, and jacks-of-all-trades.

Starting Features

A 1st level character who chooses Charismatic Hero as a starting class receives the following starting features:

Hit Points: 6
Skill Points: (7 + Int modifier) x4
Feats: The 1st level Hero can choose any two feats.
Bonus Starting Feats: In addition to two starting feats, the Charismatic hero gains Armor Proficiency (light) and Simple Weapons Proficiency.
Core Skill: A starting Charismatic Hero may choose an additional Charisma-based skill as a core skill.

A character who chooses Charismatic Hero as a multiclass does not receive these starting features.

Charismatic Hero Advancement

Charismatic Heroes advancing beyond first level receive the following features as normal:

Hit Die: 1d6
Skill Points Each Additional Level: 7 + Int modifier.

Class Features

Talents

At 1st level and every odd-numbered level thereafter, (3rd, 5th, 7th, 9th, etc.) the Charismatic hero may choose a talent from the following basic talents. As long as the hero qualifies for all prerequisites, he or she can select freely from any talents. No talent can be selected more than once unless expressly indicated.

Basic Talents

Charm (Favor, Captivate); Coordinate (Inspiration, Greater Inspiration); Fast Talk (Dazzle, Taunt).

Advanced Talents

A character with at least 3 Charismatic class levels may also choose Advanced Talents available to Charismatic heroes, including those from the following list:

Aura of Grace (Aura of Courage, Aura of Health); Magical Adept (Improved Caster Level, Master Eldritch Flow), Turn Undead (Command Undead), Wild Empathy.

Bonus Feats

At 2nd level and every even-numbered level thereafter, (4th, 6th, 8th, 10th, etc.) the Charismatic hero gains a bonus feat. The bonus feat must be chosen from the following list:

Combat Reflexes, Dodge (Agile Riposte, Mobility, Sidestep), (Elusive Target), Frightful Presence, (Improved Feint), Iron Will, Lightning Reflexes, Low Profile, Point Blank Shot, Renown, Skill Familiarity (any Charisma-based skill), Skill Focus (any Charisma-based skill), (Streetfighting), (Unbalance Opponent), Weapon Finesse, Windfall

Table 1-6: The Charismatic Hero							
Level	BAB	Fort	Ref	Will	Class Features	Defense	Reputation
1	+0	+1	+1	+0	Charismatic Talent	+0	+2
2	+1	+2	+2	+0	Charismatic bonus Feat	+1	+2
3	+1	+2	+2	+1	Charismatic Talent	+1	+2
4	+2	+2	+2	+1	Charismatic bonus Feat	+1	+3
5	+2	+3	+3	+1	Charismatic Talent	+2	+3
6	+3	+3	+3	+2	Charismatic bonus Feat	+2	+3
7	+3	+4	+4	+2	Charismatic Talent	+2	+4
8	+4	+4	+4	+2	Charismatic bonus Feat	+3	+4
9	+4	+4	+4	+3	Charismatic Talent	+3	+4
10	+5	+5	+5	+3	Charismatic bonus Feat	+3	+5
11	+5	+5	+5	+3	Charismatic Talent	+4	+5
12	+6/+1	+6	+6	+4	Charismatic bonus Feat	+4	+5
13	+6/+1	+6	+6	+4	Charismatic Talent	+4	+6
14	+7/+2	+6	+6	+4	Charismatic bonus Feat	+5	+6
15	+7/+2	+7	+7	+5	Charismatic Talent	+5	+6
16	+8/+3	+7	+7	+5	Charismatic bonus Feat	+5	+7
17	+8/+3	+8	+8	+5	Charismatic Talent	+6	+7
18	+9/+4	+8	+8	+6	Charismatic bonus Feat	+6	+7
19	+9/+4	+8	+8	+6	Charismatic Talent	+6	+8
20	+10/+5	+9	+9	+6	Charismatic bonus Feat	+7	+8

SKILLS

During character creation, every character chooses a Background. Your chosen background offers you a limited number of background skills to begin your *core skill list*.

Now, choose your career skills. These are skills that a character would generally use to support himself. Choose one Craft sub-skill, one Knowledge sub-skill, and one Profession sub-skill as core skills.

Finally, add any three skills of your choice to your core skills. These "player's choice" skills allow your character to have competencies that are not necessarily related to your background or career.

To sum up, your core skill list consists of:

- 3-5 background skills;
- 3 career skills;
- 3 "player's choice" skills.

Thus, every character has at least nine core skills to choose from when spending skill points.

Skill Ranks

A character's number of ranks in a skill is based on how many skill points a character has invested in a skill. Many skills can be used even if the character has no ranks in them; doing this is called making an untrained skill check.

If you buy a core skill, your character gets 1 rank (equal to a +1 bonus on checks with that skill) for each skill point. If you buy a skill that is not on your core skill list (non-core skills), you get 1/2 rank per skill point.

Your maximum rank in a core skill is your character level + 3. Your maximum rank in a non-core skill is one-half of this number (do not round up or down).

Using Skills

To make a skill check, roll 1d20 and add your character's skill modifier for that skill. The skill modifier incorporates the character's ranks in that skill and the ability modifier for that skill's key ability, plus any other miscellaneous modifiers that may apply, including racial bonuses and armor check penalties. The higher the result, the better. Unlike with attack rolls and saving throws, a natural roll of 20 on the d20 is not an automatic success, and a natural roll of 1 is not an automatic failure (see *Critical Failures and Successes*, below).

Otherwise, this roll works just like an attack roll or a saving throw– the higher the roll, the better. Either you're trying to match or exceed a certain Difficulty Class (DC), or you're trying to beat another character's check result (an "opposed roll").

Circumstances can affect your check. A character who is free to work without distractions can make a careful attempt and avoid simple mistakes ("take 10"). A character who has lots of time can try over and over again, thereby assuring the best outcome ("take 20"). If others help, the character may succeed where otherwise he or she would fail ("aid another").

Ability Modifier

The ability modifier used in a skill check is the modifier for the key ability (the ability associated with the skill's use). The key ability of each skill is noted in its description.

Miscellaneous Modifiers

Miscellaneous modifiers include racial bonuses, armor check penalties, and bonuses provided by feats, among others.

Difficulty Class

Some checks are made against a Difficulty Class (DC). The DC is a number that you must score as a result on your skill check in order to succeed.

Difficulty Class Examples

Difficulty (DC)	Example (Skill Used)
Very easy (0)	Notice something large in plain sight (Spot)
Easy (5)	Climb a knotted rope (Climb)
Average (10)	Hear an approaching guard (Listen)
Tough (15)	Rig a wagon wheel to fall off (Disable Device)
Challenging (20)	Swim in stormy water (Swim)
Formidable (25)	Find a hidden trap (Search)
Heroic (30)	Leap across a 30-foot chasm (Jump)
Nearly Impossible (40)	Track an enemy across hard ground after 24 hours of rainfall (Survival)

Opposed Checks

An opposed check is a check whose success or failure is determined by comparing the check result to another character's check result. In an opposed check, the higher result succeeds, while the lower result fails. In case of a tie, the higher skill modifier wins. If these scores are the same, roll again to break the tie.

Trying Again

In general, you can try a skill check again if you fail, and you can keep trying indefinitely. Some skills, however, have consequences of failure that must be taken into account. A few skills are virtually useless once a check has failed on an attempt to accomplish a particular task.

Table 2-1: Skills					
Skill Name	**Ability**	**Untrained?**	**Retry?**	**Action**	**Example Use**
Appraise	Int	Yes	No	1 minute	Determine the value of a gem
Balance	Dex	Yes	No	Move or React	Walk across a slippery ledge
Bluff	Cha	Yes	varies (see text)	Standard	Convince a guard to look away
Climb	Str	Yes	Yes	Full or Move	Climb a sheer cliff
Concentration	Con	Yes	No (see text)	none	Concentrate in the middle of a windstorm
Craft	Int	Yes	Yes (see text)	na	Craft a masterwork sword
Decipher Script	Int	No	No	1 minute +	Read an ancient and forgotten text
Diplomacy	Cha	Yes	No	1 minute +	Convince the king to raise his reward
Disable Device	Int	No	varies (see text)	varies (see text)	Open a locked chest
Disguise	Cha	Yes	Yes (see text)	10 minutes +	Impersonate the Duke
Drive	Dex	Yes	No	Full or Move	Steer a chariot, ride a bike, drive a car
Escape Artist	Dex	Yes	No (see text)	varies (see text)	Free yourself from a straightjacket
Forgery	Int	Yes	No	1 minute +	Create false travelling papers
Gather Information	Cha	Yes	Yes	1 hour +	Get the "word on the street"
Handle Animal	Cha	No	Yes (see text)	varies (see text)	Calm a nervous animal
Heal	Wis	Yes	Yes (see text)	varies (see text)	Care for a snakebite victim
Hide	Dex	Yes	varies (see text)	Free (w/ Move)	Conceal yourself in a shadowy alcove
Intimidate	Cha	Yes	No	varies (see text)	Force a bully to back down
Jump	Str	Yes	Yes	Free (w/ Move)	Jump a chasm during an earthquake
Knowledge	Int	No	No	none	Recall pertinent facts about your situation
Listen	Wis	Yes	Yes	Move or React	Hear the footsteps of an approaching guard
Move Silently	Dex	Yes	No	Free (w/Move)	Follow someone without them noticing
Perform	Cha	Yes	Yes (see text)	varies (see text)	Sing a song, play a guitar, recite a poem
Profession	Wis	No	varies (see text)	varies (see text)	Use your abilities to earn a living wage
Research	Int	Yes	varies (see text)	varies (see text)	Use a library or an archive to find info
Ride	Dex	Yes	No	varies (see text)	Ride a horse, a whale, or a giant eagle
Search	Int	Yes	Yes	Full (or more)	Find a cleverly hidden secret door
Sense Motive	Wis	Yes	No	1 minute +	Determine if someone is lying to you
Sleight of Hand	Dex	No	Yes (see text)	Standard (see text)	Make a coin disappear— or pick a pocket
Speak Language	None	No	na	na	Learn to speak another language
Spot	Wis	Yes	Yes	varies (see text)	Notice when someone is sneaking up on you
Survival	Wis	Yes	varies (see text)	varies (see text)	Find food, shelter, and your way home
Swim	Str	Yes	No (see text)	Move or Full	Swim in rough or choppy waters
Tumble	Dex	No	No	Free (w/Move)	Roll between the legs of a giant enemy
Use Unknown Device	Cha	No	Yes	none (see text)	Activate a magical or technological device
Use Rope	Dex	Yes	Yes	varies (see text)	Securely tie a rope around a prisoner

Untrained Skill Checks

Generally, if your character attempts to use a skill he or she does not possess, you make a skill check as normal. The skill modifier doesn't have a skill rank added in because the character has no ranks in the skill. Any other applicable modifiers, such as the modifier for the skill's key ability, are applied to the check.

However, many skills can be used only by someone who is trained in them. These skills are noted as "Trained Only" in the skill description and cannot be used untrained.

Favorable and Unfavorable Conditions

Some situations may make a skill easier or harder to use, resulting in a bonus or penalty to the skill modifier for a skill check or a change to the DC of the skill check.

The chance of success can be altered in four ways to take into account exceptional circumstances.

1. Give the skill user a +2 circumstance bonus to represent conditions that improve performance, such as having the perfect tool for the job, getting help from another

character (see Combining Skill Attempts), or possessing unusually accurate information.

2. Give the skill user a -2 circumstance penalty to represent conditions that hamper performance, such as being forced to use improvised tools or having misleading information.
3. Reduce the DC by 2 to represent circumstances that make the task easier, such as having a friendly audience or doing work that can be subpar.
4. Increase the DC by 2 to represent circumstances that make the task harder, such as having an uncooperative audience or doing work that must be flawless.

When conditions affect your character's ability to perform the skill, change the skill modifier. When conditions modify how well the character has to perform the skill to succeed, change the DC. A bonus to the skill modifier and a reduction in the check's DC have the same result: They create a better chance of success. But they represent different circumstances, and sometimes that difference is important.

Time and Skill Checks

Using a skill might take a round, take no time, or take several rounds or even longer. Most skill uses are standard actions, move actions, or full-round actions. Types of actions define how long activities take to perform within the framework of a combat round (6 seconds) and how movement is treated with respect to the activity. Some skill checks are instant and represent reactions to an event, or are included as part of an action.

Checks without Rolls

A skill check represents an attempt to accomplish some goal, usually while under some sort of time pressure or distraction. Sometimes, though, a character can use a skill under more favorable conditions and eliminate the luck factor.

Taking 10

When your character is not being threatened or distracted, you may choose to take 10. Instead of rolling 1d20 for the skill check, calculate your result as if you had rolled a 10. For many routine tasks, taking 10 makes them automatically successful. Distractions or threats (such as combat) make it impossible for a character to take 10. In most cases, taking 10 is purely a safety measure —you know (or expect) that an average roll will succeed but fear that a poor roll might fail, so you elect to settle for the average roll (a 10). Taking 10 is especially useful in situations where a particularly high roll wouldn't help.

Taking 20

When you have plenty of time (generally 2 minutes for a skill that can normally be checked in 1 round, one full-round action, or one standard action), you are faced with no threats or distractions, and the skill being attempted carries no penalties for failure, you can take 20. In other words, eventually you will get a 20 on 1d20 if you roll enough times. Instead of rolling 1d20 for the skill check, just calculate your result as if you had rolled a 20.

Taking 20 means you are trying until you get it right, and it assumes that you fail many times before succeeding. Taking 20 takes twenty times as long as making a single check would take.

Since taking 20 assumes that the character will fail many times before succeeding, if you did attempt to take 20 on a skill that carries penalties for failure, your character would automatically incur those penalties before he or she could complete the task.

Ability Checks and Caster Level Checks

The normal take 10 and take 20 rules apply for ability checks. Neither rule applies to caster level checks.

Critical Failures and Critical Successes

Skill checks are subject to critical failures and critical successes—results below or above the norm. Each skill description contains an entry to describe extraordinary results for both critical failures and critical successes.

Critical Failures

If you roll a natural 1 (the d20 actually shows a "1" result) your check may result in a critical failure. Not all skill checks are appropriate for critical failures; activating a critical failure is at the discretion of the GM. In order to activate a critical failure, your GM must award you an action point. If the GM chooses not to award you an action point to activate the critical failure, the skill check proceeds as normal—in fact, you may have enough bonuses, or the DC may be so low, that a "1" result could very well indicate a success anyway.

However, if the GM activates a critical failure, your skill check is an automatic failure, and in fact may carry harsher penalties than an "ordinary" failed skill check. You may not spend the action point awarded by the GM—indeed, you may not spend any action points at all—to improve the result of a critical failure. The results may be harsh, but the awarding of an additional action point softens the blow somewhat: Your character learns quickly from critical failures and is invigorated to do better next time—if he survives the critical failure, of course!

Some skill checks are made secretly, by the GM. In these cases, the action point is not awarded until you become aware of your failure.

Critical Successes

If you roll a natural 20 (the d20 actually shows a "20" result) your check may result in a critical success. In this case, you must spend an action point in order to activate the critical success. You are not required to activate a critical success; again, a critical success is not appropriate or required in all situations. You should carefully read the description of the critical success in your skill entry to decide if it is worth spending the action point.

Note that if you spend an action point to activate a critical success, but your roll of 20 plus all bonuses still indicates a failure due to a particularly high DC, your skill check still fails. Some successes are out of reach, even when your character performs flawlessly. Your GM may advise you if such is the case before you spend your action point, though he is not required to do so.

Combining Skill Attempts

When more than one character tries the same skill at the same time and for the same purpose, their efforts may overlap.

Individual Events

Often, several characters attempt some action and each succeeds or fails independently. For example, the result of one character's Climb check does not influence the results of other characters' Climb checks.

Aid Another

You can help another character achieve success on his or her skill check by making the same kind of skill check in a cooperative effort. If you roll a 10 or higher on your check, the character you are helping gets a +2 bonus to his or her check, as per the rule for favorable conditions. (You can't take 10 on a skill check to aid another.) In many cases, a character's help won't be beneficial, or only a limited number of characters can help at once.

At the GM's option, when multiple characters attempt the same task as a group effort, each character should make a skill check. The player with the highest result is considered the acting character, and every other character who beats DC10 adds +2 to the acting character's total.

Skill Synergy

It's possible for a character to have two skills that work well together. In general, having 5 or more ranks in one skill gives the character a +2 bonus on skill checks with each of its synergistic skills, as noted in the skill description. In some cases, this bonus applies only to specific uses of the skill in question, and not to all checks. Some skills provide benefits on other checks made by a character, such as those checks required to use certain class features.

Sub-Skill Synergies

Skills with sub-skills have *sub-skill synergy*: your ability with two or more very closely related skills is improved as you purchase additional sub-skills. The synergy bonus for sub-skill synergy is reduced from +2 to +1.

Craft:

Every Craft skill you have works to make you a better craftsman in general. For example, your ability to manage time and raw materials carries over from one Craft skill to the next. If you have 5 or more ranks in a Craft sub-skill, it provides a +1 synergy bonus to every other Craft sub-skill. For example, if you had Craft (blacksmithing): 5 ranks, Craft (armorsmithing): 5 ranks, and Craft (weaponsmithing): 2 ranks, your Craft (blacksmithing) receives a +1 synergy bonus for your 5 ranks of armorsmithing, your Craft (armorsmithing) receives a +1 synergy bonus from your 5 ranks of blacksmithing; and your Craft (weaponsmithing) receives a +2 bonus, +1 each from your 5 ranks of blacksmithing and armorsmithing.

Drive:

Every Drive skill you have hones your senses, your timing, and your instincts a bit better for every other Drive skill. If you have 5 or more ranks in a Drive sub-skill, you receive a +1 synergy bonus to every other Drive sub-skill.

Knowledge:

Every Knowledge skill gives you some clue that can be applied to your other Knowledge skills; even two widely different and seemingly unrelated knowledge skills can benefit your ability to absorb and recall information. If you have 5 or more ranks in a Knowledge sub-skill, you receive a +1 synergy bonus to every other Knowledge sub-skill.

Perform:

Every Perform skill you have makes you a more well-rounded entertainer and increases your ability with other kinds of performances; the ability to sing, for example, can improve your rhythm and your ability to dance; the ability to dance may give you an edge when acting. If you have 5 or more ranks in a Perform sub-skill, you receive a +1 synergy bonus to every other Perform sub-skill.

Ride:

Every Ride skill you have improves your ability to anticipate and control your mount, making you a better rider in general. If you have 5 or more ranks in a Ride sub-skill, you receive a +1 synergy bonus to every other Ride sub-skill.

Ability Checks

Sometimes a character tries to do something to which no specific skill really applies. In these cases, you make an ability check. An ability check is a roll of 1d20 plus the appropriate ability modifier. Essentially, you're making an untrained skill check.

In some cases, an action is a straight test of one's ability with no luck involved. Just as you wouldn't make a height check to see who is taller, you don't make a Strength check to see who is stronger.

Skill Descriptions

This section describes each skill, including common uses and typical modifiers. Characters can sometimes use skills for purposes other than those noted here. Here is the format for skill descriptions:

Skill Name (KEY; Trained; Armor Check)

The skill name line includes (in addition to the name of the skill) the following information.

Key Ability: The abbreviation of the ability whose modifier applies to the skill check. Exception: Speak Language has "None" as its key ability because the use of this skill does not require a check.

Trained Only: If this notation is included in the skill name line, you must have at least 1 rank in the skill to use it. If it is omitted, the skill can be used untrained (with a rank of 0). If any special notes apply to trained or untrained use, they are covered in the Untrained section (see below).

Armor Check Penalty: If this notation is included in the skill name line, an armor check penalty applies (when appropriate) to checks using this skill. If this entry is absent, an armor check penalty does not apply.

The skill name line is followed by a general description of what using the skill represents. After the description are a few other types of information:

Check: What a character ("you" in the skill description) can do with a successful skill check and the check's DC.

Action: The type of action using the skill requires, or the amount of time required for a check.

Try Again: Any conditions that apply to successive attempts to use the skill successfully. If the skill doesn't allow you to attempt the same task more than once, or if failure carries an inherent penalty (such as with the Climb skill), you can't take 20. If this paragraph is omitted, the skill can be retried without any inherent penalty, other than the additional time required.

Special: Any extra facts that apply to the skill, such as special effects deriving from its use or bonuses that certain characters receive because of class, feat choices, or race.

Synergy: Some skills grant a bonus to the use of one or more other skills because of a synergistic effect. This entry, when present, indicates what bonuses this skill may grant or receive because of such synergies. See Table 4-5 for a complete list of bonuses granted by synergy between skills (or between a skill and a class feature).

Restriction: The full utility of certain skills is restricted to characters of certain classes or characters who possess certain feats. This entry indicates whether any such restrictions exist for the skill.

Untrained: This entry indicates what a character without at least 1 rank in the skill can do with it. If this entry doesn't appear, it means that the skill functions normally for untrained characters (if it can be used untrained) or that an untrained character can't attempt checks with this skill (for skills that are designated as "Trained Only").

Critical Failure: Details on the results of a critical failure can be found here. The GM must award the player an action point in order to activate a critical failure.

Critical Success: The results of a critical success can be found here. The player must spend an action point to activate a critical success.

Appraise (INT)

Use this skill to approximate the value of an item, whether it be an ancient tome, a finely-crafted weapon, or a piece of advanced technology. This skill is typically used to determine the value of an item you wish to buy or sell.

Check: The GM should secretly roll the d20 skill check, along with the 2d6 estimate, so the player does not know whether he succeeded or failed.

Appraising common or well-known objects requires a DC 12 Appraise check. Failure means that you estimate the value at 50% to 150% (2d6+3 times 10%,) of its actual value.

Appraising a rare or exotic item requires a successful check against DC 15, 20, or higher. If the check is successful, you estimate the value correctly; failure means you cannot estimate the item's value at all.

A magnifying glass gives you a +2 circumstance bonus on Appraise checks involving any item that is small or highly detailed, such as a gem. A merchant's scale gives you a +2 circumstance bonus on Appraise checks involving any items that are valued by weight, including anything made of precious metals.These bonuses stack.

Action: Appraising an item takes 1 minute (ten consecutive full-round actions).

Try Again: No. You cannot try again on the same object, regardless of success.

Synergy: If you have 5 ranks in an applicable Craft skill, you gain a +2 bonus on Appraise checks related to items made with that Craft skill.

Untrained: For common items, failure on an untrained check means no estimate. For rare items, success means an estimate of 50% to 150% (2d6+3 times 10%).

Critical Failure: If you are attempting to sell the item, you estimate its value at 50%. If you are attempting to buy the item, you estimate its value at 150%.

Critical Success: You estimate the item's value with perfect accuracy, and in addition you notice some overlooked detail—a hidden code word, a maker's mark or owner's mark, a valuable gem hidden amongst a multitude of rhinestones. As a result of your obscure knowledge, you gain a +2 competence bonus to any other skill checks involving this item—whether haggling to buy or sell, attempting to activate or identify the item, etc.

Balance (DEX; Armor Check Penalty)

Use this skill to keep your balance on a slippery surface, to stand up in the back of a moving vehicle, or to walk across a narrow ledge.

Check: You can walk on a precarious surface. A successful check lets you move at half your speed along the surface for 1 round. A failure by 4 or less means you can't move for 1 round. A failure by 5 or more means you fall. The difficulty varies with the surface, as follows:

Type of Surface	Balance DC[1]
Narrow Surface	
7-12 inches wide	10
2-6 inches wide	15
Less than 2 inches wide	20
1 Add Narrow Surface Modifiers, below, as appropriate.	
Lightly obstructed	+2
Severely obstructed	+5
Lightly slippery	+2
Severely slippery	+5
Sloped or angled	+2
Surface shifts or moves	+1 to +4
Difficult Surface	
Uneven flagstone	10[2]
Hewn stone floor	10[2]
Sloped or angled floor	10[2]
2 Only if running or charging. Failure by 4 or less means you can't run or charge, but may otherwise act normally.	

Being Attacked while Balancing: You are considered flat-footed while balancing, since you can't move to avoid a blow, and thus you lose your Dexterity bonus to AC (if any). If you have 5 or more ranks in Balance, you aren't considered flat-footed while balancing. If you take damage while balancing, you must make another Balance check against the same DC to remain standing.

Accelerated Movement: You can try to walk across a precarious surface more quickly than normal. If you accept a -5 penalty, you can move your full speed as a move action. (Moving twice your speed in a round requires two Balance checks, one for each move action used.) You may also accept this penalty in order to charge across a precarious surface; charging requires one Balance check for each multiple of your speed (or fraction thereof) that you charge.

Action: None. A Balance check doesn't require an action; it is made as part of another action or as a reaction to a situation.

Synergy: If you have 5 or more ranks in Tumble, you get a +2 bonus on Balance checks.

Critical Failure: You are wildly off balance and you fall. You cannot use any other skill (such as Jump or Tumble) to reduce the damage of your fall. Alternately, you freeze up, forcing someone else to come to your rescue.

Critical Success: You may move at twice the speed you were trying to move, up to the limit of your movement rate.

Bluff (CHA)

Check: A Bluff check is opposed by the target's Sense Motive check. See the accompanying table for examples of different kinds of bluffs and the modifier to the target's Sense Motive check for each one.

Example Circumstances	Sense Motive Modifier
The target wants to believe you.	-5
The bluff is believable and doesn't affect the target much.	+0
The bluff is a little hard to believe or puts the target at some risk.	+5
The bluff is hard to believe or puts the target at significant risk.	+10
The bluff is way out there, almost too incredible to consider.	+20

Favorable and unfavorable circumstances weigh heavily on the outcome of a bluff. Two circumstances can weigh against you: The bluff is hard to believe, or the action that the target is asked to take goes against its self-interest, nature, personality, orders, or the like. If it is important, you can distinguish between a bluff that fails because the target doesn't believe it and one that fails because it just asks too much of the target. For instance, if the target gets a +10 bonus on its Sense Motive check because the bluff demands something risky, and the Sense Motive check succeeds by 10 or less, then the target didn't so much see through the bluff as prove reluctant to go along with it. A target that succeeds by 11 or more has seen through the bluff.

A successful Bluff check indicates that the target reacts as you wish, at least for a short time (usually 1 round or less) or believes something that you want it to believe.

A bluff requires interaction between you and the target, and may require that you and the target speak the same language. Creatures unaware of you cannot be bluffed.

Feinting in Combat: You can also use Bluff to mislead an opponent in melee combat (so that it can't dodge your next attack effectively). To feint, make a Bluff check opposed by your target's Sense Motive check, but in this case, the target may add its base attack bonus to the roll along with any other applicable modifiers.

If your Bluff check result exceeds the opponent's Sense Motive check result, your target is denied its Dexterity bonus to AC (if any) for the next melee attack you make against it. This attack must be made on or before your next turn.

Feinting in this way against a non-humanoid is difficult because it is harder to read a strange creature's body language; you take a -4 penalty on your Bluff check. Against a creature of animal Intelligence (1 or 2) it is even harder: you take a -8 penalty. Against a non-intelligent creature, it is impossible.

Feinting in combat does not provoke an attack of opportunity.

Creating a Diversion to Hide: You can use the Bluff skill to help you hide. A successful Bluff check gives you the momentary diversion you need to attempt a Hide check while people are aware of you. This usage does not provoke an attack of opportunity.

Delivering a Secret Message: You can use Bluff to get a message across to another character without others understanding it. The DC is 15 for simple messages, or 20 for complex messages, especially those that rely on getting across new information. Failure by 4 or less means you can't get the message across. Failure by 5 or more means that some false information has been implied or inferred. Anyone listening to the exchange can make a Sense Motive check opposed by the Bluff check you made to transmit in order to intercept your message (see Sense Motive).

Action: Varies. A Bluff check made as part of general interaction always takes at least 1 round (and is at least a full-round action), but it can take much longer if you try something elaborate. A Bluff check made to feint in combat or create a diversion to hide is a standard action. A Bluff check made to deliver a secret message doesn't take an action; it is part of normal communication.

Try Again: Varies. Generally, a failed Bluff check in social interaction makes the target too suspicious for you to try again in the same circumstances, but you may retry freely on Bluff checks made to feint in combat. Retries are also allowed when you are trying to send a message, but you may attempt such a retry only once per round. Each retry carries the same chance of miscommunication.

Synergy: If you have 5 or more ranks in Bluff, you get a +2 bonus on Diplomacy, Intimidate, and Sleight of Hand checks, as well as on Disguise checks made when you know you are being observed and you try to act in character.

Critical Failure: The target isn't fooled by your Bluff, and is insulted at the attempt. The target's attitude immediately shifts one category worse. If you are feinting in combat, your bluff provokes an attack of opportunity. If attempting to create a diversion to hide, your bluff gives your position away; any targets within line of sight who were not already aware of you are able to pinpoint your position. If delivering a secret message, the target interprets your meaning as the opposite of what you intended, or in the worst possible way.

Critical Success: The target is completely fooled. You receive a +2 bonus to Bluff, Diplomacy, Hide, or even to your attack roll, depending on how you were using your Bluff skill. If you were attempting to use Bluff to deliver a secret message, your meaning is crystal clear to your intended recipient; he does not need to roll a Sense Motive check to understand your meaning, though eavesdroppers must still check as normal.

Climb (STR; Armor Check Penalty)

Check: With a successful Climb check, you can advance up, down, or across a slope, a wall, or some other steep incline (or even a ceiling with handholds) at one-quarter your normal speed. A slope is considered to be any incline at an angle measuring less than 60 degrees; a wall is any incline at an angle measuring 60 degrees or more.

A Climb check that fails by 4 or less means that you make no progress, and one that fails by 5 or more means that you fall from whatever height you have already attained.

A climber's kit gives you a +2 circumstance bonus on Climb checks.

The DC of the check depends on the conditions of the climb. Compare the task with those on the following table to determine an appropriate DC.

You need both hands free to climb, but you may cling to a wall with one hand while you cast a spell or take some other action that requires only one hand. While climbing, you can't move to avoid a blow, so you lose your Dexterity bonus to AC (if any). You also can't use a shield while climbing.

Any time you take damage while climbing, make a Climb check against the DC of the slope or wall. Failure means you fall from your current height and sustain the appropriate falling damage.

Accelerated Climbing: You try to climb more quickly than normal. By accepting a –5 penalty, you can move half your speed (instead of one-quarter your speed).

Making Your Own Handholds and Footholds: You can make your own handholds and footholds by pounding pitons into a wall. Doing so takes 1 minute per piton, and one piton is needed per 3 feet of distance. As with any surface that offers handholds and footholds, a wall with pitons in it has a DC of 15. In the same way, a climber with a hand-axe or similar implement can cut handholds in an ice wall.

Climb DC	Example Surface or Activity
0	A slope too steep to walk up, or a knotted rope with a wall to brace against.
5	A rope with a wall to brace against, or a knotted rope, or a rope affected by the *rope trick* spell.
10	A surface with ledges to hold on to and stand on, such as a very rough wall or a ship's rigging.
15	Any surface with adequate handholds and footholds (natural or artificial), such as a very rough natural rock surface or a tree, or an unknotted rope, or pulling yourself up when dangling by your hands.
20	An uneven surface with some narrow handholds and footholds, such as a typical wall in a dungeon or ruins.
25	A rough surface, such as a natural rock wall or a brick wall.
25	An overhang or ceiling with handholds but no footholds.
–	A perfectly smooth, flat, vertical surface cannot be climbed.
Climb DC Modifier[1]	**Example Surface or Activity**
-10	Climbing a chimney (artificial or natural) or other location where you can brace against two opposite walls (reduces DC by 10).
-5	Climbing a corner where you can brace against perpendicular walls (reduces DC by 5).
+5	Surface is slippery (increases DC by 5).
1 These modifiers are cumulative; use any that apply.	

Catching Yourself When Falling: It is practically impossible to catch yourself on a wall while falling. Make a Climb check (DC = wall's DC + 20) to do so. It is much easier to catch yourself on a slope (DC = slope's DC + 10).

Catching a Falling Character While Climbing: If someone climbing above you or adjacent to you falls, you can attempt to catch the falling character if he is within your reach. Doing so requires a successful melee touch attack against the falling character (though he can voluntarily forego any Dexterity bonus to AC if desired). If you hit, you must immediately attempt a Climb check (DC = wall's DC + 10). Success indicates that you catch the falling character, but his total weight, including equipment, cannot exceed your heavy load limit or you automatically fall. If you fail your Climb check by 4 or less, you fail to stop the character's fall but don't lose your grip on the wall. If you fail by 5 or more, you fail to stop the character's fall and begin falling as well.

Action: Climbing is part of movement, so it is generally part of a move action (and may be combined with other types of movement in a move action). Each move action that includes any climbing requires a separate Climb check. Catching yourself or another falling character doesn't take an action.

Special: You can use a rope to haul a character upward (or lower a character) through sheer strength. You can lift double your maximum load in this manner.

A creature with a listed climb speed has a +8 racial bonus on all Climb checks. The creature must make a Climb check to climb any wall or slope with a DC higher than 0, but it always can choose to take 10, even if rushed or threatened while climbing. If a creature with a climb speed chooses an accelerated climb (see above), it moves at double its climb speed (or at its land speed, whichever is slower) and makes a single Climb check at a -5 penalty. Such a creature retains its Dexterity bonus to Armor Class (if any) while climbing, and opponents get no special bonus to their attacks against it. It cannot, however, use the run action while climbing.

Synergy: If you have 5 or more ranks in Use Rope, you get a +2 bonus on Climb checks made to climb a rope, a knotted rope, or a rope-and-wall combination.

Critical Failure: You fall. You cannot use any other skill (such as Jump or Tumble) to reduce the damage of your fall. Alternately, you freeze up, forcing someone else to come to your rescue.

Critical Success: You may move at twice the speed you were trying to move, up to the limit of your movement rate.

Concentration (CON)

Check: You must make a Concentration check whenever you might potentially be distracted (by taking damage, by harsh weather, and so on) while engaged in some action that requires your full attention. Such actions include casting a spell, concentrating on an active spell, directing a spell, using a spell-like ability, or using a skill that would provoke an attack of opportunity. In general, if an action wouldn't normally provoke an attack of opportunity, you need not make a Concentration check to avoid being distracted.

If the Concentration check succeeds, you may continue with the action as normal. If the check fails, the action automatically fails and is wasted. If you were in the process of casting a spell, the spell is lost. If you were concentrating on an active spell, the spell ends as if you had ceased concentrating on it. If you were directing a spell, the direction fails but the spell remains active. If you were using a spell-like ability, that use of the ability is lost. A skill use also fails, and in some cases a failed skill check may have other ramifications as well.

The table summarizes various types of distractions that cause you to make a Concentration check. If the distraction occurs while you are trying to cast a spell, you

Concentration DC[1]	Distraction
10 + damage dealt	Damaged during the action.[2]
10 + half damage dealt	Taking continuous damage[3] during the action.
Distracting spell's save DC	Distracted by nondamaging spell (including magical weather effects).[4]
10	Vigorous motion (on a moving mount, taking a bouncy wagon ride, in a small boat in rough water, belowdecks in a storm-tossed ship).
15	Violent motion (on a galloping horse, taking a very rough wagon ride, in a small boat in rapids, on the deck of a storm-tossed ship).
20	Extraordinarily violent motion (earthquake).
15	Entangled.
20	Grappling or pinned. (You can cast only spells without somatic components for which you have any required material component in hand.)
5	Weather is a high wind carrying blinding rain or sleet.
10	Weather is wind-driven hail, dust, or debris.

1 If you are trying to cast, concentrate on, or direct a spell when the distraction occurs, add the level of the spell to the indicated DC.
2 Such as during the casting of a spell with a casting time of 1 round or more, or the execution of an activity that takes more than a single full-round action (such as Disable Device). Also, damage stemming from an attack of opportunity or readied attack made in response to the spell being cast (for spells with a casting time of 1 action) or the action being taken (for activities requiring no more than a full-round action).
3 Such as from *fire, acid,* or other damaging effects that last from round to round.
4 If the spell allows no save, use the save DC it would have if it did allow a save.

must add the level of the spell you are trying to cast to the appropriate Concentration DC. If more than one type of distraction is present, make a check for each one; any failed Concentration check indicates that the task is not completed.

Action: None. Making a Concentration check doesn't take an action; it is either a free action (when attempted reactively) or part of another action (when attempted actively).

Try Again: Yes, though a success doesn't cancel the effect of a previous failure, such as the loss of a spell you were casting or the disruption of a spell you were concentrating on.

Special: You can make a Concentration check to perform certain actions "defensively" so as to avoid attacks of opportunity. You may use Concentration in this way when casting a spell, using a spell-like ability, or using a skill. This doesn't apply to other actions that might provoke attacks of opportunity.

The DC of the check is 15 (plus the spell's level, if casting a spell or using a spell-like ability defensively). If the Concentration check succeeds, you may attempt the action normally without provoking any attacks of opportunity. A successful Concentration check still doesn't allow you to take 10 on another check if you are in a stressful situation; you must make the check normally. If the Concentration check fails, the related action also automatically fails (with any appropriate ramifications), and the action is wasted, just as if your concentration had been disrupted by a distraction.

Critical Failure: You concentration is completely foiled. You cannot attempt the action again until the source of the distraction is removed.

Critical Success: Your concentration is flawless. No further Concentration checks are required until after you complete your current task (if possible).

Craft (INT)

Like Drive, Knowledge, Perform, Profession, and Ride, Craft is actually a number of separate skills. You could have several Craft skills, each with its own ranks, each purchased as a separate skill.

A Craft skill is specifically focused on creating something tangible. If nothing is created by the endeavor, it probably falls under the heading of a Profession skill.

Check: You can practice your trade and make a decent living. You know how to use the tools of your trade, how to perform the craft's daily tasks, how to supervise untrained helpers, and how to handle common problems.

The basic function of the Craft skill, however, is to allow you to make an item of the appropriate type. The DC depends on the complexity of the item to be created. The DC, your check results, and the price of the item determine how long it takes to make a particular item. The item's finished price also determines the cost of raw materials.

All crafts require craftsman's tools to give the best chance of success. If improvised tools are used, the check is made with a –2 circumstance penalty. On the other hand, masterwork tools provide a +2 circumstance bonus on the check.

To determine how much time and money it takes to make an item, follow these steps:

1. Find the item's price (market value) in currency units (see Chapter Five: Economy and Equipment).
2. Obtain the Craft DC from the GM or from the table below.
3. Pay one-third of the item's price (or make a Wealth check) for the cost of raw materials.

A Craft check represents one week's work. If the check succeeds, multiply your check result by the DC. If the result x the DC equals the item's value, then you have completed the item. (If the result x the DC equals double or triple the value, then you've completed the task in one-half or one-third of the time. Other multiples of the DC reduce the time in the same manner.) If the result x the DC doesn't equal the value, then it represents the progress you've made this week towards the completion of the task. Record the result and make a new Craft check for the next week. Each week, you make more progress until your total reaches the value of the item.

If you fail a check by 4 or less, you make no progress that week.

If you fail by 5 or more, you ruin half the raw materials and have to pay half the original raw material cost again.

Typical Craft DCs

Item Complexity/Rarity	Example	DC
Simple Item	iron pot, wooden staff	5
Average Item	simple weapon	10
High Quality Item	martial weapon	15
Complex Item / Masterwork	exotic weapon	20
Common Item	-	+0
Unusual Item	-	+5
Rare/Restricted Item	-	+10

- Simple items have no moving parts, and are constructed from a single raw material (i.e., solid clay, iron, wood, etc.).
- Average items may have moving parts, or are constructed of two or more solid raw materials (i.e. iron and leather, bone and sinew, etc.).
- High quality items are constructed of higher quality raw materials (e.g. steel instead of iron) or materials that are difficult or dangerous to work with (e.g. chemicals).
- Complex Items have moving parts and are constructed of two or more kinds of raw materials.
- Common items can be found nearly anywhere in the campaign world.
- Unusual items can be found only in specific shops or locales.
- Rare items can rarely be found in any shop, or are restricted by local laws, trade guilds, etc.

Creating Masterwork Items: You can make a masterwork item (such as a weapon or tool) that conveys a bonus on its use through its exceptional craftsmanship. To create a masterwork item, you create the masterwork component as if it were a separate item in addition to the standard item. The masterwork component has its own price (your GM will inform you of the details) and a Craft DC of 20. Once both the standard component and the masterwork component are completed, the masterwork item is finished.

Repairing Items: Generally, you can repair an item by making checks against the same DC that it took to make the item in the first place, but you receive a +5 bonus to your check result. The cost of repairing an item is one-fifth of the item's price and the value of a repair is one-fifth the value of a new item.

Action: Does not apply. Craft checks are made by the week (see above).

Try Again: Yes, but each time you miss by 5 or more, you ruin half the raw materials and have to pay half the original raw material cost again.

Special: You may voluntarily add +10 to the indicated DC to craft an item as a "rush job." This allows you to create the item more quickly (since you'll be multiplying this higher DC by your Craft check result to determine progress). You must decide whether to increase the DC before you make each weekly check.

Synergy: If you have 5 ranks in a Craft skill, you get a +2 bonus on Appraise checks related to items made with that Craft skill.

If you have 5 ranks in any other Craft skill, you get a sub-skill synergy bonus of +1 to every other Craft skill.

Critical Failure: All of your raw materials are ruined, and all progress is lost. You must start anew.

Critical Success: You make twice the progress towards completion with this check; if the check was sufficient to complete the item anyway, you complete the item in half the time.

Decipher Script (INT; Trained Only)

Check: You can decipher a piece of writing (about one page long, or the equivalent) in an unfamiliar language or a message written in an incomplete or archaic form. The base DC is 20 for the simplest messages, 25 for standard texts, and 30 or higher for intricate, exotic, or very old writing.

The GM will make your Decipher Script check secretly, as there is a possibility that you will draw some false conclusion about the meaning of the writing. You can't tell whether the conclusion you draw is true or false.

If the check succeeds, you understand the general content or meaning of the writing, though not a precise translation of the text. If the check fails, you cannot understand the writing.

Action: Deciphering the equivalent of a single page of script takes 1 minute (ten consecutive full-round actions).

Try Again: No.

Special: A character with the Diligent feat gets a +2 bonus on Decipher Script checks.

Synergy: If you have 5 or more ranks in Decipher Script, you get a +2 bonus on Use Unknown Device checks involving scrolls.

Critical Failure: You draw a false conclusion about the text.

Critical Success: You understand the text perfectly, gaining a precise reading of the text (as opposed to merely the general meaning or content of the writing).

Diplomacy (CHA)

Check: You can change the attitudes of others (non-player characters) with a successful Diplomacy check; see the Influencing NPC Attitudes sidebar below for basic DCs. In negotiations, participants roll opposed Diplomacy checks, and the winner gains the advantage. Opposed checks also resolve situations when two advocates or diplomats plead opposite cases in a hearing before a third party.

Action: Changing others' attitudes with Diplomacy generally takes at least 1 full minute (10 consecutive full-round actions). In some situations, this time requirement may greatly increase. A rushed Diplomacy check can be made as a full-round action, but you take a –10 penalty on the check.

Try Again: Optional, but not recommended because retries usually do not work. Even if the initial Diplomacy check succeeds, the other character can be persuaded only so far, and a retry may do more harm than good. If the initial check fails, the other character has probably become more firmly committed to his position, and a retry is futile.

Synergy: If you have 5 or more ranks in Bluff, Knowledge (nobility and royalty), or Sense Motive, you get a +2 bonus on Diplomacy checks.

Critical Failure: Your diplomacy fails spectacularly. You may even have insulted your target. The target's attitude immediately shifts down one step to the next worse category.

Critical Success: Your diplomacy is successful, and your target's attitude shifts up an additional category for the better.

Disable Device (INT; Trained Only)

Check: The Disable Device check is made secretly by the GM, so that you don't necessarily know whether you've succeeded.

The DC depends on how tricky the device is. Disabling (or rigging or jamming) a fairly simple device has a DC of 10; more intricate and complex devices have higher DCs.

Device	Time	Disable Device DC[1]
Simple	Full round	10
Tricky	1d4 rounds	15
Difficult	2d4 rounds	20
Wicked	2d4 rounds	25
Very simple lock	Full round	20
Average lock	Full round	25
Good lock	Full round	30
Amazing lock	Full round	40

1 If you attempt to leave behind no trace of your tampering, add 5 to the DC.

If the check succeeds, you disable the device. If it fails by 4 or less, you have failed but can try again. If you fail by 5 or more, something goes wrong. If the device is a trap, you spring it. If you are attempting some sort of sabotage, you think the device is disabled, but it still works normally.

You also can rig simple devices such as saddles or wagon wheels to work normally for a while and then fail some time later (usually after 1d4 rounds or minutes of use).

Attempting to open a lock without a set of thieves' tools or lock picks imposes a –2 circumstance penalty on the check, even if a simple tool is employed. If you use masterwork tools, you gain a +2 circumstance bonus on the check.

Diplomacy: Influencing NPC Attitudes

Use the table below to determine the effectiveness of Diplomacy checks (or Charisma checks) made to influence the attitude of a non-player character. Find the target's initial attitude in the left-hand column, then read across the row to the result of your Diplomacy check. The target's new attitude is at the top of the column.

			Target's Adjusted Attitude vs. Diplomacy Check Result				
Initial Attitude	What it means	Possible actions	Hostile	Unfriendly	Indifferent	Friendly	Helpful
Hostile	Will take risks to hurt you	Attack, interfere, berate, flee	Less than 20	20-24	25-34	35-49	50+
Unfriendly	Wishes you ill	Mislead, gossip, avoid, watch suspiciously, insult	Less than 5	5-14	15-24	25-39	40+
Indifferent	Doesn't much care	Socially expected interaction	—	Less than 1	1-14	15-29	30+
Friendly	Wishes you well	Chat, advise, offer limited help, advocate	—	—	Less than 1	1-19	20+
Helpful	Will take risks to help you	Protect, back up, heal, aid	—	—	—	Less than 1	1+

Action: The amount of time needed to make a Disable Device check depends on the task, as noted above. Disabling a simple device takes 1 round and is a full-round action. An intricate or complex device requires 1d4 or 2d4 rounds.

Untrained: You cannot pick locks untrained (you might try forcing them open instead).

Try Again: Varies. You can retry if you have missed the check by 4 or less, though you must be aware that you have failed in order to try again.

Restriction: Only characters with the trapfinding talent can disarm magic traps. A magic trap generally has a DC of 25 + the spell level of the magic used to create it.

Critical Failure: If the device is a trap, you cannot defend against it. You are considered flat-footed, and you automatically fail any Reflex save. If the device is a lock, you have fouled the lock. It will not open even with the key, and must be forced open. If you are attempting sabotage, the item not only continues to work, but evidence of your tampering is readily apparent.

Critical Success: If the device is a trap, you can study it, figure out how it works, and bypass it (along with your companions) without disarming it. If the device is a lock, you understand it fully; you can lock and unlock it with your tools without the need for further checks, as if you had a key. If you are trying to sabotage some other device, your sabotage is perfect, and goes off at the best possible time (depending on your intent).

Disguise (CHA)

Check: The Disguise check is made secretly by the GM, so that you can't be sure how good the result is.

Your Disguise check result determines how good the disguise is, and it is opposed by others' Spot check results. If you don't draw any attention to yourself, others do not get to make Spot checks. If you come to the attention of people who are suspicious (such as a guard who is watching commoners walking through a city gate), it can be assumed that such observers are taking 10 on their Spot checks.

You get only one Disguise check per use of the skill, even if several people are making Spot checks against it.

The effectiveness of your disguise depends in part on how much you are attempting to change your appearance.

Disguise	Check Modifier
Minor details only	+5
Disguised as different gender[1]	-2
Disguised as different race[1]	-2
Disguised as different age category[1]	-2[2]

1 These modifiers are cumulative; use any that apply.
2 Per step of difference between your actual age category and your disguised age category. The steps are: young (younger than adulthood), adulthood, middle age, old, and venerable.

If you are impersonating a particular individual, those who know what that person looks like get a bonus on their Spot checks according to the table below. Furthermore, they are automatically considered to be suspicious of you, so opposed checks are always called for.

Familiarity	Spot Check Bonus
Would normally recognize on sight	+4
Friends or associates	+6
Close friends	+8
Intimate	+10

Usually, an individual makes a Spot check to see through your disguise immediately upon meeting you and each hour thereafter. If you casually meet many different creatures, each for a short time, check once per day or hour, using an average Spot modifier for the group.

Action: Creating a disguise requires 1d3×10 minutes.

Try Again: Yes. You may try to redo a failed disguise, but once others know that a disguise was attempted, they'll be more suspicious.

Synergy: If you have 5 or more ranks in Bluff, you get a +2 bonus on Disguise checks when you know that you are being observed and you try to act in character.

Critical Failure: Your disguise is a complete failure—your wig is sliding off or your fake nose has melted, and you, unfortunately, are completely oblivious to the fact. All observers immediately spot the fact that you are disguised without the need for a Spot check.

Critical Success: The disguise is flawless. Individuals observing the disguise are not automatically suspicious of you; they must have reason to be suspicious of you (odd behavior, conversations, etc.) in order to make a Spot check.

Drive (DEX)

Like Craft, Knowledge, Perform, Profession, and Ride, Drive is actually a number of separate skills. You could have several Drive skills, each with its own ranks, each purchased as a separate skill. Like the Ride skill, the Drive sub-skills are grouped according to the vehicle's type of movement—on the ground, on water, or in the air. The basic Drive sub-skills are Drive (ground transport), Drive (nautical), and Drive (aerospace).

The Drive skill applies whenever the character is seated or mounted in or on a vehicle and must maintain control over the vehicle's operation. A horse-drawn wagon or chariot uses the Drive skill, not the Ride skill, even though the vehicle is powered by animals.

Check: Routine tasks, such as ordinary driving, don't require a skill check. Make a check only when some unusual circumstance exists (such as inclement weather or an icy surface), or when the character is driving during a dramatic situation (the character is being chased or attacked, for example, or is trying to reach a destination in a limited amount of time). When driving, the character can attempt simple maneuvers or stunts. See Chapter Eleven: Vehicles for more details.

Action: A Drive check is a move action.

Try Again: Most driving checks have consequences for failure that make trying again impossible.

Special: A character can take 10 when driving, but can't take 20. You may not take 10 if you are involved in a chase, combat, or other stressful situation.

Synergy: If you have 5 ranks in any other Drive skill, you get a sub-skill synergy bonus of +1 to every other Drive skill.

Critical Failure: The vehicle strikes an obstacle, goes out of control, or stalls. This is equivalent to failing a Crash check.

Critical Success: You receive a +4 bonus to your next Drive check. In addition, if you are involved in a chase or dogfight and attempt a maneuver, your maneuver is automatically successful unless your opponent also scores a critical success.

Escape Artist (DEX; Armor Check Penalty)

Check: The table below gives the DCs to escape various forms of restraints.

Ropes: Your Escape Artist check is opposed by the binder's Use Rope check. Since it is easier to tie someone up than to escape from being tied up, the binder gets a +10 bonus on his check.

Manacles and Masterwork Manacles: The DC for manacles is set by their construction.

Tight Space: The DC noted on the table is for getting through a space where your head fits but your shoulders don't. If the space is long you may need to make multiple checks. You can't get through a space that your head does not fit through.

Grappler: You can make an Escape Artist check opposed by your enemy's grapple check to get out of a grapple or out of a pinned condition (so that you are only grappling).

Restraint	Escape Artist DC
Ropes	Binder's Use Rope check at +10
Net, bolas, or similar entanglement	20
Manacles, straight-jacket	30
Tight space	30
Masterwork manacles, handcuffs	35
Grappler	Grappler's grapple check result

Action: Making an Escape Artist check to escape from rope bindings, manacles, hand-cuffs, a straight-jacket, or other restraints (except a grappler) requires 1 minute of work. Escaping from a net or similar entanglements is a full-round action. Escaping from a grapple or pin is a standard action. Squeezing through a tight space takes at least 1 minute, maybe longer, depending on how long the space is; if the space is especially long, requiring several minutes to move through, you may need to make additional checks.

Try Again: Varies. You can make another check after a failed check if you are squeezing your way through a tight space, making multiple checks. If the situation permits, you can make additional checks, or even take 20, as long as you are not being actively opposed.

Special: If you are trying to escape without being noticed, the observers must beat your Escape Artist check with an opposed Spot check in order to notice that you have escaped.

Synergy: If you have 5 or more ranks in Escape Artist, you get a +2 bonus on Use Rope checks to bind someone.

If you have 5 or more ranks in Use Rope, you get a +2 bonus on Escape Artist checks when escaping from rope bonds.

Critical Failure: You are trapped. If you were trying to escape from bonds, you cannot escape and you cannot try again. If you were trying to move through a tight space, you are trapped halfway through and someone must free you. If you are grappling, your opponent immediately does his normal grappling damage to you.

Critical Success: You escape in half the time. If you are in a tight space, you do not need to check again. If you are attempting to escape without being noticed, your captors do not notice that you have escaped, and you gain a surprise round against them when you choose to act. If you are grappling, you escape as a free action and can immediately take any remaining actions. If all you do is move away, you do not provoke an attack of opportunity.

Forgery (INT)

Check: The Forgery check is made secretly by the GM, so that you are not sure how good your forgery is.

Forgery requires writing materials appropriate to the document being forged, enough light or sufficient visual acuity to see the details of what you are writing, wax for seals (if appropriate), and some time. To forge a document on which the handwriting is not specific to a person (military orders, a government decree, a business ledger, or the like), you need only to have seen a similar document before, and you gain a +8 bonus on your check. To forge a signature, you need an autograph of that person to copy, and you gain a +4 bonus on the check. A longer document written in the hand of some particular person cannot be attempted without a large sample of that person's handwriting.

As with Disguise, you don't even need to make a check until someone examines the work. Your Forgery check is opposed by the Forgery check of the person who examines the document to check its authenticity. The examiner gains modifiers on his check if any of the conditions on the table below exist.

A document that contradicts procedure, orders, or previous knowledge, or one that requires sacrifice on the part of the person checking the document can increase that character's suspicion (and thus create favorable circumstances for the checker's opposing Forgery check).

Condition	Reader's Forgery Check Modifier
Document unknown to reader	-2
Document somewhat known to reader	+0
Document well known to reader	+2
Handwriting not known to reader	-2
Handwriting somewhat known to reader	+0
Handwriting intimately known to reader	+2
Reader only casually reviews the document	-2

Action: Forging a very short and simple document takes about 1 minute. A longer or more complex document takes 1d4 minutes per page.

Try Again: Usually, no. A retry is never possible after a particular reader detects a particular forgery. But the document created by the forger might still fool someone else. The result of a Forgery check for a particular document must be used for every instance of a different reader examining the document. No reader can attempt to detect a particular forgery more than once; if that one opposed check goes in favor of the forger, then the reader can't try using his own skill again, even if he's suspicious about the document.

Restriction: Forgery is language-dependent; thus, to forge documents and detect forgeries, you must be able to read and write the language in question.

Critical Failure: The document is automatically detected as a forgery the first time it is presented for inspection.

Critical Success: The forgery is perfect. It can only be detected with a critical success on the opposed roll.

Gather Information (CHA)

Check: The Gather Information check is made secretly by the GM, so that you are not sure how good your information is. An evening's time, drinks bought to make friends, and a DC 10 Gather Information check get you a general idea of a city's major news items, assuming there are no obvious reasons why the information would be withheld. The higher your check result, the better the information.

If you want to find out about a specific rumor, or a specific item, or obtain a map, or do something else along those lines, the DC for the check is 15 to 25, or even higher.

Action: A typical Gather Information check takes 1d4+1 hours.

Try Again: Yes, but it takes time for each check. Furthermore, you may draw attention to yourself if you repeatedly pursue a certain type of information.

Synergy: If you have 5 or more ranks in Knowledge (local) or Knowledge (streetwise), you get a +2 bonus on Gather Information checks.

Critical Failure: The person you are asking deduces your intention (or has had word passed to him from your prior efforts). You are given deliberately faulty information.

Critical Success: You not only receive the information you were looking for, you receive additional, related information you didn't even know you needed.

Handle Animal (CHA; Trained Only)

Check: The DC depends on what you are trying to do.

Task	Handle Animal DC
Handle an animal	10
"Push" an animal	25
Teach an animal a trick	15 or 20[1]
Train an animal for a general purpose	15 or 20[1]
Rear a wild animal	15 + HD of animal
1 See the specific trick or purpose below.	

Handle an Animal: This task involves commanding an animal to perform a task or trick that it knows. If the animal is wounded or has taken any nonlethal damage or ability score damage, the DC increases by 2. If your check succeeds, the animal performs the task or trick on its next action.

"Push" an Animal: To push an animal means to get it to perform a task or trick that it doesn't know but is physically capable of performing. This category also covers making an animal perform a forced march or forcing it to hustle for more than 1 hour between sleep cycles. If the animal is wounded or has taken any nonlethal damage or ability score damage, the DC increases by 2. If your check succeeds, the animal performs the task or trick on its next action.

Teach an Animal a Trick: You can teach an animal a specific trick with one week of work and a successful Handle Animal check against the indicated DC. An animal with an Intelligence score of 1 can learn a maximum of three tricks, while an animal with an Intelligence score of 2 can learn a maximum of six tricks. Possible tricks (and their associated DCs) include, but are not necessarily limited to, the following.

Attack (DC 20): The animal attacks apparent enemies. You may point to a particular creature that you wish the animal to attack, and it will comply if able. Normally, an animal will attack only humanoids, monstrous humanoids, giants, or other animals. Teaching an animal to attack all creatures (including such unnatural creatures as undead and aberrations) counts as two tricks.

Come (DC 15): The animal comes to you, even if it normally would not do so.

Defend (DC 20): The animal defends you (or is ready to defend you if no threat is present), even without any command being given. Alternatively, you can command the animal to defend a specific other character.

Down (DC 15): The animal breaks off from combat or otherwise backs down. An animal that doesn't know this trick continues to fight until it must flee (due to injury, a fear effect, or the like) or its opponent is defeated.

Fetch (DC 15): The animal goes and gets something. If you do not point out a specific item, the animal fetches some random object.

Guard (DC 20): The animal stays in place and prevents others from approaching.

Heel (DC 15): The animal follows you closely, even to places where it normally wouldn't go.

Perform (DC 15): The animal performs a variety of simple tricks, such as sitting up, rolling over, roaring or barking, and so on.

Seek (DC 15): The animal moves into an area and looks around for anything that is obviously alive or animate.

Stay (DC 15): The animal stays in place, waiting for you to return. It does not challenge other creatures that come by, though it still defends itself if it needs to.

Track (DC 20): The animal tracks the scent presented to it. (This requires the animal to have the scent ability.)

Work (DC 15): The animal pulls or pushes a medium or heavy load.

Train an Animal for a Purpose: Rather than teaching an animal individual tricks, you can simply train it for a general purpose. Essentially, an animal's purpose represents a preselected set of known tricks that fit into a common scheme, such as guarding or heavy labor. The animal must meet all the normal prerequisites for all tricks included in the training package. If the package includes more than three tricks, the animal must have an Intelligence score of 2.

An animal can be trained for only one general purpose, though if the creature is capable of learning additional tricks (above and beyond those included in its general purpose), it may do so. Training an animal for a purpose requires fewer checks than teaching individual tricks does, but no less time.

Combat Riding (DC 20): An animal trained to bear a rider into combat knows the tricks attack, come,

General Purpose	DC
Combat riding	20
Fighting	20
Guarding	20
Heavy labor	15
Hunting	20
Performance	15
Riding	15

defend, down, guard, and heel. Training an animal for combat riding takes six weeks. You may also "upgrade" an animal trained for riding to one trained for combat riding by spending three weeks and making a successful DC 20 Handle Animal check. The new general purpose and tricks completely replace the animal's previous purpose and any tricks it once knew. Warhorses and riding dogs are already trained to bear riders into combat, and they don't require any additional training for this purpose.

Fighting (DC 20): An animal trained to engage in combat knows the tricks attack, down, and stay. Training an animal for fighting takes three weeks.

Guarding (DC 20): An animal trained to guard knows the tricks attack, defend, down, and guard. Training an animal for guarding takes four weeks.

Heavy Labor (DC 15): An animal trained for heavy labor knows the tricks come and work. Training an animal for heavy labor takes two weeks.

Hunting (DC 20): An animal trained for hunting knows the tricks attack, down, fetch, heel, seek, and track. Training an animal for hunting takes six weeks.

Performance (DC 15): An animal trained for performance knows the tricks come, fetch, heel, perform, and stay. Training an animal for performance takes five weeks.

Riding (DC 15): An animal trained to bear a rider knows the tricks come, heel, and stay. Training an animal for riding takes three weeks.

Rear a Wild Animal: To rear an animal means to raise a wild creature from infancy so that it becomes domesticated. A handler can rear as many as three creatures of the same kind at once.

A successfully domesticated animal can be taught tricks at the same time it is being raised, or it can be taught as a domesticated animal later.

Action: Varies. Handling an animal is a move action, while pushing an animal is a full-round action. (A character with the wild empathy talent can handle her animal companion as a free action or push it as a move action.) For tasks with specific time frames noted above, you must spend half this time (at the rate of 3 hours per day per animal being handled) working toward completion of the task before you attempt the Handle Animal check. If the check fails, your attempt to teach, rear, or train the animal fails and you need not complete the teaching, rearing, or training time. If the check succeeds, you must invest the remainder of the time to complete the teaching, rearing, or training. If the time is interrupted or the task is not followed through to completion, the attempt to teach, rear, or train the animal automatically fails.

Try Again: Yes, except for rearing an animal.

Special: You can use this skill on a creature with an Intelligence score of 1 or 2 that is not an animal, but the DC of any such check increases by 5. Such creatures have the same limit on tricks known as animals do.

Synergy: If you have 5 or more ranks in Handle Animal, you get a +2 bonus on Ride checks.

Untrained: If you have no ranks in Handle Animal, you can use a Charisma check to handle and push domestic animals, but you can't teach, rear, or train animals.

Critical Failure: The animal immediately bucks, rears, flees, or attacks you unexpectedly, as appropriate for an animal of its type. You are considered *flat-footed* against its attack, if any. Its attitude is hostile.

Critical Success: If you are handling the animal or pushing it, the animal receives a +2 bonus to a d20 roll on its action (skill check, ability check, attack roll, etc.) If you are attempting to teach an animal a trick, it has a natural aptitude for the trick; the trick does not count against its limit of tricks. If you are training the animal for a general purpose, the training is completed in half the time.

Heal (WIS)

Check: The DC and effect depend on the task you attempt.

Task	Heal DC
Stabilize (first aid)	15
Restore hit points	15
Revive a character	15
Long-term care	15
Treat poison	Poison's save DC
Treat disease	Disease's save DC
Surgery	20 or more

Stabilize a Dying Character (DC15): You usually use first aid to save a *dying* character. If a character has negative hit points and is losing hit points (at the rate of 1 per round, 1 per hour, or 1 per day), you can make him or her stable. A stable character regains no hit points but stops losing them.

Restore Hit Points (DC 15): With a healer's kit, if a character has lost hit points, the character can restore some of them. A successful check, as a full-round action, restores 1d4 hit points. The number restored can never exceed the character's full normal total of hit points. This application of the skill can be used successfully on a character only once per day. You may not attempt to restore hit points on a *dying* character; they must be stabilized first.

Revive Dazed, Stunned, Crippled, or Unconscious Character (DC 15): With a healer's kit, the character can remove the dazed, stunned, crippled, or unconscious condition from a character. This check is a standard action.

A successful check removes the dazed, stunned, crippled, or unconscious condition from an affected character. You cannot revive an unconscious character who is at -1 hit points or lower without first stabilizing the character and restoring them to 0 or more hit points.

Long-Term Care (DC 15): Providing long-term care means treating a wounded person for a day or more. With the proper supplies (bandages, salves, and other items commonly found in a healer's kit), the successful application of this skill allows a patient to recover hit points and ability points lost to temporary damage at an advanced rate. If your Heal check is successful, the patient recovers hit points or ability score points (lost to ability damage) at twice the normal rate, according to the patient's character level: 2 hit points per level for a full 8 hours of rest in a day, or 4 hit points per level for each full day of complete rest; 2 ability score points for a full 8 hours of rest in a day, or 4 ability score points for each full day of complete rest.

A character can tend up to as many patients as she has ranks in the skill. The character needs to devote at least a half an hour each day to each patient the character is caring for. Giving long-term care counts as light activity for the healer. You cannot give long-term care to yourself.

Type of Damage	Normal (unassisted)	With Long Term Care
Hit points (8 hours rest)	1 hp/level	2 hp/level
Hit points (full day's rest)	2 hp/level	4 hp/level
Ability damage (8 hours rest)	1 point/ability	2 points/ability
Ability damage (full day's rest)	2 points/ability	4 points/ability

Treat Poison (DC 15): A character can tend to a poisoned character. Before a poisoned character makes a saving throw against a poison's secondary effect, the healer first makes a Heal check as a standard action. If the healer's check succeeds, the character provides a bonus on the poisoned character's saving throw equal to her ranks in this skill.

Treat Disease (DC 15): A character can tend to a character infected with a treatable disease. Every time the diseased character makes a saving throw against disease effects (after the initial contamination), the healer first makes a Heal check to help the diseased character fend off secondary damage. This activity takes 10 minutes. If the healer's check succeeds, she provides a bonus on the diseased character's saving throw equal to her ranks in this skill.

Surgery (DC 20+): With a surgery kit, a character can perform surgery. This application of the skill (as with all applications of the Heal skill at DC20 and above) can only be attempted with the Surgery feat.

Surgery requires 1d4 hours; if the patient is at negative hit points, add an additional hour for every point below 0 the patient has fallen, and increase the DC by +1 for every negative hit point.

Surgery restores 1d6 hit points for every character level of the patient (up to the patient's full normal total of hit points) with a successful skill check.

Surgery can be used for other purposes besides the restoration of hit points: setting bones, amputating limbs, etc. Your GM will advise the DC and the details of such uses on a case-by-case basis.

Surgery can only be used successfully on a character once in a 24-hour period.

A character who undergoes surgery is fatigued for 24 hours, minus 2 hours for every point above the DC the surgeon achieves. The period of fatigue can never be reduced below 6 hours in this fashion (except through a critical success, see below).

Try Again: Yes, for restoring hit points, reviving dazed, stunned, crippled, or unconscious characters, stabilizing *dying* characters, and surgery. No, for all other uses of the skill.

Special: The Surgery feat gives a character the extra training she needs to use the Heal skill to help a wounded character by means of an operation.

A character can take 10 when making a Heal check. A character can take 20 only when restoring hit points or attempting to revive dazed, stunned, or unconscious characters.

Most uses of the Heal skill require a healer's kit. Surgery requires a surgery kit. If the character does not have the appropriate kit, she takes a –4 penalty on the check.

A character can use the Heal skill on herself only to administer first aid, treat disease, or treat poison. The character takes a –5 penalty on the check any time she treats herself.

Action: Providing first aid or treating poison is a standard action. Treating a diseased creature or reviving a creature takes 10 minutes of work. Providing long-term care requires 8 hours of light activity. Surgery can require an hour or more.

Try Again: Varies. Generally speaking, you can't try a Heal check again without proof of the original check's failure. You can always retry a check to provide first aid, assuming the target of the previous attempt is still alive.

Special: A healer's kit (or similar) gives you a +2 circumstance bonus on Heal checks.

Critical Failure: If you are trying to stabilize a *dying* character, restore hit points, revive a character, or providing long term care, the character does not stabilize, gain any hit points, or revive, and in addition, loses 1 hit point. If you are assisting a save vs. poison or disease, the patient's saving throw automatically fails. If you are attempting surgery, the patient immediately drops to –1 hit points (unless his previous total was already lower) and begins *dying*.

Critical Success: If you are trying to stabilize a *dying* character, the character is stabilized and gains hit points as if you had also attempted to restore hit points. If you are trying to restore hit points or providing long term care, the patient regains twice as many hit points. If you are assisting a patient with a save vs. poison or disease, the saving throw automatically succeeds. If you are attempting surgery, the surgery is successful; the patient recovers twice as many hit points, and/or the patient's recovery time is halved.

Hide (DEX; Armor Check Penalty)

Check: Your Hide check is opposed by the Spot check of anyone who might see you. You can move up to one-half your normal speed and hide at no penalty. When moving at a speed greater than one-half but less than your normal speed, you take a –5 penalty. It is practically impossible (–20 penalty) to hide while attacking, running or charging.

A creature larger or smaller than Medium takes a size bonus or penalty on Hide checks depending on its size category: Fine +16, Diminutive +12, Tiny +8, Small +4, Large –4, Huge –8, Gargantuan –12, Colossal –16.

You need cover or concealment in order to attempt a Hide check. Total cover or total concealment usually (but not always; see Special, below) obviates the need for a Hide check, since nothing can see you anyway.

If people are observing you, even casually, you can't hide. You can run around a corner or behind cover so that you are out of sight and then hide, but the others then know at least where you went.

If your observers are momentarily distracted (such as by a Bluff check; see below), though, you can attempt to hide. While the others turn their attention from you, you can attempt a Hide check if you can get to a hiding place of some kind. (As a general guideline, the hiding place has to be within 1 foot per rank you have in Hide.) This check, however, is made at a –10 penalty because you have to move fast.

Sniping: If you've already successfully hidden at least 10 feet from your target, you can make one ranged attack, then immediately hide again. You take a –20 penalty on your Hide check to conceal yourself after the shot.

Creating a Diversion to Hide: You can use Bluff to help you hide. A successful Bluff check can give you the momentary diversion you need to attempt a Hide check while people are aware of you.

Action: Usually none. Normally, you make a Hide check as part of movement, so it doesn't take a separate action. However, hiding immediately after a ranged attack (see Sniping, above) is a move action.

Special: If you are invisible, you gain a +40 bonus on Hide checks if you are standing still, or a +20 bonus on Hide checks if you are moving.

Critical Failure: Everyone with line of sight to your position automatically spots you trying to hide. You cannot attempt to hide again until you find concealment or cover out of line of sight of these observers.

Critical Success: You have found a perfect hiding place. Provided you do not move, attempts to Spot you automatically fail (unless they also score a critical success).

Intimidate (CHA)

Check: You can change another's behavior with a successful check. Your Intimidate check is opposed by the target's modified level check (1d20 + character level or Hit Dice + target's Wisdom bonus [if any] + target's modifiers on saves against fear). If you beat your target's check result, you may treat the target as friendly, but only for the purpose of actions taken while it remains intimidated. (That is, the target retains its normal attitude, but will chat, advise, offer limited help, or advocate on your behalf while intimidated. See the Diplomacy skill, above, for additional details.) The effect lasts as long as the target remains in your presence, and for 1d6×10 minutes afterward. After this time, the target's default attitude toward you shifts to unfriendly (or, if normally unfriendly, to hostile).

If you fail the check by 5 or more, the target provides you with incorrect or useless information, or otherwise frustrates your efforts.

Demoralize Opponent: You can also use Intimidate to weaken an opponent's resolve in combat. To do so, make an Intimidate check as a standard action, opposed by the target's modified level check (see above). If you win, the

target becomes shaken for 1 round. A shaken character takes a –2 penalty on attack rolls, ability checks, and saving throws. You can intimidate only an opponent that you threaten in melee combat and that can see you.

Action: Varies. Changing another's behavior requires 1 minute of interaction. Intimidating an opponent in combat is a standard action.

Try Again: Optional, but not recommended because retries usually do not work. Even if the initial check succeeds, the other character can be intimidated only so far, and a retry doesn't help. If the initial check fails, the other character has probably become more firmly resolved to resist the intimidator, and a retry is futile.

Special: You gain a +4 bonus on your Intimidate check for every size category that you are larger than your target. Conversely, you take a –4 penalty on your Intimidate check for every size category that you are smaller than your target.

A character immune to fear can't be intimidated, nor can non-intelligent creatures.

Synergy: If you have 5 or more ranks in Bluff, you get a +2 bonus on Intimidate checks.

Critical Failure: The target's resolve against your intimidation is hardened. His attitude immediately shifts to hostile, all future intimidation checks against this opponent suffer a -5 penalty.

Critical Success: The target is deeply affected by your intimidation. All future intimidation checks against this opponent receive a +5 bonus.

Jump (STR; Armor Check Penalty)

Check: The DC and the distance you can cover vary according to the type of jump you are attempting (see below).

Your Jump check is modified by your speed. If your speed is 30 feet then no modifier based on speed applies to the check. If your speed is less than 30 feet, you take a -6 penalty for every 10 feet of speed less than 30 feet. If your speed is greater than 30 feet, you gain a +4 bonus for every 10 feet beyond 30 feet.

All Jump DCs given here assume that you get a running start, which requires that you move at least 20 feet in a straight line before attempting the jump. If you do not get a running start, the DC for the jump is doubled.

Distance moved by jumping is counted against your normal maximum movement in a round.

If you have ranks in Jump and you succeed on a Jump check, you land on your feet (when appropriate). If you attempt a Jump check untrained, you land prone unless you beat the DC by 5 or more.

Long Jump: A long jump is a horizontal jump, made across a gap like a chasm or stream. At the midpoint of the jump, you attain a vertical height equal to one-quarter of the horizontal distance. The DC for the jump is equal to the distance jumped (in feet).

If your check succeeds, you land on your feet at the far end. If you fail the check by less than 5, you don't clear the distance, but you can make a DC 15 Reflex save to grab the far edge of the gap. You end your movement grasping the far edge. If that leaves you dangling over a chasm or gap, getting up requires a move action and a DC 15 Climb check.

Long Jump Distance	Jump DC[1]
5 feet	5
10 feet	10
15 feet	15
20 feet	20
25 feet	25
30 feet	30

1 Requires a 20-foot running start. Without a running start, double the DC.

High Jump: A high jump is a vertical leap made to reach a ledge high above or to grasp something overhead. The DC is equal to 4 times the distance to be cleared.

High Jump Distance[2]	Jump DC[3]
1 foot	4
2 feet	8
3 feet	12
4 feet	16
5 feet	20
6 feet	24
7 feet	28
8 feet	32

2 Not including vertical reach; see below.
3 Requires a 20-foot running start. Without a running start, double the DC.

If you jumped up to grab something, a successful check indicates that you reached the desired height. If you wish to pull yourself up, you can do so with a move action and a DC 15 Climb check. If you fail the Jump check, you do not reach the height, and you land on your feet in the same spot from which you jumped. As with a long jump, the DC is doubled if you do not get a running start of at least 20 feet.

Obviously, the difficulty of reaching a given height varies according to the size of the character or creature. The maximum vertical reach (height the creature can reach without jumping) for an average creature of a given size is shown on the table below. (As a Medium creature, a typical human can reach 8 feet without jumping.)

Quadrupedal creatures don't have the same vertical reach as a bipedal creature; treat them as being one size category smaller.

Creature Size	Vertical Reach
Colossal	128 ft.
Gargantuan	64 ft.
Huge	32 ft.
Large	16 ft.
Medium	8 ft.
Small	4 ft.
Tiny	2 ft.
Diminutive	1 ft.
Fine	1/2 ft.

Hop Up: You can jump up onto an object as tall as your waist, such as a table or small boulder, with a DC 10 Jump check. Doing so counts as 10 feet of movement, so if your speed is 30 feet, you could move 20 feet, then hop up onto a counter. You do not need to get a running start to hop up, so the DC is not doubled if you do not get a running start.

Jumping Down: If you intentionally jump from a height, you take less damage than you would if you just fell. The DC to jump down from a height is 15. You do not have to get a running start to jump down, so the DC is not doubled if you do not get a running start.

If you succeed on the check, you take falling damage as if you had dropped 10 fewer feet than you actually did.

Action: None. A Jump check is included in your movement, so it is part of a move action. If you run out of movement mid-jump, your next action (either on this turn or, if necessary, on your next turn) must be a move action to complete the jump.

Special: Effects that increase your movement also increase your jumping distance, since your check is modified by your speed.

If you have the Run feat, you get a +4 bonus on Jump checks for any jumps made after a running start.

Synergy: If you have 5 or more ranks in Tumble, you get a +2 bonus on Jump checks.

If you have 5 or more ranks in Jump, you get a +2 bonus on Tumble checks.

Critical Failure: You jump only a fraction of the distance you intended. If you were attempting to jump across a gap, you fall, suffering the normal effects for the fall. In addition, you land badly, and are crippled until you receive first aid.

Critical Success: The distance jumped only counts as ½ against your movement for the round. If you have additional movement remaining at the end of your jump, you may continue your movement.

Knowledge (INT; Trained Only)

Like the Craft and Profession skills, Knowledge actually encompasses a number of unrelated skills. Knowledge represents a study of some body of lore, possibly an academic or even scientific discipline.

The DC of a Knowledge check is based on how easy the question is for someone with your field of knowledge to answer.

Within the context of the campaign setting (archaic, modern, or apocalyptic), and with the GM's permission, you may define your field of knowledge as broadly or as narrowly as you like. Broad fields of knowledge will make the skill more generally applicable; narrow fields of knowledge may restrict the applicability of the skill, but on a successful check, you will gain more specifically useful information, and the DC for such specific information is generally lower than it would be for a character with only broad knowledge.

For example, a character with Knowledge (geography) may find it easy to locate Imperial City on a map, but would have a harder time describing the city itself; a character with Knowledge (Imperial City) would find it easy to describe the city, its inhabitants, customs, etc.

Check: The Knowledge check is made secretly by the GM, so that you are not sure how reliable your knowledge is.

Answering a question within your field of study has a DC of 10 (for really easy questions), 15 (for basic questions), or 20 to 30 (for really tough questions). The GM decides the difficulty of the question based on how narrowly you have defined your Knowledge sub-category. For example, suppose you want to know the name of a Spanish sovereign as well as the dates during which he reigned. If you have Knowledge (history), this may be a DC15 question. If you have Knowledge (Spanish Royalty), this would be an easy question.

For every 5 points by which your check result exceeds the DC, you recall another piece of useful information.

Action: Usually none. In most cases, making a Knowledge check doesn't take an action—you simply know the answer or you don't.

Try Again: No. The check represents what you know, and thinking about a topic a second time doesn't let you know something that you never learned in the first place.

Synergy: If you have 5 ranks in any other Knowledge sub-skill, you get a sub-skill synergy bonus of +1 to every other Knowledge skill.

Many Knowledge skills grant a synergy bonus with other skills, and the GM is encouraged to be generous in this regard. Some examples:

If you have 5 or more ranks in Knowledge (geography), you get a +2 bonus on Survival checks made to keep from getting lost or to avoid natural hazards.

If you have 5 or more ranks in Knowledge (history), you get a +2 bonus on obscure knowledge checks.

If you have 5 or more ranks in Knowledge (local), you get a +2 bonus on Gather Information checks.

If you have 5 or more ranks in an applicable Knowledge sub-skill for your current environment, you get a +2 bonus on Survival checks made in that environment. For example, if you had 5 ranks of Knowledge (nature), you get a +2 bonus to Survival checks made in above-ground natural environments (aquatic, desert, forest, hill, marsh, mountains, or plains).

If you have 5 or more ranks in Knowledge (nobility and royalty), you get a +2 bonus on Diplomacy checks.

If you have 5 or more ranks in Knowledge (religion), you get a +2 bonus on turning checks against undead.

If you have 5 or more ranks in Survival, you get a +2 bonus on Knowledge (nature) checks.

Untrained: An untrained Knowledge check is simply an Intelligence check. Without actual training, you know only common knowledge (DC 10 or lower).

Critical Failure: You remember incorrect information.

Critical Success: Your recall of this specific piece of knowledge is as detailed and complete as possible.

Listen (WIS)

Check: The Listen check may be made secretly by the GM, so that you are not sure how good your hearing is.

Your Listen check is either made against a DC that reflects how quiet the noise is that you might hear, or it is opposed by your target's Move Silently check.

Listen DC	Sound
-10	A battle
0	People talking[1]
5	A person in medium armor walking at a slow pace (10 feet/round) trying not to make any noise.
10	An unarmored person walking at a slow pace (15 feet/round) trying not to make any noise
15	A 1st-level hero using Move Silently to sneak past the listener
15	People whispering[1]
19	A cat stalking
30	An owl gliding in for a kill

1 If you beat the DC by 10 or more, you can make out what's being said, assuming that you understand the language.

Listen DC Modifier	Condition
+5	Through a door
+15	Through a stone wall
+1	Per 10 feet of distance
+5	Listener distracted

In the case of people trying to be quiet, the DCs given on the table could be replaced by Move Silently checks, in which case the indicated DC would be their average check result.

Action: Varies. Every time you have a chance to hear something in a reactive manner (such as when someone makes a noise or you move into a new area), you can make a Listen check without using an action. Trying to hear something you failed to hear previously is a move action.

Try Again: Yes. You can try to hear something that you failed to hear previously with no penalty.

Special: When several characters are listening to the same thing, a single 1d20 roll can be used for all the individuals' Listen checks.

If you have the Alertness feat, you get a +2 bonus on Listen checks.

A sleeping character may make Listen checks at a -10 penalty. A successful check awakens the sleeper.

Critical Failure: You mishear something, with unfavorable, perhaps disastrous, results. You automatically lose any opposed check, unless the opposing roll is also a critical failure.

Critical Success: You know exactly what you heard. You automatically win any opposed check, unless the opposing roll is also a critical success.

Move Silently (DEX; Armor Check Penalty)

Check: Your Move Silently check is opposed by the Listen check of anyone who might hear you. You can move up to one-half your normal speed at no penalty. When moving at a speed greater than one-half but less than your full speed, you take a -5 penalty. It is practically impossible (-20 penalty) to move silently while running or charging.

Noisy surfaces, such as bogs or undergrowth, are tough to move silently across. When you try to sneak across such a surface, you take a penalty on your Move Silently check as indicated below.

Surface	Check Modifier
Noisy (scree, shallow or deep bog, undergrowth, dense rubble)	-2
Very noisy (dense undergrowth, deep snow)	-5

Action: None. A Move Silently check is included in your movement or other activity, so it is part of another action.

Critical Failure: You make a loud noise that alerts everyone in the area to your presence. You automatically lose any opposed check, unless the opposing roll is also a critical failure.

Critical Success: You move so silently there is nothing to hear. You automatically win any opposed check, unless the opposing roll is also a critical success.

Perform (CHA)

Like Craft, Knowledge, and Profession, Perform is actually a number of separate skills.

You could have several Perform skills, each with its own ranks, each purchased as a separate skill.

Each of the nine categories of the Perform skill includes a variety of methods, instruments, or techniques, a small list of which is provided for each category below.

- Act (comedy, drama, mime)
- Comedy (buffoonery, limericks, joke-telling)
- Dance (ballet, waltz, jig)
- Keyboard instruments (harpsichord, piano, pipe organ)
- Oratory (epic, ode, storytelling)
- Percussion instruments (bells, chimes, drums, gong)
- String instruments (fiddle, harp, lute, mandolin)
- Wind instruments (flute, pan pipes, recorder, trumpet)
- Song (ballad, chant, melody)

Check: You can impress audiences with your talent and skill.

Perform Check Result	Performance
10	Routine performance. Trying to earn money by playing in public is essentially begging. You can earn up to 1 ₵/day.
15	Enjoyable performance. In a prosperous city, you can earn 1d10 ₵/day.
20	Great performance. In a prosperous city, you can earn 3d10 ₵/day. In time, you may be invited to join a professional troupe and may develop a regional reputation.
25	Memorable performance. In a prosperous city, you can earn 1d6 x10 ₵/day. In time, you may come to the attention of patrons and develop a national reputation.
30	Extraordinary performance. In a prosperous city, you can earn 3d6 x10 ₵/day. In time, you may draw attention from distant, powerful, or influential patrons.

A masterwork musical instrument gives you a +2 circumstance bonus on Perform checks that involve its use.

Action: Varies. Trying to earn money by playing in public requires anywhere from an evening's work to a full day's performance.

Try Again: Yes. Retries are allowed, but they don't negate previous failures, and an audience that has been unimpressed in the past is likely to be prejudiced against future performances. (Increase the DC by 2 for each previous failure.)

Synergy: If you have 5 ranks in any other Perform sub-skill, you get a sub-skill synergy bonus of +1 to every other Perform skill.

Critical Failure: Your performance is abysmal. If you attempt to perform for this audience again, your check is at a -10 penalty.

Critical Success: You have given a truly memorable performance. If you perform for this audience again, your check is at a +10 bonus.

Profession (WIS; Trained Only)

Like Craft, Knowledge, and Perform, Profession is actually a number of separate skills. You could have several Profession skills, each with its own ranks, each purchased as a separate skill. While a Craft skill represents ability in creating or making an item, a Profession skill represents an aptitude in a vocation requiring a broader range of less specific knowledge.

Check: You can practice your trade and make a decent living, earning about 5 ₵ x your check result per week of dedicated work. You know how to use the tools of your trade, how to perform the profession's daily tasks, how to supervise helpers, and how to handle common problems.

Action: Not applicable. A single check generally represents a week of work.

Try Again: Varies. An attempt to use a Profession skill to earn an income cannot be retried. You are stuck with whatever weekly wage your check result brought you. Another check may be made after a week to determine a new income for the next period of time. An attempt to accomplish some specific task can usually be retried.

Synergy: If you have 5 or more ranks in an applicable Profession skill (at the GM's discretion) you may receive a +2 synergy bonus to other skill checks. For example, a character with Profession (guide) may receive a +2 synergy bonus to Survival checks.

Untrained: Untrained laborers and assistants (that is, characters without any ranks in Profession) earn an average of 1-10 ₵/day.

Critical Failure: You earn no money this week. You may have performed so poorly as to draw the ire or your employer or supervisors.

Critical Success: You earn twice as much money this week.

Research (INT)

Check: A Research skill check is similar to a Gather Information check; but rather than emphasizing interpersonal and social skills, research is the ability to find information through books, libraries, archives, and other impersonal means.

Researching a topic takes time, skill, and some luck. The GM determines how obscure a particular topic is (the more obscure, the higher the DC) and what kind of information might be available depending on where the character is conducting her research.

Information ranges from general to protected. Given enough time (usually 1d4 hours) and a successful skill check, the character gets a general idea about a given topic. This assumes that no obvious reasons exist why such information would be unavailable, and that the character has a way to acquire restricted or protected information.

The higher the check result, the better and more complete the information. If the character wants to discover a specific fact, date, map, or similar bit of information, add +5 to +15 to the DC.

Action: A Research check takes 1d4 hours.

Try Again: Yes.

Special: A character can take 10 or take 20 on a Research check.

Synergy: Knowledge (computers) can provide a +2 synergy bonus on a Research check when searching computer records for data (see Skill Synergy).

Critical Failure: Your research is fruitless and heavy-handed. Interested parties (if any) become aware of your research attempts.

Critical Success: You gain the information you were looking for, and may even gain relevant information you didn't even know you needed.

Ride (DEX)

Like Craft, Drive, Knowledge, Perform, and Profession, Ride is actually a number of separate skills. You could have several Ride skills, each with its own ranks, each purchased as a separate skill. Like the Drive skill, the Ride sub-skills are grouped according to the mount's type of movement—on the ground, on water, in the air, or some other type of movement. The basic Ride sub-skills are Ride (ground), Ride (flight), and Ride (swim). It is conceivable that you could even have a Ride (burrow)!

If a creature has more than one movement type, you must purchase your Ride skill separately for each type of movement.

If you attempt to ride a creature that is ill suited as a mount, you take a -5 penalty on your Ride check.

Check: Typical riding actions don't require checks. You can saddle, mount, ride, and dismount from a mount without a check, even untrained.

The following tasks do require checks:

Guide with Knees: You can react instantly to guide your mount with your knees so that you can use both hands in combat. Make your Ride check at the start of your turn. If you fail, you can use only one hand this round because you need to use the other to control your mount.

Stay in Saddle: You can react instantly to try to avoid falling when your mount rears or bolts unexpectedly or when you take damage. This usage does not take an action.

Fight with Warhorse/Warbeast: If you direct your war-trained mount to attack in battle, you can still make your own attack or attacks normally. This usage is a free action.

Cover: You can react instantly to drop down and hang alongside your mount, using it as cover. You can't attack or cast spells while using your mount as cover. If you fail your Ride check, you don't get the cover benefit. This usage does not take an action.

Soft Fall: You can react instantly to try to take no damage when you fall off a mount—when it is killed or when it falls, for example. If you fail your Ride check, you take 1d6 points of falling damage. This usage does not take an action.

Leap: You can get your mount to leap obstacles as part of its movement. Use your Ride modifier or the mount's Jump modifier, whichever is lower, to see how far the creature can jump. If you fail your Ride check, you fall off the mount when it leaps and take the appropriate falling damage (at least 1d6 points). This usage does not take an action, but is part of the mount's movement.

Spur Mount: You can spur your mount to greater speed with a move action. A successful Ride check increases the mount's speed by 10 feet for 1 round but deals 1 point of damage to the creature. You can use this ability every round, but each consecutive round of additional speed deals twice as much damage to the mount as the previous round (2 points, 4 points, 8 points, and so on).

Control Mount in Battle: As a move action, you can attempt to control a light horse, pony, heavy horse, or other mount not trained for combat riding while in battle.

If you fail the Ride check, you can do nothing else in that round. You do not need to roll for warhorses or warponies.

Fast Mount or Dismount: You can attempt to mount or dismount from a mount of up to one size category larger than yourself as a free action, provided that you still have a move action available that round. If you fail the Ride check, mounting or dismounting is a move action. You can't use fast mount or dismount on a mount more than one size category larger than yourself.

Task	Ride DC	Task	Ride DC
Guide with knees	5	Leap	15
Stay in saddle	5	Spur mount	15
Fight with warhorse	10	Control mount in battle	20
Cover	15	Fast mount or dismount	20[1]
Soft fall	15		

1 Armor check penalty applies.

Action: Varies. Mounting or dismounting normally is a move action. Other checks are a move action, a free action, or no action at all, as noted above.

Special: If you are riding bareback, you take a –5 penalty on Ride checks.

If your mount has a military saddle you get a +2 circumstance bonus on Ride checks related to staying in the saddle.

The Ride skill is a prerequisite for the feats Mounted Archery, Mounted Combat, Ride-By Attack, Spirited Charge, Trample.

Synergy: If you have 5 ranks in any other Ride sub-skill, you get a sub-skill synergy bonus of +1 to every other Ride skill.

If you have 5 or more ranks in Handle Animal, you get a +2 bonus on Ride checks.

Critical Failure: You fall from your mount. Both you and your mount must make a Reflex save (DC15) or become crippled from your cumbersome fall. A mount is crippled in the mode of movement you were attempting: a flying mount is crippled for flight, but can still walk, for example.

Critical Success: If your mount is attempting an action this round that requires a d20 check, it may use the result of your Ride check instead of rolling. If your mount is not attempting a d20 check this round, but you are, you receive a +2 bonus to your roll— as if your mount was reading your mind and aiding your actions!

Search (INT)

Check: You generally must be within 10 feet of the object or surface to be searched. The table below gives DCs for typical tasks involving the Search skill.

Task	Search DC
Ransack a chest full of junk to find a certain item	10
Notice a typical secret door or a simple trap	20
Find a difficult trap (trapfinding only)	21 or higher
Find a magic trap (trapfinding only)	25 + level of spell
Notice a well-hidden secret door	30
Find a footprint	Varies[1]

1 A successful Search check can find a footprint or similar sign of a creature's passage, but it won't let you find or follow a trail. See the Track feat for the appropriate DC.

Action: It takes a full-round action to search a 5-foot-by-5-foot area or a volume of goods 5 feet on a side.

Special: Some spells create magic traps that a character with the trapfinding talent can find by making a successful Search check, and can then attempt to disarm by using Disable Device. See the individual spell descriptions for details.

Active abjuration spells within 10 feet of each other for 24 hours or more create barely visible energy fluctuations. These fluctuations give you a +4 bonus on Search checks to locate such abjuration spells.

Synergy: If you have 5 or more ranks in Search, you get a +2 bonus on Survival checks to find or follow tracks.

If you have 5 or more ranks in Knowledge (architecture and engineering), you get a +2 bonus on Search checks to find secret doors or hidden compartments.

Restriction: While anyone can use Search to find a trap whose DC is 20 or lower, only a character with the trapfinding talent can use Search to locate traps with higher DCs.

Critical Failure: If you are searching for a trap, you trigger it. If you are searching for tracks or clues, your blundering attempt destroys the tracks or clue.

Critical Success: You find everything hidden in the square you are searching as well as all adjacent squares; or, your search takes only half the time.

Sense Motive (WIS)

Check: A successful check lets you avoid being bluffed (see the Bluff skill). You can also use this skill to determine when "something is up" (that is, something odd is going on) or to assess someone's trustworthiness.

Hunch (DC20): This use of the skill involves making a gut assessment of the social situation. You can get the feeling from another's behavior that something is wrong, such as when you are talking to an impostor. Alternatively, you can get the feeling that someone is trustworthy.

Sense Enchantment (DC25 or 15): You can tell that someone's behavior is being influenced by an enchantment effect (by definition, a mind-affecting effect), even if that person isn't aware of it. The usual DC is 25, but if the target is *dominated*, the DC is only 15 because of the limited range of the target's activities.

Discern Secret Message (DC varies): You may use Sense Motive to detect that a hidden message is being transmitted via the Bluff skill. In this case, your Sense Motive check is opposed by the Bluff check of the character transmitting the message. For each piece of information relating to the message that you are missing, you take a –2 penalty on your Sense Motive check. If you succeed by 4 or less, you know that something hidden is being communicated, but you can't learn anything specific about its content. If you beat the DC by 5 or more, you intercept and understand the message. If you fail by 4 or less, you don't detect any hidden communication. If you fail by 5 or more, you infer some false information.

Action: Trying to gain information with Sense Motive generally takes at least 1 minute, and you could spend a whole evening trying to get a sense of the people around you.

Try Again: No, though you may make a Sense Motive check for each Bluff check made against you.

Synergy: If you have 5 or more ranks in Sense Motive, you get a +2 bonus on Diplomacy checks.

Critical Failure: You are misled by your senses, drawing a false conclusion or completely misreading the intentions of the target.

Critical Success: You gain incredibly accurate insight into the target. Not only can you tell if the target is trying to mislead you, you may gain some insight into *why* the target is trying to mislead you.

Sleight of Hand (DEX; Trained Only; Armor Check Penalty)

Check: A DC 10 Sleight of Hand check lets you palm a coin-sized, unattended object. Performing a minor feat of legerdemain, such as making a coin disappear, also has a DC of 10 unless an observer is determined to note where the item went.

When you use this skill under close observation, your skill check is opposed by the observer's Spot check. The observer's success doesn't prevent you from performing the action, just from doing it unnoticed.

You can hide a small object (including a light weapon or an easily concealed ranged weapon) on your body. Your Sleight of Hand check is opposed by the Spot check of anyone observing you or the Search check of anyone frisking you. In the latter case, the searcher gains a +4 bonus on the Search check, since it is generally easier to find such an object than to hide it. An extraordinarily small object, such as a coin, shuriken, or ring, grants you a +4 bonus on your Sleight of Hand check to conceal it, and heavy or baggy clothing (such as a cloak) grants you a +2 bonus on the check.

Drawing a hidden weapon is a standard action and doesn't provoke an attack of opportunity.

If you try to take something from another creature, you must make a DC 20 Sleight of Hand check to obtain it. The opponent makes a Spot check to detect the attempt, opposed by the same Sleight of Hand check result you achieved when you tried to grab the item. An opponent who succeeds on this check notices the attempt, regardless of whether you got the item.

You can also use Sleight of Hand to entertain an audience as though you were using the Perform skill. In such a case, your "act" encompasses elements of legerdemain, juggling, and the like.

Sleight of Hand DC	Task
10	Palm a coin-sized object, make a coin disappear
20	Lift a small object from a person

Action: Any Sleight of Hand check normally is a standard action. However, you may perform a Sleight of Hand check as a free action by taking a –20 penalty on the check.

Try Again: Yes, but after an initial failure, a second Sleight of Hand attempt against the same target (or while you are being watched by the same observer who noticed your previous attempt) increases the DC for the task by 10.

Synergy: If you have 5 or more ranks in Bluff, you get a +2 bonus on Sleight of Hand checks.

Untrained: An untrained Sleight of Hand check is simply a Dexterity check. Without actual training, you can't succeed on any Sleight of Hand check with a DC higher than 10, except for hiding an object on your body.

Critical Failure: Your Sleight of Hand attempt is automatically noticed by anyone observing you. You automatically lose any opposed check, unless the opposing check is also a critical failure.

Critical Success: A flawless attempt. You automatically win any opposed check, unless the opposing check is also a critical success.

Speak Language (NONE; Trained Only)

Action: Not applicable.

Try Again: Not applicable. There are no Speak Language checks to fail.

The Speak Language skill doesn't work like other skills. Languages work as follows.

- You start at 1st level knowing one or two languages (a "common" language such as English, plus the language of your race or country of origin), plus an additional number of languages equal to your starting Intelligence bonus.
- You can purchase Speak Language just like any other skill, but instead of buying a rank in it, you choose a new language that you can speak.
- You don't make Speak Language checks. You either know a language or you don't.
- A literate character can read and write any language she speaks. Each language has an alphabet, though sometimes several spoken languages share a single alphabet.

Spot (WIS)

Check: The Spot skill is used primarily to detect characters or creatures who are hiding. Typically, your Spot check is opposed by the Hide check of the creature trying not to be seen.

Spot is also used to detect someone in disguise (see the Disguise skill), and to read lips when you can't hear or understand what someone is saying.

Spot checks may be called for to determine the distance at which an encounter begins. A penalty applies on such checks, depending on the distance between the two individuals or groups, and an additional penalty may apply if the character making the Spot check is distracted (not concentrating on being observant).

Condition	Penalty
Per 10 feet of distance	-1
Spotter distracted	-5

Read Lips: To understand what someone is saying by reading lips, you must be within 30 feet of the speaker, be able to see him or her speak, and understand the speaker's language. (This use of the skill is language-dependent.) The base DC is 15, but it increases for complex speech or an inarticulate speaker. You must maintain a line of sight to the lips being read.

If your Spot check succeeds, you can understand the general content of a minute's worth of speaking, but you usually still miss certain details. If the check fails by 4 or less, you can't read the speaker's lips. If the check fails by 5 or more, you draw some incorrect conclusion about the speech. The check is rolled secretly by the GM in this case, so that you don't know whether you succeeded or missed by 5.

Action: Varies. Every time you have a chance to spot something in a reactive manner you can make a Spot check without using an action. Trying to spot something you failed to see previously is a move action. To read lips, you must concentrate for a full minute before making a Spot check, and you can't perform any other action (other than moving at up to half speed) during this minute.

Try Again: Yes. You can try to spot something that you failed to see previously at no penalty. You can attempt to read lips once per minute.

Special: A fascinated creature takes a -4 penalty on Spot checks made as reactions.

If you have the Alertness feat, you get a +2 bonus on Spot checks.

Critical Failure: You notice nothing. You automatically lose any opposed check, unless the opposing roll is also a critical failure.

Critical Success: You automatically win any opposed check, unless the opposing roll is also a critical success.

Survival (WIS)

Check: You can keep yourself and others safe and fed in the wild, and can find your way without getting lost. The table below gives the DCs for various tasks that require Survival checks.

Action: Varies. A single Survival check may represent activity over the course of hours or a full day. A Survival check made to find tracks is at least a full-round action, and it may take even longer.

Intuit Direction: When faced with multiple choices, such as at a branch in a tunnel, a character can make a Survival check (DC 20) to intuit the choice that takes the character toward a known destination. If unsuccessful, the character chooses the wrong path, but at the next juncture, with a successful check, the character realizes her mistake.

A character cannot use this function of Survival to find a path to a site if the character has no idea where the site is located. The GM may choose to make the check for the

Survival DC	Task
10	Get along in the wild. Move up to one-half your overland speed while hunting and foraging (no food or water supplies needed). You can provide food and water for one other person for every 2 points by which your check result exceeds 10.
15	Gain a +2 bonus on all Fortitude saves against severe weather while moving up to one-half your overland speed, or gain a +4 bonus if you remain stationary. You may grant the same bonus to one other character for every 1 point by which your Survival check result exceeds 15.
15	Avoid natural hazards, such as quicksand.
15	Predict the weather up to 24 hours in advance. For every 5 points by which your Survival check result exceeds 15, you can predict the weather for one additional day in advance.
20	Intuit direction when faced with a branching choice.
15	Determine absolute position.
Varies	Follow tracks (see the Track feat).

character in secret, so she doesn't know from the result whether the character is following the right or wrong path.

Determine Location: A character can use Survival to determine her position on earth without the use of any high-tech equipment by checking the constellations or other natural landmarks. The character must have a clear view of the night sky to make this check. The DC is 15.

Navigation: Make a Survival check when a character is trying to find her way to a distant location without directions or other specific guidance. Generally, a character does not need to make a check to find a local street or other common urban site, or to follow an accurate map. However, the character might make a check to wend her way through a dense forest or a labyrinth of underground storm drains.

For movement over a great distance, make a Survival check. The DC depends on the length of the trip. If the character succeeds, she moves via the best reasonable course toward her goal. If the character fails, she still reaches the goal, but it takes the character twice as long (the character loses time backtracking and correcting her path). If the character fails by more than 5, she travels the expected time, but only gets halfway to her destination, at which point the character becomes lost.

A character may make a second check (DC 20) to regain her path. If the character succeeds, she continues on to her destination; the total time for the trip is twice the normal time. If the character fails, she loses half a day before the character can try again. The character keeps trying until she succeeds, losing half a day for each failure.

Try Again: Varies. For getting along in the wild or for gaining the Fortitude save bonus noted in the table above, you make a Survival check once every 24 hours. The result of that check applies until the next check is made. To avoid getting lost or avoid natural hazards, you make a

Survival: Navigation	
Survival DC	**Length of Trip**
20	Short (a few hours)
22	Moderate (a day or two)
25	Long (up to a week)
28	Extreme (more than a week)

Survival check whenever the situation calls for one. Retries to avoid getting lost in a specific situation or to avoid a specific natural hazard are not allowed. For finding tracks, you can retry a failed check after 1 hour (outdoors) or 10 minutes (indoors) of searching.

Restriction: While anyone can use Survival to find tracks (regardless of the DC), or to follow tracks when the DC for the task is 10 or lower, only a character with the Track feat can use Survival to follow tracks when the task has a higher DC.

Special: A character can take 10 when making a navigation check. A character can take 20 only when determining her location, not when traveling.

If you have 5 or more ranks in Survival, you can automatically determine where true north lies in relation to yourself.

Synergy: If you have 5 or more ranks in Survival, you get a +2 bonus on Knowledge (nature) checks.

If you have 5 or more ranks in a Knowledge skill applicable to your current environment, you get a +2 bonus on

Survival checks made while in that environment. For example, if you have 5 or more ranks in Knowledge (nature), you get a +2 bonus on Survival checks in above-ground natural environments (aquatic, desert, forest, hill, marsh, mountains, and plains).

If you have 5 or more ranks in Search, you get a +2 bonus on Survival checks to find or follow tracks.

Critical Failure: If you are attempting to move through the wild or forage, you make no progress, find no food, and become lost. If you are attempting to avoid the effects of severe weather, you fail, and suffer twice the normal effects. If you are attempting to intuit direction, determine your location, or navigate, you become lost. If you are attempting to follow tracks, not only do you lose the trail, you foul the existing trail.

Critical Success: You move at twice the desired speed, find twice the required forage, and suffer no ill effects from weather for the duration of your trip. If you are attempting to intuit direction, in addition to choosing the correct path, you also intuit a rough estimate of the distance to your destination (i.e., minutes, hours, or days away). If you are attempting to follow tracks, you move at twice the desired speed.

Swim (STR; Armor Check Penalty)

Check: Make a Swim check once per round while you are in the water. Success means you may swim at up to one-half your speed (as a full-round action) or at one-quarter your speed (as a move action). If you fail by 4 or less, you make no progress through the water. If you fail by 5 or more, you go underwater.

The DC for the Swim check depends on the water, as given on the table below.

Water	Swim DC
Calm water	10
Rough water	15
Stormy water	20[1]
1 You can't take 10 on a Swim check in stormy water, even if you aren't otherwise being threatened or distracted.	

Each hour that you swim, make a DC 20 Swim check or take 1d6 points of nonlethal damage from fatigue.

For details on holding your breath and drowning, see Chapter Seven, Hazardous Environments, Water Hazards.

Action: A successful Swim check allows you to swim one-quarter of your speed as a move action or one-half your speed as a full-round action.

Special: Swim checks are subject to double the normal armor check penalty and encumbrance penalty.

If you have the Endurance feat, you get a +4 bonus on Swim checks made to avoid fatigue.

Critical Failure: You do not move, and immediately begin drowning.

Critical Success: You move twice the attempted speed.

Tumble (DEX; Trained Only; Armor Check Penalty)

Check: You can land softly when you fall or tumble past opponents. You can also tumble to entertain an audience (as if using the Perform skill). The DCs for various tasks involving the Tumble skill are given below.

Tumble DC	Task
15	Treat a fall as if it were 10 feet shorter than it really is when determining damage.
opponent's BAB +10[1]	Tumble at one-half speed as part of normal movement, provoking no attacks of opportunity while doing so. Failure means you provoke attacks of opportunity normally.
opponent's BAB +20[1]	Tumble at one-half speed through an area occupied by an enemy (over, under, or around the opponent) as part of normal movement, provoking no attacks of opportunity while doing so. Failure means you stop before entering the enemy-occupied area and provoke an attack of opportunity from that enemy.
1 Make a single Tumble check and apply the result against each opponent you move past, in the order in which you pass them (player's choice of order in case of a tie). Each additional enemy after the first adds +2 to the Tumble DC.	

Obstructed or otherwise treacherous surfaces, such as natural cavern floors or undergrowth, are tough to tumble through. The DC for any Tumble check made to tumble into such a square is modified as indicated on the table below.

Surface Is . . .	DC Modifier
Lightly obstructed (scree, light rubble, shallow bog[1], undergrowth)	+2
Severely obstructed (natural cavern floor, dense rubble, dense undergrowth)	+5
Lightly slippery (wet floor)	+2
Severely slippery (ice sheet)	+5
Sloped or angled	+2
1 Tumbling is impossible in a deep bog.	

Accelerated Tumbling: You try to tumble past or through enemies more quickly than normal. By accepting a -10 penalty on your Tumble checks, you can move at your full speed instead of one-half your speed.

Action: Not applicable. Tumbling is part of movement, so a Tumble check is part of a move action.

Try Again: Usually no. An audience, once it has judged a tumbler as an uninteresting performer, is not receptive to repeat performances.

You can try to reduce damage from a fall as an instant reaction only once per fall.

Special: You can't use this skill if your speed has been reduced by armor or encumbrance.

If you have 5 or more ranks in Tumble, you gain a +3 dodge bonus to AC when fighting defensively instead of the usual +2 dodge bonus to AC.

If you have 5 or more ranks in Tumble, you gain a +6 dodge bonus to AC when executing the total defense standard action instead of the usual +4 dodge bonus to AC.

Synergy: If you have 5 or more ranks in Tumble, you get a +2 bonus on Balance and Jump checks.

If you have 5 or more ranks in Jump, you get a +2 bonus on Tumble checks.

Critical Failure: You fall prone during your tumble (at a location chosen at the GMs whim) ending your movement and your actions for the round.

Critical Success: Your tumbling movement counts as only one-half the distance tumbled (you may continue your move action with the remaining movement).

Use Rope (DEX)

Check: Most tasks with a rope are relatively simple. The DCs for various tasks utilizing this skill are summarized on the table below.

Use Rope DC	Task
10	Tie a firm knot
10[1]	Secure a grappling hook
15	Tie a special knot, such as one that slips, slides slowly, or loosens with a tug
15	Tie a rope around yourself one-handed
15	Splice two ropes together
Varies	Bind a character
1 Add 2 to the DC for every 10 feet the hook is thrown.	

Secure a Grappling Hook: Securing a grappling hook requires a Use Rope check (DC 10, +2 for every 10 feet of distance the grappling hook is thrown, to a maximum DC of 20 at 50 feet). Failure by 4 or less indicates that the hook fails to catch and falls, allowing you to try again. Failure by 5 or more indicates that the grappling hook initially holds, but comes loose after 1d4 rounds of supporting weight. This check is made secretly by the GM, so that you don't know whether the rope will hold your weight.

Bind a Character: When you bind someone, their Escape Artist check is opposed by your Use Rope check.

You get a +10 bonus on this check because it is easier to bind someone than to escape from bonds. You don't even make your Use Rope check until someone tries to escape.

Action: Varies. Throwing a grappling hook is a standard action that provokes an attack of opportunity. Tying a knot, tying a special knot, or tying a rope around yourself one-handed is a full-round action that provokes an attack of opportunity. Splicing two ropes together takes 5 minutes. Binding a character takes 1 minute.

Synergy: If you have 5 or more ranks in Use Rope, you get a +2 bonus on Climb checks made to climb a rope, a knotted rope, or a rope-and-wall combination.

If you have 5 or more ranks in Use Rope, you get a +2 bonus on Escape Artist checks to escape from rope bonds.

If you have 5 or more ranks in Escape Artist, you get a +2 bonus on Use Rope checks made to bind someone.

Critical Failure: The knot comes undone at a critical moment. You automatically lose any opposed check, unless the opposing roll is also a critical failure.

Critical Success: You've tied a veritable Gordian knot. You automatically win any opposed check unless the opposing roll is also a critical success.

Use Unknown Device (CHA; Trained Only)

Characters with this skill have a knack for getting unknown or unfamiliar items to work for them. This skill is used equally to activate magic items or advanced technology that you are unfamiliar with.

Check: You make a Use Unknown Device check each time you try to activate a device. If you are using the check to emulate some quality in an ongoing manner (for example, if you were trying to convince a holy sword that you were a devout worshipper, or trying to convince a cerebral enhancer that you were an alien noble), you need to make the relevant Use Unknown Device check once per hour.

You must know what you are trying to emulate when you make a Use Unknown Device check for that purpose. The DCs for various tasks involving Use Unknown Device checks are summarized on the table below.

Task	Use Unknown Device DC
Activate blindly	25
Decipher a written spell	25 + spell level
Use a magic scroll	20 + caster level
Use a trigger item (wand, ray gun, etc.)	20
Emulate a talent or class feature	20 + class level
Emulate an ability score	15 + desired score
Emulate another race, type, or sub-type	25
Emulate an allegiance	30

Activate Blindly: Some items are activated by special words, thoughts, or sequences of actions. You can activate such an item as if you were using the activation word, thought, or action, even when you are not and even if you don't know it. You must still speak, wave the item around, push buttons and pull levers, or otherwise attempt to get it to activate. You get a special +2 bonus on your Use Unknown Device check if you've activated the item in question at least once before. If you fail by 9 or less, you can't activate the device. If you fail by 10 or more, you suffer a mishap. A mishap means that something happens but it doesn't do what you wanted it to do. The default mishaps are that the item affects the wrong target or that uncontrolled energy is released, dealing 2d6 points of damage to you. This mishap is in addition to any chance for a mishap that you normally risk when using the item.

Decipher a Written Spell: As the Spellcraft skill (see Chapter Eight: Spells and Magic, except that the DC is 5 points higher. Deciphering a written spell requires 1 minute of concentration.

Emulate an Ability Score: Some items require a minimum ability score in order to activate them; this will commonly be magical items such as scrolls, but could also include alien technology that requires certain physiologies. Your effective ability score is your Use Unknown Device check result minus 15. If you already have a high enough score in the appropriate ability, you don't need to make this check.

Emulate an Allegiance: Some items have effects based on the user's allegiances. Use Unknown Device lets you use these items as if you had an allegiance of your choice. You can emulate only one allegiance at a time.

Emulate a Talent or Class Feature: Sometimes you need to use a talent or class feature to activate an item. In cases where it is relevant, your effective level in the appropriate class equals your Use Unknown Device check result minus 20. This skill does not let you actually use the talent or class feature of another class. It just lets you activate items as if you had the required talent or feature. If the class whose feature you are emulating has an allegiance requirement that you do not meet, you must emulate it with a separate Use Unknown Device check (see above).

Emulate a Race or Creature Type: Some items work only for members of certain races, or work better for members of those races. You can use such an item as if you were a race of your choice. You can emulate only one race, type, or sub-type at a time.

Use a Scroll: If you are not a magical adept, and are attempting to cast a spell from a scroll, you have to decipher it first (see above). The DC to use the scroll is equal to 20 + the caster level of the spell you are trying to cast from the scroll. In addition, casting a spell from a scroll requires a minimum score (10 + spell level) in the appropriate ability (Intelligence, Wisdom, or Charisma). If you don't have a sufficient score in that ability, you must emulate the ability score with a separate Use Unknown Device check (see above).

Use a Trigger Item: Many items require only a simple trigger to activate their effects. This includes magical items such as wands or staves, or technological devices like alien ray guns or grenades. This use of the skill allows you the minimum knowledge to activate the device.

Action: None. The Use Unknown Device check is made as part of the action (if any) required to activate the item.

Try Again: Yes, but if you ever roll a natural 1 while attempting to activate an item and you fail, then you can't try to activate that item again for 24 hours.

Special: You cannot take 10 with this skill.

You can't aid another on Use Unknown Device checks. Only the user of the item may attempt such a check.

Synergy: If you have 5 or more ranks in Spellcraft, you get a +2 bonus on Use Unknown Device checks related to magical scrolls.

If you have 5 or more ranks in Decipher Script, you get a +2 bonus on Use Unknown Device checks with scrolls.

If you have 5 or more ranks in Use Unknown Device, you get a +2 bonus to Spellcraft checks to decipher scrolls.

If you have 5 or more ranks in a relevant Craft, Knowledge, or Profession (at the GM's discretion) you gain a +2 bonus to Use Unknown Device checks related to similar unknown technology. This synergy bonus is cumulative with each separate relevant skill.

Critical Failure: You suffer a mishap, and the item in question is destroyed or rendered useless. (At the GM's discretion, it may be repaired.)

Critical Success: You have gained a thorough understanding of the item. It activates properly, and you need not check for this specific item again for the duration of the current session of play.

FEATS

Feats enable you to direct the growth of your character and to develop unique competencies to set your character apart from ordinary folk, and your fellow heroes. Feats can improve your offensive options, your defensive capabilities, or even open up entirely new abilities.

Feats are not generally as powerful as talents, but they are generally more inclusive. As long as your character meets the prerequisites, you can select any feat, regardless of your class. Talents represent abilities that are only available to a chosen few (the adherents of a particular class) while feats can be learned by anyone.

Prerequisites

Some feats have prerequisites. Your character must have the indicated ability score, class feature, feat, skill, base attack bonus, or other quality designated in order to select or use that feat. A character can gain a feat at the same level at which he or she gains the prerequisite.

A character can't use a feat if he or she has lost a prerequisite.

Types of Feats

Most of the following feats are general, meaning that no special rules govern them as a group. The remaining feats are grouped together according to the chapter that governs their use. If your GM does not allow Firearms in his campaign, for example, you cannot choose feats that are marked [*Firearms*].

Bonus Feats

Feats are further categorized according to class (Strong, Fast, Tough, Dedicated, Smart, Charismatic). To determine If a feat appears on the list of bonus feats for your class, simply look for the appropriate tag. This designation does not restrict characters of other classes from selecting these feats, assuming that they meet any prerequisites. This designation simply means that the feat appears on the list of bonus feats for the class listed.

Feat Descriptions

General Feats

Agile Riposte

[Fast, Smart, Charismatic]
Prerequisites: Dexterity 13, Dodge.

Benefit: Once per round, if the opponent the character has designated as his or her dodge target (see the Dodge feat) makes a melee attack or melee touch attack against the character and misses, the character may make an attack of opportunity with a melee weapon against that opponent. Resolve and apply the effects from both attacks simultaneously.

Even a character with the Combat Reflexes feat can't use the Agile Riposte feat more than once per round. This feat does not grant more attacks of opportunity than the character is normally allowed in a round.

Alertness

[Tough, Smart, Dedicated]
Benefit: The character gets a +2 bonus on all Listen checks and Spot checks.

Special: Alertness is an example of two related skills linked with a Skill Focus (see below).

Armor Proficiency (heavy)

Prerequisites: Armor Proficiency (light), Armor Proficiency (medium).

Benefit: See Armor Proficiency (light).

Normal: See Armor Proficiency (light).

Armor Proficiency (light)

Benefit: When the character wears a type of armor with which the character is proficient, the character suffers

only the armor check penalty listed for the armor and only for those skills to which the armor check penalty applies.

Normal: A character who wears armor with which he or she is not proficient applies its armor check penalty to attack rolls and to any skill check that involves movement, including Ride.

Armor Proficiency (medium)
Prerequisite: Armor Proficiency (light).

Benefit: See Armor Proficiency (light).

Normal: See Armor Proficiency (light).

Back Off
[Fast]
Prerequisites: Dex 13+, Dodge, Mobility, Sidestep

Benefit: If an opponent's actions grant you an attack of opportunity, you may take a single 5-foot step instead of attacking. You may not step into a square that is threatened by any of your opponents. Use of this feat counts as one of your attacks of opportunity. After your 5-foot step, your opponent's action continues normally.

Normal: Attacks of opportunity do not allow you to move, only to make a single attack.

Blind-Fight
[Strong, Smart, Dedicated]
Benefit: In melee combat, every time the character misses because of concealment, the character can re-roll the miss chance roll one time to see if the character actually hits.

The character takes only half the usual penalty to speed for being unable to see. Darkness and poor visibility in general reduces the character's speed to three-quarters of normal, instead of one-half.

Brawl
[Strong, Tough]
Benefit: When making an unarmed attack, the character receives a +1 competence bonus on attack rolls, and the character deals nonlethal damage equal to 1d6 + his or her Strength modifier.

Normal: Unarmed attacks normally deal nonlethal damage equal to 1d3 + Strength modifier.

Cleave
[Strong, Tough]
Prerequisites: Strength 13, Power Attack.

Benefit: If the character deals an opponent enough damage to make the opponent drop (either by knocking the opponent out due to massive damage or by reducing the opponent's hit points to less than 0), the character gets an immediate extra melee attack against another opponent adjacent to the character. The character can't take a 5-foot step before making this extra attack. The extra attack is with the same weapon and at the same bonus as the attack that dropped the previous opponent. The character can use this ability once per round.

Combat Expertise
[Fast, Smart]
Prerequisite: Intelligence 13.

Benefit: When the character uses the attack action or the full attack action in melee, the character can take a penalty of up to -5 on his or her attack roll and add the same number (up to +5) to the character's AC. This number may not exceed the character's base attack bonus. The changes to attack rolls and AC last until the character's next action. The bonus to the character's AC is a dodge bonus (and as such it stacks with other dodge bonuses the character may have).

Normal: A character without the Combat Expertise feat can fight defensively while using the attack or full attack action to take a -4 penalty on attacks and gain a +2 dodge bonus to AC.

Combat Reflexes
[Strong, Fast, Charismatic]
Benefit: The maximum number of attacks of opportunity the character may make each round is equal to the character's Dexterity modifier + 1. The character can still only make one attack of opportunity on a single opponent.

With this feat, the character may also make attacks of opportunity when flat-footed.

Normal: A character without the Combat Reflexes feat can make only one attack of opportunity per round and can't make attacks of opportunity when flat-footed.

Special: The Combat Reflexes feat doesn't allow a Fast hero with the opportunist talent to use that talent more than once per round.

Combat Throw
[Fast]
Prerequisite: Defensive Expertise.

Benefit: The character gains a +2 bonus on opposed Strength and Dexterity checks any time the character attempts trip or grapple attacks, or when the character tries to avoid a trip or grapple attack made against him or her.

Defensive Expertise
[Fast]
Benefit: The character gains a +1 dodge bonus to AC against all melee attacks.

Special: A condition that makes the character lose his or her Dexterity bonus to AC also makes the character lose dodge bonuses. Also, dodge bonuses stack, unlike most other types of bonuses.

Table 3-1: Alphabetical Listing of Feats

Feat Name	Type	Benefit
Alertness	Tough, Smart, Dedicated	+2 to Spot and Listen
Armor Proficiency (light, medium, heavy)		No armor check penalty to attack rolls for non-proficient use
Blind-Fight	Strong, Smart, Dedicated	Re-roll misses due to concealment
Brawl	Strong, Tough	Unarmed attacks +1 to hit, do 1d6 non-lethal damage
↳ Improved Brawl	Strong, Tough	As above, +2 to hit, 1d8 non-lethal
↳ Knockout Punch	Strong, Tough	If opponent is flat-footed, any successful unarmed attack is a critical
↳ Improved Knockout Punch		Brawl attacks improve to x3 critical
↳ Streetfighting	Tough, Charismatic	+1d4 damage once per round
↳ Improved Feint	Tough, Smart, Charismatic	Feint in combat as move action
Combat Expertise	Fast, Smart	Trade attack bonus to increase AC
↳ Improved Disarm	Fast, Smart	Does not provoke attack of opportunity; +4 bonus
↳ Improved Trip	Smart	Does not provoke attack of opportunity; +4 bonus
Combat Reflexes	Strong, Fast, Charismatic	Make additional attack of opportunity (up to Dex mod)
Defensive Expertise	Fast	+1 AC bonus vs. all melee opponents
↳ Combat Throw	Fast	+2 Str, Dex w/ trip, grapple attempts
↳ Improved Combat Throw		Free trip attack if opponent misses
↳ Elusive Target	Fast, Smart, Charismatic	Ranged attacks -4 to hit you in melee
↳ Unbalance Opponent	Fast, Charismatic	Opponent gets no Str bonus to damage
Dodge	Fast, Smart, Charismatic	+1 AC bonus vs. a specific opponent
↳ Agile Riposte	Fast, Smart, Charismatic	Attack of opportunity if opponent misses you
↳ Mobility	Fast, Charismatic	+4 AC vs. attack of opportunity when moving
↳ Shot on the Run	Fast	Move before and after ranged attack
↳ Sidestep	Fast, Charismatic	Switch places with your opponent
↳ Back Off	Fast	Take a 5-foot step instead of taking an attack of opportunity
↳ Spring Attack		Move before and after melee attack
↳ Whirlwind Attack	Strong	Make one melee attack vs each opponent within reach
Endurance	Tough, Dedicated	+4 on certain Con based checks, saves
↳ Die Hard	Tough, Dedicated	Continue fighting at -1 hp and below
Exotic Weapon Proficiency		Proficiency with one exotic weapon
Far Shot	Smart, Dedicated	Increase range increment
↳ Improved Aim	Dedicated	Maintain aim even while moving
Frightful Presence	Tough, Dedicated, Charismatic	Some foes may be *shaken*
Great Fortitude	Tough, Dedicated	+2 bonus to Fortitude saves
Heroic Surge		Extra move or attack action
Improved Damage Threshold	Tough, Dedicated	Increase Massive Damage Threshold by +3
Improved Initiative		+4 bonus to initiative
Improved Unarmed Strike	Strong	Unarmed attacks do 1d4 lethal damage
↳ Improved Grapple	Strong	No attack of opportunity for grapple; +4 bonus
↳ Greater Unarmed Strike		Unarmed attack improves to x3 critical
↳ Stunning Fist	Dedicated	Opponent must save or be *stunned*

Table 3-1: Alphabetical Listing of Feats (continued)		
Feat Name	**Type**	**Benefit**
Iron Will	Smart, Dedicated, Charismatic	+2 bonus to Will saves
Lightning Reflexes	Fast, Smart, Charismatic	+2 bonus to Reflex saves
Low Profile	Charismatic	Reduce Reputation bonus by 3
Martial Weapon Proficiency		Proficiency with one martial weapon
Mounted Combat	Strong, Dedicated	Negate hits on mount with Ride check
↳ Mounted Shot		Half penalty for ranged attacks
↳ Ride-by Attack	Strong	Move before and after mounted attack
↳ Spirited Charge	Dedicated	Double damage with mounted charge
↳ Trample		Target of mounted overrun can't move
Point Blank Shot	Fast, Charismatic	Ranged attacks +1 to hit and damage
↳ Improved Point Blank Shot	Fast	Sacrifice accuracy for damage
↳ Precise Shot	Smart	No penalty for shooting into melee
↳ Improved Precise Shot		Ignore anything less than total cover
↳ Rapid Shot		One extra ranged attack each round
Power Attack	Strong, Tough	Trade attack bonus to increase damage
↳ Cleave	Strong, Tough	Drop target for one additional attack
↳ Great Cleave	Strong	As above; no limit to extra attacks
↳ Improved Bull Rush	Strong, Tough	Does not provoke attack of opportunity; +4 bonus
↳ Improved Overrun		Does not provoke attack of opportunity; +4 bonus
↳ Improved Sunder	Strong, Tough	Does not provoke attack of opportunity; +4 bonus
Quick Draw	Fast	Draw weapons as a free action
Renown	Charismatic	+3 Reputation bonus
Run	Fast	Move up to x5; +2 on running Jump
Shield Proficiency		Gain proficiency with all shields
↳ Improved Shield Bash	Strong	Retain shield bonus after shield bash
Simple Weapon Proficiency		Proficiency with all simple weapons
Skill Familiarity	Special	Add another skill to your core skill list
Skill Focus	Special	+3 to one skill or +2 to two skills
Skill Supremacy	Dedicated	Add your Reputation bonus to a skill
Surgery	Smart	Use Heal skill to perform surgery
Toughness	Tough, Dedicated	+3 hit points
Track	Dedicated	Use Survival skill to track
Two-Weapon Fighting	Fast	+2 bonus when fighting with 2 weapons
↳ Improved Two Weapon Fighting		Additional off-hand attack at -5
↳ Greater Two Weapon Fighting		Additional off-hand attack at -10
↳ Two-Weapon Defense	Fast	Off-hand weapon grants +1 AC bonus
Weapon Finesse	Fast, Charismatic	Use Dex instead of Str for to hit bonus
Weapon Focus	Strong, Smart, Dedicated	+1 to hit with chosen weapon
↳ Greater Weapon Focus	Strong, Dedicated	+2 to hit with chosen weapon
Windfall	Smart, Charismatic	+3 Wealth; +1 bonus to Profession checks

Die Hard
[Tough, Dedicated]
Prerequisite: Endurance.

Benefit: When you are *disabled*, you automatically become stable. You don't have to roll to stabilize each round.

When reduced to negative hit points, you may choose to act as if you were *disabled*, rather than *dying*. You must make this decision as soon as you are *disabled* (even if it isn't your turn). If you do not choose to act as if you were *disabled*, you immediately fall unconscious.

When using this feat, you can take either a single move or standard action each turn, but not both, and you cannot take a full round action.
You can take a move action without further injuring yourself, but if you perform any standard action (or any other action deemed as strenuous, including some free actions, such as casting a quickened spell) you take 1 point of damage after completing the act. If your negative hit points exceed your Constitution score, you immediately die.

Dodge
[Fast, Smart, Charismatic]
Prerequisite: Dexterity 13.

Benefit: During the character's action, the character designates an opponent and receives a +1 dodge bonus to AC against any subsequent attacks from that opponent. The character can select a new opponent on any action.

Special: A condition that makes the character lose his or her Dexterity bonus to AC also makes the character lose dodge bonuses. Also, dodge bonuses stack with each other, unlike most other types of bonuses.

Elusive Target
[Fast, Smart, Charismatic]
Prerequisites: Dexterity 13, Defensive Expertise.

Benefit: When fighting an opponent or multiple opponents in melee, other opponents attempting to target the character with ranged attacks take a -4 penalty. This penalty is in addition to the normal -4 penalty for firing into melee, making the penalty to target to character -8.

Special: An opponent with the Precise Shot feat has the penalty lessened to -4 when targeting the character.

Endurance
[Tough, Dedicated]
Benefit: The character gains a +4 bonus on the following checks and saves: hourly Swim checks to avoid becoming fatigued, Constitution checks to continue running, Constitution checks to hold the character's breath, Constitution checks to avoid damage from starvation or thirst, Fortitude saves to avoid damage from hot or cold environments, and Fortitude saves to resist suffocation or drowning.

Also, the character may sleep in medium or light armor without becoming fatigued.

Normal: A character without this feat who sleeps in armor is automatically fatigued the following day.

Exotic Weapon Proficiency
Choose one exotic weapon. The character is proficient with that weapon in combat.

Prerequisite: Base attack bonus +1.

Benefit: The character makes attack rolls with the weapon normally.

Normal: A character who uses a weapon without being proficient with it takes a -4 penalty on attack rolls.

Special: A character can gain this feat multiple times. Each time the character takes the feat, he or she selects a different exotic melee weapon.

Far Shot
[Smart, Dedicated]
Benefit: When the character uses a ranged weapon, its range increment increases by one-half (multiply by 1.5). When the character throws a weapon, its range increment is doubled.

Frightful Presence
[Tough, Dedicated, Charismatic]
Prerequisites: Charisma 15, Intimidate 9 ranks.

Benefit: When the character uses this feat, all opponents within 10 feet who have fewer levels than the character must make a Will saving throw (DC 10 + ½ the character's level + the character's Charisma modifier). An opponent who fails his or her save is shaken, taking a -2 penalty on attack rolls, saves, and skill checks for a number of rounds equal to 1d6 + the character's Charisma modifier. The character can use the feat once per round as a free action.

A successful save indicates that the opponent is immune to the character's use of this feat for 24 hours. This feat does not affect creatures with an Intelligence of 3 or lower.

If the character has the Renown feat, the Will saving throw's DC increases by 5.

Great Cleave
[Strong]
Prerequisites: Strength 13, Power Attack, Cleave, base attack bonus +4.

Benefit: As Cleave, except that the character has no limit to the number of times he or she can use it per round.

Great Fortitude
[Tough, Dedicated]
Benefit: The character gets a +2 bonus on all Fortitude saving throws.

Greater Two-Weapon Fighting
Prerequisites: Dexterity 13, Two-Weapon Fighting, Improved Two-Weapon Fighting, base attack bonus +11.

Benefit: The character gets a third attack with his or her offhand weapon, albeit at a -10 penalty. This feat also allows the character to use a melee weapon in one hand and a ranged weapon in the other.

Greater Unarmed Strike
Prerequisites: Improved Unarmed Strike, base attack bonus +8.

Benefit: When the character scores a critical hit on an opponent with an unarmed strike, the character deals triple damage.

Normal: An unarmed strike critical hit deals double damage.

Greater Weapon Focus
[Strong, Dedicated]
Choose one type of weapon for which you have already selected Weapon Focus. You can also choose unarmed strike or grapple as your weapon for purposes of this feat.

Prerequisites: Proficiency with selected weapon, Weapon Focus with selected weapon, base attack bonus +8.

Benefit: You gain a +1 bonus on all attack rolls you make using the selected weapon. This bonus stacks with other bonuses on attack rolls, including the one from Weapon Focus (see below).

Special: You can gain Greater Weapon Focus multiple times. Its effects do not stack. Each time you take the feat, it applies to a new type of weapon.

Heroic Surge
Benefit: The character may take an extra move action or attack action in a round, either before or after the character's regular actions. The character may use Heroic Surge a number of times per day depending on his or her character level (as shown below), but never more than once per round.

Character Level	Times per Day
1st-4th	1
5th-8th	2
9th-12th	3
13th-16th	4
17th-20th	5

Improved Aim
[Dedicated]
Prerequisites: Wisdom 13, Far Shot.

Benefit: You may move up to 30 feet while aiming without losing your bonus. If you are attacked or your concentration is otherwise disrupted, you may make a Concentration check (DC15 or 10 + damage dealt) to retain your aiming bonus.

Normal: If you move or your concentration is disrupted, you lose your aiming bonus.

Improved Brawl
[Strong, Tough]
Prerequisites: Brawl, base attack bonus +3.

Benefit: When making an unarmed attack, the character receives a +2 competence bonus on his or her attack roll, and the character deals nonlethal damage equal to 1d8 + the character's Strength modifier.

Normal: Unarmed attacks normally deal nonlethal damage equal to 1d3 + Strength modifier.

Improved Bull Rush
[Strong, Tough]
Prerequisites: Strength 13, Power Attack.

Benefit: When the character performs a bull rush, the character does not provoke an attack of opportunity from the defender. You also gain a +4 bonus on the opposed Strength check you make to push back the defender.

Improved Combat Throw
Prerequisites: Defensive Expertise, Combat Throw, base attack bonus +3.

Benefit: In melee combat, if an opponent attacks and misses the character, the character may immediately make a trip attack against the opponent. This counts as an attack of opportunity.

Special: This feat doesn't grant the character more attacks of opportunity than he or she is normally allowed in a round.

Improved Damage Threshold

[Tough, Dedicated]
Benefit: The character increases his or her massive damage threshold by 3 points.

Special: A character may gain this feat multiple times. Its effects stack.

Improved Disarm

[Fast, Smart]
Prerequisites: Intelligence 13, Combat Expertise.

Benefit: The character does not provoke an attack of opportunity when the character attempts to disarm an opponent, nor does the opponent get a chance to disarm the character. You also gain a +4 bonus on the opposed attack roll you make to disarm your opponent.

Improved Feint

[Tough, Smart, Charismatic]
Prerequisites: Intelligence 13, Brawl, Streetfighting.

Benefit: The character can make a Bluff check in combat as a move action. The character receives a +2 bonus on Bluff checks made to feint in melee combat.

Normal: Feinting in combat requires an attack action.

Improved Grapple

[Strong]
Prerequisites: Dex 13, Improved Unarmed Strike.

Benefit: You do not provoke an attack of opportunity when you make a touch attack to start a grapple. You also gain a +4 bonus on all grapple checks, regardless of whether you started the grapple.

Normal: Without this feat, you provoke an attack of opportunity when you make a touch attack to start a grapple.

Improved Initiative]

Benefit: The character gets a +4 bonus on initiative checks.

Improved Knockout Punch

Prerequisites: Brawl, Knockout Punch, base attack bonus +6.

Benefit: When making the character's first unarmed attack against a flat-footed opponent, treat a successful attack as a critical hit. This critical hit deals triple damage and does not require the expenditure of an action point. The damage is nonlethal damage.

Special: Even if the character has the ability to treat unarmed damage as lethal damage, the damage from a knockout punch is always nonlethal.

Improved Overrun

Prerequisites: Str 13, Power Attack.

Benefit: When you attempt to overrun an opponent, the target may not choose to avoid you. You also gain a +4 bonus on your Strength check to knock down your opponent.

Normal: Without this feat, the target of an overrun can choose to avoid you or to block you.

Improved Point Blank Shot

[Fast]
Prerequisites: Point Blank Shot, base attack bonus +3.

Benefit: On your action, before making attack rolls for the round, you may choose to subtract a number from all ranged attack rolls and add the same number to all ranged damage rolls to targets within 30 feet. This number may not exceed the character's base attack bonus. The penalty on attacks and bonus on damage applies until the character's next action.

Special: You may not use this ability against targets that are immune to critical hits. If your ranged attack fires multiple missiles with a single attack roll, the added damage applies only to the first missile.

Improved Precise Shot

Prerequisites: Dex 13, Point Blank Shot, Precise Shot, base attack bonus +11.

Benefit: Your ranged attacks ignore the AC bonus granted to targets by anything less than total cover, and the miss chance granted to targets by anything less than total concealment. Total cover and total concealment provide their normal benefits against your ranged attacks.

In addition, when you shoot or throw ranged weapons at a grappling opponent, you automatically strike at the opponent you have chosen.

Normal: See the normal rules on the effects of cover and concealment. Without this feat, a character who shoots or throws a ranged weapon at a target involved in a grapple must roll randomly to see which grappling combatant the attack strikes.

Improved Shield Bash

[Strong]
Prerequisite: Shield Proficiency.

Benefit: When you perform a shield bash, you do not lose the shield bonus to your AC.

Normal: Without this feat, a character who performs a shield bash loses the shield's shield bonus to AC until his or her next turn.

Improved Sunder
[Strong, Tough]
Prerequisites: Strength 13, Power Attack.

Benefit: When the character strikes an object held or carried by an opponent, such as a weapon, the character does not provoke an attack of opportunity.

The character gains a +4 bonus on any attack roll made to attack an object held or carried by another character. The character deals double normal damage to objects, whether they are held or carried or not.

Normal: A character without this feat incurs an attack of opportunity when he or she strikes at an object held or carried by another character.

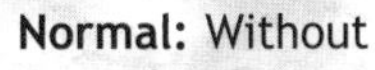

Improved Trip
[Smart]
Prerequisites: Intelligence 13, Combat Expertise.

Benefit: The character does not provoke an attack of opportunity when the character tries to trip an opponent while the character is unarmed. You also gain a +4 bonus on the opposed attack roll you make to trip your opponent.

If the character trips an opponent in melee combat, the character immediately gets to make a melee attack against that opponent as if the character had not used his or her attack action for the trip attempt.

Improved Two-Weapon Fighting
Prerequisites: Dexterity 13, Two-Weapon Fighting, base attack bonus +6.

Benefit: The character gets a second attack with his or her offhand weapon, albeit at a -5 penalty. Also, this feat allows the character to use a melee weapon in one hand and a ranged weapon in the other.

Normal: Without this feat, a character can only get a single extra attack with an off-hand weapon, and both weapons must be of the same type (either both ranged weapons or both melee weapons).

Improved Unarmed Strike
[Strong]
Prerequisite: Base attack bonus +1.

Benefit: With an unarmed strike, the character deals lethal or nonlethal damage (the character's choice) equal to 1d4 + the character's Strength modifier. The character's unarmed attacks count as armed, which means that opponents do not get attacks of opportunity when the character attacks them unarmed. The character may make attacks of opportunity against opponents who provoke such attacks.

Normal: Without this feat, a character deals only 1d3 points of nonlethal damage. Unarmed attacks normally provoke attacks of opportunity, and unarmed combatants cannot normally make attacks of opportunity.

Iron Will
[Smart, Dedicated, Charismatic]
Benefit: The character gets a +2 bonus on all Will saving throws.

Knockout Punch
[Strong, Tough]
Prerequisites: Brawl, base attack bonus +3.

Benefit: When making the character's first unarmed attack against a flat-footed opponent, treat a successful attack as a critical hit. You do not need to spend an action point to activate this critical hit. This damage is nonlethal damage.

Special: Even if the character has the ability to treat unarmed damage as lethal damage, the damage from a knockout punch is always nonlethal.

Lightning Reflexes
[Fast, Charismatic]
Benefit: The character gets a +2 bonus on all Reflex saving throws.

Low Profile
[Charismatic]
Benefit: Reduce the character's Reputation bonus by 3 points.

Martial Weapon Proficiency
Choose a type of martial weapon. You understand how to use that type of martial weapon in combat.

Benefit: You make attack rolls with the selected weapon normally.

Normal: When using a weapon with which you are not proficient, you take a -4 penalty on attack rolls.

Special: You can gain Martial Weapon Proficiency multiple times. Each time you take the feat, it applies to a new type of weapon.

Mobility
[Fast, Charismatic]
Prerequisites: Dexterity 13, Dodge.

Benefit: The character gets a +4 dodge bonus to AC against attacks of opportunity provoked when the character moves out of a threatened square.

Special: A condition that makes a character lose his or her Dexterity bonus to AC also makes the character lose dodge bonuses. Also, dodge bonuses stack with each other, unlike most other types of bonuses.

Mounted Combat
[Strong, Dedicated]
Prerequisite: Ride 1 rank.

Benefit: Once per round when your mount is hit in combat, you may attempt a Ride check (as a reaction) to negate the hit. The hit is negated if your Ride check result is greater than the opponent's attack roll. (Essentially, the Ride check result becomes the mount's Armor Class if it's higher than the mount's regular AC.)

Mounted Shot
Prerequisites: Ride 1 rank, Mounted Combat.

Benefit: The penalty you take when using a ranged weapon while mounted is halved: -2 instead of -4 if your mount is taking a double move, and -4 instead of -8 if your mount is running.

Point Blank Shot
[Fast, Charismatic]
Benefit: The character gets a +1 bonus on attack and damage rolls with ranged weapons against opponents within 30 feet.

Power Attack
[Strong, Tough]
Prerequisite: Strength 13.

Benefit: On the character's action, before making attack rolls for a round, the character may choose to subtract a number from all melee attack rolls and add the same number to all melee damage rolls. This number may not exceed the character's base attack bonus. The penalty on attacks and bonus on damage applies until the character's next action.

Precise Shot
[Smart]
Prerequisite: Point Blank Shot.

Benefit: The character can shoot or throw ranged weapons at an opponent engaged in melee without penalty.

Normal: A character takes a -4 penalty when using a ranged weapon to attack an opponent who is engaged in melee combat.

Quick Draw
[Fast]
Prerequisite: Base attack bonus +1.

Benefit: The character can draw a weapon as a free action.

A character with this feat may throw weapons at his or her full normal rate of attacks.

Normal: A character can draw a weapon as a move action. If a character has a base attack bonus of +1 or higher, the character can draw a weapon as a free action when moving.

Rapid Shot
Benefit: You can get one extra attack per round with a ranged weapon. The attack is at your highest base attack bonus, but each attack you make in that round (the extra one and the normal ones) takes a -2 penalty. You must use the full attack action to use this feat.

Renown
[Charismatic]
Benefit: The character's Reputation bonus increases by +3.

Ride-By Attack
[Strong]
Prerequisites: Ride 1 rank, Mounted Combat.

Benefit: When you are mounted and use the charge action, you may move and attack as if with a standard charge and then move again (continuing the straight line of the charge). Your total movement for the round can't exceed double your mounted speed. You and your mount do not provoke an attack of opportunity from the opponent that you attack.

Run
[Fast]
Benefit: When running, the character moves a maximum of five times his or her normal speed instead of four times. If the character is in heavy armor, the character can move four times his or her speed rather than three times. If the character makes a long jump, the character gains a +2 competence bonus on his or her Jump check.

Shield Proficiency
Benefit: You can use a shield and take only the standard penalties.

Normal: When you are using a shield with which you are not proficient, you take the shield's armor check penalty on attack rolls and on all skill checks that involve moving, including Ride checks.

Shot on the Run
[Fast]
Prerequisites: Dexterity 13, Point Blank Shot, Dodge, Mobility.

Benefit: When using an attack action with a ranged weapon, the character can move both before and after the attack, provided that the character's total distance moved is not greater than his or her speed.

Moving in this way does not provoke an attack of opportunity from the defender the character is attacking (though it can provoke attacks of opportunity from others, as normal).

Sidestep
[Fast, Charismatic]
Prerequisites: Dex 13+, Dodge, Mobility

Benefit: When an opponent in an adjacent square takes a single 5-foot step into a square that you threaten, you may spend 1 action point to move into the square your opponent just left.

Simple Weapons Proficiency
Benefit: The character makes attack rolls with simple weapons normally.

Normal: A character without this feat takes the –4 non-proficiency penalty when making attacks with simple weapons.

Skill Familiarity
[all classes]
Benefit: Choose one skill. This skill is now considered a core skill.

Special: Skill Familiarity is a bonus feat choice for every core class. When chosen as a bonus feat, you must choose a skill corresponding to the primary attribute for your class.

Skill Focus
[all classes]
Benefit: Choose one skill with which you receive a +3 bonus, or two related skills with which you receive a +2 bonus to each skill.

Special: A character can select this feat multiple times. Each time, you must select a different skill or skills.

Skill Focus is a bonus feat choice for every core class. When chosen as a bonus feat, you must choose a skill or skills corresponding to the primary attribute for your class.

Skill Supremacy
[Dedicated]
Prerequisites: At least 1 rank in the chosen skill.

Benefit: Choose a single skill for this feat. When making checks with the selected skill, you may use your Reputation bonus instead of the usual ability modifier.

Special: A character can select this feat multiple times. Each time, you must choose a different skill.

Spirited Charge
[Dedicated]
Prerequisites: Ride 1 rank, Mounted Combat, Ride-By Attack.

Benefit: When mounted and using the charge action, you deal double damage with a melee weapon (or triple damage with a lance).

Spring Attack
Prerequisites: Dexterity 13, Dodge, Mobility, base attack bonus +4.

Benefit: When using an attack action with a melee weapon, the character can move both before and after the attack, provided that the total distance moved is not greater than the character's speed.

Moving in this way does not provoke an attack of opportunity from the defender the character is attacking (though it can provoke attacks of opportunity from others, as normal).

A character can't use this feat if he or she is carrying a heavy load or wearing heavy armor.

Streetfighting
[Tough, Charismatic]
Prerequisites: Brawl, base attack bonus +2.

Benefit: Once per round, if the character makes a successful melee attack with an unarmed strike or a light weapon, the character deals an extra 1d4 points of damage.

Stunning Fist

[Dedicated]
Prerequisites: Dex 13, Wis 13, Improved Unarmed Strike, base attack bonus +8.

Benefit: You must declare that you are using this feat and spend an action point before you make your attack roll (thus, a failed attack roll ruins the attempt, and the action point is lost). Stunning Fist forces a foe damaged by your unarmed attack to make a Fortitude saving throw (DC 10 + 1/2 your character level + your Wis modifier), in addition to dealing damage normally. A defender who fails this saving throw is *stunned* for 1 round (until just before your next action). A *stunned* character can't act, loses any Dexterity bonus to AC, and takes a –2 penalty to AC. Constructs, oozes, plants, undead, incorporeal creatures, and creatures immune to critical hits cannot be *stunned*.

Surgery

[Smart]
Prerequisite: Heal skill 4 ranks.

Benefit: The character can use the Heal skill to perform surgery.

Normal: Characters without this feat cannot perform surgery.

Toughness

[Tough]
Benefit: The character gains +3 hit points.

Special: A character may gain this feat multiple times. Its effects stack.

Track

[Dedicated]
Benefit: To find tracks or follow them for one mile requires a Survival check. The character must make another Survival check every time the tracks become difficult to follow.

The character moves at half his or her normal speed (or at the character's normal speed with a –5 penalty on the check, or at up to twice the character's speed with a –20 penalty on the check). The DC depends on the surface and the prevailing conditions.

Surface	Track DC
Very soft	5
Soft	10
Firm	15
Hard	20

Very Soft: Any surface (fresh snow, thick dust, wet mud) that holds deep, clear impressions of footprints.

Soft: Any surface soft enough to yield to pressure, but firmer than wet mud or fresh snow, in which the quarry leaves frequent but shallow footprints.

Firm: Most normal outdoor or exceptionally soft or dirty indoor surfaces. The quarry might leave some traces of its passage, but only occasional or partial footprints can be found.

Hard: Any surface that doesn't hold footprints at all, such as bare rock, concrete, metal catwalks, or indoor floors. The quarry leaves only traces, such as scuff marks.

If the character fails a Survival check, he or she can retry after 1 hour (outdoors) or 10 minutes (indoors) of searching.

Normal: A character without this feat can use the Survival skill to find tracks, but can only follow tracks if the DC is 10 or less. A character can use the Search skill to find individual footprints, but cannot follow tracks using Search.

Trample

Prerequisites: Ride 1 rank, Mounted Combat.

Benefit: When you attempt to overrun an opponent while mounted, your target may not choose to avoid you. Your mount may make one hoof attack against any target you knock down, gaining the standard +4 bonus on attack rolls against prone targets.

Two-Weapon Defense

[Fast]
Prerequisites: Dex 15, Two-Weapon Fighting.

Benefit: When wielding a double weapon or two weapons (not including natural weapons or unarmed strikes), you gain a +1 shield bonus to your AC.

Track DC modifiers	
Condition	DC Modifier
General Modifiers	
Every three targets in the group being tracked	-1
Every 24 hours since the trail was made	+1
Every hour of rain since the trail was made	+1
Fresh snow cover since the trail was made	+10
Tracked target hides trail (and moves at half speed)	+5
Size of targets being tracked: [1]	
Fine	+8
Diminutive	+4
Tiny	+2
Small	+1
Medium-size	+0
Large	-1
Huge	-2
Gargantuan	-4
Colossal	-8
Poor visibility: [2]	
Overcast or moonless night	+6
Moonlight	+3
Fog or precipitation	+3

1 For a group of mixed sizes, apply only the modifier for the largest size category represented.
2 Apply only the largest modifier from this category.

When you are fighting defensively or using the total defense action, this shield bonus increases to +2.

Two-Weapon Fighting
[Fast]
Prerequisite: Dexterity 13.

Benefit: The character's penalties for fighting with two weapons are lessened by 2.

The weapons used must both be melee weapons or both be ranged weapons (the character can't mix the types).

Unbalance Opponent
[Fast, Charismatic]
Prerequisites: Defensive Expertise, base attack bonus +6.

Benefit: During the character's action, the character designates an opponent no more than one size category larger or smaller than the character. That opponent doesn't get to add his or her Strength modifier to attack rolls when targeting the character. (If the opponent has a Strength penalty, he or she still takes that penalty.)

The opponent's Strength modifier applies to damage, as usual.

The character can select a new opponent on any action.

Weapon Finesse
[Fast, Charismatic]
Choose one light melee weapon, a rapier (if the character can use it with one hand), or a chain.

Prerequisites: Proficient with weapon, base attack bonus +1.

Benefit: With the selected melee weapon, the character may use his or her Dexterity modifier instead of his or her Strength modifier on attack rolls.

Special: A character can gain this feat multiple times. Each time the character takes the feat, the character selects a different weapon.

Weapon Focus
[Strong, Smart, Dedicated]
Choose a specific weapon. A character can choose unarmed strike or grapple for your weapon for purposes of this feat.

Prerequisites: Proficient with weapon, base attack bonus +1.

Benefit: The character adds +1 to all attack rolls he or she makes using the selected weapon.

Special: A character can gain this feat multiple times. Each time the character takes the feat, the character must select a different weapon.

Whirlwind Attack
[Strong]
Prerequisites: Dexterity 13, Intelligence 13, Dodge, Mobility, Spring Attack, Combat Expertise, base attack bonus +4.

Benefit: When the character performs a full-round action, the character can give up his or her regular attacks and instead make one melee attack at the character's highest base attack bonus against each adjacent opponent.

Windfall
[Smart, Charismatic]
Benefit: The character's Wealth bonus increases by +3. Also, this feat provides a +1 bonus on all Profession checks.

Special: A character can select this feat multiple times. Each time, both of its effects stack.

Spellcasting Feats

In campaigns where the GM has decided that spells, magical items, and magical adepts exist, the following feats are recommended for use.

Spellcasting feats are grouped into three categories: General Spellcasting, Metamagic, and Item Creation. Even if the campaign features spellcasting, it may not include Metamagic or Item Creation feats.

General Spellcasting Feats

Augment Summoning

[General] [Spellcasting] [Charismatic]
Prerequisite: Spell Focus (conjuration).

Benefit: Each creature you conjure with any summon spell gains a +4 enhancement bonus to Strength and Constitution for the duration of the spell that summoned it.

Combat Casting

[General] [Spellcasting]
Benefit: You get a +4 bonus on Concentration checks made to cast a spell or use a spell-like ability while on the defensive or while you are grappling or pinned.

Eschew Materials

[General] [Spellcasting] [Charismatic]
Benefit: You can cast any spell that has a material component costing 10 ¢ or less without needing that component. (The casting of the spell still provokes attacks of opportunity as normal.) If the spell requires a material component that costs more than 10 ¢, you must have the material component at hand to cast the spell, just as normal.

Greater Spell Focus

[General] [Spellcasting]
Choose a school of magic to which you already have applied the Spell Focus feat.

Benefit: Add +1 to the Difficulty Class for all saving throws against spells from the school of magic you select. This bonus stacks with the bonus from Spell Focus.

Special: You can gain this feat multiple times. Its effects do not stack. Each time you take the feat, it applies to a new school of magic to which you already have applied the Spell Focus feat.

Greater Spell Penetration

[General] [Spellcasting]
Prerequisite: Spell Penetration.

Benefit: You get a +2 bonus on caster level checks (1d20 + caster level) made to overcome a creature's spell resistance. This bonus stacks with the one from Spell Penetration.

Improved Counterspell

[General] [Spellcasting] [Smart]
Benefit: When counterspelling, you may use a spell of the same school that is one or more spell levels higher than the target spell.

Normal: Without this feat, you may counter a spell only with the same spell or with a spell specifically designated as countering the target spell.

Spell Focus

[General] [Spellcasting] [Dedicated]
Choose a school of magic.

Benefit: Add +1 to the Difficulty Class for all saving throws against spells from the school of magic you select.

Special: You can gain this feat multiple times. Its effects do not stack. Each time you take the feat, it applies to a new school of magic.

Spell Penetration

[General] [Spellcasting] [Smart]
Benefit: You get a +2 bonus on caster level checks (1d20 + caster level) made to overcome a creature's spell resistance.

Spell Preparation

[General] [Spellcasting] [Smart, Dedicated]
Prerequisites: Magical Adept, caster level 1+.

Benefit: Magical adepts generally cast spells spontaneously, choosing from their spells known as the need arises. Spellcasters with this feat are able to prepare spells ahead of time to lessen the effects of spell burn.

An adept can prepare any of her spells known in advance of casting. An adept may prepare up to 2 spell levels per caster level, plus one bonus spell level for each point of spellcasting attribute modifier, if positive (Intelligence for arcane adepts, Wisdom for divine adepts, and Charisma for wild adepts).

Preparing spells requires at least 8 hours of sleep with no more than one interruption. In addition, the caster must study or meditate for 1 hour to prepare her full allotment of spell levels. Preparing fewer spell levels requires proportionately less time, but always at least 15 minutes. Spell preparation is usually done at the beginning of the day in a safe and secluded place.

> *Example: A wild adept with a Charisma of 16 (+3 modifier) and a caster level of 5 can prepare up to 13 spell levels (5x2 + 3). She can divide these spell levels in any way she chooses, for example: 3 x 1st level spells (3 spell levels), 3 x 2nd level spells (6 spell levels) and 1 x 4th level spell (4 spell levels), for a total of 13 spell levels.*

When casting a prepared spell, the adept can choose to re-roll the spell burn dice after seeing the results of her first roll. She must re-roll all of the dice, and she must accept the result of the re-roll.

A 0-level spell counts as 1/2 spell level.

Metamagic Feats

As a spellcaster's knowledge of magic grows, she can learn to cast spells in ways slightly different from the ways in which the spells were originally designed or learned. Spells modified by a metamagic feat add additional spell burn dice, as if they were a higher level spell. However, this does not change the actual level of the spell, so the DC for saving throws against it does not go up.

Metamagic feats that eliminate the verbal, somatic, or material components of a spell don't eliminate the attack of opportunity provoked by casting a spell while threatened. However, casting a spell modified by Quicken Spell does not provoke an attack of opportunity.

Metamagic feats cannot be used with all spells. See the specific feat descriptions for the spells that a particular feat can't modify.

A spellcaster can apply multiple metamagic feats to a single spell, and the increases to spell burn are cumulative. You can't apply the same metamagic feat more than once to a single spell.

The modifications made by these feats only apply to spells cast directly by the feat user. A spellcaster can't use a metamagic feat to alter a spell that is triggered or released from a wand, scroll, or other device.

However, with the right Item Creation feat, you can store a metamagic version of a spell in a scroll, potion, or wand. In this case, the level limits for potions and wands apply to the spell's higher spell level (after the application of the metamagic feat). A character doesn't need the metamagic feat to activate an item storing a metamagic version of a spell.

Whether or not a spell has been enhanced by a metamagic feat does not affect its vulnerability to counterspelling.

Empower Spell

[Metamagic] [Spellcasting]
Benefit: All variable, numeric effects of an empowered spell are increased by one-half. Saving throws and opposed rolls are not affected, nor are spells without random variables. An empowered spell causes spell burn as if it were two levels higher than the spell's actual level.

Enlarge Spell

[Metamagic] [Spellcasting]

Benefit: You can alter a spell with a range of close, medium, or long to increase its range by 100%. An enlarged spell with a range of close now has a range of 50 ft. + 5 ft./level, while medium-range spells have a range of 200 ft. + 20 ft./level and long-range spells have a range of 800 ft. + 80 ft./level. An enlarged spell causes spell burn as if it were one level higher than the spell's actual level. Spells whose ranges are not defined by distance, as well as spells whose ranges are not close, medium, or long, do not have increased ranges.

Extend Spell

[Metamagic] [Spellcasting]

Benefit: An extended spell lasts twice as long as normal. A spell with a duration of concentration, instantaneous, or permanent is not affected by this feat. An extended spell causes spell burn as if it were one level higher than the spell's actual level.

Heighten Spell

[Metamagic] [Spellcasting]

Benefit: A heightened spell has a higher spell level than normal (up to a maximum of 9th level). Unlike other metamagic feats, Heighten Spell actually increases the effective level of the spell that it modifies. All effects dependent on spell level (such as saving throw DCs and ability to penetrate defensive spells) are calculated according to the heightened level. A heightened spell causes spell burn as a spell of its effective level.

Maximize Spell

[Metamagic] [Spellcasting]

Benefit: All variable, numeric effects of a spell modified by this feat are maximized. Saving throws and opposed rolls are not affected, nor are spells without random variables. A maximized spell causes spell burn as if it were three levels higher than the spell's actual level.

An empowered, maximized spell gains the separate benefits of each feat: the maximum result plus one-half the normally rolled result.

Quicken Spell

[Metamagic] [Spellcasting]

Benefit: Casting a quickened spell is a free action. You can perform another action, even casting another spell, in the same round as you cast a quickened spell. You may cast only one quickened spell per round. A spell whose casting time is more than 1 full round action cannot be quickened. A quickened spell causes spell burn as if it were four levels higher than the spell's actual level. Casting a quickened spell doesn't provoke an attack of opportunity.

Silent Spell

[Metamagic] [Spellcasting]

Benefit: A silent spell can be cast with no verbal components. Spells without verbal components are not affected. A silent spell causes spell burn as if it were one level higher than the spell's actual level.

Still Spell

[Metamagic] [Spellcasting]

Benefit: A stilled spell can be cast with no somatic components. Spells without somatic components are not affected. A stilled spell causes spell burn as if it were one level higher than the spell's actual level.

Widen Spell

[Metamagic] [Spellcasting]

Benefit: You can alter a burst, emanation, line, or spread shaped spell to increase its area. Any numeric measurements of the spell's area increase by 100%. A widened spell causes spell burn as if it were three levels higher than the spell's actual level. Spells that do not have an area of one of these types (in particular, cones of a fixed size) are not affected by this feat.

Item Creation Feats

An item creation feat lets a spellcaster create a magic item of a certain type.

Item Creation Feat	Min. Caster Level
Craft Spell Completion Item	1
Craft Single Use Item	3
Craft Constant Item	3-12[1]
Craft Spell Trigger Item	5
Craft Arms and Armor	5

1 Caster Level 12 or higher is only achievable by a spellcaster in extraordinary circumstances.

Regardless of the type of items they involve, the various item creation feats all have certain features in common.

Item Cost

Magic items have a cost in XP, wealth, time, or some combination thereof.

XP Cost: Experience that the spellcaster would normally keep is expended when making a magic item. A character cannot spend so much XP on an item that he or she loses a level. However, upon gaining enough XP to attain a new level, he or she can immediately expend XP on creating an item rather than keeping the XP to advance a level.

The XP costs for various items are shown on the table at the right.

Converting XP Cost From Other Sources: Multiply the item's base price x 0.14 to find the XP cost within Grim Tales. This calculation supplants the normal creation cost of 1/2 the base price in raw materials and 1/25 the base price in XP.

Creation Time: The creation time for magic items ranges from 1 day per 100 XP (slower creation) to 1 day per 200 XP (faster creation); the standard is 1 day per 140 XP. The minimum time to create any magic item is one day.

In order to infuse the item with magical energy, the creator must cast each of the spells required for the item at least once per day. Spell burn applies as normal for each casting. It is not unheard of for inexperienced casters to die from spell burn while trying to create an item beyond their means.

Raw Materials Cost: Magic items can be crafted only from superior quality components. Scrolls require ink and parchment or vellum upon which to write; potions require flasks to store them; weapons, armor, clothing and the like must be masterwork (at additional cost). The cost of assembling these basic raw materials must be met without exception.

Using an item creation feat usually requires access to a laboratory or magical workshop, special tools, and so on. If the character does not have personal access to such requirements, the GM must determine the likelihood of finding those materials "for rent" in the current community.

Reducing XP Costs

The standard rules assume that the bulk of an item's cost is paid in XP. At the GM's discretion, the creator may be able to defer a portion of the XP cost by increasing the raw materials cost or creation times.

Once the base creation time is determined, the XP cost can be reduced by 25% for each extension of the creation time interval: days turn to weeks, weeks turn to months, months turn to years. This option allows even spellcasters who do not "adventure" to create magic items without being on a rushed timetable. The caster must cast the necessary spells once per week, month, or year until the item is completed, suffering spell burn as normal.

Creation Time	XP Discount
1 day per 100-200 XP	standard (no discount)
1 week per 100-200 XP	25%
1 month per 100-200 XP	50%
1 year per 100-200 XP	75%

At the GM's discretion, a portion of the XP cost can be deferred by investing in additional high quality materials. The creator can convert up to 25% of the XP cost of an item to currency at a rate of 1:50: for every 1 XP reduction, increase the cost of the item by 50 ¢.

If the GM allows these cost reductions, they must be performed in the order presented: creation time first, raw materials second.

Example:

A spellcaster wishes to create a magic wand of fireball with 10 charges. The XP cost for a wand is 21 x spell level (3rd) x caster level (5th) for a total XP cost of 315. The creation time for this item is 4 days (315 / 100).

The caster now wishes to reduce the XP cost. Being in no particular hurry, he defers his creation time to 4 months for a discount of 50%, reducing the XP cost to 158 XP.

Now he decides to invest in higher quality materials to reduce the cost even further. He converts almost 25% of the remaining XP cost (39 XP) to raw materials at a cost of 1950 ¢ (39 x 50). He reduces the XP cost to 119 XP (158 XP - 39 XP).

The final cost: 119 XP, 1950 ¢, and 4 months of creation time.

Extra Costs: Any potion, scroll, or wand that stores a spell with a costly material component or an XP cost also carries a commensurate cost. For potions and scrolls, the creator must expend the material component or pay the XP cost when creating the item.

For a wand, staff, or other item with multiple charges of a spell with an extra cost in XP or material components, the creator must pay the extra cost for each charge. These costs may not be deferred; the creator must pay the full XP cost for each charge of the spell within.

Some magic items similarly incur extra costs in material components or XP, as noted in their descriptions.

Craft Single-Use Item

[Item Creation] [Spellcasting] [Charismatic]
Prerequisite: Caster level 3rd.

Benefit: You can create a single-use item (such as a potion or pinch of dust) of any 3rd-level or lower spell that you can cast and that targets one or more creatures. You set the caster level when you create the item, but it must be at least equal to the level of the spell in question and no higher than your own caster level.

You also make any necessary choices for the spell in question when you create the item. For example, if you create a potion, you must specify a target (usually, the person who drinks the potion). If you double the cost, you can leave some of these decisions up to the end user, who makes such decisions by proxy as if they were the caster.

Magic Item Creation Costs			
Item Creation Feat	Example	Min. Caster Level	XP Cost
Craft Spell Completion Item	scroll, talisman, or fetish	1	Spell level x caster level x 3.5
Craft Single-Use Item	potion, pinch of powder, token	3	Spell level x caster level x 7
Craft Charged Item (spell-trigger)	wands	5	Spell level x caster level x 21 (per 10 charges)
Craft Magic Arms and Armor	magic sword or bow	5	Bonus squared x 280
Craft Magic Arms and Armor	magic armor or shield	5	Bonus squared x 140
Constant Item Effects			
Ability Score bonus (enhancement)	belt of Strength	5	Bonus squared x 140
AC bonus (deflection)	ring of protection	12	Bonus squared x 280
AC bonus (other)[1]	ioun stone	12	Bonus squared x 350
Natural armor bonus (enhancement)	amulet of natural armor	12	Bonus squared x 280
Save bonus (resistance)	cloak of resistance	3	Bonus squared x 140
Save bonus (other)[1]	stone of good luck	12	Bonus squared x 280
Skill bonus (competence)	gloves of climbing	3	Bonus squared x 14
Spell resistance	mantle of spell resistance	12	1400 per point over SR 12 (SR 13 minimum)
Spell effect, command word	cape of the mountebank	9	Spell level x caster level x 250
Spell effect, use-activated or continuous	lantern of revealing	12	Spell level x caster level x 280[2]
Constant Item: XP Cost Adjustments			
1 use per day 2 uses per day 3 uses per day 4 uses per day 5 or more uses per day			Multiply cost by 0.2 Multiply cost by 0.4 Multiply cost by 0.6 Multiply cost by 0.8 Multiply cost by 1.0
Charged (50 charges)			1/2 unlimited use base price
Uncustomary body affinity[3]			Multiply entire cost by 1.5
No space limitation[4]			Multiply entire cost by 2
Multiple different abilities in one item			Multiply highest item cost by 2

1 Such as a luck, insight, sacred, or profane bonus.
2 If a constant item has an effect based on a spell with a duration measured in rounds, multiply the cost by 4. If the duration of the base spell is 1 minute/level, multiply the cost by 2, and if the duration is 10 minutes/level, multiply the cost by 1.5. If the base spell has a 24-hour duration or greater, divide the cost in half.
3 See Magic Item Space Limitations in Chapter Eight: Spells and Magic.
4 An item that does not take up one of the spaces on a body costs double.

Craft Magic Arms and Armor

[Item Creation] [Spellcasting] [Dedicated]
Prerequisite: Caster level 5th.

Benefit: You can create any magic weapon, armor, or shield whose prerequisites you meet. The weapon, armor, or shield to be enhanced must be a masterwork item, and its cost is not included in the item creation cost above.

You may add an enhancement bonus to a weapon or armor (such as a +1 sword or a +2 shield), or you may add special abilities (such as keen) with an enhancement equivalent. Your caster level must be at least 3 times the total enhancement bonus.

You can also mend a broken magic weapon, suit of armor, or shield if it is one that you could make. Doing so costs only half the normal item creation costs.

Craft Charged Item

[Item Creation] [Spellcasting]
Prerequisite: Caster level 5th.

Benefit: You can create a spell-trigger item (such as a wand) charged with a limited number of uses of any spell you can cast. A newly created charged item has 10 charges, but can be created with up to 50 charges by paying the item creation cost multiple times. At the GM's discretion, you may create an item with fewer than 10 charges at a prorated cost.

A charged item may only contain spells of 4th level or lower. You set the caster level when you create the item, but it must be at least equal to the level of the spell in question and no higher than your own caster level.

You can also mend a broken charged item or recharge an item if it contains a spell that you can cast. Mending a broken item costs only have the normal item creation costs. Recharging an item costs the normal XP cost, prorated on a charge-by-charge basis.

Craft Constant Item

[Item Creation] [Spellcasting]
Prerequisite: Caster level 3rd.

Benefit: You can create a magic item whose effects work "constantly" while in use (for example, a magic belt). Constant items can have a variety of effects; some effects require a higher minimum caster level.

You can also mend a broken item if it is one that you could make. Doing so costs half the normal item creation costs.

Craft Spell-Completion Item

[Item Creation] [Spellcasting] [Smart]
Prerequisite: Caster level 1st.

Benefit: You can create a spell-completion item (such as a scroll) containing any spell that you can cast. You set the caster level when you create the item, but it must be at least equal to the level of the spell in question and no higher than your own caster level.

Firearms Feats

Action Shootist

[Fast] [Firearms]
Prerequisites: base attack +3 or higher

Benefit: Choose a type of single-shot action (single-action, bolt-action, lever-action, or pump-action). With firearms of this type, you may treat the weapon as a semi-automatic (SA) weapon. This allows you to use a single-shot weapon to make multiple attacks in a round, whether by virtue of your base attack or through another feat normally reserved for SA weapons (Rapid Shot, Triple-Tap, etc.)

Normal: Single-shot weapons (S) may not make multiple attacks in a round, even if the attacker may normally make multiple attacks with a full attack action.

Cool Under Fire

[Dedicated]
Benefit: You suffer only half the penalty (round down) when enemies use covering fire or suppressing fire against you. If you make your Concentration check, you suffer only 1/4 the normal penalty.

Exotic Weapon Proficiency (Firearms)

[Strong, Tough] [Firearms]
Prerequisites: Personal Firearms Proficiency

Benefit: You can use exotic firearms, also known as "heavy weapons." Unlike exotic melee weapons, for which proficiency is generally purchased on an individual basis, exotic firearms are usually purchased in groups of similar function, as determined by the GM. For example, all heavy machine guns can be purchased as a group, while a flamethrower might require a singular purchase. Because of the skill required to load, shoot, and maintain them, muzzle-loaders may also require this feat.

Improved Autofire

[Strong, Tough] [Firearms]
Prerequisites: base attack +6 or higher

Benefit: When taking the autofire attack action, you do not count the attack penalty for the first volley. When taking the strafe action, you suffer only a -1 penalty for each targeted square beyond the first. Finally, you may perform suppressing fire as a standard action.

Normal: Autofire attacks are at -1 per volley, including the first. Strafe attacks are at -2 per square beyond the first. Suppressing fire is a full-round action.

Improved Brace

[Dedicated] [Firearms]
Prerequisites: Wisdom 13, Far Shot, base attack bonus +1.

Benefit: When you are bracing your weapon, if you succeed at a Concentration check (DC15), your target may move up to 30 feet before your bonus due to bracing is lost. If you move, or are distracted, or your target moves more than 30 feet, you lose your bracing bonus.

Normal: If your target moves while you are bracing, the bonus is lost.

Improved Burst-Fire

[Strong, Fast, Tough] [Firearms]
Benefit: When taking the burst-fire attack action, you receive an additional +1 bonus to your attack and damage rolls. Your narrow bursts are -2 to hit and +3 to damage, and your wide bursts are +2 to hit and +1 to damage.

Normal: A narrow burst is -3 to hit and +2 to damage. A wide burst is +1 to hit and +0 to damage.

Improved Covering Fire

[Strong, Fast] [Firearms]
Prerequisites: Precise Shot, Rapid Shot, base attack bonus +3 or higher

Benefit: You may perform covering fire as a standard action.

Normal: Covering fire is a full-round action.

Marksman

[Firearms]

Prerequisites: Precise Shot, base attack bonus +3.

Benefit: You receive an additional +1 circumstance bonus to your ranged attack roll whenever you aim or brace. If you aim and brace, your marksman bonuses stack, for a total of +2.

Personal Firearms Proficiency

[Firearms]

Benefit: The character can fire any personal firearm without penalty. Personal firearms include all handguns and all longarms, but not heavy or exotic weapons.

Normal: Characters without this feat take a –4 penalty on attack rolls made with personal firearms.

Quick Reload

[Fast] [Firearms]

Prerequisite: Base attack bonus +1.

Benefit: Reloading a firearm with an already filled box magazine or speed loader is a free action. Reloading a revolver without a speed loader, or reloading any firearm with an internal magazine, is a move action.

Normal: Reloading a firearm with an already filled box magazine or speed loader is a move action. Reloading a revolver without a speed loader, or reloading any firearm with an internal magazine, is a full-round action.

Special: This feat has no effect on muzzle-loaders.

Skip Shot

[Smart] [Firearms]

Prerequisites: Point Blank Shot, Precise Shot.

Benefit: If the character has a solid, relatively smooth surface on which to skip a bullet (such as a street or a concrete wall), and a target within 10 feet of that surface, the character may ignore cover between the character and the target. However, the character receives a -2 penalty on his or her attack roll, and the character's attack deals -1 die of damage.

Special: The surface doesn't have to be perfectly smooth and level; a brick wall or an asphalt road can be used. The target can have no more than nine-tenths cover for a character to attempt a skip shot.

Snap Shot

[Fast] [Firearms]

Prerequisites: Rapid Shot

Benefit: Before rolling for initiative, you may add a number (up to your base attack bonus) to your initiative result in order to act first in the opening round of combat. Subtract this number from all ranged attacks you make this round. You may not make a melee attack this round. The effects last until the next round, at which point your initiative drops to its normal level and your ranged attacks are no longer penalized.

Sniper

[Firearms]

Prerequisites: Precise Shot, Far Shot, Marksman, base attack bonus +12.

Benefit: When you aim and brace before making a ranged attack, your weapon's threat range against that target is improved by 1 (a weapon with a threat range of 19-20 would improve to 18-20). Furthermore, you do not need to spend an action point to confirm a critical.

Triple-Tap

[Fast] [Firearms]

Prerequisites: Point Blank Shot, Rapid Shot

Benefit: When using a semi-automatic weapon (SA), you may perform firearms combat actions that normally require burst-fire (BF) capability.

Vehicle Feats

...A Gun in the Other

[Vehicle]

Prerequisites: Drive-By Attack, base attack bonus +6 or higher

Benefit: You suffer no penalty when making ranged attacks from a moving vehicle when you are the driver.

Baby It

[Vehicle]

Benefit: You can ignore any penalties caused by the first critical suffered by a vehicle you are driving.

Daredevil

[Fast] [Vehicle]

Prerequisites: Dexterity 13, Drive 6 ranks, Vehicle Combat Reflexes.

Benefit: You may choose maneuvers from the Daredevil list of maneuvers. In addition, you receive a +2 bonus to Crash checks.

Drive-By Attack

[Vehicle]

Prerequisites: base attack bonus +3 or higher

Benefit: You ignore the first -2 penalty for making an attack from a moving vehicle. (Essentially, you receive a +2 bonus that may only be used to offset any penalties.)

Greater Vehicle Focus
[Vehicle]
Prerequisites: Vehicle Focus

Benefit: Choose a type of vehicle (ground, nautical, or aerospace) for which you have the Vehicle Focus feat. You receive an additional +1 bonus to all maneuvers with this type of vehicle, for a total of +2.

You may select this feat multiple times. Its effects do not stack. Each time you select this feat, you must choose another type of vehicle.

Hold it Together
[Vehicle]
Prerequisites: Baby It, Vehicle Focus, Drive 9 ranks

Benefit: When a vehicle you are driving is reduced to 0 hit points, it continues to operate as if the vehicle were crippled (see Chapter Eleven: Vehicles). Each time the vehicle suffers damage after that, make a Crash check with a cumulative +5 modifier (+5, +10, etc.) to the Crash check DC. If you fail the Crash check, the vehicle is disabled and crashes; apply damage to the vehicle and all passengers as normal.

Maneuver Focus
[Vehicle]
Prerequisites: any Drive sub-skill 4 ranks

Benefit: Choose a vehicle maneuver (either a Chase maneuver or a Dogfight maneuver, but not a Daredevil maneuver— see Chapter Eleven). You receive a +2 bonus to Drive skill checks with this maneuver, whether acting or reacting.

You may select this feat multiple times. Its effects do not stack. Each time you select this feat, you must choose another vehicle maneuver.

Vehicle Combat Reflexes
[Vehicle]
Prerequisites: Dexterity 13, Drive 6 ranks.

Benefit: You may make more than one Drive check (including reaction rolls and Crash checks) per round. The maximum number of Drive checks that you may make each round is equal to the character's Dexterity modifier + 1.

Vehicle Dodge
[Vehicle]
Prerequisites: Dexterity 13, Drive 6 ranks, Vehicle Expert.

Benefit: When driving a vehicle, during the character's action the character designates an opposing vehicle or a single opponent. The character's vehicle and everyone aboard it receive a +1 dodge bonus to AC against attacks from that vehicle or opponent. The character can select a new vehicle or opponent on any action.

Vehicle Focus
[Vehicle]
Prerequisites: Drive 4 ranks (any sub-skill)

Benefit: Choose a type of vehicle (ground, nautical, or aerospace) for which you meet the prerequisites. You receive a +1 bonus to all maneuvers with this type of vehicle.

You may select this feat multiple times. Its effects do not stack. Each time you select this feat, you must choose another type of vehicle.

Talents

Talents are special abilities or qualities available only to heroes of a certain class. Unlike feats, which can be learned by anyone, talents represent special training available only to select members of the core classes.

Like feats, many talents require certain prerequisites before they can be chosen. Talents form talent trees, where each talent requires, and builds upon, the preceding talent. Other talents may require feats or a minimum base attack bonus as prerequisites.

Many of the talents listed below are available to more than one class. When a character gains a level and a talent in the corresponding class, he may choose any talent listed for his class (assuming he meets all other prerequisites).

Finally, of particular note are *advanced talents*. Regardless of any other prerequisites, these talents require that the character advance to a minimum of 3rd level in the corresponding class. Advanced talents are shown on Table 4-1 in *italics*.

Aura Talent Tree

Aura of Grace

[*Dedicated, Charismatic*] *[Advanced]*
The hero is blessed by Fate or the powers above with luck and protection. The hero adds her Charisma modifier (if positive) to all saving throw checks.

Aura of Courage

[*Dedicated, Charismatic*] *[Advanced]*
Prerequisite: Aura of Grace.

The hero's faith and will in the face of adversity improves his or her resistance to the effects of *fear* and Horror. The hero treats *panicked* results as *fear*; *fear* results as *shaken*; and *shaken* results as no effect. This talent has no effect on any other Horror results.

Aura of Health

[*Dedicated, Charismatic*] *[Advanced]*
Prerequisite: Aura of Grace.

The hero enjoys the blessings of perfect health. The hero is immune to all non-magical diseases, and gains a +4 bonus to saving throws against all other diseases.

Charm Talent Tree

Charm

[Charismatic]
The Charismatic hero gets a bonus on all Charisma-based skill checks made to influence members of his chosen gender. (Some characters are charming to members of the opposite gender, others to members of the same gender.) The bonus is equal to the character's Charismatic level (up to +10).

A Charismatic hero can only charm non-player characters with attitudes of indifferent or better. The charm bonus can't be used against NPCs who are unfriendly or hostile.

Favor

[Charismatic]
Prerequisite: Charm.

The Charismatic hero has the ability to acquire minor aid from anyone he or she meets. By making a favor check, a Charismatic hero can gain important information without going through the time and trouble of doing a lot of research. Favors can also be used to acquire the loan of equipment or documents, or to receive other minor assistance in the course of an adventure.

A Charismatic hero spends 1 action point to activate this talent. To make a favor check, roll a d20 and add the character's favor bonus, equal to the character's Charismatic level. The GM sets the DC based on the scope of the favor being requested. The DC ranges from 10 for a simple favor to as high as 30 for formidable and highly dangerous, expensive, or illegal favors. A Charismatic hero can't take 10 or 20 on this check, nor can the hero retry the check for the same (or virtually the same) favor. Favors should help advance the plot of an adventure. A favor that would enable a character to avoid an adventure altogether should always be unavailable to the character, regardless of the result of a favor check.

The GM should carefully monitor a Charismatic hero's use of favors to ensure that this ability isn't abused. The success or failure of a mission shouldn't hinge on the use of a favor, and getting a favor shouldn't replace good roleplaying or the use of other skills. The GM may disallow any favor deemed to be disruptive to the game.

Captivate

[Charismatic]
Prerequisites: Charm, Favor.

The Charismatic hero has the ability to temporarily beguile a target (an NPC) through the use of words and bearing. The target must have an Intelligence score of 3 or higher to be susceptible to a captivate attempt, must be within 30 feet of the hero, and must be able to see, hear, and understand the hero.

To captivate a target, the hero must use a standard action and make a Charisma check (DC 15), adding his Charismatic level as a bonus. If the Charisma check succeeds, the target can try to resist.

The target resists the captivation attempt by making a Will saving throw against DC 10 + Charismatic hero's class level (up to +10) + Charismatic hero's Cha bonus. If the saving throw fails, the hero becomes the target's sole focus. The target pays no attention to anyone else for 1 round. This focusing of the target's attention allows other characters to take actions of which the captivated target is unaware. The effect ends immediately if the target is attacked or threatened.

A Charismatic hero can concentrate to keep a target captivated for additional rounds. The Charismatic hero concentrates all his effort on the task, and the target gets to make a new Will save each round. The effect ends when the hero stops concentrating, or when the target succeeds on the save.

Damage Reduction Talent Tree

Damage Reduction

[Tough] [Advanced]
The Tough hero has an innate talent to ignore a few points of damage from most weapons, but not from energy or special attack forms (which may or may not exist, depending on the campaign).

With Damage Reduction 1/—, the Tough hero ignores 1 point of damage from all physical melee and ranged weapons (but not energy attacks). Damage cannot be reduced to less than zero.

You may choose this talent multiple times, and its effects stack. Each time you select this talent, increase your DR by +1/-.

Defensive Talent Tree

Evasion

[Fast]
If the Fast hero is exposed to any effect that normally allows a character to attempt a Reflex saving throw for half damage, the Fast hero suffers no damage if she makes a successful saving throw. Evasion can only be used when wearing light armor or no armor.

Uncanny Dodge

[Fast]
Prerequisite: Evasion.

The Fast hero retains her Dexterity bonus to AC regardless of being caught flat-footed or struck by a hidden attacker. (The hero still loses her Dexterity bonus to AC if the hero is immobilized.)

Defensive Roll

[Fast]
Prerequisites: Evasion, Uncanny Dodge.

The Fast hero can roll with a potentially lethal attack to take less damage from it. When the Fast hero would be reduced to 0 hit points or less by damage in combat (from a ranged or melee attack), the Fast hero can attempt to roll with the damage.

A Fast hero spends 1 action point to use this talent. Once the point is spent, the hero makes a Reflex saving throw (DC = damage dealt). If the save succeeds, he or she takes only half damage. The Fast hero must be able to react to the attack to execute a defensive roll—if the hero is immobilized, he or she can't use this talent.

Since this effect would not normally allow a character to make a Reflex save for half damage, the Fast hero's evasion talent doesn't apply to the defensive roll.

Improved Uncanny Dodge

[Fast]
Prerequisites: Evasion, Uncanny Dodge.

The Fast hero can no longer be flanked; the hero can react to opponents on opposite sides of him or herself as easily as he or she can react to a single attacker.

Improved Evasion

[Fast] [Advanced]
Prerequisites: Evasion, Improved Reaction +2.

This ability works like Evasion, except that while the hero still takes no damage on a successful Reflex saving throw, she only takes half damage even on a failed Reflex save. If the hero is helpless, she cannot gain the benefit of Improved Evasion.

Table 4-1: Alphabetical Summary of Talents

Talent	Type	Benefit
Aura of Grace	*Dedicated, Charismatic*	Add your Cha modifier to all saving throws
↳ *Aura of Courage*	*Dedicated, Charismatic*	Resistance to fear effects
↳ *Aura of Health*	*Dedicated, Charismatic*	Grant a bonus vs. fear to nearby allies
Charm	Charismatic	Bonus to Cha checks to charm a target
↳ Favor	Charismatic	Ask favors from NPCs
↳ ↳ Captivate	Charismatic	Beguile a target for a time
Coordinate	Charismatic	Grant a +1 bonus to your allies
↳ Inspiration	Charismatic	Grant a +2 morale bonus to allies
↳ ↳ Greater Inspiration	Charismatic	Grant a +3 morale bonus to allies
Damage Reduction ✚	*Tough*	Reduce physical damage by +1 point
Empathy	Dedicated	Bonus to social interaction skills
↳ Improved Aid Another	Dedicated	Gain an additional +1 bonus to Aid Another
↳ Intuition	Dedicated	Sense when something is amiss
↳ ↳ *Improved Intuition*	*Dedicated*	Sense the direction/location of trouble
↳ *Wild Empathy*	*Charismatic*	Use your Diplomacy skill with animals
Energy Resistance	Tough	Reduce energy damage by your Con bonus
↳ *Improved Energy Resistance*	*Tough*	Double your resistance as above
Evasion	Fast	No damage on successful Reflex saves
↳ *Improved Evasion*	*Fast*	Half damage even on failed Reflex saves
↳ ↳ *Heightened Reflexes*	*Fast*	Take 10 on Reflex saves; +10 bonus
↳ Opportunist	Fast	Bonus attack of opportunity in combat
↳ Uncanny Dodge	Fast	Retain your Dex bonus to AC at all times
↳ ↳ Defensive Roll	Fast	Roll with an attack to reduce the damage
↳ ↳ Improved Uncanny Dodge	Fast	You can no longer be flanked
Exploit Weakness	*Smart*	Add your Int mod to hit vs. chosen target
↳ *Sneak Attack* ✚	*Smart*	+1d6 bonus damage when you sneak attack
Extreme Effort ✚	Strong	Increase your Strength by +2 for one task
Fast-Talk	Charismatic	Add your Charismatic level to Cha checks
↳ Dazzle ✚	Charismatic	Target opponent receives a -1 penalty
↳ ↳ Taunt	Charismatic	Target opponent is *dazed*
Favored Enemy ✚	*Smart, Dedicated*	+2 bonus to damage, skills vs. enemy type
Flurry of Blows	*Fast*	Make an additional unarmed attack at -2
↳ *Improved Flurry of Blows*	*Fast*	Flurry attack penalty reduced to -1
↳ ↳ *Advanced Flurry of Blows*	*Fast*	Flurry attack penalty reduced to -0
↳ ↳ ↳ *Greater Flurry of Blows*	*Fast*	Make an additional flurry attack
Harm's Way	*Tough, Dedicated*	Trade places with an ally to protect against attack
↳ *Protective Strike*	*Tough, Dedicated*	Get an attack of opportunity against any who attack your ally
↳ ↳ *Protective Bonus* ✚	*Tough, Dedicated*	Improve your AC by +1 when defending an ally
Healing Knack	Dedicated	+2 bonus to Heal checks
↳ Healing Touch ✚	Dedicated	+2 hit points restored with Heal check
↳ ↳ *Minor Medical Miracle*	*Dedicated*	Revive a character who has been dead for up to 3 rounds
↳ ↳ ↳ *Major Medical Miracle*	*Dedicated*	Revive a character who has been dead for up to 3 minutes
Ignore Hardness ✚	Strong	Ignore 1 point of object hardness

Table 4-1: Alphabetical Listing of Talents (continued)		
Talent	**Type**	**Benefit**
Improved Reaction ✚	*Fast*	+2 bonus to initiative
Increased Speed ✚	Fast	Increase your movement rate by +5
Insight	Dedicated	+3 bonus to chosen skill
↳ Aware	Dedicated	Add your Will save bonus to Spot and Listen
↳ Faith	Dedicated	Add your Wis modifier to action point rolls
↳ *Cool Under Pressure*	*Dedicated*	Take 10 on select skills even under pressure
Linguist	Smart	Understand any spoken or written language
Living Weapon ✚	*Strong, Dedicated*	Increase the base damage die of your unarmed strikes
Magical Adept	*Smart, Dedicated, Charismatic*	Improve your ability to cast spells
↳ *Improved Caster Level* ✚	*Smart, Dedicated, Charismatic*	+1 caster level
↳ *Master Eldritch Flow*	*Smart, Dedicated, Charismatic*	Change the drain die
Melee Smash ✚	Strong	+1 bonus to damage with all melee attacks
Obscure Knowledge	*Smart*	Gain access to obscure lore
Plan	*Smart*	Gain a temporary bonus to skills or combat
Rage	*Tough*	+4 Str, +4 Con, +2 Will saves, -2 AC
↳ *Tireless Rage*	*Tough*	No longer *fatigued* after you rage
↳ *Mighty Rage*	*Tough*	+8 Str, +8 Con, +4 Will saves, -2 AC
Remain Conscious	Tough	Continue fighting at -1 hp or below
↳ *Stay in the Game*	*Tough*	Re-roll a failed massive damage save
Robust	Tough	+1 hit point per Tough level
↳ Stamina	Tough	Recover twice as fast
Second Wind	Tough	Regain your Con bonus in hit points
↳ *Improved Second Wind*	*Tough*	Regain Con bonus x Tough level in hit points
Savant	Smart	Add your Smart level to one skill check
Smite	*Dedicated*	Strike a powerful blow against enemies
Trapfinding	*Smart*	Gain the ability to find complex traps
↳ *Trap Sense* ✚	*Fast*	Bonus to Reflex saving throws vs. traps
Trick	*Smart*	Target opponent is *dazed*
Turn Undead	*Dedicated, Charismatic*	Turn undead
↳ *Command Undead*	*Charismatic*	Command undead who share an allegiance
↳ *Destroy Undead*	*Dedicated*	Destroy undead of an opposing allegiance
↳ *Banish Outsiders*	*Dedicated*	Banish demons and devils back to their home plane
Weapon Specialization	*Strong*	+2 to damage with chosen weapon
↳ *Greater Weapon Specialization*	*Strong*	+4 to damage with chosen weapon
↳ *Improved Critical*	*Strong*	Improve critical threat range by 1
Zen Defense	*Dedicated*	Add your Wis modifier to AC
↳ *Deflect Arrows*	*Fast*	Deflect one ranged attack per round
↳ *Snatch Arrows*	*Fast*	Catch one ranged attack per round
↳ *Deflect Bullets*	*Fast*	Deflect one bullet per round
Zen Focus	*Dedicated*	Add your Wis modifier to ranged attacks
↳ *Zen Strike*	*Dedicated*	Add your Wis modifier to unarmed damage

KEY

↳ This talent requires a prior talent pre-requisite.
✚ This talent may be chosen multiple times. See the description for details.

Heightened Reflexes
[Fast] [Advanced]
Prerequisites: Evasion, Improved Evasion, Improved Reaction +2, Increased Speed.

The Fast hero can take 10 on any Reflex save. She may also spend an action point to gain a +10 bonus to any Reflex save. She can combine both of these effects, taking 10 and spending an action point for a +10 bonus.

Empathic Talent Tree

Empathy
[Dedicated]
The Dedicated hero has a knack for being sensitive to the feelings and thoughts of others without having those feelings and thoughts communicated in any objectively explicit manner. This innate talent provides a bonus on checks involving interaction skills (Bluff, Diplomacy, Handle Animal, Intimidate, Perform, and Sense Motive), provided the hero spends at least 1 minute observing her target prior to making the skill check. The bonus is equal to the hero's Dedicated level (up to +10).

Improved Aid Another
[Dedicated]
Prerequisite: Empathy.

The Dedicated hero's bonus on attempts to aid another increases by +1 on a successful aid another check. This talent can be selected multiple times, each time increasing the bonus by +1.

Intuition
[Dedicated]
Prerequisite: Empathy.

The Dedicated hero has an innate ability to sense trouble in the air. The Dedicated hero can make a Will saving throw (DC 15). On a successful save, the hero gets a hunch that everything is all right, or the hero gets a bad feeling about a specific situation, based on the GM's best guess relating to the circumstances. This talent is usable a number of times per day equal to the character's Dedicated level.

Improved Intuition
[Dedicated] [Advanced]
Prerequisites: Empathy, Intuition.

The Dedicated hero's intuition is honed to a razor's edge. Instead of rolling a Will saving throw, the Dedicated hero may spend an action point to activate her ability. In addition to the good or bad feeling gained from above, the Dedicated hero can tell from what general direction the feeling emanates, for example, "You get a bad feeling from behind that door..."

Wild Empathy
[Charismatic]
Prerequisite: Empathy.

The hero can improve the attitude of an animal. This ability functions just like a Diplomacy check made to improve the attitude of a person. The hero rolls 1d20 and adds his Charismatic level (up to +10) and his Charisma modifier to determine the Diplomacy check result.

The typical domestic animal has a starting attitude of indifferent, while wild animals are usually unfriendly.

To use wild empathy, the hero and the animal must be able to study each other, which means that they must be within 30 feet of one another under normal conditions. Generally, influencing an animal in this way takes 1 minute but, as with influencing people, it might take more or less time.

A hero can also use this ability to influence a magical beast with an Intelligence score of 1 or 2, but he takes a -4 penalty on the check.

Energy Resistance Talent Tree

Energy Resistance
[Tough]
The Tough hero is particularly resistant to certain kinds of deadly energy effects. Upon choosing this talent, choose a type of energy from the list below:

> *Acid Resistance*: The Tough hero ignores an amount of acid damage equal to his Constitution modifier.

Cold Resistance: The Tough hero ignores an amount of cold damage equal to his Constitution modifier.

Electricity Resistance: The Tough hero ignores an amount of electricity damage equal to his Constitution modifier.

Fire Resistance: The Tough hero ignores an amount of fire damage equal to his Constitution modifier.

Sonic/Concussion Resistance: The Tough hero ignores an amount of sonic or concussion damage equal to his Constitution modifier.

Improved Energy Resistance

[Tough] [Advanced]
Prerequisites: Damage Reduction 1, Energy Resistance (chosen type).

The Tough hero improves his resistance to a specific type of energy. Choose a type of energy for which you already have Energy Resistance. Your resistance against that energy type is doubled (Con modifier x2). You may choose this talent multiple times, but each time you must select a different type of energy.

Extreme Effort Talent Tree

Extreme Effort

[Strong]
A Strong hero can push himself to make an extreme effort. The effort must relate either to a Strength check (such as forcing a door or bending the bars of a jail cell) or a Strength-based skill check (such as Jump, Climb, etc.). You must decide to use this ability before making the check. The effort requires a full-round action and provides a +2 bonus on the check.

You may select this talent multiple times, and its effects stack. Each time you select this talent, your Strength bonus for Extreme Effort increases by +2.

Fast Talk Talent Tree

Fast-Talk

[Charismatic]
The Charismatic hero has a way with words when attempting to con and deceive. With this talent, he applies his Charismatic level (up to +10) as a bonus on any Bluff, Diplomacy, or Profession (gambler) checks the hero makes while attempting to lie, cheat, or otherwise bend the truth.

Dazzle

[Charismatic]
Prerequisite: Fast-Talk.

The Charismatic hero has the ability to dazzle a target (an NPC) through sheer force of personality, a winning smile, and fast-talking. The target must have an Intelligence score of 3 or higher to be susceptible to a dazzle attempt, must be within 30 feet of the hero, and must be able to see, hear, and understand the hero.

To dazzle a target, the hero must use a standard action and make a Charisma check (DC 15), adding his Charismatic level as a bonus. If the Charisma check succeeds, the target can try to resist.

The target resists the dazzle attempt by making a Will saving throw against DC 10 + Charismatic class level (up to +10) + Charismatic hero's Cha bonus. If the save fails, the target receives a -1 penalty on attack rolls, ability checks, skill checks, and saving throws for a number of rounds equal to the character's Charismatic level.

This talent can be selected multiple times, each time worsening the dazzled penalty by -1.

Taunt

[Charismatic]
Prerequisites: Fast-talk, Dazzle.

The Charismatic hero has the ability to temporarily rattle a target (a GM character) through the use of insults and goading. The target must have an Intelligence score of 3 or higher to be susceptible to a taunt, must be within 30 feet of the hero, and must be able to hear and understand the hero.

To taunt a target, the hero must use a standard action and make a Charisma check (DC 15), adding his Charismatic level as a bonus. If the Charisma check succeeds, the target can try to resist.

The target resists the taunt by making a Will saving throw against DC 10 + Charismatic hero's class level (up to +10) + Charismatic hero's Charisma modifier. If the save fails, the target becomes dazed (unable to act, but can defend normally) for 1 round.

A taunt can be attempted against an opponent any number of times.

Flurry of Blows Talent Tree

Flurry of Blows

[Fast] [Advanced]
Prerequisite: Improved Unarmed Attack.

When the Fast hero chooses the full attack action, she may make an additional unarmed attack. This additional attack is at her highest attack bonus, but this attack and all attacks made in the round suffer a -2 penalty to hit. This penalty applies until the hero's next action.

Improved Flurry of Blows

[Fast] [Advanced]
Prerequisite: Improved Unarmed Attack (feat), Flurry of Blows, base attack bonus +4 or higher.

The hero's penalty for Flurry of Blows is reduced by 1, to -1. The extra attack and all attacks made until the start of the hero's next action suffer a -1 penalty.

Advanced Flurry of Blows

[Fast] [Advanced]
Prerequisite: Improved Unarmed Attack (feat), Flurry of Blows, Improved Flurry of Blows, base attack bonus +8 or higher.

The hero's penalty for Flurry of Blows is reduced to 0. The extra attack and all attacks made until the start of the hero's next action no longer suffer any penalty for Flurry of Blows.

Greater Flurry of Blows

[Fast] [Advanced]
Prerequisite: Improved Unarmed Attack (feat), Flurry of Blows, Improved Flurry of Blows, Advanced Flurry of Blows, base attack bonus +12 or higher.

The hero gains a second additional unarmed attack each round at her highest base attack bonus. Thus, when using the Flurry of Blows talent and combined with all prerequisites, the hero may take a full attack action to gain two additional attacks each round at her highest base attack bonus, with no penalty.

Harrier Talent Tree

Favored Enemy

[Dedicated] [Advanced]
The Dedicated hero may choose a type of creature: Aberration, Animal, Construct, Dragon, Fey, Giant, Humanoid, Magical Beast, Monstrous Humanoid, Ooze, Outsider, Plant, Undead, or Vermin. (If you choose Humanoid or Outsider, you must also choose a sub-type).

The hero gains a +2 bonus on Bluff, Listen, Sense Motive, Spot, and Survival checks when using these skills against creatures of this type. In addition, she gets a +2 bonus on weapon damage rolls against such creatures.

You may choose this talent multiple times. Each time, choose an additional favored enemy. In addition, each time you choose this talent, the bonus against any one favored enemy (including the one just selected, if so desired) increases by 2.

If a specific creature falls into more than one category of favored enemy, the hero's bonuses do not stack; she simply uses whichever bonus is higher.

Smite

[*Charismatic, Dedicated*] *[Advanced]*
The hero may spend an action point to attempt to smite an opponent of an opposing allegiance (e.g. *good* vs. *evil*) with one normal melee attack. She adds her Charisma bonus (if any) to her attack roll and deals 1 extra point of damage per Charismatic or Dedicated class level (up to +10 for each). If the hero accidentally smites a creature that does not have an opposing allegiance, the smite has no effect, but the action point is still spent.

Healing Talent Tree

Healing Knack

[Dedicated]
The hero has a knack for the healing arts. The hero receives a +2 bonus on all Heal skill checks.

Healing Touch

[Dedicated]
Prerequisite: Healing Knack.

The Dedicated hero's ability to restore damage with a medical kit or perform surgery with a surgery kit increases by +2 hit points.

You may select this talent multiple times, and its effects stack. Each time you select this talent, your bonus increases by +2 points.

Minor Medical Miracle

[Dedicated] [Advanced]
Prerequisite: Healing Knack, Healing Touch; Surgery (feat).

The Dedicated hero can restore life to a patient who has been dead (reduced to -10 or fewer hit points) for up to 3 rounds.

If the Dedicated hero can treat the patient within 3 rounds, he may make a Surgery check. The DC for this check is 20 + patient's negative hit point total— for example, a patient at -10 hit points would require a DC30 check (20 + 10 negative hit points). The hero cannot take 10 or take 20 on his Surgery check. Only other characters

with the Surgery feat may use the Aid Another action to assist with this roll.

If the check succeeds, the patient may make a Fortitude save (DC15). If the save succeeds, the dead character is stabilized and brought back to 0 hit points.

If the check fails, the patient is beyond help.

Major Medical Miracle

[Dedicated] [Advanced]
Prerequisite: Healing Knack, Healing Touch, Minor Medical Miracle; Surgery (feat).

As above, but the Dedicated hero can restore life to a patient who has been dead for up to 3 minutes.

The Surgery check for a major medical miracle is 30 + patient's negative hit point total, and the patient's Fortitude saving throw is DC20.

At the GM's discretion, a patient who has been brought back to life after an excessive period of brain death may experience side effects, both pleasant and unpleasant.

Ignore Hardness Talent Tree

Ignore Hardness

[Strong]
The Strong hero has an innate talent for finding weaknesses in objects. This allows a Strong hero to ignore some of an object's hardness when making a melee attack to break it. The Strong hero ignores 1 point of an object's hardness.

You may select this talent multiple times, and its effects stack. Each time you select this talent, you ignore an additional 1 point of hardness.

Improved Reaction Talent Tree

Improved Reaction

[Fast]
The Fast hero gains a +2 bonus to all Initiative checks. This talent stacks with the effects of the Improved Initiative feat.

You may choose this talent multiple times, and its effects stack. Each time you select this talent, your bonus to initiative increases by +2.

Opportunist

[Fast]
Prerequisite: Improved Reaction +2.

The Fast hero can spend 1 action point to use this talent. Once the point is spent, the hero can make an attack of opportunity against an opponent who has just been struck for damage in melee by another character. This attack counts as the Fast hero's attack of opportunity for that round. Even a Fast hero with the Combat Reflexes feat can't use this talent more than once per round.

Increased Speed Talent Tree

Increased Speed

[Fast]
The Fast hero increases her natural base speed by 5 feet.

You may select this talent multiple times, and its effects stack. Each time you select this talent, your base movement rate increases by +5 feet.

Insight Talent Tree

Insight

[Dedicated]
The Dedicated hero's innate insightfulness serves her well. The Dedicated hero chooses a single skill and receives a +3 bonus on all checks with that skill. This bonus does not allow the hero to make checks for a trained-only skill if the hero has no ranks in the skill.

Aware

[Dedicated]
Prerequisite: Insight.

The Dedicated hero is intuitively aware of her surroundings. The hero adds her base Will saving throw bonus to Listen or Spot checks to avoid surprise.

Faith

[Dedicated]
Prerequisite: Insight.

The Dedicated hero has a great deal of faith. It might be faith in self, in a higher power, or in both. When the Dedicated hero spends an action point to improve the result of an attack roll, skill check, saving throw, or ability check, her unswerving belief allows her to add her Wisdom modifier to the die roll as an additional bonus.

Cool Under Pressure

[Dedicated] [Advanced]
Prerequisite: Insight plus either Aware or Faith.

The Dedicated hero selects a number of skills equal to 3 + the hero's Wisdom modifier. When making a check with one of these skills, the Dedicated hero can take 10 even when distracted or under duress.

Leadership Talent Tree

Coordinate

[Charismatic]
The Charismatic hero has a knack for getting people to work together. When the hero can spend a full round directing his allies and makes a Charisma check (DC 10), the hero provides any of his allies within 30 feet a +1 bonus on their attack rolls and skill checks. The bonus lasts for a number of rounds equal to the hero's Charisma modifier.

The hero can coordinate a number of allies equal to one-half his Charismatic level, rounded down (to a minimum of one ally).

Inspiration

[Charismatic]
Prerequisite: Coordinate.

The Charismatic hero can inspire his allies, bolstering them and improving their chances of success. An ally must listen to and observe the Charismatic hero for a full round for the inspiration to take hold, and the hero must make a Charisma check (DC 10). The effect lasts for a number of rounds equal to the hero's Charisma modifier.

An inspired ally gains a +2 morale bonus on saving throws, attack rolls, and damage rolls.

A Charismatic hero can't inspire him or herself. The hero can inspire a number of allies equal to one-half his Charismatic level, rounded down (to a minimum of one ally).

Greater Inspiration

[Charismatic]
Prerequisites: Coordinate, Inspiration.

The Charismatic hero can inspire his allies to even greater heights, bolstering them and improving their chances of success. An ally must listen to and observe the Charismatic hero for a full round for the greater inspiration to take hold, and the hero must make a Charisma check (DC 10). The effect lasts for a number of rounds equal to the hero's Charisma modifier.

An inspired ally gains an additional +1 morale bonus on saving throws, attack rolls, and damage rolls, which stacks with the bonus from inspiration for a total of a +3 morale bonus.

A Charismatic hero can't inspire him or herself. The hero can inspire a number of allies equal to one-half his Charismatic level, rounded down (to a minimum of one ally).

Living Weapon Talent Tree

Living Weapon

[Strong, Dedicated] [Advanced]
Prerequisite: Improved Unarmed Strike (feat), BAB requirement (see below)

The hero's unarmed damage increases by one damage category:

Current Damage	Improved Damage	Minimum BAB
d4	d6	+3
d6	d8	+7
d8	d10	+11
d10	2d6	+14
2d6	2d8	+17

You may choose this feat multiple times. Provided you meet the BAB requirements, your unarmed damage increases one step each time you select this talent, to a maximum of 2d8.

Magical Adept Talent Tree

Check with your GM before selecting any of the talents in this tree to make certain that spellcasting is a feature of the campaign.

Magical Adept

[*Smart, Dedicated, Charismatic*] *[Advanced]*
Prerequisites: relevant ability score 10 or better.

The hero gains knowledge of a magical tradition and can henceforth cast any spells he or she knows. *Arcane adepts* use their Intelligence to cast arcane spells; *divine adepts* use their Wisdom to cast divine spells; and *wild adepts* can cast either arcane or divine spells on the force of their Charisma alone.

The hero gains a caster level of 1 and spell burn resistance equal to his or her relevant ability score modifier. Furthermore, Spellcraft becomes a core skill. For more information, see Chapter Eight: Spells and Magic.

Improved Caster Level

[*Smart, Dedicated, Charismatic*] *[Advanced]*
Prerequisites: Magical Adept (any).

The hero gains additional spellcasting ability in a chosen magical tradition (arcane, divine, or wild adept). You may choose this talent multiple times. Each time you choose this talent, your caster level in the chosen magical

tradition improves by +1, and you gain an additional +1 bonus to your spell burn resistance.

Master Eldritch Flow

[Smart, Dedicated, Charismatic] [Advanced]
Prerequisites: Magical Adept.

The hero is better able to manipulate the capricious flows of magical energy. The hero may now choose to change the spell burn die when casting a spell, either increasing or decreasing the spell burn die by one step from the standard burn die used in the campaign. For example, if the spell burn die is the standard d6, this talent allows the magical adept to lower the burn die to d4 or increase it to d8.

The procedure for determining spell burn proceeds as normal, but for each drain die that rolls a maximum result (4 on a d4, 6 on d6, etc.) the adept may increase either the caster level or the DC of the spell by +1. For more information, see Chapter Eight: Spells and Magic.

Melee Smash Talent Tree

Melee Smash

[Strong]
The Strong hero has an innate talent that increases melee damage. The Strong hero receives a +1 bonus on melee damage.

You may select this talent multiple times, and its effects stack. Each time you select this talent, your bonus to melee damage increases by +1.

Protective Talent Tree

Harm's Way

[Tough, Dedicated]
Prior to combat (generally, when initiative is determined) the hero can specify one ally to protect.

If the hero is adjacent to his ally and his ally is targeted by a direct melee or ranged attack (but not an area effect), the hero can spend an action point to switch places with his ally and subject himself to the attack instead. The hero must declare his intention to place himself in harm's way before the attack roll is made. If the attack hits the hero, he takes damage normally. If it misses, it also misses the ally.

Protective Strike

[Tough, Dedicated]
Prerequisite: Harm's Way

While the hero is protecting his ally (see Harm's Way, above), any attack against the ally provokes an attack of opportunity from the hero with this talent. Note that this talent does not grant the hero the ability to make more attacks of opportunity in a round than he otherwise could.

Protective Bonus

[Tough, Dedicated]
Prerequisite: Harm's Way.

When the hero is defending an ally using the Harm's Way talent above, he receives a +1 bonus to his AC against any attack he intercepts.

You may select this talent multiple times. Each time you select this talent, your AC bonus increases by +1 (to a maximum of +4).

Rage Talent Tree

Rage

[Tough] [Advanced]
The hero can spend an action point to fly into a rage. In a rage, the hero temporarily gains a +4 bonus to Strength, a +4 bonus to Constitution, and a +2 morale bonus on Will saves, but he takes a -2 penalty to Armor Class. The increase in Constitution increases the hero's hit points by 2 points per level, but these hit points go away at the end of the rage when his Constitution score drops back to normal. (These extra hit points are not lost first the way temporary hit points are.) While raging, the hero cannot use any Charisma-, Dexterity-, or Intelligence-based skills (except for Balance, Escape Artist, Intimidate, and Ride); he cannot use the Concentration skill, the Combat Expertise feat, nor any skill or feat that requires concentration or mental faculties, entirely at the GM's discretion.

A fit of rage lasts for a number of rounds equal to 3 + the character's (newly improved) Constitution modifier. The hero may prematurely end his rage.

At the end of the rage, the hero loses the rage modifiers and restrictions and becomes *fatigued* (-2 penalty to Strength, -2 penalty to Dexterity, can't charge or run) for the duration of the current encounter (unless he has tireless rage; see below).

The hero can fly into a rage only once per encounter, but may use his rage multiple times each day, provided he has the action points to spend. Entering a rage takes no time itself, but a hero can do it only during his action, not in response to someone else's action.

Tireless Rage

[Tough] [Advanced]
Prerequisites: Rage, base attack bonus +8 or higher.

The hero is no longer *fatigued* at the end of his rage.

Mighty Rage

[Tough] [Advanced]
Prerequisites: Rage, Tireless Rage, base attack bonus +12 or better.

The hero's bonuses for rage improve to +8 Strength, +8 Constitution, and +4 to Will saves. His penalty to AC remains at -2.

Research Talent Tree

Linguist

[Smart]
Prerequisite: At least three different Speak Language skills.

With this talent, the Smart hero becomes a master linguist. Whenever the hero encounters a new language, either spoken or written, he or she can make an Intelligence check to determine if he or she can understand it. The check is made with a bonus equal to the hero's Smart level + the hero's Intelligence modifier. For a written language, the bonus applies to a Decipher Script check instead.

The DC for the check depends on the situation: DC 15 if the language is in the same group as a language the hero has as a Read/Write Language or Speak Language skill; DC 20 if the language is unrelated to any other languages the hero knows; and DC 25 if the language is ancient or unique. With this special ability, a Smart hero can glean enough meaning from a conversation or document to ascertain the basic message, but this ability in no way simulates actually being able to converse or fluently read and write in a given language.

Savant

[Smart]
Select one of the skills listed in the following paragraph. The Smart hero gets to add a bonus equal to her Smart level (up to +10) when making checks with that skill. A Smart hero can take this talent multiple times; each time it applies to a different skill.

Craft (any single sub-skill), Decipher Script, Disable Device, Forgery, Knowledge (any single sub-skill), Research, Search.

Obscure Knowledge

[Smart] [Advanced]
The Smart hero may make a special obscure knowledge check with a bonus equal to her Smart level + her Intelligence modifier to see whether she knows some relevant information about local notable people, legendary items, or noteworthy places. (If the hero has 5 or more ranks in Knowledge (history), she gains a +2 bonus on this check.)

A successful obscure knowledge check will not reveal the powers of a magic item but may give a hint as to its general function. A hero may not take 10 or take 20 on this check; this sort of knowledge is essentially random.

In some campaigns this talent is known as *bardic knowledge*.

DC	Type of Knowledge
10	Common, known by at least a substantial minority; common legends of the local population.
20	Uncommon but available, known by only a few people; legends.
25	Obscure, known by few, hard to come by.
30	Extremely obscure, known by very few, possibly forgotten by most who once knew it, possibly known only by those who don't understand the significance of the knowledge.

Strategy Talent Tree

Exploit Weakness

[Smart] [Advanced]
After 1 round of combat, the Smart hero can designate one opponent and try to find ways to gain an advantage by using brains over brawn. The Smart hero uses a move action and makes an Intelligence check (DC 15) with a bonus equal to her Smart level. If the check succeeds, for the rest of the combat the Smart hero uses her Intelligence bonus instead of either Strength or Dexterity bonus on attack rolls, as the hero finds ways to out-think her opponent and notices weaknesses in her opponent's fighting style.

Plan

[Smart] [Advanced]
Prior to a dramatic situation, either combat- or skill-related, the Smart hero can develop a plan of action to handle the situation. Using this talent requires preparation; a Smart hero can't use this talent when surprised or otherwise unprepared for a particular situation.

The Smart hero makes an Intelligence check (DC 10) with a bonus equal to her Smart level (up to +10). The result of the check provides the Smart hero and allies with a circumstance bonus. A Smart hero can't take 10 or 20 when making this check.

Check Result	Bonus
9 or lower	+0 (check failed)
10-14	+1
15-24	+2
25 or higher	+3

This bonus can be applied to all skill checks and attack rolls made by the Smart hero and her allies, but the bonus only lasts for the first 3 rounds. After that time, reduce the bonus by 1 point (to a minimum of +0) for every additional round the situation continues, as the vagaries of circumstance begin to unravel even the best-laid plans.

Trick

[Smart] [Advanced]
The Smart hero has the ability to temporarily confuse a target (an NPC) through the use of ploy and deception. The target must have an Intelligence score of 3 or higher to be susceptible to a trick, must be within 30 feet of the hero, and must be able to hear and understand the hero.

To play a trick on a target, the hero must use a full-round action and make an Intelligence check (DC 15), adding her Smart level as a bonus. If the Intelligence check succeeds, the target can try to think quickly and ignore the trick.

The target resists the trick by making a Reflex saving throw against DC 10 + Smart hero's class level (up to +10) + Smart hero's Int bonus. If the saving throw fails, the target becomes dazed (unable to act, but can defend normally) for 1 round.

A trick can only be played on a particular target once per encounter. After the first trick in an encounter, whether the attempt succeeds or not, that target becomes wary and immune to such ploys.

Sneak Attack

[Smart] [Advanced]
Prerequisites: Exploit Weakness.

If the hero can catch an opponent when he is unable to defend himself effectively from her attack, she can strike a vital spot for extra damage.

The hero's attack deals an extra +1d6 damage any time her target would be denied a Dexterity bonus to AC (whether the target actually has a Dexterity bonus or not). This includes, but certainly is not limited to, catching an opponent flat-footed at the beginning of combat.

Should the hero score a critical hit with a sneak attack, this extra damage is not multiplied.

Ranged attacks can count as sneak attacks only if the target is within 30 feet.

With a sap (blackjack) or an unarmed strike, the hero can make a sneak attack that deals nonlethal damage instead of lethal damage. She cannot use a weapon that deals lethal damage to deal nonlethal damage in a sneak attack, not even with the usual -4 penalty.

The hero can sneak attack only living creatures with discernible anatomies—undead, constructs, oozes, plants, and incorporeal creatures lack vital areas to attack. Any creature that is immune to critical hits is not vulnerable to sneak attacks. The hero must be able to see the target well enough to pick out a vital spot and must be able to reach such a spot. She cannot sneak attack while striking a creature with concealment (as she cannot discern the vital location), or when striking the limbs of a creature whose vitals are beyond reach.

You may select this talent multiple times, and its effects stack. Each time you select this talent, your sneak attack bonus increases by +1d6.

Trapfinding

Trapfinding

[Smart] [Advanced]
Prerequisites: Search 4 ranks.

The hero can find traps with a Search DC above 20. Without this talent, a character may only find traps with a Search DC of 20 or lower; more complex traps are beyond the ability of most heroes.

Trap Sense

[Fast] [Advanced]
Prerequisites: Trapfinding.

The hero gains a +1 bonus to AC or to Reflex saving throws vs. attacks and effects from traps. You may select this talent multiple times, and its effects stack. Each time you select this talent, your Trap Sense bonus increases by an additional +1.

Turning Talent Tree

Check with your GM before selecting any of the talents in this tree to make certain that undead are a feature of the campaign.

Turn Undead

[Dedicated, Charismatic] [Advanced]
The hero has the power to affect undead creatures by channeling the power of her faith through her holy (or unholy) symbol.

The hero may attempt to turn undead a number of times per day equal to 3 + her Charisma modifier.

A hero with 5 or more ranks in Knowledge (religion) gets a +2 bonus on turning checks against undead.

Destroy Undead

[Dedicated] [Advanced]
Prerequisites: Turn Undead

If the hero has an allegiance in direct opposition to the undead targeted (e.g. *good* vs. *evil*), she gains the power to destroy any undead she would normally turn. Make a turn undead check. Any undead whose hit dice are equal to or lower than your Dedicated class level, with an opposing allegiance, and who would be successfully turned by your attempt, are destroyed instead. Other undead are turned as normal.

Command Undead

[Charismatic] [Advanced]
Prerequisites: Turn Undead

If the hero shares an allegiance (such as *evil*) in common with the target undead, he can command them. A commanded undead creature is under the mental control of the hero. The hero must take a standard action to give mental orders to a commanded undead. At any one time, the hero may command any number of undead whose total Hit Dice do not exceed his Charismatic level. He may voluntarily relinquish command on any commanded undead creature or creatures in order to command new ones.

Banish Outsiders

[*Dedicated*] *[Advanced]*
Prerequisites: Turn Undead, Destroy Undead

The hero can banish Outsiders (including demons, devils, angels, and so forth) with an allegiance in opposition to her own. Make a turn undead check and apply the result to any outsiders who could be affected. Affected outsiders are banished back to their plane of origin.

Banishing outsiders requires the hero to use one of her daily turn undead attempts (see below).

A hero with 9 or more ranks in Knowledge (religion) or Knowledge (the planes) gets a +2 bonus on turning checks against outsiders.

Unbreakable Talent Tree

Remain Conscious

[Tough]
The Tough hero gains the ability to continue to perform actions when he or she would otherwise be considered unconscious and *dying*. When the Tough hero begins *dying*, he can continue to perform as though he or she were *disabled*, making either a standard action or a move action every round until the hero dies or the hero's hit points return to 1 or higher. The hero can choose to succumb to unconsciousness at any time.

Robust

[Tough]
The Tough hero becomes especially robust, gaining a number of hit points equal to his Tough level as soon as he selects this talent. Thereafter, the hero gains +1 hit point with each level of Tough he gains.

Second Wind

[Tough]
The Tough hero can spend 1 action point to gain a second wind. When the hero does this, he recovers a number of hit points equal to his Constitution modifier. This talent does not increase the Tough hero's hit points beyond the character's full normal total.

Stamina

[Tough]
Prerequisite: Robust.

The Tough hero recovers twice as fast as normal. So, for example, the hero recovers 2 hit points per character level per evening of rest, 2 points of temporary ability damage per evening of rest, and awakens in half the normal time after being knocked unconscious.

Stay in the Game

[Tough] [Advanced]
Prerequisites: Remain Conscious, Robust, Stamina.

If the Tough hero fails a Fortitude saving throw to resist the effects of massive damage, he may spend 1 action point to re-roll the save. He must accept the result of the second roll.

Improved Second Wind

[Tough] [Advanced]
Prerequisites: Second Wind, Robust, Stamina, Remain Conscious, Stay in the Game.

When the Tough hero spends an action point to gain his second wind, he regains hit points equal to his Constitution modifier x his Tough class level.

Weapon Mastery Talent Tree

Weapon Specialization

[Strong] [Advanced]
Prerequisites: Proficiency with selected weapon, Weapon Focus (feat) with selected weapon, with selected weapon, base attack bonus +4.

Choose one type of weapon with which you have chosen the Weapon Focus feat. You can choose unarmed strike or grapple as your weapon for purposes of this feat.

You gain a +2 bonus on all damage rolls you make using the selected weapon. This bonus stacks with other bonuses on damage rolls.

You can gain Weapon Specialization multiple times. Its effects do not stack. Each time you take this talent, it must be applied to a new type of weapon.

Greater Weapon Specialization

[Strong] [Advanced]
Prerequisites: Proficiency with selected weapon, Greater Weapon Focus (feat) with selected weapon, Weapon Focus (feat) with selected weapon, Weapon Specialization with selected weapon, base attack bonus +8.

Choose one type of weapon for which you have already selected Weapon Specialization. You can choose unarmed strike or grapple as your weapon for purposes of this talent.

You gain a +2 bonus on all damage rolls you make using the selected weapon. This bonus stacks with other bonuses on damage rolls, including the one from Weapon Specialization.

You can gain Greater Weapon Specialization multiple times. Its effects do not stack. Each time you take this talent, it must be applied to a new type of weapon.

Improved Critical

[Strong] [Advanced]
Prerequisites: Proficient with weapon, Weapon Focus (feat) with chosen weapon, Greater Weapon Focus (feat) with chosen weapon, Weapon Specialization with chosen weapon, Greater Weapon Specialization with chosen weapon, base attack bonus +12.

When using your chosen weapon, your threat range improves by 1. For example, if the weapon you are using normally threatens a critical on a roll of 19-20, this feat improves the threat range to 18-20.

You may choose this talent multiple times. Its effects do not stack. Each time you select this talent, you must choose a different weapon.

Zen Talent Tree

Zen Defense

[Dedicated] [Advanced]
When the hero is unencumbered and wearing no armor, she gains a bonus to her AC equal to her Wisdom modifier. These bonuses to AC apply even against touch attacks or when the hero is flat-footed. She loses these bonuses when she is *immobilized* or *helpless*, when she wears any armor, when she carries a shield, or when she carries a medium or heavy load.

Zen Focus

[Dedicated] [Advanced]
The hero is able to clear her mind and focus on her opponent. She gains a bonus to all ranged attack rolls equal to her Wisdom modifier.

Zen Strike

[Dedicated] [Advanced]
Prerequisites: Zen Defense, Zen Focus, Improved Unarmed Strike

The hero is able to call upon her inner energy to deliver more powerful unarmed attacks. She adds her Wisdom modifier to all unarmed damage.

Deflect Arrows

[Fast] [Advanced]
Prerequisites: Dex 13, Zen Defense, Improved Unarmed Strike (feat).

Once per round when the hero would normally be hit with a ranged weapon, she may deflect it with her bare hand, weapon, shield, or other suitable object, so that she takes no damage from it. The character must be aware of the attack and not flat-footed.

Attempting to deflect a ranged weapon doesn't count as an action. Unusually massive ranged weapons, ballistic attacks (such as firearms), and ranged attacks generated by spell effects can't be deflected.

Snatch Arrows

[Fast] [Advanced]
Prerequisites: Dex 13, Zen Defense, Deflect Arrows, Improved Unarmed Strike (feat).

When using the Deflect Arrows talent the hero may catch the weapon instead of just deflecting it. Thrown weapons can immediately be thrown back at the original attacker (even though it isn't your turn) or kept for later use.

The hero must have at least one hand free (holding nothing) to use this feat.

Deflect Bullets

[Fast] [Advanced]
Prerequisites: Dex 15, Zen Defense, Deflect Arrows, Snatch Arrows, Improved Unarmed Strike (feat)

The hero must be holding something the GM deems capable of deflecting a bullet (a knife, a sword, a serving tray, etc.) to use this talent. Once per round when the hero would normally be hit with a bullet or other ballistic attack, she may deflect it so that she takes no damage from it. The hero may only deflect a single bullet; she cannot deflect burst fire or autofire. The hero must be aware of the attack and not flat-footed.

Attempting to deflect a bullet doesn't count as an action. Unusually massive ballistic weapons and ranged attacks generated by spell effects can't be deflected.

Economy & Equipment

Grim Tales is designed for play in almost any genre or setting. Some Archaic settings, particularly traditional sword-and-sorcery settings, focus on the acquisition of treasure, and players like to keep track of their wealth down to the last copper piece. In Modern settings, however, the complexities of checking accounts and credit ratings require a different economic model.

Rather than list multiple prices for each setting, all prices in this book are listed in *currency units (cu, or ¢)*.

The basic currency unit is based on the smallest denomination in which daily living wages are normally paid.

For Archaic games, this is generally the ***silver piece***; in Modern games, the ***dollar***. The currency used in Apocalyptic games varies wildly; some settings may use a standard unit of currency, some dark future "anti-corporate" settings may be better served with an abstract model, and in some settings it may depend entirely on whether there is sufficient society left to even have a system of currency!

As a point of reference, the cost of an entry-level, average weapon (be it a longsword or a handgun) should be about 200 ¢, which in turn is about 10% of the starting wealth for a 1st level character.

Economic Models

Before starting play, the GM must decide which economic model the campaign will use. Most campaigns will use the currency model; Modern campaigns, or indeed any campaign where the GM wishes to divert the focus of the game away from the acquisition of wealth and onto the action, should use the Wealth model.

Currency Model

The currency model is the model common to most games and requires little explanation. Players keep track of their total wealth in concrete numbers, recording each coin, gem, or other unit of currency. Items for purchase have a set price and that price is deducted from the player's total wealth upon purchase.

Wealth Model

In this model, the economy is much more abstract. Every character has a Wealth bonus that reflects his or her buying power—a composite of income, credit rating, and savings. A character's Wealth bonus serves as the basis of the character's Wealth check, which is used to purchase equipment and services for the character.

Wealth Bonus

To determine a character's starting Wealth bonus, roll 2d4 plus (if appropriate) the bonus from the Windfall feat.

Over the course of play, the hero's Wealth bonus will decrease as the hero purchases expensive items and increase as the hero gains levels.

A character's Wealth bonus can never fall below +0, and there is no limit to how high the Wealth bonus can climb.

Since Wealth is an abstract concept, it's sometimes difficult to determine how financially well off a character is. To get a general sense of how financially solvent a character is at any given time, check the table below.

Wealth Bonus	Financial Condition
+0	Impoverished or in debt
+1 to +4	Struggling
+5 to +10	Middle class
+11 to +15	Affluent
+16 to +20	Wealthy
+21 to +30	Rich
+31 or higher	Very rich

Purchasing Equipment

Wealth checks are used to determine what characters can afford and what gear they might reasonably have access to. Every character has a Wealth bonus that reflects his or her buying power. Every object and service has a purchase DC. To purchase an object, make a Wealth check against the purchase DC.

Wealth Check Summary

A Wealth check is a 1d20 roll plus a character's current Wealth bonus.

If the character's current Wealth bonus is equal to or greater than the DC, the character automatically succeeds; no roll is necessary.

If the character succeeds on the Wealth check, the character gains the object. If the character fails, he or she can't afford the object at the time.

If the character successfully purchases an object or service with a purchase DC higher than his or her current Wealth bonus, the character's Wealth bonus decreases. This represents the character spending beyond his means; because his Wealth bonus decreases when purchasing expensive items, he will find it harder to purchase next time.

Shopping and Time

Buying less common objects generally takes a number of hours equal to the purchase DC of the object or service, reflecting the time needed to locate the wanted materials and close the deal. Getting a license or buying an object with a restriction rating increases the time needed to make purchases.

Taking 10 and Taking 20

A character can usually take 10 or take 20 when making a Wealth check. Taking 20 requires 20 times as long as normal.

Also, there is a penalty for spending beyond a character's means. Whenever a character buys an object that has a purchase DC higher than his or her current Wealth bonus, the character's Wealth bonus decreases (see below).

Try Again?

A character can try again if he or she fails a Wealth check, but not until the character has spent an additional number of hours shopping equal to the purchase DC of the object or service. If the GM is using the Supply and Demand rules (see below) you may have a better chance at finding the item you seek if you are willing to pay a little more.

Aid Another

One other character can make an aid another attempt to help a character purchase an object or service. If the attempt is successful, that character provides the purchaser with a +2 bonus on his or her Wealth check. The character who provides the aid reduces his or her Wealth bonus by +1.

Purchasing Items: Decreasing Wealth

Any time a character purchases an object or service with a purchase DC higher than his or her current Wealth bonus, or one with a purchase DC of 15 or higher, the character's Wealth bonus goes down. How much the Wealth bonus is reduced depends on how expensive the object is (see the Wealth Increase/Decrease table below).

Along with this loss, any time a character buys an object or service with a purchase DC of 15 or higher, the character reduces his or her current Wealth bonus by an additional 1 point.

A character's Wealth bonus only goes down if he or she successfully buys an object or service. If the character attempts to buy something and the check fails, his or her Wealth bonus is unaffected.

Selling Stuff: Increasing Wealth

To sell something, a character first needs to determine its sale value. Assuming the object is undamaged and in working condition, the sale value is equal to the object's purchase DC (as if purchased new) minus 3.

Selling an object can provide an increase to a character's Wealth bonus. The increase is the same amount as the Wealth bonus loss the character would experience if the character purchased an object with a purchase DC equal to the sale value (see the Wealth Increase/Decrease table below).

Regardless of the character's current Wealth bonus, he or she gains a Wealth bonus increase of 1 whenever the character sells an object with a sale value of 15 or higher.

If A character sells an object with a sale value less than or equal to his or her current Wealth bonus, and that sale value is 14 or lower, the character gains nothing.

Wealth Decrease/Increase

Purchase DC / Sale Value	Wealth Bonus Change
DC equal or lower than current Wealth	no change
Any item DC15 or higher	1 point
1-10 points higher than current Wealth bonus	1 point
11-15 points higher than current Wealth bonus	1d6 points
16 or more points higher than current Wealth bonus	2d6 points

Wealth Bonus of +0

A character's Wealth bonus can never decrease to less than +0. If a character's Wealth bonus is +0, the character doesn't have the buying power to purchase any object or service that has a purchase DC of 10 or higher, and can't take 10 or take 20.

Regaining Wealth

A character's Wealth bonus recovers as the character advances.

Every time a character gains a new level, make a Profession check. (Profession is a core skill for all heroes, but if the character has no ranks in the skill, this check is a Wisdom check.) The DC is equal to the character's current Wealth bonus. If the character succeeds, his or her current Wealth bonus increases by +1. For every 5 points by which the character exceeds the DC, he or she gains an additional +1 to his or her Wealth bonus.

Wealth Awards

Adventuring may result in characters finding valuable items. In such cases, the benefit translates into a Wealth award.

Economic Model Conversions

If you wish to use material from another published setting that uses a different economic model, use the following chart to convert between currency units and Purchase DC.

If you are converting from the currency model to the Wealth model, scroll down the left hand column to find the first value that is equal to or greater than the item's value, then read across to find the Purchase DC. For items whose value falls in between two rows, you may tweak the Purchase DC by +1.

Remember to convert all prices into the correct currency unit before converting to a Purchase DC. For example, in a standard fantasy campaign, a longsword that sells for 20 gold pieces would have a Purchase DC of 12— the equivalent of 200 currency units (silver pieces).

Converting Prices and Purchase DCs	
Item's Price (currency units)	Purchase DC
Up to 10 ₵	2
20 ₵	4
50 ₵	7
100 ₵	10
200 ₵	12
500 ₵	15
1000 ₵	18
2000 ₵	20
5000 ₵	23
10,000 ₵	26
20,000 ₵	28
50,000 ₵	31
100,000 ₵	34
200,000 ₵	36
500,000 ₵	39
1,000,000 ₵	42
2,000,000 ₵	44
5,000,000 ₵	47
Each additional x10	+8

If you are converting from the Wealth model, find the Purchase DC in the right hand column then read across the row to the left to find the approximate currency value of the item. Always err towards the higher end of the cost listed.

Supply and Demand

The GM may wish to add an additional level of complexity to his campaign economics in order to model supply and demand. In this model, the heroes are not guaranteed to find the item they want at the time they need it and at the price they want to pay. By travelling to larger communities and/or paying more for the item, they increase their chances of finding the item they desire.

- Step 1: The GM sets a Supply DC for the item. The Supply DC is based on the item's rarity as well as its base price.

Base Supply DCs	
Rarity	Base Supply DC
Very Common	5
Common	10
Uncommon	15
Rare	20

Remember that just because an item is rare, does not mean it is expensive; and just because an item is expensive does not make it rare. The rarity of an item fluctuates primarily by location. For example, a Sli'ess *gurak* blade may be a rare and exotic weapon on Earth, but it is a common sight in the slave pits of Cydonia.

The GM should set the rarity by region, however, and not by the population of the locale (see below).

The GM should further adjust the Supply DC according to the base price of the item using the table below.

Supply DC Adjustment by Item Price		
Item Price		Supply DC adjustment
Wealth Model	Currency Model	
DC 2	less than 10 ₵	-1
DC 2 - DC 15	10-500 ₵	+0
DC 15 - DC 20	501-2000 ₵	+1
DC 20 - DC 23	2001-5000 ₵	+2
DC 23 - DC 26	5001-10,000 ₵	+3
DC 26 - DC 28	10,001-20,000 ₵	+4
DC 28 - DC 31	20,001-50,000 ₵	+5
Each additional Wealth bracket		(+1)

- Step 2: Once the GM has calculated the Supply DC of the item, the player may now roll to find the item. Purchasing the item requires a Supply check; this roll simply determines whether the item is in supply in the location where the player is attempting his purchase.

The Supply check is adjusted (penalty or bonus) according to the size of the community in which the purchase is attempted, and by the buyer's offered price. The buyer can attempt to find the item either below cost (haggling for a better price) or above cost (increasing his "demand" to improve the "supply").

Supply Check modifier by Community Size	
Community Size	Supply check penalty/bonus
Thorp population 20 - 80	-3
Hamlet population 81 - 400	-2
Village population 401 - 900	-1
Small Town population 901 - 2000	+0
Large Town population 2001 - 5000	+3
Small City population 5001 - 12,000	+6
Large City population 12,001 - 25,000	+9
Metropolis population 25,001 or more	+12

The populations listed are appropriate for most Archaic and Apocalyptic campaigns. In most modern campaigns, adjust these population densities by x10 (e.g., a small town is 9,000 to 20,000 people).

Supply Check modifier by Offered Price		
Price Offered (base price increase/multiplier)		Supply check penalty/bonus
Wealth Model	Currency Model	
Purchase DC -1	0.70	-24
	0.75	-20
	0.80	-16
	0.85	-12
	0.90	-8
	0.95	-4
Purchase DC +0	1.00	+0
	1.25	+1
Purchase DC +1	1.50	+2
	1.75	+3
Purchase DC +2	2.00	+4
	3.00	+5
Purchase DC +4	4.00	+6

- Step 3: Once the Supply DC is set and all modifiers to the Supply check are calculated, the player rolls d20, applies all modifiers, and compares it to the Supply DC. If the roll equals or exceeds the Supply DC, he may purchase the item.

Wealth Model Example

In this example, our hero is attempting to purchase a hunting rifle (common, base Supply DC10). The rifle has a base purchase DC16; the Supply DC adjustment for an item of this price is +1, for a final Supply DC11.

The hero goes to a small city to make his purchase. This grants him a +3 bonus to his Supply check. He rolls a d20 and gets a 5, for a total of 8. The item is not in supply, so he cannot purchase it at this time.

Our hero decides to shop around a while longer, increasing his offered price. The Supply DC remains the same (DC16) but he offers a bit more (increasing the item's purchase DC by +1 gives him an additional +2 bonus to his Supply check. He rolls again and gets an 8, +3 for shopping in a small city, +2 for offering over the base price, for a total of 13. This beats the Supply DC11, and he finds the rifle.

The player must now make his Wealth check as normal, figuring in the increased Purchase DC17, to see how much his Wealth score decreases.

Currency Model Example

Now we will try the same example, using the currency model. The hunting rifle has a hard cost of 500 ¢. The currency model offers a bit more flexibility in the price offerings. Our hero offers 125% of the base price (x1.25) for a Supply check modifier of +1. He rolls an 8, +3 for a small city, +1 for offering 1.25 the base price, for a total of 12. Once again, this beats the Supply DC and the purchase is available. Our hero subtracts 625 ¢ (500 x 1.25) from his account and the deal is done.

Equipping The Campaign

The quickest and easiest way to generate equipment lists for your campaign is to use the information provided in the Players' Handbook (if you are creating a fantasy campaign) or the d20 Modern Roleplaying Game (if you are creating a modern campaign). If you are playing in another published setting, you can use the equipment lists found therein.

You can generate additional equipment for a modern campaign by simply browsing through your newspapers, catalogs, or the internet to find the going price for common equipment.

Custom Equipment for Unique Campaigns

The GM may wish to create unique weapons, armor, or other equipment for his campaign. If you choose to do so, use the following guidelines.

Custom Weapons

You can create custom melee weapons for your campaign, and using the following rules, be certain that they are balanced against each other. Do not overburden your campaign with weapon options. The danger in making too many weapons is that players will tend to sift through each weapon to find the most mathematically superior weapon offered. Keep your weapon offerings to broad groupings and use the following guidelines to balance them.

Simple Melee Weapons

The standard simple melee weapon has the following statistics:

Simple Melee Weapon			
Damage	Threat Range	Multiplier	Size
d6	20	x3	Medium

- Decrease the multiplier to x2 to improve the threat range to 19-20.
- Decrease the damage die to d4 to reduce the size to Small.
- Decrease the multiplier to x2 to improve the damage die by one step (d4/d6/d8). A simple weapon may not do more than d8 damage.
- Decrease the multiplier to x2 to allow the weapon to be thrown. Slashing and bludgeoning weapons have a range increment of 10; piercing weapons have a range increment of 20.
- Increase the size to Large to improve the damage die by one step (d4/d6/d8). A simple weapon may not do more than d8 damage.

Martial Melee Weapons

The standard martial melee weapon has the following statistics:

Martial Melee Weapon			
Damage	Threat Range	Multiplier	Size
d8	20	x3	Medium

- Decrease the multiplier to x2 to improve the threat range by 1 (20 becomes 19-20, 19-20 becomes 18-20, etc.).
- Decrease the damage die by one step (d8/d6/d4) to improve the threat range by 1.
- Decrease the damage die by one step to reduce the size to Small.
- Decrease the multiplier to x2 to improve the damage die by one step.
- Decrease the damage die by one step to increase the multiplier by one (x2/x3/x4).
- Decrease the multiplier to x2 to allow the weapon to be thrown. Slashing and bludgeoning weapons have a range increment of 10; piercing weapons have a range increment of 20. Decrease the damage die by one step to increase the range increment by +10.
- Decrease the damage die by one step to allow the weapon the use of two of the following combat maneuvers:

    Disarm: The weapon grants a +2 bonus to all disarm attempts.

    Mounted: When you use the weapon from a charging mount, you inflict double damage. If the weapon is Large, you may wield it one handed while mounted.

    Reach: If the weapon is size Large, it is a reach weapon. You may strike opponents up to 10 feet away.

    Set: When you use a ready action to set this weapon against an opponent's charge, you inflict double damage on a successful hit.

    Trip: You can use this weapon to make trip attacks. If you are tripped in your attempt, you can drop the weapon instead.

- Increase the size to Large to improve the damage die by two steps (d4/d6/d8/d10/d12).
- Increase the size to Large to improve the multiplier by one (x2/x3/x4).

Exotic Weapons

Exotic weapons should be built as martial weapons first. Applying the exotic weapon option means that these weapons require the Exotic Weapon Proficiency feat, but they may then apply any of the following adjustments:

- If the weapon is size Medium, it may be a double weapon. Essentially you may create two martial weapons and join them together into a single exotic weapon. Both ends of the weapon must be size M or smaller, and the combined double weapon is Large.
- If the weapon is Large, drop the damage die by one step to create a "hand-and-a-half" weapon. Such a weapon normally requires two hands to wield, but it may be wielded one-handed by those with the Exotic Weapon Proficiency feat for the weapon.

Typical Melee Weapons				
Simple Weapons				
Weapon	Damage	Critical	Size	Range
small club	d4	20/x2	S	10
small blade	d4	19-20/x2	S	-
small axe	d4	20/x3	S	-
club or axe	d6	20/x3	M	-
short spear	d6	20/x2	M	20
large club	d8	20/x3	L	
Martial Weapons				
short sword	d6	19-20/x2	S	-
broad sword	d8	19-20/x2	M	-
great sword	d12	19-20/x2	L	-
hand axe	d6	20/x3	S	-
throwing axe	d6	20/x2	S	10
battle axe	d8	20/x3	M	-
war club	d8	20/x2	M	10
great axe	d12	20/x3	L	-
spear	d8	20/x2	M	20
polearm[1]	d10	20/x3	L	
light flail[2]	d6	20/x2	S	
flail[2]	d8	20/x2	M	
heavy flail[2]	d10	19-20/x2	L	
small pick	d4	20/x4	S	
pick	d6	20/x4	M	
heavy pick	d10	20/x4	L	

1 Reach weapon. Can be set vs. charge.
2 Can be used to make trip and disarm attacks.

Ranged Weapons

Archaic ranged weapons such as crossbows, shortbows, longbows, and the like can use the statistics shown below, taken from the Players' Handbook. The GM can tweak these statistics by changing the range and reload times, and he can change the basic damage of the ammunition by using the same guidelines given above for melee weapons.

For gunpowder and other advanced technology ranged weapons, please see Chapter Nine: Firearms.

Typical Ranged Weapons[1]

Weapon	Damage	Critical	Size	Range
Simple Weapons				
light crossbow[2]	d8	19-20/x2	M	80
heavy crossbow[3]	d10	19-20/x2	M	120
sling	d4	20/x2	M	50
Martial Weapons				
short bow	d6	20/x3	M	60
long bow	d8	20/x3	L	100
composite short bow	d6	20/x3	M	70
composite long bow	d8	20/x3	L	110

1 All ranged weapons require two hands to reload. Once loaded, a crossbow or sling may be fired one handed.
2 Requires a move-equivalent action to reload.
3 Requires a full-round action to reload.

Cost as a Design Consideration

Generally speaking, cost is a poor design consideration when creating custom weapons for your campaign. There is little difference between a weapon costing 120¢ and 150¢— indeed, using the Wealth economic system, such differences in price may be completely transparent.

Cost becomes a valid design consideration only when a weapon is priced so high as to be out of reach of a starting character. Such cases are fine, provided they are not used to balance out the statistics of the weapon, and are instead used only to add flavor to the campaign.

Generally speaking, the cost of basic "self-defense" for a character in any campaign should be around 200 ¢ (Purchase DC12). The majority of custom weapons you design should cluster around this cost.

Custom Armor

You can also create custom armor for your campaign. The main design consideration with armor is that as protection increases, mobility should decrease. Your players will invariably choose the most protection they can afford to trade off with movement rates and DEX penalties.

Armor Statistics

Unlike weapons, the cost of armor is a valid design consideration— for starting characters. Most players will want to afford the best armor in a given category, but will often settle with the worst armor in the category and graduate to better armor as they can afford it. Generally speaking, the best armor in a given category shows a huge jump in cost.

Do Materials Matter?

In some campaigns, it is necessary to draw distinctions between armors based on the materials from which they are made. For example, in many fantasy campaigns, druids and other nature priests are barred from wearing metal armor. This restriction loses any meaningful significance, however, in the modern world, where the heaviest combat armor may be made of kevlar and ceraplast and not a trace of metal to be seen. Generally speaking, drawing distinctions between armor materials is a background choice, and not a design consideration that impacts the basic statistics of armor.

Typical Armors

Armor Name/Type	AC Bonus	Max. Dex bonus	Armor Check Penalty	Speed	Price	
					Currency	Wealth
Light Armors						
thick/heavy clothing	+1	+7	0	30	50 ¢	DC7
soft leather	+2	+6	0	30	100 ¢	DC10
hard leather	+3	+5	-1	30	200 ¢	DC12
light chain	+4	+4	-2	30	1000 ¢	DC18
Medium Armors						
scale/hide	+3	+4	-3	20	200 ¢	DC12
medium chain	+4	+3	-4	20	500 ¢	DC15
breastplate	+5	+2	-5	20	1500 ¢	DC19
Heavy Armors						
light combat (splint, banded, reinforced)	+6	+2	-6	20	3000 ¢	DC21
heavy combat (field plate, sealed suit)	+7	+1	-7	20	6000 ¢	DC24
super-heavy combat (full plate, power armor, etc.)	+8	+0	-8	20	12,000 ¢	DC27

Light Armor				
AC	Max. Dex bonus	Armor Check Penalty	Speed	Price
+1	+7	0	30	x1
+2	+6	0	30	x2
+3	+5	-1	30	x4
+4	+4	-2	30	x20

- Improve max Dex bonus by +1 (one time only): add x1 to cost
- Reduce armor check penalty by 1: add x1 to cost
- Worsen max Dex bonus by 1: subtract x1 cost
- Worsen armor check penalty by 1: subtract x1 cost

Medium Armor				
AC	Max. Dex bonus	Armor Check Penalty	Speed	Price
+3	+4	-3	20	x4
+4	+3	-4	20	x10
+5	+2	-5	20	x30

- Improve max Dex bonus by +1 (one time only): add x4 to cost
- Improve armor check penalty by 1: add x4 to cost
- Worsen max Dex bonus by 1: subtract x4 cost
- Worsen armor check penalty by 1: subtract x4 cost

Heavy Armor				
AC	Max. Dex bonus	Armor Check Penalty	Speed	Price
+6	+2	-6	20	x60
+7	+1	-7	20	x120
+8	+0	-8	20	x240

- Improve max Dex bonus by +1 (one time only): add x10 to cost
- Improve armor check penalty by 1: add x10 to cost
- Worsen max Dex bonus by 1: subtract x10 cost
- Worsen armor check penalty by 1: subtract x10 cost

When combining price multipliers, add them together. For example, a x4 multiplier and a x10 multiplier combine to a x14 multiplier.

When creating custom armor for your campaign, remember to leave room for masterwork armor (which grants a bonus of +1 to the armor check penalty). If your armor selections already include every possible permutation of AC, max Dex bonus, and armor check penalty, there is little incentive for players to seek out masterwork armor.

Miscellaneous Equipment

The following table lists some of the most common "adventuring gear." While this is by no means an exhaustive list, for those lacking any supplementary equipment lists, it is a good place to start. You can use the prices shown as a guideline for similar items within the same category: clothing, containers, provisions, and tools.

Miscellaneous Equipment		
	Price	
Item	Currency	Wealth
Clothing		
Adventurer's gear	100 ₵	DC 10
Business	200 ₵	DC 12
Casual	50 ₵	DC 7
Cold weather gear	80 ₵	DC 9
Formal	500 ₵	DC 15
Containers		
Backpack	20 ₵	DC 4
Basket	4 ₵	DC 2
Belt Pouch	10 ₵	DC 2
Case (map or scroll)	10 ₵	DC 2
Chest (wooden 1x1x6")	20 ₵	DC 4
Chest (iron 1x1x6")	50 ₵	DC 7
Sack	1 ₵	-
Food/Provisions/Shelter		
Bedroll	1 ₵	-
Blanket	5 ₵	DC 2
Bread (per loaf)	0.2 ₵	-
Butter (1 lb.)	2 ₵	-
Cheese (1 lb.)	1 ₵	-
Meat (1/2 lb)	3 ₵	-
Rations, trail, per day (1 lb.)	5 ₵	DC2
Wine (bottle)	20 ₵	DC 4
Tent	100 ₵	DC 10
Tools and Gear		
Chain (10 feet)	300 ₵	DC 13
Climber's Kit	800 ₵	DC 17
Craftsman's Tools	50 ₵	DC 7
Crowbar	20 ₵	DC 4
Disguise Kit	500 ₵	DC 15
Grappling Hook	10 ₵	DC 2
Hammer	5 ₵	DC 2
Healer's Kit	50 ₵	DC 7
Holy Symbol	250 ₵	DC13
Pitons/Spikes (dozen)	10 ₵	DC 2
Rope (hemp 50')	10 ₵	DC 2
Rope (nylon/silk)	100 ₵	DC10
Shovel	10 ₵	DC 2
Sledgehammer	10 ₵	DC 2
Surgery Kit	750 ₵	DC 16
Thieves' Tools	300 ₵	DC 13

Carrying Capacity (Encumbrance)

A character's carrying capacity depends directly on the character's Strength score, as shown on the table below.

Unencumbered (Light Load)

If the weight of everything a character is wearing or carrying amounts to no more than his light load figure, he can move and perform any actions normally (though his speed might already be slowed by other means).

Encumbered (Medium and Heavy Load)

If the weight of the character's gear falls in the medium or heavy load range, he is considered encumbered. An encumbered character's speed is reduced to the value given below, if the character is not already slowed to that speed for some other reason (for example, wearing armor).

Previous Base Speed	Medium Load	Heavy Load
20 ft.	15 ft.	10 ft.
30 ft.	20 ft.	15 ft.
40 ft.	30 ft.	20 ft.
50 ft.	40 ft.	25 ft.
60 ft.	50 ft.	30 ft.

A character encumbered with a medium load has a maximum Dex bonus of +3. In addition, he takes a -3 encumbrance penalty on attack rolls and checks with the following skills: Balance, Climb, Escape Artist, Hide, Jump, Move Silently, and Tumble. This encumbrance penalty stacks with any armor check penalty.

A heavily encumbered character has a maximum Dex bonus of +1, and suffers a -6 encumbrance penalty as above. His maximum running speed is x3 instead of speed x4.

The figure at the upper end of a character's heavy load range is his or her maximum load. No character can move or perform any other actions while carrying more than his or her maximum load.

Lifting and Dragging

A character can lift up to his maximum load over his head.

A character can lift up to double his or her maximum load off the ground, but he or she can only stagger around with it. While overloaded in this way, the character loses any Dexterity bonus to AC and can only move 5 feet per round (as a full-round action).

A character can generally push or drag along the ground up to five times his or her maximum load. Favorable conditions (smooth ground, dragging a slick object) can double these numbers, and bad circumstances (broken ground, pushing an object that snags) can reduce them to one-half or less.

Bigger and Smaller Creatures

The figures on Table: Carrying Capacity are for Medium-size bipedal creatures. Larger bipedal creatures can carry more weight depending on size category: Large x2, Huge x4, Gargantuan x8, and Colossal x16. Smaller creatures can carry less weight depending on size category: Small x3/4, Tiny x1/2, Diminutive x1/4, and Fine x1/8.

Quadrupeds, such as horses, can carry heavier loads than characters can. Use these multipliers instead of the ones given above: Fine x1/4, Diminutive x1/2, Tiny x3/4, Small x1, Medium-size x1.5, Large x3, Huge x6, Gargantuan x12, and Colossal x24.

Carrying Capacity

Strength	Light	Medium	Heavy
1	up to 3 lb.	4-6 lb.	7-10 lb.
2	up to 6 lb.	7-13 lb.	14-20 lb.
3	up to 10 lb.	11-20 lb.	21-30 lb.
4	up to 13 lb.	14-26 lb.	27-40 lb.
5	up to 16 lb.	17-33 lb.	34-50 lb.
6	up to 20 lb.	21-40 lb.	41-60 lb.
7	up to 23 lb.	24-46 lb.	47-70 lb.
8	up to 26 lb.	27-53 lb.	54-80 lb.
9	up to 30 lb.	31-60 lb.	61-90 lb.
10	up to 33 lb.	34-66 lb.	67-100 lb.
11	up to 38 lb.	39-76 lb.	77-115 lb.
12	up to 43 lb.	44-86 lb.	87-130 lb.
13	up to 50 lb.	51-100 lb.	101-150 lb.
14	up to 58 lb.	59-116 lb.	117-175 lb.
15	up to 66 lb.	67-133 lb.	134-200 lb.
16	up to 76 lb.	77-153 lb.	154-230 lb.
17	up to 86 lb.	87-173 lb.	174-260 lb.
18	up to 100 lb.	101-200 lb.	201-300 lb.
19	up to 116 lb.	117-233 lb.	234-350 lb.
20	up to 133 lb.	134-266 lb.	267-400 lb.
21	up to 153 lb.	154-306 lb.	307-460 lb.
22	up to 173 lb.	174-346 lb.	347-520 lb.
23	up to 200 lb.	201-400 lb.	401-600 lb.
24	up to 233 lb.	234-466 lb.	467-700 lb.
25	up to 266 lb.	267-533 lb.	534-800 lb.
26	up to 306 lb.	307-613 lb.	614-920 lb.
27	up to 346 lb.	347-693 lb.	694-1,040 lb.
28	up to 400 lb.	401-800 lb.	801-1,200 lb.
29	up to 466 lb.	467-933 lb.	934-1,400 lb.
each +10	x4	x4	x4

Tremendous Strength

For Strength scores not listed, find the Strength score between 20 and 29 that has the same ones digit as the creature's Strength score. Multiply the figures by x4 if the creature's Strength is in the 30s, x16 if it's in the 40s, x64 if it's in the 50s, and so on.

Combat in Grim Tales is cyclical and is measured in *rounds*. Each round, each combatant acts in turn, according to his initiative, until all combatants have acted. This signals the end of the round, at which point the next round begins, starting again at the top with the combatant with the highest initiative.

Combat follows this sequence:

1. Each combatant starts out flat-footed. Once a combatant acts, he is no longer flat-footed.
2. Determine which characters are aware of their opponents at the start of the battle. If some but not all of the combatants are aware of their opponents, a surprise round happens before regular rounds of combat begin.

   The combatants who are aware of their opponents can act in the surprise round, so they roll for initiative. In initiative order (highest to lowest), combatants who started the battle aware of their opponents each take one action (either a standard action or a move action) during the surprise round. Combatants who were unaware do not get to act in the surprise round. If no one or everyone starts the battle aware, there is no surprise round.
3. Combatants who have not yet rolled initiative do so. All combatants are now ready to begin their first regular round of combat.
4. Combatants act in initiative order (highest to lowest).
5. When everyone has had a turn, the combatant with the highest initiative acts again, and steps 4 and 5 repeat until combat ends.

Surprise

When a combat starts, if you are not aware of your opponents and they are aware of you, you are surprised.

Determining Awareness

Sometimes all the combatants on a side are aware of their opponents, sometimes none are, and sometimes only some of them are. Sometimes a few combatants on each side are aware and the other combatants on each side are unaware.

Determining awareness may call for Listen checks, Spot checks, or other checks as the GM requires.

The Surprise Round

If some but not all of the combatants are aware of their opponents, a surprise round happens before regular rounds begin. Any combatants aware of the opponents can act in the surprise round, so they roll for initiative. In initiative order (highest to lowest), combatants who started the battle aware of their opponents each take a standard action during the surprise round. You can also take free actions during the surprise round. If no one or everyone is surprised, no surprise round occurs.

Unaware Combatants

Combatants who are unaware at the start of battle don't get to act in the surprise round. Unaware combatants are flat-footed because they have not acted yet, so they lose any Dexterity bonus to AC.

Initiative

At the start of a battle, each combatant makes an initiative check. An initiative check is a d20 roll plus your Dexterity modifier, plus any extra modifiers (such as from the Improved Initiative feat).

Characters act in order, counting down from highest result to lowest. In every round that follows, the characters act in the same order (unless a character takes an action that results in his initiative changing; see Special Initiative Actions).

If two or more combatants have the same initiative check result, the combatants who are tied act in order of total initiative modifier (highest first). If there is still a tie, the tied characters should roll again to determine which one of them goes before the other. Note that this step is unnecessary if the combatants are on the same side (such as two player characters tied for initiative); one may simply defer the higher initiative to the other.

Flat-Footed

At the start of a battle, before you have had a chance to act (specifically, before your first action in the initiative order), you are flat-footed. You can't use your Dexterity bonus to AC (if any) while flat-footed.

Many characters have the *uncanny dodge* talent, which allows them to avoid losing their Dexterity bonus to AC due to being flat-footed.

A flat-footed character can't make attacks of opportunity.

Inaction

Even if you can't take actions, you retain your initiative score for the duration of the encounter.

Essentials of Combat

The essential combat statistics needed to resolve the effects of a single attack roll are:

- Attack Bonus
- Armor Class
- Damage
- Hit Points

Attack Roll

An attack roll represents your attempt to strike your opponent on your turn in a round. When you make an attack roll, you roll a d20 and add your attack bonus.

If your result equals or beats the target's Armor Class (AC), you hit and deal damage.

Automatic Misses and Hits: Regardless of any other penalties or bonuses, a natural 1 (the d20 comes up 1) on an attack roll is always a miss (an automatic miss). A natural 20 (the d20 comes up 20) is always a hit (an automatic hit).

Attack Bonus

Your attack bonus with a melee weapon is:

Base attack bonus + Strength modifier + size modifier

With a ranged weapon, your attack bonus is:

Base attack bonus + Dexterity modifier + size modifier + range penalty

Strength Modifier: Strength helps a character swing a weapon harder and faster, so a character's Strength modifier applies to melee attack rolls.

Dexterity Modifier: Dexterity measures coordination and steadiness, so a character's Dexterity modifier applies when the character attacks with a ranged weapon.

Range Penalty: The range penalty for a ranged weapon depends on what weapon the character is using and how far away the target is. All ranged weapons and thrown weapons have a range increment. Any attack from a distance of less than one range increment is not penalized for range. However, each full range increment causes a cumulative -2 penalty on the attack roll. A thrown weapon has a maximum range of five range increments, while ranged weapons that fire projectiles can generally shoot up to ten increments.

Size Modifier: The size modifier applies to a creature's size (not the size of the weapon). As noted below, the size modifier also applies to AC, so that two creatures of the same size category strike each other normally.

Size Modifiers to Attack Roll / AC bonus			
Size	Modifier	Size	Modifier
Colossal	-8	Small	+1
Gargantuan	-4	Tiny	+2
Huge	-2	Diminutive	+4
Large	-1	Fine	+8
Medium	+0		

Armor Class

Your Armor Class (AC) represents how hard it is for opponents to land a solid, damaging blow on you. Your AC is the attack roll result that an opponent needs to achieve to hit you.

A character or creature's AC is equal to 10 + any of the following that apply:

+ armor bonus
+ shield bonus
+ natural armor bonus
+ Dexterity modifier
+ deflection bonus
+ size modifier
+ Defense bonus
+ dodge bonuses

Armor Bonus: The type of armor you wear (if any) adds to your AC. Conceptually speaking, armor does not make you harder to hit; it makes you harder to hurt; nevertheless, the end result is that armor adds to your AC.

Note that heavier armor progressively limits your Dexterity bonus. If you are wearing armor, you might not be able to apply your whole Dexterity bonus to your AC. You may add only up to the maximum Dexterity bonus listed for the type of armor you are wearing.

Shield Bonus: If you are carrying a shield, it also provides a bonus to AC.

☠☠☠ In grittier campaigns, a shield must be readied in combat before it can provide an AC bonus. At the GM's discretion, a combatant who is flat-footed or denied his Dex bonus does not receive a shield bonus, either.

Natural Armor Bonus: Natural armor improves your AC. Whereas the armor bonus represents equipment that is worn over the body, natural armor represents thick scales, skin, dense muscle, or other physical parts of the body that nevertheless reduce the effectiveness of each blow.

Dexterity Bonus: Your Dexterity bonus represents your ability to actively avoid a blow. If you cannot react to a blow (such as when you are surprised or flat-footed), you may not add your Dexterity bonus to AC.

Deflection Bonus: Deflection bonuses are invisible, intangible effects that slow down, ward off, or otherwise deflect blows and improve your AC.

Size Modifier: Larger creatures are easier to hit, while smaller creatures are harder to hit. Most characters are Medium sized and will have a size modifier of +0. Note that due to the size modifiers to hit (see above), combatants of the same size effectively cancel out their size modifiers.

Defense Bonuses: Player characters (and some creatures with core class levels) gain a Defense bonus to their AC. This bonus represents the improved luck and training of higher level characters.

☠☠☠ In grittier campaigns, the Defense bonus is an active bonus that requires the combatant to be aware of his opponents. At the GM's discretion, combatants who are flat-footed or otherwise denied their Dex or dodge bonuses for any reason, do not get to add their Defense bonus to AC, either.

Dodge Bonuses: Some other AC bonuses represent actively avoiding blows. These bonuses are called dodge bonuses. Any situation that denies you your Dexterity bonus also denies you dodge bonuses. (Wearing armor, however, does not limit these bonuses the way it limits a Dexterity bonus to AC.) Unlike most sorts of bonuses, dodge bonuses stack with each other.

Touch Attacks / Touch AC: Some attacks disregard armor, including shields and natural armor. In these cases, the attacker makes a touch attack roll (either ranged or melee). Touch AC does not include any armor bonus, shield bonus, or natural armor bonus. All other modifiers, such as size modifier, Dexterity modifier, Defense modifier, dodge bonuses, and especially deflection bonuses (if any) apply normally.

Damage

When your attack succeeds, you deal damage. The type of weapon used determines the amount of damage you deal. Effects that modify weapon damage apply to unarmed strikes and the natural physical attack forms of creatures.

Damage reduces a target's current hit points.

Minimum Damage: If penalties reduce the damage result to less than 1, a hit still deals 1 point of damage. Note that this includes only penalties to damage (such as from low Strength) and does *not* apply to damage reduction, energy resistance, or other effects that may reduce damage to zero.

Strength Bonus: When you hit with a melee or thrown weapon, including a sling, add your Strength modifier to the damage result. A Strength penalty, but not a bonus, applies on attacks made with a bow that is not a composite bow.

Off-Hand Weapon: When you deal damage with a weapon in your off hand, you add only 1/2 your Strength bonus (round down).

Wielding a Weapon Two-Handed: When you deal damage with a weapon that you are wielding two-handed, you add 1-1/2 times your Strength bonus (round down). However, you don't get this higher Strength bonus when using a *light* weapon with two hands.

Multiplying Damage: Sometimes you multiply damage by some factor, such as on a critical hit. Roll the damage (with all modifiers) multiple times and total the results. Note: When you multiply damage more than once, each multiplier works off the original, unmultiplied damage.

Exception: Extra damage *dice* over and above a weapon's normal damage are never multiplied.

Ability Damage: Certain creatures and magical effects can cause temporary ability damage (a reduction to an ability score).

Critical Hits

When you make an attack roll and get a natural 20 (the d20 actually shows 20), you hit regardless of your target's Armor Class, and you have scored a threat: a potential critical hit (or "crit").

If the attack roll would normally hit the target's AC— that is, the attack roll is a hit regardless of being an automatic hit— you may spend an action point to score a critical hit. Any attack roll that wouldn't ordinarily result in a hit is not a threat.

A critical hit means that you roll your damage more than once, with all your usual bonuses, and add the rolls together. Unless otherwise specified, the threat range for a critical hit on an attack roll is 20, and the multiplier is x2; the natural attacks of most monsters fall into this category.

When a critical hit is scored, multiply the weapon's base damage dice as well all damage bonuses, such as Strength modifiers to damage. Note that bonus damage *dice* (such as from the *sneak attack* talent, or a magical *flaming burst* weapon) are never multiplied.

Increased Threat Range: Sometimes your threat range is greater than 20. That is, you can score a threat on a lower number. In such cases, a roll of lower than 20 is not an automatic hit. Any attack roll that doesn't result in a hit is not a threat.

Increased Critical Multiplier: Some weapons deal better than x2 damage on a critical hit.

Critical Misses

When you make an attack roll and get a natural 1 (the d20 actually shows 1) your attack automatically misses. In addition, this is a threat for a critical miss.

If the attack roll would normally hit (despite rolling a 1) the attack simply misses. The GM may not activate a critical miss.

However, if the attack roll is a 1 and would normally have resulted in a miss despite being an automatic miss, the GM may award you an action point and activate a critical miss.

The GM is free to determine the effect of a critical miss as he sees fit. Some common examples include dropping your weapon, being *stunned* for a round, striking another adjacent target by mistake, or even striking yourself. There is no limit to the depravity of the GM in these situations, so take what comfort you can from your extra action point.

Hit Points

Hit points mean two things in the game world: the ability to take physical punishment and keep going, and the ability to turn a serious blow into a less serious one.

Injury and Death

Your hit points measure how hard you are to kill. No matter how many hit points you lose, your character isn't hindered in any way until your hit points drop to 0 or lower.

Loss of Hit Points

The most common way that your character gets hurt is to take lethal damage and lose hit points.

Disabled

When your current hit points drop to 0, you are *disabled*.

You may continue to act as if *disabled* until your negative hit point total exceeds your Constitution modifier. For example, if your Con modifier is +3, you are *disabled* from 0 to -3 hit points.

You can only take a single move or standard action each turn (but not both, nor can you take full-round actions). You can take move actions without further injuring yourself, but if you perform any standard action (or any other strenuous action) you take 1 point of damage after the completing the act. Unless your activity increased your hit points, you may now be *dying*.

A disabled character who takes any non-lethal damage becomes *unconscious*, but does not begin *dying*.

Healing that raises your hit points above 0 makes you fully functional again, just as if you'd never been reduced to 0 or fewer hit points.

You can also become *disabled* when recovering from *dying*. In this case, it's a step toward recovery, and you can have fewer than 0 hit points (see *Stabilizing and Recovery*, below).

Dying

When your character's negative hit point total is greater than your Constitution modifier but still less than your Constitution score, he's *dying*.

A *dying* character immediately falls unconscious and can take no actions.

A *dying* character loses 1 hit point every round. This continues until the character dies or becomes stable (see *Stabilizing and Recovery*, below).

Dead

When your character's negative hit point total exceeds his Constitution score, he's dead.

A character can also die from ability damage or drain that reduces his Constitution to 0.

Massive Damage

If you sustain damage from a single attack that exceeds your Massive Damage Threshold (and the loss of hit points doesn't kill you outright!) you must still make a Fortitude save (DC15). If this saving throw fails, you immediately drop to -1 hit points and begin *dying*, regardless of your previous hit point total.

If you take damage from multiple attacks, no single attack of which exceeds your Massive Damage Threshold, the massive damage rule does not apply.

☠ In standard campaigns, your Massive Damage Threshold is equal to your Constitution score plus your armor, shield, and natural armor bonus. In this variant, even if an attack exceeds your Constitution score, it must do sufficient damage to pierce your armor before it can kill you from massive damage.

☠☠ In grittier campaigns, your Massive Damage Threshold is equal to your Constitution score. You do not receive any additional Massive Damage Threshold from natural armor or equipment.

☠☠☠ In the most lethal campaigns, all characters and creatures have a Massive Damage Threshold of 10. Regardless of size, health, or armor worn, all creatures are mortal and equally vulnerable.

Variant: "Mooks" and Massive Damage

The GM can use this option to speed up play when the heroes are facing a number of "mooks" or "cannon fodder."

Creatures who qualify as mooks (generally, creatures whose CR is 1/4 or less than the average level of the characters, or whose individual EL is 8 less than the party EL), at the GMs discretion, are assumed to automatically fail their Fortitude save vs. Massive Damage.

The GM does not roll a Fortitude save for mooks: any hit that exceeds their Massive Damage Threshold slays them instantly, regardless of hit points. This allows the heroes to wade through lesser foes and come to grips with more interesting (and evenly matched) adversaries.

To speed play even further and make the GM's book-keeping easier, the GM can dispense with hit points for mooks entirely. A mook that is struck in combat once (and not slain from Massive Damage) is marked as *wounded*, and the next successful hit (regardless of damage) slays the mook outright.

The GM may wish to reduce or eliminate any experience point awards for mooks when using these options. Instead, he can grant a lump sum experience award if the heroes overcome the mooks and move on to the next scene.

Stabilizing and Recovery

On the next turn after a character is *dying* and on all subsequent turns, he must make a Fortitude save (DC20) to see whether he becomes stable. If the saving throw succeeds, he becomes stable. If the saving throw fails, he loses 1 more hit point. (A character who is unconscious or *dying* can't use any special action that changes the initiative count on which his action occurs.)

You can keep a *dying* character from losing any more hit points and make him stable with a DC 15 Heal check.

If any sort of healing cures the *dying* character of even 1 point of damage, he stops losing hit points and becomes stable.

Healing can raise a *dying* character's hit point total. Depending on his new total, his status can improve to *disabled* or better. Healing that raises his hit points to 1 or more makes him fully functional again, just as if he had never been reduced to 0 or lower.

A stable character who has been tended by a healer or who has been magically healed eventually regains consciousness and recovers hit points naturally. If the character has no one to tend him, however, his life is still in danger, and he may yet slip away, as detailed below.

Recovering with Help: One hour after a tended, *dying* character becomes stable, he must succeed at another Fortitude save (DC20), at which point he is *disabled.*

If the save is failed, he remains unconscious, though he may make a new saving throw every hour to revive and become *disabled*. Even if unconscious, he recovers hit points naturally through rest. He is back to normal when his hit points rise to 1 or higher.

Recovering without Help: Recovering without anyone to tend to you is difficult and dangerous, but it can be done. Though a severely wounded character left alone usually dies, he has a small chance of recovering on his own.

A character who becomes stable on his own (by making the Fortitude save while *dying*) and who has no one to tend to him still loses hit points, just at a slower rate. Once each hour as above, he must make a Fortitude saving throw (DC20) to regain consciousness. If the save is successful, he regains consciousness, though his hit point total remains where it is, even if negative.

If the hourly Fortitude save to become conscious is failed, he loses 1 hit point. He can not recover hit points through natural healing until he becomes conscious.

Even once he becomes conscious and is *disabled*, an unaided character still does not recover hit points naturally. Instead, each day he must make a Fortitude save (DC20) to start recovering hit points naturally (starting with that day); otherwise, he loses 1 hit point.

Once an unaided character starts recovering hit points naturally, he is no longer in danger of naturally losing hit points (even if his current hit point total is negative).

Healing

After taking damage, you can recover hit points through natural healing (or, if your campaign features spellcasting, through magical healing). In any case, you can't regain hit points past your full normal hit point total.

Natural Healing: With a full night's rest (8 hours of sleep or more), you recover 1 hit point per character level. Any significant interruption during your rest prevents you from healing that night.

If you undergo complete bed rest for an entire day and night, you recover twice your character level in hit points.

Healing Limits: You can never recover more hit points than you lost.

Healing Ability Damage: Ability damage is temporary, just as hit point damage is. Ability damage returns at the rate of 1 point per night of rest (8 hours) for each affected ability score. Complete bed rest restores 2 points per day (24 hours) for each affected ability score.

Rapid Healing: Note that characters with the Heal skill, and some Talents, can improve upon the natural rates of healing listed above.

Temporary Hit Points

Certain effects give a character temporary hit points. When a character gains temporary hit points, note his current hit point total. When the temporary hit points go away the character's hit points drop to his current hit point total. If the character's hit points are below his current hit point total at that time, all the temporary hit points have already been lost and the character's hit point total does not drop further.

When temporary hit points are lost, they cannot be restored as real hit points can be, not even by magic.

Increases in Constitution Score and Current Hit Points: An increase in a character's Constitution score, even a temporary one, can give her more hit points (an effective hit point increase), but these are not temporary hit points. They can be restored and they are not lost first as temporary hit points are. If your Constitution score subsequently drops, you immediately lose any added hit points.

Non-Lethal Damage

Certain attacks deal nonlethal damage. Other effects, such as heat or being *exhausted*, also deal nonlethal damage. When you take nonlethal damage, keep a running total of how much you've accumulated. Do not deduct the nonlethal damage number from your current hit points. It is not "real" damage. Instead, when your nonlethal damage equals your current hit points, you're *staggered*, and when it exceeds your current hit points, you fall unconscious. It doesn't matter whether the nonlethal damage equals or exceeds your current hit points because the nonlethal damage has gone up or because your current hit points have gone down.

Nonlethal Damage with a Weapon that Deals Lethal Damage: You can use a melee weapon that deals lethal damage to deal nonlethal damage instead, but you take a -4 penalty on your attack roll.

Lethal Damage with a Weapon that Deals Nonlethal Damage: You can use a weapon that deals nonlethal damage, including an unarmed strike, to deal lethal damage instead, but you take a -4 penalty on your attack roll.

Staggered and Unconscious: When your nonlethal damage equals your current hit points, you're *staggered*. You can only take a standard action or a move action in each round. You cease being *staggered* when your current hit points once again exceed your nonlethal damage.

When your nonlethal damage exceeds your current hit points, you fall unconscious. While unconscious, you are *helpless*.

Healing Nonlethal Damage: You heal nonlethal damage at the rate of 1 hit point per character level, per hour. In addition, any effect that heals lethal damage (whether by magic, spending an action die, application of the Heal skill, or some other means) heals an equal amount of non-lethal damage.

Variant: Fewer Dead Heroes

In this variant, armor helps to protect combatants by converting a portion of lethal damage from every attack into non-lethal damage.

For every successful attack, roll damage normally, but before applying the damage to the defender's hit points, subtract the armor bonus from the damage done. This damage is instead converted to non-lethal damage.

If the attack normally does non-lethal damage, the armor absorbs up to its armor bonus, negating the damage completely.

Only the defender's armor bonus converts damage in this way. Natural armor, shields, and other bonuses to AC do not apply. Furthermore, armor can only convert physical damage; energy damage (such as from heat or cold) is not converted or absorbed.

Example:
A warrior in heavy armor (+8 armor bonus) is struck for 10 points of lethal damage. The first 8 points of this damage is converted to non-lethal damage, and 2 points of lethal damage are applied to his hit points.

Later, the same fighter is involved in a bar brawl. His attacker strikes him for 4 points of non-lethal damage. The warrior's armor completely negates all of this non-lethal damage.

Because a combatant is knocked unconscious when his non-lethal damage exceeds his current hit points, this variant will not change the duration of combat. However, combatants will be knocked unconscious before they are killed.

The GM should note that this will have the side effect of leaving the victors in control of the battlefield with their opponents at their mercy. For the heroes, this leaves them in the delicate position of having to decide between allowing their opponents to escape, burdening themselves with prisoners, or grimly stalking the battlefield to finish off their fallen foes.

Saving Throws

Generally, when you are subject to an unusual attack, you get a saving throw to avoid or reduce the effect. Like an attack roll, a saving throw is a d20 roll plus a bonus based on your class, level, and an ability score. Your saving throw modifier is:

Base save bonus + ability modifier

Saving Throw Types

The three different kinds of saving throws are Fortitude, Reflex, and Will:

Fortitude: These saves measure your ability to stand up to physical punishment or attacks against your vitality and health. Apply your Constitution modifier to your Fortitude saving throws.

Reflex: These saves test your ability to dodge area attacks. Apply your Dexterity modifier to your Reflex saving throws.

Will: These saves reflect your resistance to mental influence as well as many magical effects. Apply your Wisdom modifier to your Will saving throws.

Automatic Failures and Successes

A natural 1 (the d20 comes up 1) on a saving throw is always a failure (and may cause damage to exposed items carried by the character). A natural 20 (the d20 comes up 20) is always a success.

Visualizing Combat: Using the Battle Grid

Combat is generally played out on the tabletop with the help of miniatures (25mm to 30mm scale) and a battle grid marked with one-inch squares.

When using a grid to represent character's movement, the standard scale equates 1 inch (or a 1 inch square) to 5 feet in the game world.

Measuring Distance

Diagonals: When measuring distance, the first diagonal counts as 1 square, the second counts as 2 squares, the third counts as 1, the fourth as 2, and so on.

- You can't move diagonally past a corner (even by taking a 5-foot step).
- You can move diagonally past a creature, even an opponent.
- You can also move diagonally past other impassable obstacles, such as pits.

Closest Creature: When it's important to determine the closest square or creature to a location, if two squares or creatures are equally close, randomly determine which one counts as closest by rolling a die.

Unusual Sized Creatures

Creatures smaller than Small or larger than Medium have special rules relating to their positioning on the battle grid.

Tiny, Diminutive, and Fine Creatures: Very small creatures take up less than 1 square of space. This means that more than one such creature can fit into a single square.

A Tiny creature typically occupies a space only 2-1/2 feet across, so four can fit into a single square. Twenty-five Diminutive creatures or 100 Fine creatures can fit into a single square.

Creatures that take up less than 1 square of space typically have a natural reach of 0 feet, meaning they can't reach into adjacent squares. They must enter an opponent's square to attack in melee. This provokes an attack of opportunity from the opponent. You can attack into your own square if you need to, so you can attack such creatures normally. Since they have no natural reach, they do not threaten the squares around them. You can move past them without provoking attacks of opportunity. They also can't flank an enemy.

Large, Huge, Gargantuan, and Colossal Creatures: Very large creatures take up more than 1 square.

Creatures that take up more than 1 square typically have a natural reach of 10 feet or more, meaning that they can reach targets even if they aren't in adjacent squares.

Table 6-1: Creature Size, Scale, and Reach

Creature Size	Space[1]	Reach[1]
Fine	1/2 ft.	0
Diminutive	1 ft.	0
Tiny	2-1/2 ft.	0
Small	5 ft.	5 ft.
Medium	5 ft.	5 ft.
Large (tall)	10 ft.	10 ft.
Large (long)	10 ft.	5 ft.
Huge (tall)	15 ft.	15 ft.
Huge (long)	15 ft.	10 ft.
Gargantuan (tall)	20 ft.	20 ft.
Gargantuan (long)	20 ft.	15 ft.
Colossal (tall)	30 ft.	30 ft.
Colossal (long)	30 ft.	20 ft.

1 These values are typical for creatures of the indicated size. Some exceptions exist.

Unlike when a character uses a reach weapon, a creature with greater than normal natural reach (more than 5 feet) still threatens squares adjacent to it. A creature with greater than normal natural reach usually gets an attack of opportunity against you if you approach it, because you must enter and move within the range of its reach before you can attack it. (This attack of opportunity is not provoked if you take a 5-foot step.)

Large or larger creatures using reach weapons can strike up to double their natural reach but can't strike at their natural reach or less.

Tactical Movement

Where can a character move, how long it takes to get there, and whether he is vulnerable to *attacks of opportunity* (see below) while moving are key questions in combat.

Speed

Your speed tells you how far you can move in a round with a single move action. Most characters move 30 feet (6 squares), although armor can slow a character down. Some creatures move faster or slower. A character's speed when unarmored is sometimes called *base speed.*

If you use two move actions in a round (sometimes called a "double move" action), you can move up to double your speed. If you spend the entire round to run all out, you can move up to quadruple your speed (or triple if you are in heavy armor).

Encumbrance: A character encumbered by carrying a large amount of gear or a fallen comrade may move slower than normal.

Movement in Darkness: If a character moves when he can't see, such as in total darkness, his speed is limited to one-half normal. The Blind-Fight feat reduces this penalty.

Moving through a Square

Friend: You can move through a square occupied by a friendly character, unless you are charging. When you move through a square occupied by a friendly character, that character doesn't provide you with cover.

Opponent: You can't move through a square occupied by an opponent, unless the opponent is helpless. You can move through a square occupied by a helpless opponent without penalty. (Some creatures, particularly very large ones, may present an obstacle even when helpless. In such cases, each square you move through counts as 2 squares.)

Ending Your Movement: You can't end your movement in the same square as another creature unless it is helpless.

Overrun: During your movement or as part of a charge, you can attempt to move through a square occupied by an opponent.

Tumbling: A trained character can attempt to tumble through a square occupied by an opponent (see the Tumble skill).

Very Small Creature: A Fine, Diminutive, or Tiny creature can move into or through an occupied square. The creature provokes attacks of opportunity when doing so.

Square Occupied by Creature Three Sizes Larger or Smaller: Any creature can move through a square occupied by a creature three size categories larger than it is.

A big creature can move through a square occupied by a creature three size categories smaller than it is.

Designated Exceptions: Some creatures break the above rules. A creature that completely fills the squares it occupies (such as a gelatinous blob) cannot be moved past, even with the Tumble skill or similar special abilities.

Terrain and Obstacles

Difficult Terrain: Difficult terrain hampers movement. Each square of difficult terrain counts as 2 squares of movement. (Each diagonal move into a difficult terrain square counts as 3 squares.) You can't run or charge across difficult terrain.

If you occupy squares with different kinds of terrain, you can move only as fast as the most difficult terrain you occupy will allow.

Flying and incorporeal creatures are not hampered by difficult terrain.

Obstacles: Like difficult terrain, obstacles can hamper movement. If an obstacle hampers movement but doesn't completely block it each obstructed square or obstacle between squares counts as 2 squares of movement. You must pay this cost to cross the barrier, in addition to the cost to move into the square on the other side. If you don't have sufficient movement to cross the barrier and move into the square on the other side, you can't cross the barrier. Some obstacles may also require a skill check to cross.

On the other hand, some obstacles block movement entirely. A character can't move through a blocking obstacle.

Flying and incorporeal creatures can avoid most obstacles.

Squeezing: In some cases, you may have to squeeze into or through an area that isn't as wide as the space you take up. You can squeeze through or into a space that is at least half as wide as your normal space. Each move into or through a narrow space counts as if it were 2 squares, and while squeezed in a narrow space you take a -4 penalty on attack rolls and a -4 penalty to AC.

When a Large creature (which normally takes up four squares, 2x2) squeezes into a space that's one square wide, the creature's miniature figure occupies two squares, centered on the line between the two squares. For a bigger creature, center the creature likewise in the area it squeezes into.

A creature can squeeze past an opponent while moving but it can't end its movement in an occupied square.

To squeeze through or into a space less than half your space's width, you must use the Escape Artist skill. You can't attack while using Escape Artist to squeeze through or into a narrow space, you take a -4 penalty to AC, and you lose any Dexterity bonus to AC.

Special Movement Rules

These rules cover special movement situations.

Accidentally Ending Movement in an Illegal Space: Sometimes a character ends its movement while moving through a space where it's not allowed to stop. When that happens, put your miniature in the last legal position you occupied, or the closest legal position, if there's a legal position that's closer.

Double Movement Cost: When your movement is hampered in some way, your movement usually costs double. For example, each square of movement through difficult terrain counts as 2 squares, and each diagonal move through such terrain counts as 3 squares (just as two diagonal moves normally do).

If movement cost is doubled twice, then each square counts as 4 squares (or as 6 squares if moving diagonally). If movement cost is doubled three times, then each square counts as 8 squares (12 if diagonal) and so on. This is

an exception to the general rule that two doublings are equivalent to a tripling.

Minimum Movement: Despite penalties to movement, you can take a full-round action to move 5 feet (1 square) in any direction, even diagonally. (This rule doesn't allow you to move through impassable terrain or to move when all movement is prohibited.) Such movement provokes attacks of opportunity as normal (despite the distance covered, this move isn't a 5-foot step).

Flanking

If a character is making a melee attack against an opponent, and an ally directly opposite the character is threatening the opponent, the character and his ally flank the opponent. The character gains a +2 bonus on his attack roll. The ally must be on the other side of the opponent so that the opponent is directly between the character and the ally.

A character doesn't gain a bonus for flanking when making a ranged attack.

Attacks of Opportunity

Sometimes a combatant in a melee lets her guard down. In this case, combatants near her can take advantage of her lapse in defense to attack her for free. These free attacks are called attacks of opportunity.

Threatened Squares: You threaten all squares into which you can make a melee attack, even when it is not your action. Generally, that means everything in all squares adjacent to your space (including diagonally). An enemy that takes certain actions while in a threatened square provokes an attack of opportunity from you. If you're unarmed, you don't normally threaten any squares and thus can't make attacks of opportunity.

Reach Weapons: Most creatures of Medium or smaller size have a reach of only 5 feet. This means that they can make melee attacks only against creatures up to 5 feet (1 square) away. However, Small and Medium creatures wielding reach weapons threaten more squares than a typical creature. In addition, most creatures larger than Medium have a natural reach of 10 feet or more.

Provoking an Attack of Opportunity: Two kinds of actions can provoke attacks of opportunity: moving out of a threatened square and performing an action within a threatened square.

Moving: Moving out of a threatened square usually provokes an attack of opportunity from the threatening opponent. There are two common methods of avoiding such an attack—the 5-foot step and the withdraw action (see below).

Performing a Distracting Act: Some actions, when performed in a threatened square, provoke attacks of opportunity as you divert your attention from the battle.

Attack Roll Modifiers

Attacker is . . .	Melee	Ranged
Dazzled	-1	-1
Entangled	-2[1]	-2[1]
Flanking defender	+2	—
Invisible	+2[2]	+2[2]
On higher ground	+1	+0
Prone	-4	—[3]
Shaken or frightened	-2	-2
Squeezing through a space	-4	-4

1 An entangled character also takes a -4 penalty to Dexterity, which may affect his attack roll.
2 The defender loses any Dexterity bonus to AC. This bonus doesn't apply if the target is blinded.
3 Most ranged weapons can't be used while the attacker is prone; you can use a crossbow, firearm, or other mechanically propelled ranged weapon while prone at no penalty.

Armor Class Modifiers

Defender is . . .	Melee	Ranged
Behind cover	+4	+4
Blinded	-2[1]	-2[1]
Concealed or invisible	— See Concealment —	
Cowering	-2[1]	-2[1]
Entangled	+0[2]	+0[2]
Flat-footed (such as surprised, balancing, climbing)	+0[1]	+0[1]
Grappling (but attacker is not)	+0[1]	+0[1, 3]
Helpless (such as paralyzed, sleeping, or bound)	-4[4]	+0[4]
Kneeling or sitting	-2	+2
Pinned	-4[4]	+0[4]
Prone	-4	+4
Squeezing through a space	-4	-4
Stunned	-2[1]	-2[1]

1 The defender loses any Dexterity bonus to AC.
2 An entangled character takes a -4 penalty to Dexterity.
3 Roll randomly to see which grappling combatant you strike. That defender loses any Dexterity bonus to AC.
4 Treat the defender's Dexterity as 0 (-5 modifier). You can use the sneak attack talent against helpless or pinned defenders.

Remember that even actions that normally provoke attacks of opportunity may have exceptions to this rule.

Making an Attack of Opportunity: An attack of opportunity is a single melee attack, and you can only make one per round. You don't have to make an attack of opportunity if you don't want to.

You make your attack of opportunity at your highest normal attack bonus—even if you've already attacked in the round.

An attack of opportunity "interrupts" the normal flow of actions in the round. If an attack of opportunity is provoked, immediately resolve the attack of opportunity, then continue with the next character's turn (or complete the current turn, if the attack of opportunity was provoked in the midst of a character's turn).

Combat Reflexes and Additional Attacks of Opportunity: If you have the Combat Reflexes feat you can add your Dexterity modifier to the number of attacks of opportunity you can make in a round. This feat does not let you make more than one attack for a given opportunity, but if the same opponent provokes two attacks of opportunity from you, you could make two separate attacks of opportunity (since each one represents a different opportunity). Moving out of more than one square threatened by the same opponent in the same round doesn't count as more than one opportunity for that opponent. All these attacks are at your full normal attack bonus.

Combat Modifiers

This section covers offensive and defensive modifiers provided by position or battlefield conditions, such as the relative positions of the attacker and defender, cover, concealment, helpless defenders, and so on.

Favorable and Unfavorable Conditions

Generally speaking, any situational modifier created by the attacker's position or tactics applies to the attack roll, while any situational modifier created by the defender's position, state, or tactics applies to the defender's Armor Class. The GM judges what bonuses and penalties apply, using the Attack Roll Modifier and Armor Class Modifier tables, above, as guides.

Cover

To determine whether your target has cover from your ranged attack, choose a corner of your square. If any line from this corner to any corner of the target's square passes through a square or border that blocks line of effect or provides cover, or through a square occupied by a creature, the target has cover (+4 to AC).

When making a melee attack against an adjacent target, your target has cover if any line from your square to the target's square goes through a wall (including a low wall). When making a melee attack against a target that isn't adjacent to you (such as with a reach weapon), use the rules for determining cover from ranged attacks.

Low Obstacles and Cover: A low obstacle (such as a wall no higher than half your height) provides cover, but only to creatures within 30 feet. The attacker can ignore the cover if he's closer to the obstacle than his target.

Cover and Attacks of Opportunity: You can't execute an attack of opportunity against an opponent with cover relative to you.

Cover and Reflex Saves: Cover grants you a +2 bonus on Reflex saves against attacks that originate or burst out from a point on the other side of the cover from you. Note that spread effects can extend around corners and thus negate this cover bonus.

Cover and Hide Checks: You can use cover to make a Hide check. Without cover, you usually need concealment (see below) to make a Hide check.

Soft Cover: Creatures, even your enemies, can provide you with cover against melee attacks, giving you a +4 bonus to AC. However, such soft cover provides no bonus on Reflex saves, nor does soft cover allow you to make a Hide check.

Big Creatures and Cover: Any creature with a space larger than 5 feet (1 square) determines cover against melee attacks slightly differently than smaller creatures do. Such a creature can choose any square that it occupies to determine if an opponent has cover against its melee attacks. Similarly, when making a melee attack against such a creature, you can pick any of the squares it occupies to determine if it has cover against you.

Total Cover: If you don't have line of effect to your target he is considered to have total cover from you. You can't make an attack against a target that has total cover.

Varying Degrees of Cover: In some cases, cover may provide a greater bonus to AC and Reflex saves. In such situations the normal cover bonuses to AC and Reflex saves can be doubled (to +8 and +4, respectively). A creature with this improved cover effectively gains improved evasion against any attack to which the Reflex save bonus applies. Furthermore, improved cover provides a +10 bonus on Hide checks.

Concealment

Concealment applies when the target is difficult to see, such as in darkness or fog, but there is otherwise no barrier between you and your opponent.

Ranged Attacks: To determine whether your target has concealment from your ranged attack, choose a corner of your square. If any line from this corner to any corner of the target's square passes through a square or border that provides concealment, the target has concealment.

Melee Attacks: When making a melee attack against an adjacent target, your target has concealment if his space is entirely within an effect that grants concealment. When making a melee attack against a target that isn't adjacent to you use the rules for determining concealment from ranged attacks.

In addition, some magical effects provide concealment against all attacks, regardless of whether any intervening concealment exists.

Concealment Miss Chance: Concealment gives the subject of a successful attack a 20% chance that the attacker missed because of the concealment. If the attacker hits, the defender must make a miss chance percentile roll to avoid being struck. Multiple concealment conditions do not stack.

Concealment and Hide Checks: You can use concealment to make a Hide check. Without concealment, you usually need cover to make a Hide check.

Total Concealment: If you have line of effect to a target but not line of sight he is considered to have total concealment from you. You can't attack an opponent that has total concealment, though you can attack into a square that you think he occupies. A successful attack into a square occupied by an enemy with total concealment has a 50% miss chance (instead of the normal 20% miss chance for an opponent with concealment).

You can't execute an attack of opportunity against an opponent with total concealment, even if you know what square or squares the opponent occupies.

Ignoring Concealment: Concealment isn't always effective. A shadowy area or darkness doesn't provide any concealment against an opponent with darkvision. Characters with low-light vision can see clearly for a greater distance with the same light source than other characters. Although invisibility provides total concealment, sighted opponents may still make Spot checks to notice the location of an invisible character. An invisible character gains a +20 bonus on Hide checks if moving, or a +40 bonus on Hide checks when not moving (even though opponents can't see you, they might be able to figure out where you are from other visual clues).

Varying Degrees of Concealment: Certain situations may provide more or less than typical concealment, and modify the miss chance accordingly.

Helpless Defenders

A helpless opponent is someone who is bound, sleeping, paralyzed, unconscious, or otherwise at your mercy.

Regular Attack: A helpless character is considered to have a Dexterity of 0 (AC penalty -5), and takes an additional -4 penalty to AC against melee attacks, but no penalty to AC against ranged attacks.

Coup de Grace: As a full-round action, you can use a melee weapon to deliver a *coup de grace* to a helpless opponent. You can also use a ranged weapon, provided you are adjacent to the target.

You automatically hit and score a critical hit, with no expenditure of an action point necessary, applying damage as normal. Even if the defender survives the damage, he must make a Fortitude save (DC 10 + damage dealt) or die (similar to Death from Massive Damage).

Delivering a *coup de grace* provokes attacks of opportunity from threatening opponents.

You can't deliver a *coup de grace* against a creature that is immune to critical hits. You can deliver a *coup de grace* against a creature with total concealment, but doing this requires two consecutive full-round actions (one to "find" the creature once you've determined what square it's in, and one to deliver the *coup de grace*).

Actions in Combat

Each round represents 6 seconds in the game world. A round presents an opportunity for each character involved in a combat situation to take an *action*.

Each round's activity begins with the character with the highest initiative result and then proceeds, in order, from there. Each round of a combat uses the same initiative order. When a character's turn comes up in the initiative sequence, that character performs his entire round's worth of actions.

A combat round is flexible, with essentially no beginning or end. A combat round consists of a span of time from one combatant's initiative until the same initiative count in the next round. Effects that last a certain number of rounds end just before the same initiative count that they began on.

Action Types

An action's type essentially tells you how long the action takes to perform (within the framework of the 6-second combat round) and how movement is treated. There are four types of actions: standard actions, move actions, full-round actions, and free actions.

In a normal round, you can perform a standard action and a move action, or you can perform a full-round action. You can take a move action in place of a standard action. Finally, you can perform one or more free actions.

In some situations (such as in a surprise round), you may be limited to taking only a single move action or standard action.

Standard Action: A standard action allows you to do something, most commonly to make an attack.

Move Action: A move action allows you to move your speed or perform an action that takes a similar amount of time.

You can take a move action in place of a standard action.

If you move no actual distance in a round (commonly because you have swapped your move for one or more move-equivalent actions), you can take a single 5-foot step either before, during, or after the action.

Full-Round Action: A full-round action consumes all your effort during a round. The only movement you can take during a full-round action is a 5-foot step before, during, or after the action. You can also perform free actions (see below).

Some full-round actions do not allow you to take a 5-foot step.

Some full-round actions can be taken as standard actions, but only in situations when you are limited to performing only a standard action during your round. The descriptions

Table 6-2: Actions in Combat			
Actions	Type	Attack of Opportunity[1]	Brief Description
Attack (melee)	Standard	No	Make a single attack with a melee weapon
Attack (ranged)	Standard	Yes	Make a single attack with a ranged weapon
Attack (unarmed)	Standard	Yes[2]	Punch, kick, brawl, or other unarmed attack
Attack (aid another)	Standard	No	Provide a +2 bonus to an ally's attack
Bull rush (attack)	Standard	No	Push an opponent back 5 feet or more
Feint (see the Bluff skill)	Standard	No	Negate opponent's Dex bonus to AC
Ready an action	Standard	No	Prepare an action against a specific trigger event
Sunder	Standard	Usually[3]	Attack a weapon or object
Total defense	Standard	No	+4 dodge bonus to AC
Turn undead	Standard	No	Make a Turn Undead check
Throw a splash weapon	Standard	No	Throw a volatile device (flask, grenade, etc.)
Disarm[5]	Varies	Yes	Knock a weapon from your opponent's hand
Grapple[5]	Varies	Yes	Wrestle with your opponent
Trip[5]	Varies	No	Trip an opponent
Charge	Full	No	Move up to twice your speed and attack with +2 bonus; can include a Bull Rush or Overrun
Overrun (charge)	Full	No	Plow past an opponent as you move
Coup de grace	Full	Yes	Slay a helpless opponent
Full attack (including two-weapon fighting)	Full	No	Make more than one attack in a round
Run	Full	Yes	Move more than x2 your speed
Withdraw	Full	No	A defensive retreat from combat
Move	Move	Yes	Move up to your speed
Use a piece of equipment	Move	No	
Aim a ranged weapon	Move	No	+1 circumstance bonus to hit with a ranged weapon
Climb, crawl, or swim	Move	No	
Ready a weapon[4]	Move	No	Draw a weapon
Holster/sheathe a weapon	Move	Yes	
Move a heavy object	Move	Yes	
Open a door	Move	No	
Pick up an object	Move	Yes	
Retrieve a stored object	Move	Yes	Find and retrieve an object from a backpack, etc.
Stand up from prone, sitting, or kneeling	Move	No	
Start/complete full-round action	Move	Varies	
Drop an object	Free	No	
Drop to prone, sitting, or kneeling	Free	No	
Speak	Free	No	
Hold/Delay	No action	No	Delay until a later initiative count
5-foot step	No action	No	Move a single 5-foot square in any direction

1 Regardless of the action, if a character moves out of a threatened square, the character usually provokes an attack of opportunity. This column indicates whether the action itself, not moving, provokes an attack of opportunity.

2 A character with the improved unarmed fighting feat is considered armed and does not provoke an attack of opportunity.

3 If the object is being held, carried, or worn by a creature, yes. If not, no.

4 If the character has a base attack bonus of +1 or higher, he can combine this action with a regular move. If the character has the Two-Weapon Fighting feat, he can draw two light or one-handed weapons in the time it would normally take to draw one.

5 These attack forms substitute for a melee attack, not an action. As melee attacks, they can be used once in an attack or charge action, one or more times in a full attack action, or even as an attack of opportunity.

6 The description of a feat defines its effect.

of specific actions, below, detail which actions allow this option.

Free Action: Free actions consume a very small amount of time and effort. You can perform one or more free actions while taking another action normally. However, there are reasonable limits on what you can really do for free.

No Action: Some activities are so minor that they are not even considered free actions. They literally don't take any time at all to do and are considered an inherent part of doing something else.

Restricted Activity: In some situations, you may be unable to take a full round's worth of actions. In such cases, you are restricted to taking only a single standard action or a single move action (plus free actions as normal). You can't take a full-round action (though you can start or complete a full-round action by using a standard action; see below).

Action Summary

Aid Another

Standard; Attack Of Opportunity: No

In melee combat, you can help a friend attack or defend by distracting or interfering with an opponent. If you're in position to make a melee attack on an opponent that is engaging a friend in melee combat, you can attempt to aid your friend as a standard action. You make an attack roll against AC 10. If you succeed, your friend gains either a +2 bonus on his next attack roll against that opponent or a +2 bonus to AC against that opponent's next attack (your choice), as long as that attack comes before the beginning of your next turn. Multiple characters can aid the same friend, and similar bonuses stack.

You can also use this standard action to help a friend in other ways, such as when he is affected by a spell, or to assist another character's skill check.

Aim

Move-equivalent; Attack Of Opportunity: No

As a move-equivalent action, you can aim a ranged weapon. As long as you do not move or otherwise lose your concentration, and your opponent does not move more than 5 feet, you receive a +1 circumstance bonus to your next ranged attack roll against that target.

Attack (melee)

Standard; Attack Of Opportunity: No

With a normal melee weapon, you can strike any opponent within 5 feet. (Opponents within 5 feet are considered adjacent to you.) Some melee weapons have reach, as indicated in their descriptions. With a typical reach weapon, you can strike opponents 10 feet away, but you can't strike adjacent foes (those within 5 feet are typically too close to bring the weapon to bear).

You can choose to fight defensively when attacking. If you do so, you take a –4 penalty on all attacks in a round to gain a +2 dodge bonus to AC for the same round.

A character who can make more than one attack per round must use the full attack action in order to get more than one attack.

Attack (ranged)

Standard; Attack Of Opportunity: Yes

With a ranged weapon, you can shoot or throw at any target that is within the weapon's maximum range and in line of sight.

The maximum range for a thrown weapon is five range increments. For projectile weapons, it is ten range increments. Some ranged weapons have shorter maximum ranges, as specified in their descriptions.

You can choose to fight defensively when attacking. If you do so, you take a -4 penalty on all attacks in a round to gain a +2 dodge bonus to AC for the same round.

Shooting or Throwing into a Melee: If you shoot or throw a ranged weapon at a target engaged in melee with a friendly character, you take a -4 penalty on your attack roll. Two characters are engaged in melee if they are enemies of each other and either threatens the other. (An unconscious or otherwise immobilized character is not considered engaged unless he is actually being attacked.)

If your target (or the part of your target you're aiming at, if it's a big target) is at least 10 feet away from the nearest friendly character, you can avoid the -4 penalty, even if the creature you're aiming at is engaged in melee with a friendly character.

Precise Shot: If you have the Precise Shot feat you don't take this penalty.

Attack (unarmed)

Standard; Attack Of Opportunity: Varies

Striking for damage with punches, kicks, and head butts is much like attacking with a melee weapon, except for the following:

Attacks of Opportunity: Attacking unarmed provokes an attack of opportunity from the character you attack, provided she is armed. The attack of opportunity comes before your attack. An unarmed attack does not provoke attacks of opportunity from other foes that you are not directly attacking, nor does it provoke an attack of opportunity from an unarmed foe.

An unarmed character can't take attacks of opportunity (but see "Armed" Unarmed Attacks, below).

"Armed" Unarmed Attacks: Sometimes a character's or creature's unarmed attack counts as an armed attack. A character with the Improved Unarmed Strike feat, a spellcaster delivering a touch attack spell, and a creature with natural physical weapons all count as being armed.

Note that being armed counts for both offense and defense (the character can make attacks of opportunity).

Unarmed Strike Damage: An unarmed strike from a Medium character deals 1d3 points of damage (plus your Strength modifier, as normal). A Small character's unarmed strike deals 1d2 points of damage, while a Large character's unarmed strike deals 1d4 points of damage. All damage from unarmed strikes is nonlethal damage. Unarmed strikes count as light weapons (for purposes of two-weapon attack penalties and so on).

Dealing Lethal Damage: You can specify that your unarmed strike will deal lethal damage before you make your attack roll, but you take a -4 penalty on your attack roll. If you have the Improved Unarmed Strike feat, you can deal lethal damage with an unarmed strike without taking a penalty on the attack roll.

You can choose to fight defensively when attacking. If you do so, you take a -4 penalty on all attacks in a round to gain a +2 dodge bonus to AC for the same round.

Bull Rush

Standard; Attack Of Opportunity: Yes

You can make a bull rush as a standard action (an attack) or as part of a charge (see Charge, below). When you make a bull rush, you attempt to push an opponent straight back instead of damaging him. You can only bull rush an opponent who is one size category larger than you, the same size, or smaller.

- Step 1: Initiating a Bull Rush. First, you move into the defender's space. Doing this provokes an attack of opportunity from each opponent that threatens you, including the defender. (If you have the Improved Bull Rush feat, you don't provoke an attack of opportunity from the defender.) Any attack of opportunity made by anyone other than the defender against you during a bull rush has a 25% chance of accidentally targeting the defender instead, and any attack of opportunity by anyone other than you against the defender likewise has a 25% chance of accidentally targeting you. (When someone makes an attack of opportunity, make the attack roll and then roll to see whether the attack went astray.)
- Step 2: You and the defender make opposed Strength checks. You each add a +4 bonus for each size category you are larger than Medium or a -4 penalty for each size category you are smaller than Medium. You get a +2 bonus if you are charging. The defender gets a +4 bonus if he has more than two legs or is otherwise exceptionally stable.
- Step 3: Bull Rush Results. If you beat the defender's Strength check result, you push him back 5 feet. If you wish to move with the defender, you can push him back an additional 5 feet for each 5 points by which your check result is greater than the defender's check result. You can't, however, exceed your normal movement limit. (Note: The defender provokes attacks of opportunity if he is moved. So do you, if you move with him. The two of you do not provoke attacks of opportunity from each other, however.)

If you fail to beat the defender's Strength check result, you move 5 feet straight back to where you were before you moved into his space. If that space is occupied, you fall prone in that space.

Charge

Full; Attack Of Opportunity: No

Charging is a special full-round action that allows you to move up to twice your speed and attack during the action. However, it carries tight restrictions on how you can move.

Movement During a Charge: You must move before your attack, not after. You must move at least 10 feet (2 squares) and may move up to double your speed directly toward the designated opponent.

You must have a clear path toward the opponent, and nothing can hinder your movement (such as difficult terrain or obstacles). Here's what it means to have a clear path. First, you must move to the closest space from which you can attack the opponent. (If this space is occupied or otherwise blocked, you can't charge.) Second, if any line from your starting space to the ending space passes through a square that blocks movement, slows movement, or contains a creature (even an ally), you can't charge. (Helpless creatures don't stop a charge.)

If you don't have line of sight to the opponent at the start of your turn, you can't charge that opponent.

You can't take a 5-foot step in the same round as a charge.

If you are able to take only a standard action or a move action on your turn, you can still charge, but you are only allowed to move up to your speed (instead of up to double your speed). You can't use this option unless you are restricted to taking only a standard action or move action on your turn.

Attacking on a Charge: After moving, you may make a single melee attack. You get a +2 bonus on the attack roll, and take a -2 penalty to your AC until the start of your next turn.

A charging character gets a +2 bonus on the Strength check made to bull rush or overrun an opponent (see Bull Rush, above, and Overrun, below).

Even if you have extra attacks, such as from having a high enough base attack bonus or from using multiple weapons, you only get to make one attack during a charge.

Lances and Charge Attacks: A lance deals double damage if employed by a mounted character in a charge.

Weapons Readied against a Charge: Spears, tridents, and certain other piercing weapons deal double damage when readied (set) and used against a charging character.

Coup de Grace

Full; Attack Of Opportunity: Yes

You can use a melee weapon to deliver a killing blow to a helpless foe. You can also use a ranged weapon, provided you are adjacent to the target. The attack automatically hits and scores a critical hit (no action point expenditure is necessary). Even if the target survives the damage, he must still succeed at a Fortitude save (DC10 + damage dealt) or die. You cannot deliver a coup de grace against creatures that are immune to critical hits.

Delay/Hold

Not an Action; Attack Of Opportunity: No

You can voluntarily reduce your initiative count until a later point in the round. When you delay, you can jump back in and take your action after any other character who acts on that initiative count has completed his action. If two or more characters are delaying, the character with the highest initiative bonus may go first.

Disarm

Standard; Attack Of Opportunity: Yes

As a melee attack, you may attempt to disarm your opponent. If you do so with a weapon, you knock the opponent's weapon out of his hands and to the ground. If you attempt the disarm while unarmed, you end up with the weapon in your hand.

If you're attempting to disarm a melee weapon, follow the steps outlined here. If the item you are attempting to disarm isn't a melee weapon the defender may still oppose you with an attack roll, but takes a penalty and can't attempt to disarm you in return if your attempt fails.

- Step 1: Attack of Opportunity. You provoke an attack of opportunity from the target you are trying to disarm. (If you have the Improved Disarm feat, you don't incur an attack of opportunity for making a disarm attempt.) If the defender's attack of opportunity deals any damage, your disarm attempt fails.
- Step 2: Opposed Rolls. You and the defender make opposed attack rolls with your respective weapons. The wielder of a two-handed weapon on a disarm attempt gets a +4 bonus on this roll, and the wielder of a light weapon takes a -4 penalty. (An unarmed strike is considered a light weapon, so you always take a penalty when trying to disarm an opponent by using an unarmed strike.) If the combatants are of different sizes, the larger combatant gets a bonus on the attack roll of +4 per difference in size category. If the targeted item isn't a melee weapon, the defender takes a -4 penalty on the roll.
- Step 3: Consequences. If you beat the defender, the defender is disarmed. If you attempted the disarm action unarmed, you now have the weapon. If you were armed, the defender's weapon is on the ground in the defender's square.

  If you fail on the disarm attempt, the defender may immediately react and attempt to disarm you with the same sort of opposed melee attack roll. His attempt does not provoke an attack of opportunity from you. If he fails his disarm attempt, you do not subsequently get a free disarm attempt against him.

Note: A defender wearing spiked gauntlets can't be disarmed. A defender using a weapon attached to a locked gauntlet gets a +10 bonus to resist being disarmed.

Grabbing Items

You can use a disarm action to snatch an item worn by the target. If you want to have the item in your hand, the disarm must be made as an unarmed attack.

If the item is poorly secured or otherwise easy to snatch or cut away the attacker gets a +4 bonus. Unlike on a normal disarm attempt, failing the attempt doesn't allow the defender to attempt to disarm you. This otherwise functions identically to a disarm attempt, as noted above.

You can't snatch an item that is well secured unless you have pinned the wearer (see Grapple). Even then, the defender gains a +4 bonus on his roll to resist the attempt.

Drop an Item

Free; Attack Of Opportunity: No

You can drop an item you are holding. It lands in the space you currently occupy.

Drop Prone

Free; Attack Of Opportunity: No

You can drop down into the prone position as a free action. (It will cost a move-equivalent action to stand back up.)

Feint

Standard; Attack Of Opportunity: No

Feinting is a standard action. To feint, make a Bluff check opposed by a Sense Motive check by your target. The target may add his base attack bonus to this Sense Motive check. If your Bluff check result exceeds your target's Sense Motive check result, the next melee attack you make against the target does not allow him to use his Dexterity bonus to AC (if any). This attack must be made on or before your next turn.

When feinting in this way against a non-humanoid you take a -4 penalty. Against a creature of animal Intelligence (1 or 2), you take a -8 penalty. Against a non-intelligent creature, it's impossible.

Feinting in combat does not provoke attacks of opportunity.

Feinting as a Move Action: With the Improved Feint feat, you can attempt a feint as a move action instead of as a standard action.

Full Attack

Full; Attack Of Opportunity: No

If you get more than one attack per round because your base attack bonus is high enough, because you fight with two weapons or a double weapon, or for some other special reason, you must use a full-round action to get your additional attacks. You do not need to specify the targets of your attacks ahead of time. You can see how the earlier attacks turn out before assigning the later ones.

The only movement you can take during a full attack is a 5-foot step. You may take the step before, after, or between your attacks.

If you get multiple attacks because your base attack bonus is high enough, you must make the attacks in order from highest bonus to lowest. If you are using two weapons, you can strike with either weapon first. If you are using a double weapon, you can strike with either part of the weapon first.

Cleave: The extra attack granted by the Cleave feat or Great Cleave feat can be taken whenever they apply. This is an exception to the normal limit to the number of attacks you can take when not using a full attack action.

After your first attack, you can decide to forgo the full attack, taking a move action instead of making your remaining attacks, depending on how the first attack turns out. If you've already taken a 5-foot step, you can't use your move action to move any distance, but you could still use a different kind of move action.

You can choose to fight defensively when taking a full attack action. If you do so, you take a -4 penalty on all attacks in a round to gain a +2 dodge bonus to AC for the same round.

Grapple

Varies; Attack Of Opportunity: Yes

A grapple check is an unarmed attack where the intent is to grab the opponent with your bare hands to injure or subdue him.

Grapple Checks

Repeatedly in a grapple, you need to make opposed grapple checks against an opponent. A grapple check is like a melee attack roll. Your attack bonus on a grapple check is:

Base attack bonus + Strength modifier + special size modifier

Special Size Modifier: The special size modifier for a grapple check is as follows: Colossal +16, Gargantuan +12, Huge +8, Large +4, Medium +0, Small -4, Tiny -8, Diminutive -12, Fine -16. Use this number in place of the normal size modifier you use when making an attack roll.

Starting a Grapple

To start a grapple, you need to grab and hold your target. Starting a grapple requires a successful melee attack roll. If you get multiple attacks, you can attempt to start a grapple multiple times (at successively lower base attack bonuses).

- Step 1: Attack of Opportunity. You provoke an attack of opportunity from the target you are trying to grapple. If the attack of opportunity deals damage, the grapple attempt fails. (Certain monsters do not provoke attacks of opportunity when they attempt to grapple, nor do characters with the Improved Grapple feat.) If the attack of opportunity misses or fails to deal damage, proceed to Step 2.
- Step 2: Grab. You make a melee touch attack to grab the target. If you fail to hit the target, the grapple attempt fails. If you succeed, proceed to Step 3.
- Step 3: Hold. Make an opposed grapple check as a free action. If you succeed, you and your target are now grappling, and you deal damage to the target as if with an unarmed strike.

  If you lose, you fail to start the grapple. You automatically lose an attempt to hold if the target is two or more size categories larger than you are.

  In case of a tie, the combatant with the higher grapple check modifier wins. If this is a tie, roll again to break the tie.
- Step 4: Maintain Grapple. To maintain the grapple for later rounds, you must move into the target's space. (This movement is free and doesn't count as part of your movement in the round.)

  Moving, as normal, provokes attacks of opportunity from threatening opponents, but not from your target.

  If you can't move into your target's space, you can't maintain the grapple and must immediately let go of the target. To grapple again, you must begin at Step 1.

Grappling Consequences

While you're grappling, your ability to attack others and defend yourself is limited.

No Threatened Squares: You don't threaten any squares while grappling.

No Dexterity Bonus: You lose your Dexterity bonus to AC (if you have one) against opponents you aren't grappling. (You can still use it against opponents you are grappling.)

No Movement: You can't move normally while grappling. You may, however, make an opposed grapple check (see below) to move while grappling.

If You're Grappling

When you are grappling (regardless of who started the grapple), you can perform any of the following actions. Some of these actions take the place of an attack (rather than being a standard action or a move action). If your base attack bonus allows you multiple attacks, you can attempt one of these actions in place of each of your attacks, but at successively lower base attack bonuses.

- Attack Your Opponent: You can make an attack with an unarmed strike, natural weapon, or light weapon against another character you are grappling. You take a -4 penalty on such attacks.

You can't attack with two weapons while grappling, even if both are light weapons.

- Damage Your Opponent: While grappling, you can deal damage to your opponent equivalent to an unarmed strike. Make an opposed grapple check in place of an attack. If you win, you deal nonlethal damage as normal for your unarmed strike (1d3 points for Medium attackers or 1d2 points for Small attackers, plus Strength modifiers). If you want to deal lethal damage, you take a -4 penalty on your grapple check.

  Exception: Characters with the Improved Unarmed Strike talent deal more damage on an unarmed strike than other characters, and the damage is lethal. However, they can choose to deal their damage as nonlethal damage when grappling without taking the usual -4 penalty for changing lethal damage to nonlethal damage.

- Draw a Light Weapon: You can draw a light weapon as a move action with a successful grapple check.

- Escape from Grapple: You can escape a grapple by winning an opposed grapple check in place of making an attack. You can make an Escape Artist check in place of your grapple check if you so desire, but this requires a standard action. If more than one opponent is grappling you, your grapple check result has to beat all their individual check results to escape. (Opponents don't have to try to hold you if they don't want to.) If you escape, you finish the action by moving into any space adjacent to your opponent(s).

- Move: You can move half your speed (bringing all others engaged in the grapple with you) by winning an opposed grapple check. This requires a standard action, and you must beat all the other individual check results to move the grapple.

  Note: You get a +4 bonus on your grapple check to move a pinned opponent, but only if no one else is involved in the grapple.

- Pin Your Opponent: You can hold your opponent immobile for 1 round by winning an opposed grapple check (made in place of an attack). Once you have an opponent pinned, you have a few options available to you (see below).

- Break Another's Pin: If you are grappling an opponent who has another character pinned, you can make an opposed grapple check in place of an attack. If you win, you break the hold that the opponent has over the other character. The character is still grappling, but is no longer pinned.

- Use Opponent's Weapon: If your opponent is holding a light weapon, you can use it to attack him. Make an opposed grapple check (in place of an attack). If you win, make an attack roll with the weapon with a -4 penalty (doing this doesn't require another action). You don't gain possession of the weapon by performing this action.

If the campaign features spells and magic items, you also have the following options:

- Activate a Magic Item: You can activate a magic item, as long as the item doesn't require a spell completion trigger. You don't need to make a grapple check to activate the item.

- Retrieve a Spell Component: You can produce a spell component from your pouch while grappling by using a full-round action. Doing so does not require a successful grapple check.

- Cast a Spell: If your campaign features spellcasting, you can attempt to cast a spell while grappling or even while pinned (see below), provided its casting time is no more than 1 standard action, it has no somatic component, and you have in hand any material components or focuses you might need. Any spell that requires precise and careful action is impossible to cast while grappling or being pinned. If the spell is one that you can cast while grappling, you must make a Concentration check (DC 20 + spell level) or lose the spell. You don't have to make a successful grapple check to cast the spell.

If You're Pinning an Opponent

You can attempt to damage your opponent with an opposed grapple check, you can attempt to use your opponent's weapon against him, or you can attempt to move the grapple (all described above). At your option, you can prevent a pinned opponent from speaking.

- If you're pinning your opponent and you take an additional -4 penalty on your grapple check, you can deal damage or use your opponent's weapon against him *and* bypass his armor bonus. You may only bypass the armor; you cannot bypass natural armor, defense, dodge, or deflection bonuses, or any other bonuses to AC.

- You can use a disarm action to remove or grab away a well secured object worn by a pinned opponent, but he gets a +4 bonus on his roll to resist your attempt (see Disarm).

- You may voluntarily release a pinned character as a free action; if you do so, you are no longer considered to be grappling that character (and vice versa).

- You can't draw or use a weapon (against the pinned character or any other character), escape another's grapple, retrieve a spell component, pin another character, or break another's pin while you are pinning an opponent.

If You're Pinned by an Opponent

When an opponent has pinned you, you are held immobile (but not helpless) for 1 round. While you're pinned, you take a -4 penalty to your AC against opponents other than the one pinning you. At your opponent's option, you may also be unable to speak. On your turn, you can try to escape the pin by making an opposed grapple check in place of an attack. You can make an Escape Artist check in place of your grapple check if you want, but this requires a standard action. If you win, you escape the pin, but you're still grappling.

Joining a Grapple

If your target is already grappling someone else, you can use an attack to start a grapple, as above, except that the target doesn't get an attack of opportunity against you, and your grab automatically succeeds. You still have to make a successful opposed grapple check to become part of the grapple.

If there are multiple opponents involved in the grapple, you pick one to make the opposed grapple check against.

Multiple Grapplers

Several combatants can be in a single grapple. Up to four combatants can grapple a single opponent in a given round. Creatures that are one or more size categories smaller than you count for half, creatures that are one size category larger than you count double, and creatures two or more size categories larger count quadruple.

When you are grappling with multiple opponents, you choose one opponent to make an opposed check against. The exception is an attempt to escape from the grapple; to successfully escape, your grapple check must beat the check results of each opponent.

Heroic Strike

Free; Attack Of Opportunity: No

As a free action, you may spend an action point to "strike true" against an opponent with damage reduction. Until the start of your next action, your attacks count as magical weapons with an enhancement bonus equal to your Charisma modifier (if positive). This bonus only applies for purposes of bypassing damage reduction; you do not receive any bonus to hit or damage.

Mount/Dismount

Move-equivalent; Attack Of Opportunity: No

You can mount or dismount as a free action with a DC 20 Ride check (your armor check penalty, if any, applies to this check). If you fail the check, mounting or dismounting is a move action instead. (You can't attempt a fast mount or fast dismount unless you can perform the mount or dismount as a move action in the current round.)

Mounted Combat

Varies; Attack Of Opportunity: Varies

Horses in Combat: Warhorses and warponies can serve readily as combat steeds. Light horses, ponies, and heavy horses, however, are frightened by combat. If you don't dismount, you must make a DC 20 Ride check each round as a move action to control such a horse. If you succeed, you can perform a standard action after the move action. If you fail, the move action becomes a full round action and you can't do anything else until your next turn.

Your mount acts on your initiative count as you direct it. You move at its speed, but the mount uses its action to move.

A horse (not a pony) is a Large creature and thus takes up a space 10 feet (2 squares) across. For simplicity, assume that you share your mount's space during combat.

Combat while Mounted: With a DC 5 Ride check, you can guide your mount with your knees so as to use both hands to attack or defend yourself. This is a free action.

When you attack a creature smaller than your mount that is on foot, you get the +1 bonus on melee attacks for being on higher ground. If your mount moves more than 5 feet, you can only make a single melee attack. Essentially, you have to wait until the mount gets to your enemy before attacking, so you can't make a full attack. Even at your mount's full speed, you don't take any penalty on melee attacks while mounted.

If your mount charges, you also take the AC penalty associated with a charge. If you make an attack at the end of the charge, you receive the bonus gained from the charge. When charging on horseback, you deal double damage with a lance (see Charge).

You can use ranged weapons while your mount is taking a double move, but at a –4 penalty on the attack roll. You can use ranged weapons while your mount is running (quadruple speed), at a –8 penalty. In either case, you make the attack roll when your mount has completed half its movement. You can make a full attack with a ranged weapon while your mount is moving. Likewise, you can take move actions normally.

Casting Spells while Mounted: If your campaign features spellcasting, you can cast spells while mounted. You can cast a spell normally if your mount moves up to a normal move (its speed) either before or after you cast. If you have your mount move both before and after you cast a spell, then you're casting the spell while the mount is moving, and you have to make a Concentration check due to the vigorous motion (DC 10 + spell level) or the spell fails. If the mount is running (quadruple speed), you can cast a spell when your mount has moved up to twice its speed, but your Concentration check is more difficult due to the violent motion (DC 15 + spell level).

If Your Mount Falls in Battle: If your mount falls, you have to succeed on a DC 15 Ride check to make a soft fall and take no damage. If the check fails, you take 1d6 points of damage.

If You Are Dropped: If you are knocked unconscious, you have a 50% chance to stay in the saddle (or 75% if you're in a military saddle). Otherwise you fall and take 1d6 points of damage.

Without you to guide it, your mount avoids combat.

Move

Varies; Attack Of Opportunity: Varies

With the exception of specific movement-related skills, most move actions don't require a check.

Move

The simplest move action is moving your speed. If you take this kind of move action during your turn, you can't also take a 5-foot step. If you take any other action in your turn besides another move action, you provoke attacks of opportunity when you move through a threatened space.

Climb

As a full round action, you can move at one-half your base speed. As a move-equivalent action, you can move at one-quarter your base speed. You can climb at double these rates if you accept a -5 penalty to your Climb check.

Crawl

If you are prone, you can crawl 5 feet as a move action. Crawling incurs attacks of opportunity from any attackers who threaten you at any point of your crawl.

Run

You can run as a full-round action. (If you do, you do not also get a 5-foot step.) When you run, you can move up to four times your speed in a straight line (or three times your speed if you're in heavy armor). You may not run around corners or obstacles. You lose any Dexterity bonus to AC unless you have the Run feat.

You can run for a number of rounds equal to your Constitution score, but after that you must make a DC 10 Constitution check to continue running. You must check again each round in which you continue to run, and the DC of this check increases by 1 for each check you have made. When you fail this check, you must stop running. A character who has run to his limit must rest for 1 minute (10 rounds) before running again. During a rest period, a character can move no faster than a normal move action.

You can't run across difficult terrain or if you can't see where you're going.

A run represents a speed of about 12 miles per hour for an unencumbered human.

Move 5 Feet through Difficult Terrain

In some situations, your movement may be so hampered that you don't have sufficient speed even to move 5 feet (a single square). In such a case, you may spend a full-round action to move 5 feet (1 square) in any direction, even diagonally. Even though this looks like a 5-foot step, it's not, and thus it provokes attacks of opportunity normally.

Stand Up

Standing up from a prone position requires a move action and provokes attacks of opportunity.

Take a 5-Foot Step

If you do not make any other kind of movement in a round, you may take a 5 foot step as a free action. If your movement is hampered or restricted, or your base move is 5 feet, you cannot take a 5-foot step as a free action.

Withdraw

Withdrawing from melee combat is a full-round action. When you withdraw, you can move up to double your speed. The square you start out in is not considered threatened by any opponent you can see, and therefore visible enemies do not get attacks of opportunity against you when you move from that square. (Invisible enemies still get attacks of opportunity against you, and you can't withdraw from combat if you're blinded.) You can't take a 5-foot step during the same round in which you withdraw.

If, during the process of withdrawing, you move out of a threatened square *other than the one you started in*, enemies get attacks of opportunity as normal.

You may not withdraw using a form of movement for which you don't have a listed speed.

Note that despite the name of this action, you don't actually have to leave combat entirely.

Restricted Withdraw: If you are limited to taking only a standard action each round you can withdraw as a standard action. In this case, you may move up to your speed (rather than up to double your speed).

Move a Heavy Object

Move-equivalent; Attack Of Opportunity: Yes

You can lift, drag, push, or topple a heavy object. You must devote your attention (and usually both hands) to the task.

Open a Door

Move-equivalent; Attack Of Opportunity: No

You can open a normal (unlocked, unstuck) door.

Overrun

Standard; Attack Of Opportunity: Maybe (see below)

You can attempt an overrun as a standard action taken during your move, or as part of a charge. (In general, you cannot take a standard action during a move; this is an exception.) With an overrun, you attempt to plow past or over your opponent (and move through his square) as you move. You can only overrun an opponent who is one size category larger than you, the same size, or smaller. You can make only one overrun attempt per round.

If you're attempting to overrun an opponent, follow these steps.

- Step 1: Attack of Opportunity. Since you begin the overrun by moving into the defender's space, you provoke an attack of opportunity from the defender.

- Step 2: Opponent Avoids? Unless you have the Improved Overrun feat, the defender has the option to simply avoid you. If he avoids you, he doesn't suffer any ill effect.

  If you were attempting the overrun as part of a charge, you may keep moving. (You can always move through a square occupied by someone who lets you by.) In either case, the overrun attempt doesn't count against your actions this round (except for any movement required to enter the opponent's square). If your opponent doesn't avoid you, move to Step 3.

- Step 3: Opponent Blocks? If your opponent blocks you, make a Strength check opposed by the defender's Dexterity or Strength check (whichever ability score has the higher modifier). A combatant gets a +4 bonus on the check for every size category he is larger than Medium or a –4 penalty for every size category he is smaller than Medium. You gain a +2 bonus on your Strength check if you made the overrun as part of a charge. The defender gets a +4 bonus on his check if he has more than two legs or is otherwise more stable than a normal humanoid. If you win, you knock the defender prone. If you lose, the defender may immediately react and make a Strength check opposed by your Dexterity or Strength check (including the size modifiers noted above, but no other modifiers) to try to knock you prone.

- Step 4: Consequences. If you succeed in knocking your opponent prone, you can continue your movement as normal. If you fail and are knocked prone in turn, you have to move 5 feet back the way you came and fall prone, ending your movement there. If you fail but are not knocked prone, you have to move 5 feet back the way you came, ending your movement there. If that square is occupied, you fall prone in that square.

Improved Overrun: If you have the Improved Overrun feat, your target may not choose to avoid you.

Mounted Overrun (Trample): If you attempt an overrun while mounted, your mount makes the Strength check to determine the success or failure of the overrun attack (and applies its size modifier, rather than yours). If you have the Trample feat and attempt an overrun while mounted, your target may not choose to avoid you, and if you knock your opponent prone with the overrun, your mount may make one hoof attack against your opponent.

Pick Up an Object

Move-equivalent; Attack Of Opportunity: Yes

You can pick up an object in the same space as you.

Ready

Standard; Attack Of Opportunity: No

The ready action lets you prepare to take an action later, after your turn is over but before your next one has begun. Readying is a standard action. It does not provoke an attack of opportunity (though the action that you ready might do so).

You can ready a standard action, a move action, or a free action. To do so, specify the action you will take and the conditions under which you will take it. Then, any time before your next action, you may take the readied action in response to that condition. The action occurs just before the action that triggers it. If the triggered action is part of another character's activities, you interrupt the other character. Assuming he is still capable of doing so, he continues his actions once you complete your readied action. Your initiative result changes. For the rest of the encounter, your initiative result is the count on which you took the readied action, and you act immediately ahead of the character whose action triggered your readied action.

You can take a 5-foot step as part of your readied action, but only if you don't otherwise move any distance during the round.

Initiative Consequences of Readying: Your initiative result becomes the count on which you took the readied action. If you come to your next action and have not yet performed your readied action, you don't get to take the readied action (though you can ready the same action again). If you take your readied action in the next round, before your regular turn comes up, your initiative count rises to that new point in the order of battle, and you do not get your regular action that round.

Readying a Weapon against a Charge: You can ready certain piercing weapons, setting them to receive charges. A readied weapon of this type deals double damage if you score a hit with it against a charging character.

Ready or Loose a Shield

Move-equivalent; Attack Of Opportunity: No

Strapping a shield to your arm to gain its shield bonus to your AC, or unstrapping a shield so you can use your shield hand for another purpose, requires a move action. If you have a base attack bonus of +1 or higher, you can ready or loose a shield as a free action combined with a regular move.

Dropping a carried (but not readied) shield is a free action.

Ready/Sheathe a Weapon

Move-Equivalent; Attack Of Opportunity: Varies

As a move-equivalent action, you can draw and ready a weapon. A character with a +1 BAB or higher can combine this action with a move. If you have the Two Weapon Fighting feat, you can draw two light or one-handed weapons at once.

Drawing ammunition for use with a ranged weapon (such as arrows, bolts, sling bullets, or shuriken) is a free action.

You can also sheathe or holster your weapon (as opposed to dropping it) as a move-equivalent action. Sheathing a weapon provokes an attack of opportunity.

Retrieve a Stored Item

Move-Equivalent; Attack Of Opportunity: Yes

You can rummage through a bag, pack, pouch, or other container and retrieve an item that you know is stored there.

Speak

Free; Attack Of Opportunity: No

In general, speaking is a free action that you can perform even when it isn't your turn. Speaking more than a few sentences is generally beyond the limit of a free action.

Start/Complete Full-Round Action

Standard; Attack Of Opportunity: No

The "Start a full-round action" standard action lets you start undertaking a full-round action, which you can complete in the following round by using another standard action. You can't use this action to start or complete a full attack, charge, run, or withdraw.

Sunder

Standard; Attack Of Opportunity: Yes

You can use a melee attack with a slashing or bludgeoning weapon to strike a weapon or shield that your opponent is holding. If you're attempting to sunder a weapon or shield, follow the steps outlined here. (Attacking held objects other than weapons or shields is covered below.)

Common Item Hardness and Hit Points

Weapon or Shield	Hardness	HP[1]
Light blade	10	2
One-handed blade	10	5
Two-handed blade	10	10
Light metal-hafted weapon	10	10
One-handed metal-hafted weapon	10	20
Light hafted weapon	5	2
One-handed hafted weapon	5	5
Two-handed hafted weapon	5	10
Bow or Crossbow	5	5
Armor	special[2]	armor bonus x5
Buckler	10	5
Light wooden shield	5	7
Heavy wooden shield	5	15
Light steel shield	10	10
Heavy steel shield	10	20
Tower shield	5	20

1 The hp value given is for Medium armor, weapons, and shields. Divide hit points by 2 for each size category of the item smaller than Medium, or multiply it by 2 for each size category larger than Medium.
2 Varies by material.

- Step 1: Attack of Opportunity. You provoke an attack of opportunity from the target whose weapon or shield you are trying to sunder. (If you have the Improved Sunder feat, you don't incur an attack of opportunity for making the attempt.)
- Step 2: Opposed Rolls. You and the defender make opposed attack rolls with your respective weapons. The wielder of a two-handed weapon on a sunder attempt gets a +4 bonus on this roll, and the wielder of a light weapon takes a –4 penalty. If the combatants are of different sizes, the larger combatant gets a bonus on the attack roll of +4 per difference in size category.
- Step 3: Consequences. If you beat the defender, roll damage and deal it to the weapon or shield. See Table: Common Armor, Weapon, and Shield Hardness and Hit Points to determine how much damage you must deal to destroy the weapon or shield.

If you fail the sunder attempt, you don't deal any damage.

Sundering a Carried or Worn Object: You don't use an opposed attack roll to damage a carried or worn object. Instead, just make an attack roll against the object's AC. A carried or worn object's AC is equal to 10 + its size modifier + the Dexterity modifier of the carrying or wearing character. Attacking a carried or worn object provokes an attack of opportunity just as attacking a held object does. To attempt to snatch away an item worn by a defender rather than damage it, see Disarm. You can't sunder armor worn by another character.

Throw a Splash Weapon

Standard; Attack Of Opportunity: Yes

A splash weapon is a ranged weapon that breaks on impact, splashing or scattering its contents over its target and nearby creatures or objects. To attack with a splash weapon, make a ranged touch attack against the target. Thrown weapons require no weapon proficiency, so you don't take the -4 non-proficiency penalty. A hit deals direct hit damage to the target, and splash damage to all creatures within 5 feet of the target.

You can instead target a specific grid intersection. Treat this as a ranged attack against AC 5. However, if you target a grid intersection, creatures in all adjacent squares are dealt the splash damage, and the direct hit damage is not dealt to any creature. (You can't target a grid intersection occupied by a creature, such as a Large or larger creature; in this case, you're aiming at the creature.)

If you miss the target (whether aiming at a creature or a grid intersection), roll 1d8. This determines the misdirection of the throw, with 1 being straight back at you and 2 through 8 counting clockwise around the grid intersection or target creature. Then, count a number of squares in the indicated direction equal to the range increment of the throw.

After you determine where the weapon landed, it deals splash damage to all creatures in adjacent squares.

Total Defense

Standard; Attack Of Opportunity: No

You can defend yourself as a standard action. You get a +4 dodge bonus to your AC for 1 round. Your AC improves at the start of this action. You can't combine total defense with fighting defensively or with the benefit of the Combat Expertise feat (since both of those require you to declare an attack or full attack). You can't make attacks of opportunity while using total defense.

Trip

Standard; Attack Of Opportunity: Yes

You can try to trip an opponent as an unarmed melee attack. You can only trip an opponent who is one size category larger than you, the same size, or smaller.

Making a Trip Attack: Make an unarmed melee touch attack against your target. This provokes an attack of opportunity from your target as normal for unarmed attacks.

If your attack succeeds, make a Strength check opposed by the defender's Dexterity or Strength check (whichever ability score has the higher modifier). A combatant gets a +4 bonus for every size category he is larger than Medium or a -4 penalty for every size category he is smaller than Medium. The defender gets a +4 bonus on his check if he has more than two legs or is otherwise more stable than a normal humanoid. If you win, you trip the defender. If you lose, the defender may immediately react and make a Strength check opposed by your Dexterity or Strength check to try to trip you.

Avoiding Attacks of Opportunity: If you have the Improved Trip feat, or if you are tripping with a weapon (see below), you don't provoke an attack of opportunity for making a trip attack.

Being Tripped (Prone): A tripped character is prone. Standing up is a move action.

Tripping a Mounted Opponent: You may make a trip attack against a mounted opponent. The defender may make a Ride check in place of his Dexterity or Strength check. If you succeed, you pull the rider from his mount.

Tripping with a Weapon: Some weapons can be used to make trip attacks. In this case, you make a melee touch attack with the weapon instead of an unarmed melee touch attack, and you don't provoke an attack of opportunity. If you are tripped during your own trip attempt, you can drop the weapon to avoid being tripped.

Turn Undead

Standard; Attack Of Opportunity: No

Turning undead is a supernatural ability that a character can perform as a standard action. It does not provoke attacks of opportunity.

You must present your holy symbol to turn undead. Turning is considered an attack.

Times per Day: You may attempt to turn undead a number of times per day equal to 3 + your Charisma modifier. You can increase this number by taking the Extra Turning feat.

Range: You turn the closest turnable undead first, and you can't turn undead that are more than 60 feet away or that have total cover relative to you.

Turning Check: Roll a turning check to see how powerful a creature you can turn. This is a Charisma check (1d20 + your Charisma modifier). The table below gives you the Hit Dice of the most powerful undead you can affect, relative to your level. On a given turning attempt, you can turn no undead creature whose Hit Dice exceed this result.

Turning Check Result	Most Powerful Undead Affected (Maximum Hit Dice)
0 or lower	Character level - 4
1-3	Character level - 3
4-6	Character level - 2
7-9	Character level - 1
10-12	Character level
13-15	Character level + 1
16-18	Character level + 2
19-21	Character level + 3
22 or higher	Character level + 4

Turning Damage: If your roll is high enough to let you turn at least some of the undead within 60 feet, roll 2d6 + your character level + your Charisma modifier to determine the total Hit Dice of undead you can turn. If your Charisma score is average or low, it's possible to roll fewer Hit Dice of undead turned than indicated on the table.

You may skip over already turned undead that are still within range, so that you do not waste your turning capacity on them.

Effect and Duration of Turning: Mindless undead (skeletons and zombies) immediately stop and *cower*. Fettered undead (such as shadows, ghouls, and ghasts) *panic* and flee from you by the best and fastest means available to them for 1 minute. If they cannot flee, they also cower.

If you approach within 10 feet of them, however, they overcome being turned and act normally. (You can stand within 10 feet without breaking the turning effect—you just can't approach them.) You can attack them with ranged attacks (from at least 10 feet away), and others can attack them in any fashion, without breaking the turning effect.

Free-willled undead (such as vampires and liches) who are turned are *shaken* and cannot approach you, and though they are otherwise free to act, they will generally retreat.

Commanded: A commanded undead creature is under the mental control of the turning character. He must take a standard action to give mental orders to a commanded undead. At any one time, he may command any number of undead whose total Hit Dice do not exceed his level. He may voluntarily relinquish command on any commanded undead creature or creatures in order to command new ones.

Two-Weapon Fighting

Standard; Attack Of Opportunity: No

If you wield a second weapon in your off hand, you can get one extra attack per round with that weapon when you perform a full attack action. You suffer a -6 penalty with your regular attack or attacks with your primary hand and a -10 penalty to the attack with your off hand when you fight this way. You can reduce these penalties in two ways:

- If your off-hand weapon is light, the penalties are reduced by 2 each. (An unarmed strike is always considered light.)
- The Two-Weapon Fighting feat lessens the primary hand penalty by 2, and the off-hand penalty by 6.

Two-Weapon Fighting Penalties

Circumstances	Primary Hand	Off Hand
Normal penalties	-6	-10
Off-hand weapon is light	-4	-8
Two-Weapon Fighting feat	-4	-4
Off-hand weapon is light and Two-Weapon Fighting feat	-2	-2

Double Weapons: You can use a double weapon to make an extra attack with the off-hand end of the weapon as if you were fighting with two weapons. The penalties apply as if the off-hand end of the weapon were a light weapon.

Thrown Weapons: The same rules apply when you throw a weapon from each hand. Treat a dart or shuriken as a light weapon when used in this manner, and treat a bolas, javelin, net, or sling as a one-handed weapon.

Use a Feat

Standard; Attack Of Opportunity: Varies

Certain feats let you take special actions in combat. Other feats do not require actions themselves, but they give you a bonus when attempting something you can already do. Some feats are not meant to be used within the framework of combat. The individual feat descriptions tell you what you need to know about them.

Use a Skill

Standard; Attack Of Opportunity: Varies

Most skill uses are standard actions, but some might be move actions, full-round actions, free actions, or something else entirely.

The individual skill descriptions tell you what sorts of actions are required to perform skills.

Use Special Ability

Standard; Attack Of Opportunity: Varies

Using a special ability is usually a standard action, but whether it is a standard action, a full-round action, or not an action at all is defined by the ability itself.

Spell-Like Abilities: Using a spell-like ability works like casting a spell in that it requires concentration and provokes attacks of opportunity. Spell-like abilities can be disrupted. If your concentration is broken, the attempt to use the ability fails, but the attempt counts as if you had used the ability. The casting time of a spell-like ability is 1 standard action, unless the ability description notes otherwise. For additional details on spellcasting, see Chapter Eight

Using a Spell-Like Ability on the Defensive: You may attempt to use a spell-like ability on the defensive, just as with casting a spell. If the Concentration check (DC 15 + spell level) fails, you can't use the ability, but the attempt counts as if you had used the ability.

Supernatural Abilities: Using a supernatural ability is usually a standard action (unless defined otherwise by the ability's description). Its use cannot be disrupted, does not require concentration, and does not provoke attacks of opportunity.

Extraordinary Abilities: Using an extraordinary ability is usually not an action because most extraordinary abilities automatically happen in a reactive fashion. Those extraordinary abilities that are actions are usually standard actions that cannot be disrupted, do not require concentration, and do not provoke attacks of opportunity.

Condition Summary

The following defined terms are used throughout Grim Tales and apply primarily to the combat conditions or effectiveness of the characters or their foes.

If more than one condition affects a character, apply them all. If effects can't combine, apply the most severe effect.

Ability Damage

The character has temporarily lost 1 or more ability score points. Lost points return at a rate of 1 per day unless noted otherwise by the condition dealing the damage. A character with Strength 0 falls to the ground and is helpless. A character with Dexterity 0 is paralyzed. A character with Constitution 0 is dead. A character with Intelligence, Wisdom, or Charisma 0 is unconscious. Ability damage is different from penalties to ability scores, which go away when the conditions causing them go away.

Ability Drain

The character has permanently lost 1 or more ability score points. The character can regain these points only through magical means. A character with Strength 0 falls to the ground and is helpless. A character with Dexterity 0 is paralyzed. A character with Constitution 0 is dead. A character with Intelligence, Wisdom, or Charisma 0 is unconscious.

Berserk

A *berserk* creature fights with wild ferocity, unable to tell friend from foe. Generally speaking, a berserk creature will use whatever weapon is in hand against the nearest foe.

If there is a target within melee reach of the *berserk* creature, the *berserk* creature must use a full attack action against that target. (If there are two or more targets within reach, the *berserk* creature may choose).

If there are no targets within reach of melee and the *berserk* creature does not have a ready ranged weapon, he must move towards the nearest target, charging if possible, and using a double-move if not.

If there are no targets within reach, and the *berserk* creature has a ranged weapon in hand, he may use that weapon against the nearest target.

In essence, the only actions a *berserk* creature may take is an attack, a full attack, or a move. They may not perform special attack actions, draw or ready a weapon, use skills, cast spells, etc.

Blinded

The character cannot see. He takes a -2 penalty to Armor Class, loses his Dexterity bonus to AC (if any), moves at half speed, and takes a -4 penalty on Search checks and on most Strength- and Dexterity-based skill checks. All checks and activities that rely on vision (such as reading and Spot checks) automatically fail. All opponents are considered to have total concealment (50% miss chance) to the blinded character. Characters who remain blinded for a long time grow accustomed to these drawbacks and can overcome some of them.

Blown Away

Depending on its size, a creature can be blown away by winds of high velocity. A creature on the ground that is

Hazardous Environments

Acid

Corrosive acid deals 1d6 points of damage per round of exposure except in the case of total immersion (such as into a vat of acid), which deals 10d6 points of damage per round. An attack with acid, such as from a hurled vial or a monster's spittle, counts as a round of exposure.

The fumes from most acids are inhaled poisons. Those who come close enough to a large body of acid to dunk a creature in it must make a DC 13 Fortitude save or take 1 point of Constitution damage. All such characters must make a second save 1 minute later or take another 1d4 points of Constitution damage.

Creatures immune to acid's caustic properties might still drown in it if they are totally immersed (see Drowning).

Cold

Cold and exposure deal nonlethal damage to the victim. This nonlethal damage cannot be recovered until the character gets out of the cold and warms up again.

Once rendered unconscious through the accumulation of nonlethal damage, the cold and exposure begins to deal lethal damage at the same rate.

A character with the Survival skill may receive a bonus to the saving throw for cold exposure, and may be able to apply this bonus to other characters as well (see the skill description).

An unprotected character in cold weather (below 40° F) must make a Fortitude save each hour (DC 15, + 1 per previous check) or take 1d6 points of nonlethal damage.

In conditions of severe cold or exposure (below 0° F), an unprotected character must make a Fortitude save once every 10 minutes (DC 15, +1 per previous check), taking 1d6 points of nonlethal damage on each failed save.

Extreme cold (below -20° F) deals 1d6 points of lethal damage per minute (no save), and 1d4 points of nonlethal damage (Fortitude save DC15 + 1 per previous check negates).

A character who takes any nonlethal damage from cold or exposure is beset by frostbite or hypothermia (treat as fatigued). These penalties end when the character recovers the nonlethal damage taken from the cold and exposure.

Those wearing metal armor or coming into contact with very cold metal take 1d4 points of lethal damage per round of contact.

Snow

Falling snow has the same effects on visibility, ranged weapon attacks, and skill checks as rain, and it costs 2 squares of movement to enter a snow-covered square. A day of snowfall leaves 1d6 inches of snow on the ground.

Heavy Snow

Heavy snow has the same effects as normal snowfall, but also restricts visibility as fog does (see Fog, below). A day of heavy snow leaves 1d4 feet of snow on the ground, and it costs 4 squares of movement to enter a square covered with heavy snow. Heavy snow accompanied by strong or severe winds may result in snowdrifts 1d4×5 feet deep, especially in and around objects big enough to deflect the wind—a cabin or a large tent, for instance. There is a 10% chance that a heavy snowfall is accompanied by lightning (see Thunderstorm, below). Snow has the same effect on flames as moderate wind.

Sleet

Essentially frozen rain, sleet has the same effect as rain while falling (except that its chance to extinguish protected flames is 75%) and the same effect as snow once on the ground.

Hail

Hail does not reduce visibility, but the sound of falling hail makes Listen checks more difficult (-4 penalty). Sometimes (5% chance) hail can become large enough to deal 1 point of lethal damage (per storm) to anything in the open. Once on the ground, hail has the same effect on movement as snow.

Ice

Characters walking on ice must spend 2 squares of movement to enter a square covered by ice, and the DC for Balance and Tumble checks increases by +5. Characters in prolonged contact with ice may run the risk of taking damage from severe cold (see above).

Avalanches

Avalanches are a deadly peril in many mountainous areas. While avalanches of snow and ice are common, it's also possible to have an avalanche of rock and soil.

An avalanche can be spotted from as far away as 1d10×500 feet downslope by a character who makes a DC 20 Spot check, treating the avalanche as a Colossal creature. If all characters fail their Spot checks to determine the encounter distance, the avalanche moves closer to them, and they automatically become aware of it when it closes to half the original distance. It's possible to hear an avalanche coming even if you can't see it. Under optimum conditions (no other loud noises occurring), a character

blown away is knocked down and rolls 1d4 x 10 feet, taking 1d4 points of nonlethal damage per 10 feet. A flying creature that is blown away is blown back 2d6 x 10 feet and takes 2d6 points of nonlethal damage due to battering and buffering.

Checked

Prevented from achieving forward motion by an applied force, such as wind. Checked creatures on the ground merely stop. Checked flying creatures move back a distance specified in the description of the effect.

Confused

A confused character's actions are determined by rolling d10 at the beginning of his turn:

1	Attack last perceived threat with melee or ranged weapons (or close with target if attacking is not possible)
2	Act normally
3-5	Do nothing but babble incoherently
6-7	Flee away from last perceived target at top possible speed
8-10	Attack nearest creature

A confused character who can't carry out the indicated action does nothing but babble incoherently. Attackers are not at any special advantage when attacking a confused character. Any confused character who is attacked automatically attacks its attackers on its next turn, as long as it is still confused when its turn comes. A confused character does not make attacks of opportunity against any creature that it is not already devoted to attacking (either because of its most recent action or because it has just been attacked).

Cowering

The character is frozen in fear and can take no actions. A cowering character takes a -2 penalty to Armor Class and loses her Dexterity bonus (if any).

Crippled

A crippled creature's movement is impaired. The creature's movement rate is reduced to one-half and the creature cannot charge or run. A creature can be crippled in one form of movement (for example, flight) while maintaining full mobility in another form of movement (e.g. ground).

Dazed

The creature is unable to act normally. A dazed creature can take no actions, but has no penalty to AC.

A dazed condition typically lasts 1 round.

Dazzled

The creature is unable to see well because of overstimulation of the eyes. A dazzled creature takes a -1 penalty on attack rolls, Search checks, and Spot checks.

Dead

The character's hit points are reduced to -10 or less, his Constitution drops to 0, or he is killed outright by some effect. The character's soul leaves his body. Dead characters cannot benefit from healing. A dead body decays normally unless preserved.

Deafened

A deafened character cannot hear. She takes a -4 penalty on initiative checks, automatically fails Listen checks, and has a 20% chance of spell failure when casting spells with verbal components. Characters who remain deafened for a long time grow accustomed to these drawbacks and can overcome some of them.

Disabled

A character with 0 hit points, with negative hit points that do not yet exceed his Constitution modifier, or one who has negative hit points but has become stable and conscious, is *disabled*. A *disabled* character may take a single move action or standard action each round (but not both, nor can she take full-round actions). She moves at half speed. Taking move actions doesn't risk further injury, but performing any standard action (or any other action the DM deems strenuous, including some free actions such as casting a quickened spell) deals 1 point of damage after the completion of the act. Unless the action increased the *disabled* character's hit points, she is now in negative hit points and *dying*.

A *disabled* character with negative hit points recovers hit points naturally if she is being helped. Otherwise, each day she must make a Fortitude save (DC20) to start recovering hit points naturally (starting with that day); otherwise, she loses 1 hit point. Once an unaided character starts recovering hit points naturally, she is no longer in danger of losing hit points (even if her current hit points are negative).

Dying

A *dying* character is unconscious and near death. A *dying* character can take no actions and is unconscious. At the end of each round (starting with the round in which the character was *disabled*), he must make a Fortitude save (DC20) to see whether he becomes stable. If he does not, he loses 1 hit point.

Energy Drained

The character gains one or more negative levels, which might permanently drain the character's levels. If the subject has at least as many negative levels as Hit Dice, he dies. Each negative level gives a creature the following penalties: -1 penalty on attack rolls, saving throws, skill checks, ability checks; loss of 5 hit points; and -1 to effective level (for determining the power, duration, DC, and other details of spells or special abilities).

Entangled
The character is ensnared. Being entangled impedes movement, but does not entirely prevent it unless the bonds are anchored to an immobile object or tethered by an opposing force. An entangled creature moves at half speed, cannot run or charge, and takes a -2 penalty on all attack rolls and a -4 penalty to Dexterity. An entangled character who attempts to cast a spell must make a Concentration check (DC 15 + the spell's level) or lose the spell.

Exhausted
An exhausted character moves at half speed and takes a -6 penalty to Strength and Dexterity. After 1 hour of complete rest, an exhausted character becomes fatigued. A fatigued character becomes exhausted by doing something else that would normally cause fatigue.

Fascinated
A fascinated creature is entranced by a supernatural or spell effect. The creature stands or sits quietly, taking no actions other than to pay attention to the fascinating effect, for as long as the effect lasts. It takes a -4 penalty on skill checks made as reactions, such as Listen and Spot checks. Any potential threat, such as a hostile creature approaching, allows the fascinated creature a new saving throw against the fascinating effect. Any obvious threat, such as someone drawing a weapon, casting a spell, or aiming a ranged weapon at the fascinated creature, automatically breaks the effect. A fascinated creature's ally may shake it free of the spell as a standard action.

Fatigued:
A fatigued character can neither run nor charge and takes a -2 penalty to Strength and Dexterity. Doing anything that would normally cause fatigue causes the fatigued character to become exhausted. After 8 hours of complete rest, fatigued characters are no longer fatigued.

Flat-Footed
A character who has not yet acted during a combat is flat-footed, not yet reacting normally to the situation. A flat-footed character loses his Dexterity bonus to AC (if any) and cannot make attacks of opportunity.

Frightened
A frightened creature flees from the source of its fear as best it can. If unable to flee, it may fight. A frightened creature takes a -2 penalty on all attack rolls, saving throws, skill checks, and ability checks. A frightened creature can use special abilities, including spells, to flee; indeed, the creature must use such means if they are the only way to escape.

Frightened is like shaken, except that the creature must flee if possible. Panicked is a more extreme state of fear. A character who is frightened and suffers a shaken or frightened result again is panicked.

Grappling
Engaged in wrestling or some other form of hand-to-hand struggle with one or more attackers. A grappling character can undertake only a limited number of actions. He does not threaten any squares, and loses his Dexterity bonus to AC (if any) against opponents he isn't grappling.

Helpless
A helpless character is paralyzed, held, bound, sleeping, unconscious, or otherwise completely at an opponent's mercy. A helpless target is treated as having a Dexterity of 0 (-5 modifier). Melee attacks against a helpless target get an additional +4 bonus (equivalent to attacking a prone target). Ranged attacks gets no special bonus against helpless targets. You can use the sneak attack talent against helpless targets.

As a full-round action, an enemy can use a melee weapon to deliver a coup de grace to a helpless foe. An enemy can also use a ranged weapon, provided he is adjacent to the target. The attacker automatically hits and scores a critical hit. If the defender survives, he must make a Fortitude save (DC 10 + damage dealt) or die.

Delivering a coup de grace provokes attacks of opportunity.

Creatures that are immune to critical hits do not take critical damage, nor do they need to make Fortitude saves to avoid being killed by a coup de grace.

Incorporeal
Having no physical body. Incorporeal creatures are immune to all non-magical attack forms. They can be harmed only by other incorporeal creatures, +1 or better magic weapons, spells, spell-like effects, or supernatural effects.

Invisible
Visually undetectable. An invisible creature gains a +2 bonus on attack rolls against sighted opponents, and ignores its opponents' Dexterity bonuses to AC (if any).

Knocked Down
Depending on their size, creatures can be knocked down by winds of high velocity. Creatures on the ground are knocked prone by the force of the wind. Flying creatures are instead blown back 1d6 x 10 feet.

Nauseated
Experiencing stomach distress. Nauseated creatures are unable to attack, cast spells, concentrate on spells, or do anything else requiring attention. The only action such a character can take is a single move action per turn.

Panicked
A panicked creature must drop anything it holds and flee at top speed from the source of its fear, as well as any other dangers it encounters, along a random path. It can't take any other actions. In addition, the creature takes a -2 penalty on all saving throws, skill checks, and ability checks. If cornered, a panicked creature cowers and does not attack, typically using the total defense action in combat. A panicked creature can use special abilities, including spells, to flee; indeed, the creature must use such means if they are the only way to escape.

Panicked is a more extreme state of fear than shaken or frightened.

Paralyzed
A paralyzed character is frozen in place and unable to move or act. A paralyzed character has effective Dexterity and Strength scores of 0 and is helpless, but can take purely mental actions. A winged creature flying in the air at the time that it becomes paralyzed cannot flap its wings and falls. A paralyzed swimmer can't swim and may drown. A creature can move through a space occupied by a paralyzed creature—ally or not. Each square occupied by a paralyzed creature, however, counts as 2 squares.

Petrified
A petrified character has been literally turned to stone and is considered unconscious. If a petrified character cracks or breaks, but the broken pieces are joined with the body as he returns to flesh, he is unharmed. If the character's petrified body is incomplete when it returns to flesh, the body is likewise incomplete and there is some amount of permanent hit point loss and/or debilitation.

Pinned
Held immobile (but not helpless) in a grapple.

Prone
The character is on the ground. An attacker who is prone has a -4 penalty on melee attack rolls and cannot use a ranged weapon (except for a crossbow or firearm). A defender who is prone gains a +4 bonus to Armor Class against ranged attacks, but takes a -4 penalty to AC against melee attacks.

Standing up is a move-equivalent action that provokes an attack of opportunity.

Shaken
A shaken character takes a -2 penalty on attack rolls, saving throws, skill checks, and ability checks.

Shaken is a less severe state of fear than frightened or panicked. A character who is already shaken and becomes shaken again is frightened. A character who is shaken and becomes frightened is panicked.

Sickened
The character takes a -2 penalty on all attack rolls, weapon damage rolls, saving throws, skill checks, and ability checks.

Stable
A character who was *dying* but who has stopped losing hit points and still has negative hit points is stable. The character is no longer *dying*, but is still unconscious. If the character has become stable because of aid from another character (such as a Heal check or magical healing), then the character no longer loses hit points. He has a chance each hour of becoming conscious and *disabled* (even though his hit points are still negative).

If the character became stable on his own and hasn't had help, he is still at risk of losing hit points. Each hour, he has a 10% chance of becoming conscious and *disabled*. Otherwise he loses 1 hit point.

Staggered
A character whose nonlethal damage exactly equals his current hit points is staggered. A staggered character may take a single move action or standard action each round (but not both, nor can she take full-round actions).

A character whose current hit points exceed his nonlethal damage is no longer staggered; a character whose nonlethal damage exceeds his hit points becomes unconscious.

Stunned
A stunned creature drops everything held, can't take actions, takes a -2 penalty to AC, and loses his Dexterity bonus to AC (if any).

Turned
Affected by a turn undead attempt. Turned undead cower, flee, or are shaken.

Unconscious
Knocked out and helpless. Unconsciousness can result from having current hit points between -1 and -9, or from nonlethal damage in excess of current hit points.

who makes a DC 15 Listen check can hear the avalanche or landslide when it is 1d6×500 feet away.

A landslide or avalanche consists of two distinct areas: the bury zone (in the direct path of the falling debris) and the slide zone (the area the debris spreads out to encompass). Characters in the bury zone always take damage from the avalanche; characters in the slide zone may be able to get out of the way. Characters in the bury zone take 8d6 damage (Reflex save DC15 for half). Characters in the slide zone take 3d6 points of damage (Reflex DC15 negates). Those who fail their saves are buried.

Buried characters take 1d6 points of nonlethal damage per minute. If a buried character falls unconscious, he must make a DC 15 Constitution check or take 1d6 points of lethal damage each minute thereafter until freed or dead.

The typical avalanche has a width of 1d6×100 feet, from one edge of the slide zone to the opposite edge. The bury zone in the center of the avalanche is half as wide as the avalanche's full width.

To determine the precise location of characters in the path of an avalanche, roll 1d6×20; the result is the number of feet from the center of the path taken by the bury zone to the center of the party's location. Avalanches of snow and ice advance at a speed of 500 feet per round, and rock avalanches travel at a speed of 250 feet per round.

Falling

The basic rule is simple: 1d6 points of damage per 10 feet fallen, to a maximum of 20d6.

If a character deliberately jumps instead of merely slipping or falling, the damage is the same but the first 1d6 is nonlethal damage. A DC 15 Jump check or DC 15 Tumble check allows the character to avoid any damage from the first 10 feet fallen and converts any damage from the second 10 feet to nonlethal damage. Thus, a character who slips from a ledge 30 feet up takes 3d6 damage. If the same character deliberately jumped, he takes 1d6 points of nonlethal damage and 2d6 points of lethal damage. And if the character leaps down with a successful Jump or Tumble check, he takes only 1d6 points of nonlethal damage and 1d6 points of lethal damage from the plunge.

Falls onto yielding surfaces (soft ground, mud) also convert the first 1d6 of damage to nonlethal damage. This reduction is cumulative with reduced damage due to deliberate jumps and the Jump skill.

Falling into Water

Falls into water are handled somewhat differently. If the water is at least 10 feet deep, the first 20 feet of falling do no damage. The next 20 feet do nonlethal damage (1d3 per 10-foot increment). Beyond that, falling damage is lethal damage (1d6 per additional 10-foot increment).

Characters who deliberately dive into water take no damage on a successful DC 15 Swim check or DC 15 Tumble check, so long as the water is at least 10 feet deep for every 30 feet fallen. However, the DC of the check increases by 5 for every 50 feet of the dive.

Falling Death by Massive Damage

A character's Massive Damage Threshold is never increased by armor or equipment bonuses against falling damage. If this optional rule is used, natural armor protects against falling damage as normal.

Falling Objects

Objects that fall upon characters deal damage based on their size and the distance fallen. Objects deal the initial damage listed on the table below if they fall 10 feet or less. An object deals an additional 1d6 points of damage for every 10-foot increment it falls beyond the first (to a maximum of 20d6 additional points of damage). Objects of Fine size are too small to deal damage, regardless of the distance fallen.

A successful Reflex save indicates that the target takes half damage. The size of the falling object determines the save DC.

If the save fails by 10 or more, and the object is at least three size categories larger than the character, the character is pinned under the fallen object. A pinned character cannot move but is not helpless. The character can make a Strength check to lift the object off him or herself or an Escape Artist check (DC 20) to get out from underneath. The GM can modify the DCs for these checks based on the circumstances.

Damage from Falling Objects

Object Size	Initial Damage	Reflex DC
Fine	0	n/a
Diminutive	1	0
Tiny	1d3	5
Small	1d4	10
Medium	1d6	15
Large	2d6	20
Huge	4d6	25
Gargantuan	8d6	30
Colossal	10d6	35

Fallout

Many areas of the post-apocalyptic world remain spoiled by radioactive fallout. Adventuring within these areas is extremely dangerous.

Radiation damage is measured in *rads*, and an area that poses a radiation hazard is measured in *rads per interval* (per round, per minute, per hour, or per day). The shorter the interval, the more dangerous the hazard.

For each full interval that a character is exposed to fallout, he accumulates rads. The character must make a Fortitude save (DC10 + total accumulated rads) or he takes 1 point of Constitution damage.

If a character's Con is reduced to 0, or if at any time a character's accumulated rads exceed his Con score, he dies.

Radiation Recovery/Resistance

Provided a character can retire to a fallout-free zone, his body will begin to recover.

☠ In the least grim variant, all characters recover at the rate of 1 rad per day.

☠☠ In this variant, the character must succeed at a Fortitude save (DC10 + rads) to recover 1 rad. If the check fails, the character's rad level does not change.

☠☠☠ In the most grim variant, the character must make a Fortitude save as above in order to recover 1 rad. If this check is failed, not only does the character's rad level remain, the character takes an additional 1 point of Constitution damage.

In some campaigns, PCs may be able to purchase medication to flush the body or speed the recovery rate. One such example is *prussian blue*, so named because it is literally a type of dye used in paint. A character who takes prussian blue immediately after exposure can recover an additional 1 rad per day.

Better still, of course, is the use of preventative measures prior to entering an area of fallout. Hazmat suits provide a fixed layer of radiation resistance (similar to any other energy resistance) while iodine-based tablets absorb a fixed number of rads before losing effectiveness.

Variant: Mutations

In some campaigns, fallout does not simply kill; instead, those exposed to radiation may become mutants.

Using this variant, a player whose rads exceed his Constitution score does not immediately die. Instead, the character can opt to reduce his rad level by accepting one or more mutations.

Once per day, a character who would otherwise die from radiation can instantly reduce his rad level by 2 for every 0.2 CR of mutations he accepts. (See Chapter Thirteen, Creature Creation, for the CR cost of various abilities and drawbacks.)

The nature of the mutations is entirely at the whim of the GM (though he may solicit player input). The mutations may be either entirely positive (adding 0.2 CR in new abilities per 2 rads reduced, and thus permanently increasing the character's CR) or a balance of positive and negative (for example, +0.1 CR of a positive effect and -0.1 CR of a negative effect, for a total of 0.2 CR in changes but a net CR increase of +0.0). Mutations should never be entirely negative.

Fire and Heat

Heat deals nonlethal damage that cannot be recovered until the character gets cooled off (reaches shade, survives until nightfall, gets doused in water, etc.).

Once rendered unconscious through the accumulation of nonlethal damage, the character begins to take lethal damage at the same rate.

A character with the Survival skill may receive a bonus to the saving throw for heat exposure, and may be able to apply this bonus to other characters as well (see the skill description). Characters wearing heavy clothing or armor of any sort take a –4 penalty on their saves.

A character in very hot conditions (above 90° F) must make a Fortitude saving throw each hour (DC 15, +1 for each previous check) or take 1d4 points of nonlethal damage.

In severe heat (above 110° F), a character must make a Fortitude save once every 10 minutes (DC 15, +1 for each previous check) or take 1d4 points of nonlethal damage.

A character who takes any nonlethal damage from heat exposure now suffers from heatstroke and is fatigued.

These penalties end when the character recovers the nonlethal damage she took from the heat.

Extreme heat (air temperature over 140° F, fire, boiling water, lava) deals lethal damage. Breathing air in these temperatures deals 1d6 points of damage per minute (no save). In addition, a character must make a Fortitude save every 5 minutes (DC 15, +1 per previous check) or take 1d4 points of nonlethal damage. In addition, those wearing metal armor or coming into contact with very hot metal take an additional 1d4 points of lethal damage per round.

Boiling water deals 1d6 points of scalding damage, unless the character is fully immersed, in which case it deals 10d6 points of damage per round of exposure.

Catching on Fire

Characters exposed to burning oil, bonfires, and non-instantaneous magic fires might find their clothes, hair, or equipment on fire. Spells with an instantaneous duration don't normally set a character on fire, since the heat and flame from these come and go in a flash.

Characters at risk of catching fire are allowed a DC 15 Reflex save to avoid this fate. If a character's clothes or hair catch fire, he takes 1d6 points of damage immediately. In each subsequent round, the burning character must make another Reflex saving throw. Failure means he takes another 1d6 points of damage that round. Success means that the fire has gone out. (That is, once he succeeds on his saving throw, he's no longer on fire.)

A character on fire may automatically extinguish the flames by jumping into enough water to douse himself. If no body of water is at hand, rolling on the ground or smothering the fire with cloaks or the like permits the character another save with a +4 bonus.

Those unlucky enough to have their clothes or equipment catch fire must make DC 15 Reflex saves for each item. Flammable items that fail take the same amount of damage as the character.

Lava

Lava or magma deals 2d6 points of damage per round of exposure, except in the case of total immersion (such as when a character falls into the crater of an active volcano), which deals 20d6 points of damage per round.

Damage from magma continues for 1d3 rounds after exposure ceases, but this additional damage is only half of that dealt during actual contact (that is, 1d6 or 10d6 points per round).

An immunity or resistance to fire serves as an immunity to lava or magma. However, a creature immune to fire might still drown if completely immersed in lava (see Drowning, below).

Smoke

A character who breathes heavy smoke must make a Fortitude save each round (DC 15, +1 per previous check) or spend that round choking and coughing. A character who chokes for 2 consecutive rounds takes 1d6 points of nonlethal damage.

Smoke obscures vision, giving concealment (20% miss chance) to characters within it.

High Altitude

High altitude can be extremely fatiguing—or sometimes deadly—to creatures that aren't used to it. Cold becomes extreme, and the lack of oxygen in the air can wear down even the most hardy of warriors.

Acclimated Characters

Any creature with an Environment entry that includes mountains is considered native to the area, and acclimated to the high altitude. Characters can also acclimate themselves by living at high altitude for a month. Characters who spend more than two months away from the mountains must re-acclimate themselves when they return. Undead, constructs, and other creatures that do not breathe are immune to altitude effects.

Altitude Zones

In general, mountains present three possible altitude bands: low pass, low peak/high pass, and high peak.

Low Pass (lower than 5,000 feet): Most travel in low mountains takes place in low passes, a zone consisting largely of alpine meadows and forests. Travelers may find the going difficult (which is reflected in the movement modifiers for traveling through mountains), but the altitude itself has no game effect.

Low Peak or High Pass (5,000 to 15,000 feet): Ascending to the highest slopes of low mountains, or most normal travel through high mountains, falls into this category. All non-acclimated creatures labor to breathe in the thin air at this altitude. Characters must succeed on a Fortitude save each hour (DC 15, +1 per previous check) or be fatigued. The fatigue ends when the character descends to an altitude with more air. Acclimated characters do not have to attempt the Fortitude save.

High Peak (more than 15,000 feet): The highest mountains exceed 20,000 feet in height. At these elevations, creatures are subject to both high altitude fatigue (as described above) and altitude sickness, whether or not they're acclimated to high altitudes. Altitude sickness represents long-term oxygen deprivation, and it affects mental and physical ability scores. After each 6-hour period a character spends at an altitude of over 15,000 feet, he must succeed on a Fortitude save (DC 15, +1 per previous check) or take 1 point of damage to all ability scores. Creatures acclimated to high altitude receive a +4 competence bonus on their saving throws to resist high altitude effects and altitude sickness.

Overland Travel

Characters covering long distances cross-country use overland movement. Overland movement is measured in miles per hour or miles per day. A day represents 8 hours of actual travel time. For rowed watercraft, a day represents 10 hours of rowing. For a sailing ship, it represents 24 hours.

Walk

A character or creature can walk 8 hours in a day of travel without a problem. Walking for longer than that can wear him out (see Forced March, below).

Hustle

Hustling allows a character or creature to move twice the listed hourly rate. A character or mount can hustle for 1 hour without a problem. Hustling for a second hour in between sleep cycles deals 1 point of nonlethal damage, and each additional hour deals twice the damage taken during the previous hour of hustling. A character who takes any nonlethal damage from hustling becomes fatigued.

A fatigued character can't run or charge and takes a penalty of -2 to Strength and Dexterity. Eliminating the nonlethal damage also eliminates the fatigue.

Run

Characters and creatures can't run for an extended period of time. Attempts to run and rest in cycles effectively work out to a hustle.

Terrain

The terrain through which a character travels affects how much distance he can cover in an hour or a day (see table, below). A highway is a straight, major, paved road. A road is typically a dirt track. A trail is like a road, except that it allows only single-file travel and does not benefit a party traveling with vehicles. Trackless terrain is a wild area with no paths.

Overland Movement Modifiers

Terrain	Highway	Road or Trail	Trackless
Desert, sandy	x1	x1/2	x1/2
Forest	x1	x1	x1/2
Hills	x1	x3/4	x1/2
Jungle	x1	x3/4	x1/4
Moor	x1	x1	x3/4
Mountains	x3/4	x3/4	x1/2
Plains	x1	x1	x3/4
Swamp	x1	x3/4	x1/2
Tundra, frozen	x1	x3/4	x3/4

Forced March

In a day of normal walking, a character walks for 8 hours. The rest of the daylight time is spent making and breaking camp, resting, and eating.

A character can walk for more than 8 hours in a day by making a forced march. For each hour of marching beyond 8 hours, a Constitution check (DC 10, +2 per extra hour) is required. If the check fails, the character takes 1d6 points of nonlethal damage. A character who takes any nonlethal damage from a forced march becomes fatigued. Eliminating the nonlethal damage also eliminates the fatigue. It's possible for a character to march into unconsciousness by pushing himself too hard.

Mounted Movement

A mount bearing a rider can move at a hustle. The damage it takes when doing so, however, is lethal damage, not nonlethal damage. The creature can also be ridden in a forced march, but its Constitution checks automatically fail, and, again, the damage it takes is lethal damage. Mounts also become fatigued when they take any damage from hustling or forced marches.

Table 7-1: Overland Movement Rates

Creature/Mount/Vehicle	Per Hour	Per Day
Light horse or light warhorse	6 miles	48 miles
Light horse (151-450 lb.)[1]	4 miles	32 miles
Light warhorse (231-690 lb.)[1]	4 miles	32 miles
Heavy horse or heavy warhorse	5 miles	40 miles
Heavy horse (201-600 lb.)[1]	3-1/2 miles	28 miles
Heavy warhorse (301-900 lb.)[1]	3-1/2 miles	28 miles
Human (walking, base move 30)	3 miles	24 miles
Pony or warpony	4 miles	32 miles
Pony (76-225 lb.)[1]	3 miles	24 miles
Warpony (101-300 lb.)[1]	3 miles	24 miles
Donkey or mule	3 miles	24 miles
Donkey (51-150 lb.)[1]	2 miles	16 miles
Mule (231-690 lb.)[1]	2 miles	16 miles
Dog, riding	4 miles	32 miles
Dog, riding (101-300 lb.)[1]	3 miles	24 miles
Cart or wagon	2 miles	16 miles
Archaic Watercraft		
Raft or barge (poled or towed)[2]	1/2 mile	5 miles
Keelboat (rowed)[2]	1 mile	10 miles
Rowboat (rowed)[2]	1-1/2 miles	15 miles
Sailing ship (sailed)	2 miles	48 miles
Warship (sailed and rowed)	2-1/2 miles	60 miles
Longship (sailed and rowed)	3 miles	72 miles
Galley (rowed and sailed)	4 miles	96 miles

1 Quadrupeds, such as horses, can carry heavier loads than characters can. See Chapter Five for more information.

2 If going downstream, add the speed of the current (typically 3 miles per hour) to the speed of the vehicle. In addition to 10 hours of being rowed, the vehicle can also float an additional 14 hours, if someone can guide it, so add an additional 42 miles to the daily distance traveled. These vehicles can't be rowed against any significant current, but they can be pulled upstream by draft animals on the shores.

Modern Vehicles

Modern, powered vehicles never get fatigued, but the driver certainly can. A driver can travel for up to 8 hours per day without fatigue. Travelling longer than this period is considered a hustle (as above) for the driver. A driver who becomes fatigued may continue to drive, but he must make a Crash check every hour or lose control of the vehicle. (A fatigued driver should either rest or relinquish the driving duties to another.)

A modern vehicle moves a number of miles per hour equal to 1/10th its base move.

Starvation and Thirst

Characters might find themselves without food or water and with no means to obtain them. In normal climates, Medium characters need at least a gallon of fluids and about a pound of decent food per day to avoid starvation. (Small characters need half as much.) In very hot climates, characters need two or three times as much water to avoid dehydration.

A character can go without water for 1 day plus a number of hours equal to his Constitution score. After this time, the character must make a Constitution check each hour (DC 10, +1 for each previous check) or take 1d6 points of nonlethal damage.

A character can go without food for 3 days, in growing discomfort. After this time, the character must make a Constitution check each day (DC 10, +1 for each previous check) or take 1d6 points of nonlethal damage.

Characters who have taken nonlethal damage from lack of food or water are fatigued. Nonlethal damage from thirst or starvation cannot be recovered until the character gets food or water, as needed—not even magic that restores hit points heals this damage.

Suffocation

A character who has no air to breathe can hold her breath for 2 rounds per point of Constitution. After this period of time, the character must make a DC 10 Constitution check in order to continue holding her breath. The save must be repeated each round, with the DC increasing by +1 for each previous success.

When the character fails one of these Constitution checks, she begins to suffocate. In the first round, she falls unconscious (0 hit points). In the following round, she is *dying*. In the third round, she suffocates.

Slow Suffocation: A Medium character can breathe easily for 6 hours in a sealed chamber measuring 10 feet on a side. After that time, the character takes 1d6 points of nonlethal damage every 15 minutes. Each additional Medium character or significant fire source (a torch, for example) proportionally reduces the time the air will last.

Small characters consume half as much air as Medium characters. A larger volume of air, of course, lasts for a longer time.

Visibility

In an area of bright light, all characters can see clearly. A creature can't hide in an area of bright light unless it is invisible or has cover.

In an area of shadowy illumination, a character can see dimly. Creatures within this area have concealment relative to that character. A creature in an area of shadowy illumination can make a Hide check to conceal itself.

In areas of darkness, creatures without darkvision are effectively blinded (see Darkness, below).

Creatures with low-light vision can see objects twice as far away as the given radius. Double the effective radius of bright light and of shadowy illumination for such creatures.

Creatures with darkvision can see lit areas normally as well as dark areas within 60 feet. A creature can't hide within 60 feet of a creature with darkvision unless it is invisible or has cover.

Light Sources and Illumination

Light Source	Bright	Shadowy	Duration
Candle	n/a[1]	5 ft.	1 hr.
Flashlight[2]	30 ft.	40 ft.	6 hours
Lamp, oil	15 ft.	30 ft.	6 hr./pint
Lantern, oil, bullseye[3]	60 ft.	120 ft.	6 hr./pint
Lantern, oil, hooded	30 ft.	60 ft.	6 hr./pint
Lantern, halogen	40	80	24 hours
Torch	20 ft.	40 ft.	1 hr.

1 A candle does not provide bright illumination, only shadowy illumination.
2 A flashlight creates a beam of light 30 feet long and 5 feet high.
3 A bullseye lantern illuminates a cone, not a radius.

Darkness/Blindness

Some characters and many monsters are able to see in the dark, but for most people, darkness is the same as blindness. For purposes of the following points, a blinded creature is one who simply can't see through the surrounding darkness.

- Creatures blinded by darkness lose the ability to deal extra damage due to precision (for example, point blank shot or sneak attack).
- Blinded creatures are hampered in their movement, and pay 2 squares of movement per square (double normal cost). Blinded creatures can't run or charge.
- All opponents have total concealment from a blinded creature, so the blinded creature has a 50% miss chance in combat. A blinded creature must first pinpoint the location of an opponent in order to attack the right square; if the blinded creature launches an attack without pinpointing its foe, it attacks a random square within its reach. For ranged attacks or spells against a foe whose location is not pinpointed, roll to determine which adjacent square the blinded creature is facing; its attack is directed at the closest target that lies in that direction.
- A blinded creature loses its Dexterity adjustment to AC and takes an additional –2 penalty to AC.
- A blinded creature takes a –4 penalty on Search checks and most Strength- and Dexterity-based skill checks, including any with an armor check penalty. A creature

blinded by darkness automatically fails any skill check relying on vision.

- Creatures blinded by darkness cannot use gaze attacks and are immune to gaze attacks.
- A creature blinded by darkness can make a Listen check as a free action each round in order to locate foes (DC equal to opponents' Move Silently checks). A successful check lets a blinded character hear an unseen creature "over there somewhere." It's almost impossible to pinpoint the location of an unseen creature. A Listen check that beats the DC by 20 reveals the unseen creature's square (but the unseen creature still has total concealment from the blinded creature).
- A blinded creature can grope about to find unseen creatures. A character can make a touch attack with his hands or a weapon into two adjacent squares using a standard action. If an unseen target is in the designated square, there is a 50% miss chance on the touch attack. If successful, the groping character deals no damage but has pinpointed the unseen creature's current location. (If the unseen creature moves, its location is once again unknown.)
- If a blinded creature is struck by an unseen foe, the blinded character pinpoints the location of the creature that struck him (until the unseen creature moves, of course). The only exception is if the unseen creature has a reach greater than 5 feet (in which case the blinded character knows the location of the unseen opponent, but has not pinpointed him) or uses a ranged attack (in which case, the blinded character knows the general direction of the foe, but not his location).
- A creature with the scent ability automatically pinpoints unseen creatures within 5 feet of its location.

Fog

Whether in the form of a low-lying cloud or a mist rising from the ground, fog obscures all sight, including darkvision, beyond 5 feet. Creatures 5 feet away have concealment (attacks by or against them have a 20% miss chance).

Water Dangers

Any character can wade in relatively calm water that isn't over his head, no check required. Similarly, swimming in calm water only requires skill checks with a DC of 10. Trained swimmers can just take 10. (Remember, however, that armor or heavy gear makes any attempt at swimming much more difficult. See the Swim skill description.)

By contrast, fast-moving water is much more dangerous. On a successful DC 15 Swim check or a DC 15 Strength check, it deals 1d3 points of nonlethal damage per round (1d6 points of lethal damage if flowing over rocks and cascades). On a failed check, the character must make another check that round to avoid going under.

Very deep water is not only generally pitch black, posing a navigational hazard, but worse, it deals water pressure damage of 1d6 points per minute for every 100 feet the character is below the surface. A successful Fortitude save (DC 15, +1 for each previous check) means the diver takes no damage in that minute. Very cold water deals 1d6 points of nonlethal damage from hypothermia per minute of exposure.

Drowning

Any character can hold her breath for a number of rounds equal to her Constitution score, but only if they do nothing other than take move actions or free actions. If you take a standard or full action, the duration for which you can hold your breath is reduced by 1 round.

After this period of time, the character must make a DC 10 Constitution check every round in order to continue holding her breath. Each round, the DC increases by 1.

When the character finally fails her Constitution check, she begins to drown. In the first round, she falls unconscious (0 hp). In the following round, she drops to -1 hit points and is *dying*. In the third round, she drowns.

It is possible to drown in substances other than water, such as acid, sand, quicksand, fine dust, silos full of grain, etc.

Rain

Rain reduces visibility ranges by half, resulting in a -4 penalty on Spot and Search checks. It has the same effect on flames, ranged weapon attacks, and Listen checks as severe wind (see below).

Floods

During a flood, rivers become wider, deeper, and swifter. Assume that a river rises by 1d10+10 feet during the spring flood, and its width increases by a factor of 1d4×50%. Fords may disappear for days, bridges may be swept away, and even ferries might not be able to manage the crossing of a flooded river. A river in flood makes Swim checks one category harder (calm water becomes rough, and rough water becomes stormy). Rivers also become 50% swifter.

Characters swept away by a river moving 60 feet per round or faster must make DC 20 Swim checks every round to avoid going under. If a character gets a check result of 5 or more over the minimum necessary, he arrests his motion by catching a rock, tree limb, or bottom snag—he is no longer being carried along by the flow of the water. Escaping the rapids by reaching the bank requires three DC 20 Swim checks in a row. Characters arrested by a rock, limb, or snag can't escape under their own power unless they strike out into the water and attempt to swim their way clear.

Wind and Storms

The combined effects of precipitation (or dust) and wind that accompany all storms reduce visibility ranges by three quarters, imposing a –8 penalty on Spot and Search checks. Storms make ranged attacks and Listen checks more difficult, and may extinguish candles, torches, and other flames.

Winds

The wind can create a stinging spray of dust, fan a fire, or capsize a small boat. If powerful enough, it can even knock characters down, interfere with ranged attacks, or impose penalties on some skill checks.

- **Light Wind:** A gentle breeze, having little game effect.
- **Moderate Wind:** A steady wind with a 50% chance of extinguishing small, unprotected flames, such as candles.
- **Strong Wind:** Gusts that automatically extinguish unprotected flames (candles, torches, and the like). Such gusts impose a –2 penalty on ranged attack rolls and on Listen checks.
- **Severe Wind:** In addition to automatically extinguishing any unprotected flames, winds of this magnitude cause protected flames (such as those of lanterns) to dance wildly and have a 50% chance of extinguishing these lights.
- **Windstorm:** Powerful enough to bring down branches if not whole trees, windstorms automatically extinguish unprotected flames and have a 75% chance of blowing out protected flames, such as those of lanterns.
- **Hurricane-Force Wind:** All flames are extinguished. Listen checks are impossible: All characters can hear is the roaring of the wind. Hurricane-force winds often fell trees.
- **Tornado:** All flames are extinguished. All ranged attacks and Listen checks are impossible. Instead of being blown away, characters in close proximity to a tornado who fail their Fortitude saves are sucked toward the tornado. Those who come in contact with the actual funnel cloud are picked up and whirled around for 1d10 rounds, taking 6d6 points of damage per round, before being violently expelled (falling damage may apply). While a tornado's rotational speed can be as great as 300 mph, the funnel itself moves forward at an average of 30 mph (roughly 250 feet per round). A tornado uproots trees, destroys buildings, and causes other similar forms of major destruction.

Wind Effects

Wind Force	Penalty[1]	Creature Size[2]	Effect[2]	Fort Save DC
Light (0-10 mph)	–	Any	None	–
Moderate (11-20 mph)	–	Any	None	–
Strong (21-30 mph)	-2	Tiny or smaller	Knocked down	10
		Small or larger	None	
Severe (31-50 mph)	-4	Tiny	Blown away	15
		Small	Knocked down	
		Medium	Checked	
		Large or larger	None	
Windstorm (51-74 mph)	Impossible/ -8	Small or smaller	Blown away	18
		Medium	Knocked down	
		Large or Huge	Checked	
		Gargantuan or Colossal	None	
Hurricane (75-174 mph)	Impossible	Medium or smaller	Blown away	20
		Large	Knocked down	
		Huge	Checked	
		Gargantuan or Colossal	None	
Tornado (175-300 mph)	Impossible	Large or smaller	Blown away	30
		Huge	Knocked down	
		Gargantuan or Colossal	Checked	

1 Apply this penalty to all ranged attacks and Listen checks.
2 Flying or airborne creatures are treated as one size category smaller than their actual size, so an airborne Gargantuan dragon is treated as Huge for purposes of wind effects. A Fort save prevents the listed effect.

Storms

- **Dust Storm:** A duststorm blows fine grains of sand that obscure vision, smother unprotected flames, and can even choke protected flames (50% chance). A sandstorm reduces visibility to 1d10×5 feet and provides a –4 penalty on Listen, Search, and Spot checks.

Duststorms deal 1d3 points of nonlethal damage each round to anyone caught out in the open without shelter and also pose a choking hazard (see Drowning—except that a character with a scarf or similar protection across her mouth and nose does not begin to choke until after a number of rounds equal to 10 × her Constitution score).

- **Snowstorm:** In addition to the wind and precipitation common to other storms, snowstorms leave 1d6 inches of snow on the ground afterward.
- **Thunderstorm:** In addition to wind and precipitation (usually rain, but sometimes also hail), thunderstorms are accompanied by lightning that can pose a hazard to characters without proper shelter (especially those in metal armor). As a rule of thumb, assume one bolt per minute for a 1-hour period at the center of the storm. Each bolt causes electricity damage equal to 1d10 eight-sided dice. One in ten thunderstorms is accompanied by a tornado.

SPELLS & MAGIC

In the world of Grim Tales, spellcasting is a dangerous activity, frowned upon by sane men. Still, the lure of magic and the vain hope to establish some mastery over arcane forces besets even the best-intentioned heroes.

In Grim Tales, any character can learn, and possibly even cast, spells. However, the practice of magic is dangerous, potentially even fatal, as the flow of magic saps the lifeforce directly from the spellcaster. *Magical adepts* are those heroes who have dedicated their lives to the pursuit of magic, and unlike mere dabblers, they have made some progress in the mastery of the arcane.

There are three main differences in the spellcasting system of Grim Tales as compared to the usual rule systems.

First, there are no spell slots or "spells per day." If you know a spell, you may attempt to cast it. Whether or not you are successful, the effort of spellcasting drains your character. Because magical adepts can control this effect, there is potentially no limit to the number of spells you can cast in a day.

Second, the GM is in complete control of which spells are found in his campaign. Unless your character finds, deciphers, and comprehends some ancient text, you will not know any spells to cast. No character, not even magical adepts, gain access to "automatic" spells.

Finally, because the knowledge of spells is rare and the casting of spells is so dangerous, casting a spell tends to be a relatively rare occurrence. As the process of casting a spell can cripple or kill a spellcaster, they tend to be much more judicious in their use— rare is the spellcaster who will risk spell burn just to cast a cantrip to warm his tea.

Magical Traditions

There are three magical traditions in Grim Tales. All spellcasters are magical adepts, but they are further defined according to the tradition to which they adhere.

Arcane Adepts

Arcane adepts are most often called wizards or mages. Their knowledge comes from ancient tomes, puzzled out over long hours of study. Their primary spellcasting attribute is Intelligence. Arcane adepts may cast only arcane spells.

Divine Adepts

Divine adepts are most often called priests, clerics, or shamen. Their knowledge is learned in the form of rites and incantations, passed to them from within their religious hierarchy or (much more rarely) from a powerful outsider, such as an angel or devil. Their primary spellcasting attribute is Wisdom. Divine adepts may cast only divine spells.

Wild Adepts

Wild adepts, such as sorcerers, are more rare. Their spellcasting abilities are innate, the result of capricious occult forces, demonic curses or bargains, or mysterious ancestry. Wild adepts are often granted their spells at the whim of the GM, completely out of their control. Their primary spellcasting attribute is Charisma. Wild adepts may cast any spell they know, whether it is arcane or divine, but they cast all spells as if the spell were one level higher. That is, a 1st level spell to an arcane or divine adept is a 2nd level spell for a wild adept.

Availability of Spells

Any character can learn a spell. There are no spellcasting classes nor is the knowledge of a spell the exclusive purview of a select few. PCs do not start play with any knowledge of spells; they are entirely at the mercy of the GM as to where, when, and how often new spells are discovered. The most powerful tool at the GM's disposal to control the use of magic in his game is to restrict the availability of spells.

Discovering New Spells

The first step to learning a spell, of course, is finding a source for the spell, and this is completely up to the GM. The GM may choose to seed the occasional treasure hoard or old library with a tome detailing a few spells; he may place a spellbook in the hands of a key villain; he may arrange an otherworldly visit for your character. Depending on his campaign, and if he is in a good mood, there may even be secret societies or academies where such knowledge is taught. Ultimately, however, it is completely subject to the GM's plans.

Learning Spells

Once you have found a source with the spell you wish to learn, you may attempt a Spellcraft check to learn the spell. Note that Spellcraft can not be used untrained; you must have at least 1 rank of Spellcraft to even attempt to learn the spell. As such, it is not uncommon for a character to take some time with a spellbook before learning a spell— you may find a spellbook and have to wait before purchasing your first rank of Spellcraft.

Learning a spell requires a Spellcraft roll with a DC equal to 15 + spell level.

Arcane adepts gain a +2 synergy bonus to learn arcane spells if they have 5 or more ranks of Knowledge (arcana).

Divine adepts gain a +2 synergy bonus to learn divine spells if they have 5 or more ranks of Knowledge (religion).

In modern games, the GM may allow both arcane and divine adepts a +2 synergy bonus to learn a spell if they have 5 or more ranks of Knowledge (occult).

If the check fails, you may not attempt to learn that spell again until you have gained at least one rank of Spellcraft.

If the check succeeds, you have learned the spell. Add it to your list of spells known.

There is no restriction for learning spells. Any adept— indeed, any character— who succeeds at the Spellcraft roll can add the spell to their list of spells known. Actually casting a spell, of course, is another matter...

Casting Spells

Casting a spell requires a caster level check (DC 10 + spell level). Roll a d20 and add your caster level. You may not take 10 or 20 on this check, though you may spend an action point to improve your roll.

Untrained characters have a caster level of zero. Magical adepts have a caster level of at least 1, and can increase their caster level with additional talents. An arcane or divine adept who casts a spell outside his tradition casts as an untrained caster (unless his selection of talents grants him a caster level in another tradition).

If this check is failed, the spell does not take effect. The caster still suffers spell burn (as below). Even on a failed caster level check, magical adepts gain the benefit of spell burn resistance, unless the check rolls a natural 1. In this case, they suffer spell burn without benefit of spell burn resistance.

If the check succeeds, the spell is cast successfully, and the caster suffers spell burn; magical adepts can apply spell burn resistance (see below).

For an untrained caster, regardless of whether the check succeeds or fails, he suffers spell burn to his Constitution (see below).

Magical adepts are more able to control the flow of magic when casting spells within their tradition (arcane spells for arcane adepts, divine spells for divine adepts). When casting spells whose level is equal to or less than their

The Spellcraft Skill

All characters who choose the magical adept talent gain Spellcraft as a core skill.

However, even characters who are not magical adepts may choose Spellcraft as a core skill, and even those who do not have it as a core skill may still purchase ranks (though at an increased cost of 2-for-1, as usual). This allows players to create characters who may have knowledge of spellcraft without actually having any magical ability.

Spellcraft (INT; Trained Only)

Use this skill to identify spells as they are cast or spells already in place.

Check: You can identify spells and magic effects. The DCs for Spellcraft checks relating to various tasks are summarized on the table below.

Action: Varies, as noted below.

Try Again: See below.

Synergy: If you have 5 or more ranks in Knowledge (arcana), you get a +2 bonus on Spellcraft checks.

If you have 5 or more ranks in Use Unknown Device, you get a +2 bonus on Spellcraft checks to decipher scrolls.

If you have 5 or more ranks in Spellcraft, you get a +2 bonus on Use Unknown Device checks related to scrolls.

Additionally, certain spells allow you to gain information about magic, provided that you make a successful Spellcraft check as detailed in the spell description.

Critical Failure: You misidentify the spell or effect; if you are subsequently required to make a saving throw against this specific manifestation of the spell or effect, you suffer a -2 penalty.

Critical Success: You successfully identify the spell or effect; if you are subsequently required to make a saving throw against this specific manifestation of the spell or effect, you gain a +2 bonus.

Spellcraft Standard DCs

Spellcraft DC	Task
10 + spell level	Use *read magic* to identify an inscribed spell (*glyph of warding, symbol, etc.*). No action required.
15 + spell level	Identify a spell being cast. (You must see or hear the spell's verbal or somatic components.) No action required. No retry.
15 + spell level	Learn a spell from a spellbook or scroll. No retry for that spell until you gain at least 1 rank in Spellcraft (even if you find another source to try to learn the spell from). Requires 8 hours.
15 + spell level	When casting *detect magic*, determine the school of magic involved in the aura of a single item or creature you can see. (If the aura is not a spell effect, the DC is 15 + one-half caster level.) No action required.
20 + spell level	Identify a spell you are familiar with that is already in place and in effect. You must be able to see or detect the effects of the spell. No action required. No retry.
20 + spell level	Identify materials created or shaped by magic, such as noting that an iron wall is the result of a *wall of iron* spell. No action required. No retry.
25	Identify a potion. Requires 1 minute. No retry.
30 or higher	Understand a strange or unique magical effect, such as the effects of a magic stream. Time required varies. No retry.

primary spellcasting attribute minus 10, they may apply spell burn to their Strength, instead of their Constitution. For adepts, spellcasting is more often an exhausting affair than a deadly one.

For example, an arcane adept with an Intelligence of 13 may cast arcane spells of 3rd level or less (13 minus 10) and suffer only Strength damage. He suffers Constitution damage when casting spells of 4th level or higher.

Casting Times
free action
standard action
full round
one minute
ten minutes
one hour
one day
one week
one month
one year

A magical adept whose Strength is reduced to zero is *helpless*, and any excess spell burn is applied to his Constitution.

Additional Casting Time

A spellcaster can take extra time when casting a spell in order to improve his chances of casting the spell successfully. For each increase in casting time above that required by the spell, the spellcaster receives a +1 bonus to his caster level check to determine if the spell is cast correctly. Note that this does not actually increase the adept's caster level, it merely provides a bonus to his caster level check.

Spell Burn

Spell Burn is applied as ability damage equal to 1 die per spell level. Thus, an untrained caster who casts a 3rd level spell suffers 3 dice of Constitution damage. A magical adept capable of casting 3rd level spells (at least a 13 in his primary spellcasting attribute) would suffer 3 dice of Strength damage. Ability damage recovers at the normal rate, with the exception that magical healing cannot restore ability score points lost to spell burn.

The spell burn die is set by the GM at the beginning of the campaign:

☠ A low spell burn die (d4) means that spell burn is predictably deadly, with no appreciable benefit for gifted (i.e., high attribute) spellcasters.

☠☠ The standard spell burn die is d6. There are benefits for gifted and/or trained spellcasters in this model.

☠☠☠ A high spell burn die (d8, d10, or higher) means that spell burn is wildly variable, and potentially very deadly to all but the most gifted and highly trained spellcasters.

Spell Burn Resistance

Magical adepts receive spell burn resistance equal to their primary spellcasting attribute modifier, plus any bonuses for talents. Reduce the amount of burn rolled on *each die* by their attribute modifier.

However, for each spell burn die that rolls a natural 1, the magical adept suffers 1 point of burn that *cannot be resisted*.

It is for this reason that a low burn die (such as a d4) can still be quite dangerous: there is a greater chance of rolling a natural 1.

Remember that wild adepts cast spells as if the spell were one level higher; they will always roll one more spell burn die than an arcane or divine adept casting the same spell.

Quick Spell Burn Summary

You can quickly total your spell burn and apply resistance using the following steps:

First, set aside all natural 1 results. These dice cannot be resisted.

Next, throw out all remaining results equal to or lower than your spell burn resistance. (If you have spell burn resistance of +4, for example, throw out all 2's, 3's, and 4's.

Reduce each remaining die by your spell burn resistance, total the remainder, and add them to all the natural 1 results. The remaining total is your spell burn.

Spellcasting Summary

- Make a caster level check at DC 10 + spell level;
- Apply spell burn (and resistance, if any);
- Apply spell effects (if the caster level check succeeds).

Remember that although the process for casting a spell is slightly more complicated, in the low-magic world of Grim Tales, each spell successfully cast is a major cinematic event. Spellcasting is not intended to be an everyday crutch as it is in most high-fantasy campaigns.

Spellcasting Example

A Smart hero (Intelligence 16) finds a spellbook containing *fireball*, a 3rd level spell.

Upon gaining his next level, he increases his Spellcraft skill by one rank. Because Spellcraft was not one of the core skills he selected during character creation, it costs him 2 skill points for one rank. With visions of phenomenal cosmic power dancing in his head (and skill points to spare) he considers it a small investment.

Now with 1 rank of Spellcraft, he attempts to learn the spell. The DC for this check is 18 (15+spell level 3rd). The hero succeeds; he adds *fireball* to his list of spells known.

In the next major encounter, the hero attempts to cast the spell. He makes a caster level check against DC13 (10+spell level 3rd). He fails his check. Because he is not an adept, he suffers 3d6 Constitution damage. Fortunately, the total spell burn is low, but even so, *he barely survives.*

The Smart hero's companions suggest that, if he wants to try that again, he might try becoming a magical adept. When the Smart hero gains another talent, he chooses Magical Adept. He is now an arcane adept, casting spells based upon his Intelligence. He is considered caster level 1 and he gains spell burn resistance equal to his Intelligence modifier (+3). (He also gains Spellcraft as a core skill.)

In a climactic encounter with the campaign's major villain (and a horde of minions!), the Smart hero thinks it may be time to try that *fireball* again. Because his Intelligence is 16, the Smart hero can cast up to 6th level spells (16 minus 10) and suffer Strength damage, instead of Constitution damage. Fireball is a 3rd level spell, so if things go horribly wrong this time, the worst that can happen is he will leave himself helpless at Strength 0 (instead of dead at Constitution 0).

The Smart hero tries to cast the spell. He makes a caster level check against DC13. He rolls a 12, adds his caster level of 1, and succeeds!

Now he rolls for spell burn (3d6 for a 3rd level spell) and applies spell burn resistance. He rolls a 1, a 3, and a 6. First he sets aside the 1 result— he cannot resist a 1 result. Next he throws out the 3 result— his spell burn resistance is 3, so that die is completely negated. Finally, the 6 result is reduced by his spell burn resistance (-3) to a total of 3. The Smart hero suffers 4 points (1+3) of Strength damage from spell burn.

Finally, the Smart hero gets to apply the effects of his successful spell! The *fireball* streaks from his weary fingertips and detonates on the villain, blasting him and his minions to fiery splinders...

Using Spells in Combat

Most spells require a standard action to cast. You can cast such a spell either before or after you take a move action. You retain your Dexterity bonus to AC while casting.

Spell Components: To cast a spell with a verbal (V) component, your character must speak in a firm voice. If you're gagged or silenced, you can't cast such a spell. A spellcaster who has been deafened has a 20% chance to spoil any spell with a verbal component.

To cast a spell with a somatic (S) component, you must gesture freely with at least one hand. You can't cast a spell of this type while bound, grappling, or with both your hands full or occupied.

To cast a spell with a material (M), focus (F), or divine focus (DF) component, you have to have the proper materials, as described by the spell. Unless these materials are elaborate, preparing them is a free action. For material components whose costs are not listed, you can assume that you have them among your belongings.

Some spells entail an experience point (XP) cost to you. You cannot spend so much XP that you lose a level, so you cannot cast the spell unless you have enough XP to spare. You may, on gaining enough XP to achieve a new level, immediately spend the XP on casting the spell rather than keeping it to advance a level. The XP are expended when you cast the spell, whether or not the casting succeeds.

Concentration: You must concentrate to cast a spell. If you start casting a spell but something interferes with your concentration you must make a Concentration check or lose the spell. The check's DC depends on what is threatening your concentration (see the Concentration skill). If you fail, the spell fizzles with no effect.

Concentrating to Maintain a Spell: Some spells require continued concentration to keep them going. Concentrating to maintain a spell is a standard action that doesn't provoke an attack of opportunity. Anything that could break your concentration when casting a spell can keep you from concentrating to maintain a spell. If your concentration breaks, the spell ends.

Casting Time: Most spells have a casting time of 1 standard action, and they take effect immediately.

A spell that takes 1 round to cast is a full-round action. It comes into effect just before the beginning of your turn in the round after you began casting the spell. You then act normally after the spell is completed.

A spell that takes 1 minute to cast comes into effect just before your turn 1 minute later (and for each of those 10 rounds, you are casting a spell as a full-round action). These actions must be consecutive and uninterrupted, or the spell automatically fails.

When you begin a spell that takes 1 round or longer to cast, you must continue the casting and maintain concentration from one round to just before your turn in the next round (at least). If you lose concentration before the spell is complete, it fails.

You only provoke attacks of opportunity when you begin casting a spell, even though you might continue casting for at least one full round. While casting a spell, you don't threaten any squares around you.

Attacks of Opportunity: Generally, if you cast a spell, you provoke attacks of opportunity from threatening enemies. If you take damage from an attack of opportunity, you must make a Concentration check (DC 10 + points of damage taken + spell level) or lose the spell. Spells that require only a free action to cast don't provoke attacks of opportunity.

Casting on the Defensive: Casting a spell while on the defensive does not provoke an attack of opportunity, but you must succeed at a Concentration check (DC 15 + spell level). If you fail, the spell does not take effect.

Touch Spells in Combat: Many spells have a range of touch. To use these spells, you cast the spell and then touch the target, either in the same round or any time later. You may touch the target in the same round as you cast the spell (combining the actions of casting and touching). You may take your move before casting the spell, after touching the target, or between casting the spell and touching the target. You can automatically touch one friend or use the spell on yourself, but to touch an opponent, you must succeed on an attack roll.

Touch Attacks: Touching an opponent with a touch spell is considered to be an armed attack and therefore does not provoke attacks of opportunity. However, the act of casting the spell does provoke an attack of opportunity. Touch attacks come in two types: melee touch attacks and ranged touch attacks. You can score critical hits with either type of attack. Your opponent's AC against a touch attack does not include any armor bonus, shield bonus, or natural armor bonus. His size modifier, Dexterity modifier, Defense, and deflection bonus (if any) all apply normally.

Holding the Charge: If you don't discharge a touch spell in the round when you cast the spell, you can hold the charge indefinitely. You can continue to make touch attacks round after round. You can touch one friend as a standard action or up to six friends as a full-round action. If you touch anything or anyone while holding a charge, even unintentionally, the spell discharges. If you cast another spell, the touch spell dissipates. Alternatively, you may make a normal unarmed attack (or an attack with a natural weapon) while holding a charge. In this case, you aren't considered armed and you provoke attacks of opportunity as normal for the attack. (If your unarmed attack or natural weapon attack doesn't provoke attacks of opportunity, neither does this attack.) If the attack hits, you deal normal damage for your unarmed attack or natural weapon *and* the spell discharges. If the attack misses, you are still holding the charge.

Dismiss a Spell: Dismissing an active spell is a standard action that doesn't provoke attacks of opportunity.

Direct or Redirect a Spell: Some spells allow you to redirect the effect to new targets or areas after you cast the spell. Redirecting a spell requires a move action and does not provoke attacks of opportunity or require concentration.

Spells and Critical Hits: A spell that requires an attack roll can score a critical hit. A spell attack that requires no attack roll cannot score a critical hit.

Ceasing Concentration on Spell: You can stop concentrating on an active spell as a free action.

Casting a Quickened Spell: You can cast a quickened spell (see the Quicken Spell feat) or any spell whose casting time is designated as a free action as a free action. Only one such spell can be cast in any round, and such spells don't count toward your normal limit of one spell per round. Casting a spell with a casting time of a free action doesn't incur an attack of opportunity.

Distracting Spellcasters: You can ready an attack against a spellcaster with the trigger "if she starts casting a spell." If you damage the spellcaster, she may lose the spell she was trying to cast (as determined by her Concentration check result).

Readying to Counterspell: If you ready an action to counterspell, you get a chance to identify any spell cast by your opponent. Make a Spellcraft check (DC15 + spell level). If you succeed, and you can cast the same spell (whether arcane or divine), you can cast it as a counterspell. Counterspelling requires a caster level check, as normal, but if the check succeeds, there is no spell burn. Instead, the spell energy is directed into counterspelling the opposing spell.

If you know how to cast *dispel magic*, you may use it to counterspell *any* spell, but it doesn't always work. Casting *dispel magic* requires a caster level check and causes spell burn as normal, regardless of whether it successfully dispels the opposing spell.

Magic Items

Spell Completion Items

Spell-completion items contain a spell that is mostly finished. The user need only perform the finishing parts of the spellcasting (the final gestures, words, etc.). Activating a spell completion item is a standard action and provokes attacks of opportunity exactly as casting a spell does.

Scrolls

If you find a scroll, you must first decipher the scroll before you can use it. Deciphering a spell on a scroll requires a Spellcraft check (DC20 + spell level). An adept with the Scribe Scroll feat can read any scroll she created herself.

The user does not need to have the spell on her list of spells known to activate a scroll, but the user must follow the magical tradition of the spell contained within. An arcane adept may not activate a divine scroll, nor may a divine adept activate an arcane scroll. A wild adept may activate any kind of scroll.

If the spell contained on the scroll is on the user's list of spells known, no caster level check is necessary. If the user does not know the spell, a caster level check is required as usual to complete the spellcasting process.

Upon completing the spell on the scroll, the user suffers spell burn as normal, as if he had cast the spell.

Using a scroll has two major advantages: If it is a spell you know, you need not fear failing your caster level check. On the other hand, if you find a scroll that contains a spell you do not know, you can still unleash its effects.

Spell Trigger Items

Spell trigger activation is similar to spell completion, but it's even simpler. No gestures or spell finishing are needed, just a knowledge of the spell contained within and a single word that must be spoken. Activating a spell trigger item is a standard action and does not provoke attacks of opportunity.

Wands

A wand is a spell trigger item and the spell within must be on the user's list of spells known. Triggering a spell from a wand always drains at least one charge from the wand. Wands may hold as many as 50 charges.

Triggering the spell within a wand does not require a caster level check to insure that the spell takes effect, but once the wand is triggered, spell burn affects the user as if he had cast the spell.

However, a magical adept may choose to make a caster level check to mitigate the effects of the ensuing spell burn. If the adept succeeds at a caster level check (DC 10 + spell level), any spell burn that would otherwise be suffered by the user is absorbed by the wand instead: for each point of spell burn, one additional charge is drained from the wand.

In addition, if the spell contained within the wand is on the adept's list of spells known and is within his own magical tradition (arcane or divine) he may apply his spell burn resistance before draining charges from the wand.

A wand drained below 0 charges in this way is immediately destroyed in a burst of magical energy, and the wand's user bears the full brunt of the spell burn.

Use Activated Items

This type of item simply has to be used in order to activate it. A character has to drink a potion, swing a sword, interpose a shield to deflect a blow in combat, look through a lens, sprinkle dust, wear a ring, or don a hat. Use activation is generally straightforward and self-explanatory.

Many use-activated items are objects that a character wears. Continually functioning items are practically always items that one wears. A few must simply be in the character's possession (on his person). However, some items made for wearing must still be activated. Although this activation sometimes requires a command word (see above), usually it means mentally willing the activation to happen. The description of an item states whether a command word is needed in such a case.

Unless stated otherwise, activating a use-activated magic item is either a standard action or not an action at all and does not provoke attacks of opportunity, unless the use involves performing an action that provokes an attack of opportunity in itself.

Potions

Potions store minor spell effects (3rd level or lower). Upon drinking a potion, make a caster level check using the caster level of the potion (DC 10 + spell level). If the caster level check succeeds, the potion takes effect. There is no spell burn when using a potion.

Magic Item Space Limitations

Most characters in a Grim Tales campaign will never see enough magic items to run afoul of the space limitations. Nevertheless, the guidelines below govern the number of items that can be operable on a character at one time.

A humanoid-shaped body can be decked out in magic gear consisting of one item from each of the following groups, keyed to which place on the body the item is worn.

- One headband, hat, helmet, or phylactery on the head
- One pair of eye lenses or goggles on or over the eyes
- One amulet, brooch, medallion, necklace, periapt, or scarab around the neck
- One vest, vestment, or shirt on the torso
- One robe or suit of armor on the body (over a vest, vestment, or shirt)
- One belt around the waist (over a robe or suit of armor)
- One cloak, cape, or mantle around the shoulders (over a robe or suit of armor)
- One pair of bracers or bracelets on the arms or wrists
- One glove, pair of gloves, or pair of gauntlets on the hands
- One ring on each hand (or two rings on one hand)
- One pair of boots or shoes on the feet

Using Spells From Other Sources

You may use spells from other sources, but GMs should be wary of allowing players access to certain spells:

Divination: Allow the use of *augury*, but disallow spells such as *divination* or *contact other plane* that grant players access to information that can spoil the adventure.

Teleport: The ability to travel instantly from place to place can destroy the internal logic of your campaign.

Raise Dead: The ability to restore life to the dead has obvious, far-reaching, and campaign altering ramifications.

Firearms

Using Firearms in Your Campaign

The absence or presence of firearms in your game can completely change the flavor of the entire campaign. Historically speaking, firearms were responsible for the obsolescence of armor, castles, and by extension, the entire feudal system. Even in modern times they continue to have an impact in the lives of everyday people. It does not require years of training to pick up a firearm and use it for self defense, and a gun has the same deadly potential in the hands of a frail old granny as in the hands of a vicious street punk.

As the saying goes, "God created all men, but Colt made them equal."

Thus, before you decide to include firearms in your campaign, you should carefully consider the impact that it will have on the lives and attitudes of the PCs, and especially the NPCs, in your game.

Web Enhancement
You may find it easier to navigate this chapter by first familiarizing yourself with the glossary and timeline of firearms, available for free download at www.badaxegames.com.

Designing Firearms

Now that you have perused the glossary to familiarize yourself with the terminology, and you have studied the timeline in order to choose the firearms that best fit the era of game you are planning, you can begin designing firearms.

Quick Start

The easiest way to incorporate firearms into your game is to use the firearms already detailed in existing d20 material. If you are running a modern game, for example, you could simply use the firearms presented in the *d20 Modern Roleplaying Game*. Other modern weapons are available in *Spycraft* (published by AEG) and *Ultramodern Firearms d20* (published by Green Ronin).

The firearms available from these sources come ready to play, with damage, range increments, critical threat ranges, and so forth already statted out and ready to go. However, it should be noted that there are subtle differences in how each of these sources arrives at the statistics for each firearm. If you mix and match sources, you can end up with some odd results.

Custom Firearms

Many GMs will find it more interesting to design their own firearms specifically to fit their campaign. Even if you plan on using firearms already detailed in other sources, you can use the following rules to re-stat each weapon so that they all work equally across the board.

A word of warning to the gun nuts and reality purists out there: Designing firearms that work within the context of a game will not yield results that are true to "real life." In particular, you may find that the ranges of firearms are dramatically curtailed. Why? Because even in *Grim Tales*, taking a bullet in the head from a mile away is neither fun nor heroic.

Designing Firearms

Designing firearms for your campaign is fairly simple, starting with the broad information and working down to the details of each weapon.

Step One: Choose a Firearms Era

As you may have learned from the firearms timeline, firearms improved in technology over the course of a few hundred years. For our purposes, we divide firearms into three major categories, or eras:

☠ Muzzle-Loaders
This era spans the years between the invention of the wheel lock, circa 1450, and the invention of the cartridge, circa 1830. Although the hand gonne was invented a few hundred years before the matchlock, as it was essentially an iron pot full of gunpowder on the end of a stick, most GMs will find little need for detailed statistics on the firearms of any previous era. The single defining characteristic of this era is that all firearms require the user to load both the propellant and the round before each shot.

☠☠ Cartridge
Between 1830 and 1860, several cartridge designs were invented: needlefire, rimfire, pinfire, centerfire, and so on. The clear and obvious advantage to cartridge ammunition was in the ease of loading and production. This era runs from 1830 up until about 1895. It includes a few weapons that used magazine ammunition, but such weapons did not see widespread use in this era.

☠☠☠ Automatic
Beginning in 1894, several semi-automatic pistols were invented. Perhaps the most recognizable of these was the Browning automatic pistol, invented in 1898. The advantage of the semi-automatic pistol is that, with a single squeeze of the trigger, the weapon would fire, eject the spent cartridge, and load another round of ammunition from the magazine. The firearms of this era used cartridge ammunition, like those of the era before, but the major point of difference is that the ammunition was contained in a clip or box magazine. This allowed the weapon to

be fired many more times without reloading, and at the same time allowing the user to reload an entire magazine at once, rather than cartridge by cartridge. This era runs through the present day and even into the apocalyptic era.

You will want to choose the era that best represents the impact that you want firearms to have on your game.

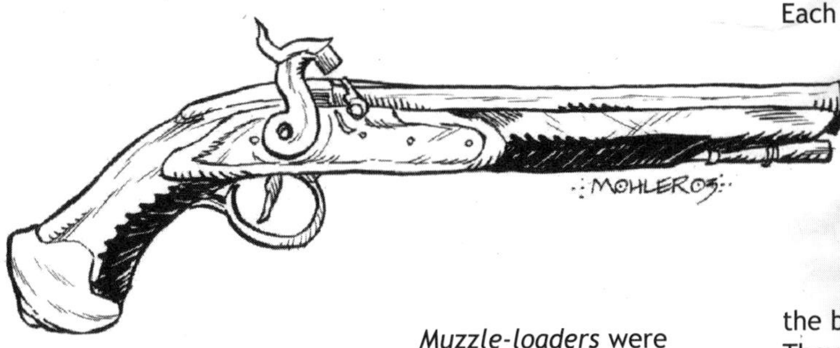

Muzzle-loaders were powerful weapons, changing the landscape of warfare and politics forever, but at the same time they remained relatively difficult to reload, clean, and maintain. This era will see firearms use relegated to the professionally trained (or the extremely patient) and only those folks with a pressing *need* for a firearm are likely to bother carrying one.

With the invention of the *cartridge*, firearms began to spread into the hands of the general populace. Even with relatively little training, one could load, aim, and fire these weapons. In this era, firearms will see widespread use, serving the common man as a great equalizer. Even so, the relatively small number of rounds contained within each weapon, and the time the firearm required for reloading, meant that the firearms of this era were not generally capable of widespread destruction or rampant shooting sprees. To be sure, a group of wanton cowboys (or a group of PCs) could get up to great mischief; but a lone gunman is not generally going to take out a room full of opponents. This era will see widespread use of firearms, but each round of ammunition remains fairly precious, lending weight and consideration to their use.

Finally, you may choose to run a game in the era of *automatic* weapons. The ability to quickly reload an entire magazine, each containing ten to thirty or even more rounds of ammunition, means that firearms users no longer need concern themselves with every round of ammunition. Whereas the era of the cartridge saw many people *carrying* firearms, the true impact of the semi-automatic age is that folks are more prone to *use* them.

Step Two: Designing the Firearm

The next step is to actually design the firearms. It is not necessary to detail every possible firearm in your game; you may simply wish to define several broad categories or representative samples, then allow the player to choose the actual weapon from some real-world gun manufacturer, based on his own style and personal preference.

It is a maxim that the more firearms you design, the more likely your players will be to min/max each weapon. Style considerations will go out the window and each player will pack the firearm that is mathematically superior to all others.

You can avoid this by designing only broad categories: .40 caliber handguns, .50 caliber handguns, etc.; or you can break it down even further by defining the action as well: .40 caliber revolvers; .40 caliber semi-automatics, etc.

Each firearm has several qualities you must specify in order to define all of its rules-related statistics:

Bore

Choose a bore for the weapon: either *smoothbore* or *rifled*.

Smoothbore weapons have a maximum range of 15 increments. There is no rifling on the inside of the bore to slow down velocity— or to improve accuracy. They suffer a range penalty of -3 per range increment beyond the first (normally, ranged weapons suffer only a -2 penalty per range increment beyond the first).

Rifled weapons sacrifice range for accuracy. They have a maximum range of 10 increments, and suffer a -2 penalty per range increment beyond the first.

Most weapons other than muzzle-loaders and shotguns will be rifled.

Range Increment

The next step is to determine the range increment of the weapon.

If you are attempting to "convert" weapons from the real world, you can get a serviceable result using the following method.

First, find the muzzle velocity of the weapon in meters/sec. Round this result to the nearest hundred. Then, divide this result by 10 to find the final range increment.

Example: A pistol has a muzzle velocity of 359 m/sec, which rounds to 400 m/sec, yielding a range increment of 40.

Example: An assault rifle has a muzzle velocity of 735 m/sec, which rounds to 700 m/sec, yielding a range increment of 70.

If you do not want to go through the trouble of converting real-world weapons in this fashion, you can simply estimate: Handguns should have a range increment from 20-50, and longarms should have a range increment from 50-100. Sniper rifles could have a range increment as high as 120, but there are better ways to improve the maximum range of the weapon than simply extending the range increment: a steady firing platform, the addition of optical sights, etc.

Critical Threat Range

It is highly recommended that all firearms have a threat range of 20. Players who wish to extend the threat range of the weapon to 19-20 should seek out a custom gunsmith, and the use of such a weapon should require an Exotic Weapon Proficiency feat.

Damage Type

All firearms use the Ballistic damage type. Shotguns can be loaded with variant ammunition that causes different damage types, such as flechettes (Piercing) or bean-bags (Bludgeoning).

Magazine

If you are creating your firearms from real world analogues, your source material will tell you the size of the magazine. Otherwise, you may determine the magazine as appropriate for the era of firearms you wish to emulate:

Muzzle-loaders do not contain a magazine. They must be reloaded after each shot.

Cartridge firearms generally contain either five or six rounds of ammunition for handguns (generally revolvers in this era), while longarms had a capacity of six, ten, twelve— even sixteen rounds of ammunition in some of the smaller calibers.

In the era of ***automatic*** weapons, pistols (but not revolvers) generally contain six to ten rounds; sub-machine guns contain ten to thirty rounds; while fully-automatic assault weapons contain thirty, thirty five, or more rounds per magazine. Sniper rifles, anti-materiel rifles, and other special-purpose weapons continue to contain only a few rounds, perhaps six or less.

Action/Rate of Fire

The action of the firearm generally influences the rate of fire. Choose one of the following:

Muzzle-loader (MZ): Muzzle-loaders do not typically have any action. You can fire once per round; reloading is a full-round action.

Single (S): A single-shot weapon requires the user to manually operate the action of the firearm to chamber a round of ammunition for each new shot. This could mean manually cocking the hammer of a revolver, or operating the mechanism of a bolt-action, lever-action, or pump-action weapon. Weapons in this category may not fire multiple shots in a round, even if the attacker normally receives multiple attacks, unless the shooter has the appropriate Action Shootist feat specific to the action of the weapon.

Semi-Automatic (SA): Semi-automatic weapons can fire one bullet per attack. If the attacker has multiple attacks, and the firearm contains multiple rounds of ammunition, he can fire additional shots. Semi-automatic weapons can make use of the Rapid Shot feat and other full-attack actions and feats.

Burst-Fire (BF): Burst-fire weapons fire bursts or volleys of three bullets at a time. These weapons can use the burst

Maximum Effective Range

Maximum effective range is defined as the maximum range at which the firearm can accurately strike the target and achieve the desired effect.

There is an understandable tendency to try to derive the range increment of a given weapon using the real-world maximum effective range. Using a simple method, such as dividing the maximum effective range by 10, will yield results that are too low for handguns and far too high for longarms— pistols will be less accurate at short ranges than archaic weapons, and longarms will have such long range increments that most PCs will never see their targets on the same battle grid (or, worse yet, they'll never see their attackers). Simply put, this method doesn't deliver ranges that are balanced for play.

Using the rules presented here, however, can lead to oddities. A 9mm pistol may have a longer range increment than a 9mm submachine gun— but this does not mean that the weapon has a greater maximum effective range.

In these cases, it is important to remember the secondary definition of maximum effective range: the weapon must deliver sufficient force to disable the target.

When choosing the damage of the weapon, use the *standard linear* method for handguns and weapons with the shortest maximum effective range; this method delivers the lowest average damage.

On the other hand, those weapons with the greatest maximum effective range use the *improved **linear*** method. This method has both less variance and a higher average damage. This improved damage capability translates into greater effectiveness.

Example: The HK 9mm P9 has a muzzle velocity of 350 m/sec; range increment = 40. The 9mm MP5 has a muzzle velocity of 400 m/sec; again, range increment = 40.

However, the real-world maximum effective range of the P9 is about 50m, while the MP5 is reliable to about 100m. Both weapons are 9mm calibre; both should have a maximum damage of 10 points. To reconcile these weapons with the concept of maximum effective range, the GM assigns the P9 a damage code of d10, while the MP5 is assigned d8+2.

attack action. Weapons that are exclusively burst-fire may not fire a single bullet (unless, of course, only a single bullet remains in the magazine...)

Full-Auto (FA): Fully automatic weapons continue to fire for as long as the trigger is depressed. Fully-automatic weapons may use the autofire, strafe, and suppressing fire attack actions.

Multiple Modes: If a firearm is marked as SA/BF, BF/FA, or SA/BF/FA, it may switch between modes through the use of a selector switch. Changing the selector switch falls under the category of "Ready a Weapon" and follows all the normal rules for that combat action.

Damage

A firearm's damage potential is, by and large, governed solely by its ammunition. Use the table and the guidelines below to fix the damage for each firearm.

Determine the maximum recommended damage for the caliber of the weapon and the type of firearm (handgun or longarm).

Next, determine the damage code that yields a result closest to the recommended maximum. There are three methods for such, presented in order of increasing utility, power, and reliability:

Standard Linear: This is the most straightforward method, which entails simply choosing the single die that is closest to the maximum damage. This method produces results that range from 1 to the maximum, with an equal chance for any result.

Bell-Curve: This method requires the user to roll two dice, the sum of which total no more than the recommended maximum. Firearms with this type of damage are highly reliable, and are more likely to produce an average result than to produce a minimum or maximum result.

Improved Linear: This method requires the user to roll a single die whose maximum result is 2 less than the recommended maximum, then to add 2 to the final result. This method should be used for more powerful firearms that do not produce minimum results and are instead weighted towards the maximum.

Magnum Rounds: Any type of ammunition can be produced as a magnum load. Find the caliber as normal, add 2 to the recommended maximum damage, then determine the die type based upon the new recommended maximum.

Example: Although it would be unusual, one could create a .22 magnum handgun as follows: The recommended maximum damage for a handgun in the 20-caliber range is 6. A magnum load increases the recommended maximum by 2 points, to 8. The GM decides that this should be a particularly powerful round and decides to use the improved linear method. He chooses a d6 (within 2 points of the recommended maximum) and adjusts its damage code by +2. The final result: a .22 magnum round that does d6+2 damage.

Shotguns

Although shotguns, for a variety of reasons, are in a category to themselves, designing them is far simpler.

All shotguns are smooth-bore weapons with a standard range increment of 20 feet. The critical threat range is 20.

The magazine on a shotgun can be 1 (a single-barrel shotgun), 2 (double-barrel), 6-8 (for most pump-action shotguns), or 10 or higher (for many modern combat shotguns).

Most shotguns are single-shot (S), though a double-barrel shotgun can fire both barrels with a single attack roll. Pump-action shotguns are common, and modern combat shotguns may have burst-fire or full-auto capability.

The caliber of a shotgun is measured in units called *gauge*, which is derived from the reciprocal weight of a ball of lead which has a diameter equivalent to that of the bore. Thus a 12-gauge has the same internal diameter as a 1/12-lb ball of lead. To put it more simply, the

Table 9-1: Firearms Damage By Caliber of Ammunition

Ammunition Caliber	Recommended Maximum Damage			
	Handguns	*Example*	Longarms	*Example*
20-caliber (.22, .25, etc.)	6	d6, 2d3, d4+2	8	d8, 2d4, d6+2
30-caliber (.30, .32, .38, etc.) *5.56mm*	8	d8, 2d4, d6+2	16	2d8, 4d4
9mm	10	d10, 2d4+2, d8+2	18	2d8+2, 3d6
40-caliber (.40, .44, .45, etc.) *7.62mm*	12	d12, 2d6, d10+2	20	2d10, 5d4
50-caliber (.50 and up)	14	d12+2, 2d6+2, 3d4+2	24	2d12, 4d6

lower the gauge, the larger the bore, and the more deadly the weapon.

The damage of a shotgun is determined by the size of the bore, or gauge. However, when firing any type of dispersal ammunition (shot, flechettes, etc.) a shotgun loses 1 die of damage per range increment beyond the first.

Table 9-2: Shotguns

Caliber	Range Increment	Damage
20-gauge	20	3d4
12-gauge	20	4d4
10-gauge	20	5d4

Example: a 12-gauge shotgun does 4d4 damage in the first range increment, 3d4 in the second, 2d4 in the third, 1d4 in the fourth, and no damage at five range increments and beyond.

Additional rules for using shotguns can be found in the following section.

Firearms in Combat

When using firearms in your game, all of the following rules apply. For clarity, the term *bullet* is used below to mean a single round of ammunition, though it is not intended to restrict the definition in any way.

Attacks of Opportunity

Unlike most ranged weapons, using a firearm does not provoke an attack of opportunity (although reloading a firearm may do so). You may not use firearms to make an attack of opportunity (other than a melee attack such as a pistol-whip, bayonet attack, etc.)

Aim

You can use the Aim combat action with firearms. See Chapter Six, Combat, for details. You may both aim and brace a firearm against the same target, stacking the circumstance bonuses for each.

Autofire (FA weapons only)

Autofire is the use of a firearm's full-auto (FA) capability to focus your fire on a single target in an attempt to take him down. This does not improve your chance of hitting the target— in fact, just the opposite— but if you hit and hit well, the target will take much more damage.

If you want to use full-auto to "hose down" an area with bullets, use the Strafe action.

As a full-round action, select a number of three-round volleys (any amount up to the remaining ammunition in your weapon, as long as each volley includes three rounds of ammunition). Make a single attack roll with a -1 penalty for each volley (in addition to all normal modifiers). For every 4 full points by which your attack roll beats the targets AC, you score an additional hit, applying the weapon's normal damage plus any modifiers. You may not score more hits than the number of volleys fired. If a critical hit is scored, only the damage from the first hit is multiplied.

Critical Hits: Autofire attacks do not score critical hits as normal. If your attack roll is a critical threat (usually, a roll of natural 20), you may spend 1 action point to roll the d20 again, adding this result to the second roll. Continue rolling as long as you continue to roll a critical threat (though you need only spend 1 action point). Total all rolls, all modifiers, and check the result against the target as above. Regardless of the total roll, you cannot score more hits than the number of volleys fired.

Example: A thug gets the drop on one of our heroes and empties the clip on his weapon. The thug fires 4 three-round volleys. His attack roll is at -4. If he hits our hero, he will deal the weapon's normal damage, and for each 4 full points by which he beats the hero's AC, he'll score another hit (and another, and another). However, no matter how well he rolls, he can't score more than 4 hits, since he only fired 4 volleys.

Because autofire uses up 3 shots per volley, and you must fire at least 2 volleys, you cannot perform this action with 5 or fewer rounds of ammunition remaining in your weapon.

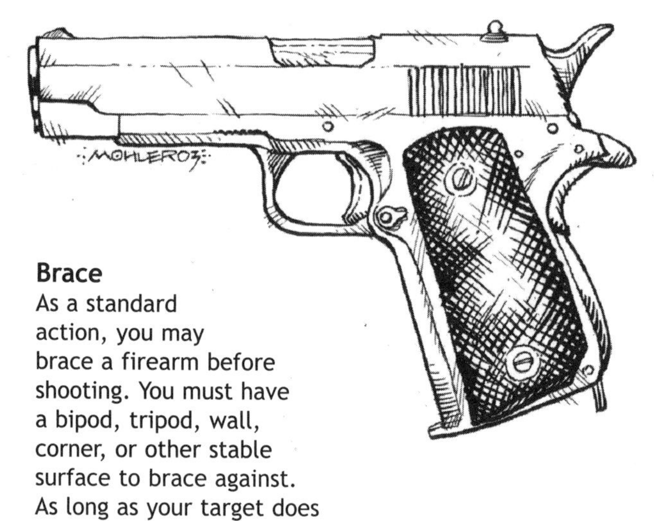

Brace

As a standard action, you may brace a firearm before shooting. You must have a bipod, tripod, wall, corner, or other stable surface to brace against. As long as your target does not move, and you do not move, lose your concentration, or do anything to disturb your weapon, you receive a +1 circumstance bonus on your next ranged attack on that target.

Provided your target does not move and you do nothing to spoil your aim, you may continue to brace your weapon using multiple standard actions, even from round to round. The bonuses stack, but your maximum bonus for bracing cannot exceed your base attack bonus.

Your bonus for bracing counts only for the first attack roll. Each attack roll beyond the first (if any) does not receive the bonus for bracing. You may brace with burst-fire, but not with auto-fire (the excessive recoil of autofire disturbs the weapon's aim.)

Example: A sniper-in-training waits patiently for her target to settle in with the evening newspaper. In the first round, she uses a move-equivalent action to aim her weapon (+1), and a standard action to brace (+1). Nervous, she continues to brace over the next five rounds (+5). However, her base attack bonus is only +3, so her total bonus for bracing cannot exceed +3. Should she ever get up the nerve to pull the trigger, her combined total for aiming and bracing is +4.

Burst-Fire (BF weapons only)

Burst-fire is the use of a weapon's burst-fire (BF) capability to fire a short spray of bullets. Burst-fire uses three bullets and can be used alternately in a narrow burst (to increase the damage against the target) or a wide burst (to increase the chances of striking the target with at least one bullet).

As a standard action, you may fire a 3-round burst. Choose either a narrow burst or a wide burst.

Narrow Burst: You receive a -3 circumstance penalty to your attack roll, but a +2 circumstance bonus to your damage.

Wide Burst: You receive a +1 circumstance bonus to your attack roll.

You may not use burst-fire if your weapon contains 2 bullets or less.

Covering Fire (SA, BF, FA weapons)

Covering fire is a hail of bullets fired towards the enemy with the sole intent of getting him to keep his head down long enough for your allies to escape, move into position, reload, etc.

As a full round action, choose a single target within range that you are aware of. Until the start of your next action, this target receives a -4 penalty to hit against any of your allies within your line of sight. Each additional character providing covering fire against the same target imposes only a -1 penalty.

The target may make a Concentration check (DC15) to reduce the penalty by one-half (round down).

Covering fire requires the expenditure of three bullets.

Special: Single-shot (S) weapons can provide covering fire provided there are enough allies to expend at least three rounds of ammunition. Every three allies armed with single-shot weapons and working in concert to provide covering fire act as a single semi-automatic shooter.

Example: A team of seven musketeers stand and fire a volley to provide covering fire for their swashbuckling ally. The first three musketeers count as a single character (imposing a -4 penalty) and the second three musketeers count as a second character (additional -1). The 7th musketeer can not provide the necessary three shots for covering fire, so he has no effect.

You cannot use covering fire against an opponent who is in melee combat nor provide covering fire to an ally who is in melee combat.

Ready a Weapon

Similar to drawing a melee weapon, you can use the Ready a Weapon action to draw or holster a firearm; to change the selector switch on a SA/BF/FA weapon; to engage/disengage the choke on a shotgun, or to engage/disengage the safety on a firearm. You may Ready a Weapon as a move-action or, if your base attack is +1 or higher, as a free action as part of movement.

Reload

Regardless of type, any reloading action requires two hands, and provokes attacks of opportunity.

Muzzle-loaders: Reloading a muzzle-loader is a full round action, and requires the Exotic Weapon Proficiency: Muzzle-loaders in order to even attempt a reload.

Cartridges: Reloading a single round of cartridge ammunition is a move-equivalent action. Completely reloading a revolver or a firearm with an internal magazine (such as a pump-action shotgun) is a full-round action.

Automatic: Reloading a firearm with an already-filled clip or box magazine is a move-equivalent action. Reloading a belt-fed weapon is a full-round action. To load individual cartridges into a clip or box magazine, use the rules above for cartridges.

Shotguns

The following special weapons govern the use of shotguns in combat:

Spread: As noted above, shotguns loaded with pellet ammunition lose 1 die of damage per range increment beyond the first as the pellets disperse.

The wide dispersal of shot has its benefits, however. A shotgun loaded with pellets has an area of effect in the first range increment equal to a single 5-foot square. Targets fully within the area of effect of this spread do not receive Dex, Defense, or dodge bonuses against the shotgun blast.

Shotguns affect an additional 5-foot square per range increment (two squares in the second range increment, three squares in the third range increment, etc.). The area of effect of multiple squares is always a straight line perpendicular to the shooter. As above, targets within the

spread do not receive Dex, Defense, or dodge bonuses against the shotgun blast.

As with Strafe, below, obstacles or intervening targets between the shooter and the spread provide cover to the target(s) beyond.

Choke: If you wish to complicate your game somewhat, you can allow the user of a shotgun to switch the barrel to *full choke*, which will narrow the dispersal of shot and add 50% to the range increment, bringing it to 30.

If the shotgun is fitted with solid ammunition, you cannot use the choke in this fashion. Setting the choke falls under the category of "Ready a Weapon" and follows all the normal rules for that combat action.

Strafe (FA weapons only)

Strafing is the use of a fully-automatic weapon to spray or "hose down" a wide area of effect.

As a full action, you may fire a 3-shot volley into any number of adjacent 5-foot squares. You may target a number of squares up to one-third the remaining ammunition in your weapon, but you must put at least 3 bullets into each square. You must have line of sight to each square and you cannot choose squares that are in front of each other.

After selecting the target squares, make a single attack roll with a -2 penalty for each square beyond the first. Compare the result of your attack roll to the AC of each target within the area you have targeted, assigning hits and misses as normal. Make a single damage roll for the weapon and apply the damage to every target that was hit.

Objects between the attacker and any target square provide cover. As with all ranged attacks, if the shot misses but is within the cover bonus, the cover is struck instead.

Suppressing Fire (FA weapons only)

Suppressing fire uses the full-auto capability of a weapon to test the morale of multiple opponents and force them to grab cover.

As a full-action, you may fire a 3-shot volley into any number of adjacent 5-foot squares. You may target a number of squares up to one-third the remaining ammo in your weapon, but you must put at least 3 bullets into each square. You must have line of sight to each square and you cannot choose squares that are in front of each other.

Until the start of your next action, any target within the affected squares suffers a -4 penalty to hit against any of your allies within your line of sight. Suppressing fire stacks with covering fire and with additional suppressing fire.

As with covering fire, the targets may make a Concentration check (DC15) to reduce the penalty by one-half (round down).

You cannot use suppressing fire against an opponent who is in melee combat nor provide suppressing fire coverage to an ally who is in melee combat.

Firearms Equipment

Bipod/Tripod

You may mount a bipod or tripod to most longarms. You may use a bipod or tripod to brace.

Flash Suppressor

A flash suppressor is used to reduce the muzzle flash of a firearm. Opponents receive a -4 penalty to Spot checks when trying to locate you by sight.

Optical Sights

When using optical sights and taking the aim action, all range penalties are halved.

Laser Sight

Laser sights are often mounted to handguns and sub machine guns. Laser sights grant a +2 circumstance bonus to hit at point blank range (30 feet or less).

Silencer

A silencer may be added to any handgun or longarm, but not shotguns. A silencer works with only a specific make and model of firearm. Opponents suffer a -4 penalty to Listen checks when trying to locate a weapon that is fired while silenced.

Alternate Ammunition

The damages listed for firearms assume standard ammunition. However, the GM may wish to allow characters to use the non-standard ammunition types described below.

Armor-Piercing (AP)
This ammunition is designed to pierce armored targets. Unfortunately, because of the bullet's tendency to pass through the target, its damage potential is compromised.

Effect: AP ammo is -2 to damage, but against opponents with an armor, natural armor, or shield bonus, it is +2 to hit.

Bean-bag/Baton
Shotguns may be armed with bean-bag or baton rounds. This ammunition is designed for crowd control.

Effect: This solid ammunition converts the shotgun's damage to *non-lethal* damage. These rounds must be loaded one at a time, restricting the shotgun to single-shot (S) action.

Flechette
This shotgun round is a shell filled with many sharp, tiny metal darts, improving armor-piercing ability at the cost of range.

Effect: The shotgun gains +2 to hit, but the range increment is halved.

Jacketed Hollow Point (JHP)
This ammunition is designed to expand upon contact with the target. This reduces the bullet's ability to penetrate armor but improves its damage potential.

Effect: JHP ammo adds +2 to damage, but is -2 to hit against opponents with an armor, natural armor, or shield bonus.

Slug
Shotguns shells may be filled with a single, solid slug instead of pellets of shot.

Effect: The shotgun loses the ability to target an area. Each shot must be applied against the AC of the target, as with any other firearm. However, because there is no dispersal, the shotgun does not lose damage with successive range increments.

Tracer
This ammunition is generally only available for longarms. Tracer rounds have a phosphorous tip that ignites and glows green when the bullet is fired, enabling the shooter to see where each shot is aimed and adjust accordingly.

Effect: Beginning on the second round of combat, a weapon equipped with tracer ammunition adds +1 to hit.

Horror & Insanity

Using Horror In Your Campaign

Many game systems use Horror as a primary component of the rules, but in many respects, the mere presence of any ruleset to govern horror ends up detracting from the mood of the game. Building suspense, dread, and a fear of the unknown that slowly escalates to a true sense of horror relies first and foremost on the storytelling skills of the GM.

Creating the Horrific Encounter

The first step for the GM is to place a horrific encounter in his adventure. The GM is well served to consider that every Horror check is like an encounter in its own right—or, at the very least, it can serve as the crowning detail of a session of play. Too-frequent Horror checks acclimate the players to the system and spoil the mood you are trying to create. One or at most two Horror checks in one session of play is acceptable; one or two Horror checks per *adventure* is even better.

It is not a necessity that you save the Horror check for the final conflict with the horrific arch-villain; indeed, a horrific encounter early in the adventure will help set the mood—particularly if the encounter goes poorly for the PCs as a result of the Horror check!

In order to use the rules for Horror checks, the GM must calculate the normal EL of the encounter ahead of time. In some cases this will be fairly straightforward: a group of ten zombies attack the PCs, for example. Other cases can get more complex: A vampire overlord captures the PCs in a trap-filled torture room and watches as his zombie minions close in for a grim feast. Despite these complexities, the underlying rule is simple: As the EL increases, it is assumed that the danger, and thus the horror, increases.

The Horror Check

The GM can require a Horror check at any point, most generally immediately after he describes the encounter and the horror of the situation is finally revealed to the players. From there, the Horror check uses a set of rules that is essentially analogous to the Turn Undead rules:

1. The GM calls for a Horror check. (If using the *Fight or Flight!* optional rules—see sidebar—the GM should call for decisions now.)
2. Each PC makes a Horror check by rolling d20 and applying the appropriate modifiers to Table 10-1.
3. The GM rolls the Horror Threshold level for the encounter (usually 2d6 + applicable modifiers from Table 10-2 and 10-3).
4. The GM compares the result of each PC's Horror check to the appropriate Encounter Level column on Table 1 (see below).
5. If the Horror Threshold is equal to or greater than the PCs Charisma, that PC suffers the effects listed on the table.

Table 10-1: The Horror Check Roll

Check Result	Effect
1-2	long term insanity
3-4	short term insanity
5-6	cowering / temporary insanity[1]
7-8	panicked / frightened[1]
9-10	frightened / berserk[1]
11-14	shaken
15-19	dazed
20 or more (or natural 20)	no effect

1 Use the entry before the slash if the party EL is lower than the horrific encounter EL. Use the number after the slash if the party EL is higher than the horrific encounter EL.

Optional Rule: *Fight! or Flight?*

This optional rule can be used to add even more uncertainty to the Horror check. After the GM calls for the Horror check, each player is given a simple choice: Fight or Flight?

If the player chooses *Fight*, he elects to leave his PC in the path of danger and take his chances with the results of the Horror check. If the PC is confident of his ability to master his fear (and to roll accordingly), this is the best choice to immediately come to grips with the horrific enemy.

If the PC chooses *Flight*, he voluntarily "fails" his Horror check and is *frightened*, fleeing for a reduced duration of 1d4+1 rounds. However, at the end of this voluntary flight, the PC fully recovers his wits (and his guts) and can return to the fight without the need for any check and without any further hindrance—he does not even suffer the normal *shaken* effects.

However, to heighten the tension and add even greater uncertainty to the process, the GM should require each player to register his choice ***secretly***—no player can be sure of what the other players are going to do!

Each player takes a d6 and, covering it with his hand to obscure his choice from his fellow players, chooses one facing of the die to place face up: a bold and daring 6 (or any even number) if he chooses to *Fight*, or a wee, pathetic 1 (or any odd number) if he chooses *Flight*. After all players are ready, the GM should have them reveal their choices at the same time.

Like the Horror check itself, the GM should resist overusing the *Fight or Flight!* option in order to keep it fresh and exciting. At any rate, if the players consistently make the same choice as a group, perhaps even working out a scheme ahead of time to ensure that the group acts in concert, he should abandon the use of this optional rule in order to avoid the foregone conclusion and speed gameplay.

Horror Check Modifiers

Each PC makes a Horror check by rolling 1d20 and applying the following modifiers:

- Add the character (or party) EL.
- Subtract the encounter EL.

If the characters are higher level than the horrific threat, the effects of a Horror check, even a failed check, are lessened.

Each PC should also add a bonus to his or her check to represent will power and guts.

- Add a Will or Wisdom bonus as described below.

In a game with a moderate threat level, this Horror check modifier is equal to the character's Wisdom bonus. However, the GM can tweak the rules to be more or less forgiving, depending on the impact that Horror should have on the campaign. Because of the possibility that one or more PCs will hesitate, panic, or cower, the higher the threat, the more likely that Horror checks will disrupt the party and derail their efforts.

☠: Each player adds his Will save modifier to all Horror checks. In this variant, high Wisdom, high level characters become more and more resistant to the effects of Horror.

☠☠: Each player adds his Wisdom modifier to all Horror checks. In this variant, high Wisdom characters (which includes most Dedicated heroes) have an advantage, but an increase in level does not make the character any more resistant to horror than normal.

☠☠☠: Players do not add any modifier to the d20 roll. In this variant, high Charisma characters tend to be the most resistant to Horror checks, due to their higher Horror Threshold. When these characters *do* fail a Horror check, the result can be devastating.

Modifiers to the Horror Threshold

The Horror Threshold roll is always modified by the Charisma modifier (if positive) of the horrifying creature. In mixed groups of creatures, use the modifier of the creature with the highest Charisma—usually, but not always, this will be the leader of a mixed group (such as a vampire at the head of a horde of zombies).

The GM should always make a note of the total after rolling the Horror Threshold; in the event that one of the PCs succumbs to a short-term or long-term psychological disorder, the Horror Threshold not only defines the extent of the horrific event, it will define the DC required to cure the PC of any disorder.

Table 10-2: Standard Horror Threshold Modifiers

Condition	*Modifier*
First time the PCs have encountered this type of foe	+2
PCs have defeated this type of foe before	-2
PCs have defeated this specific foe before	-1
Particularly horrific scene (excessive gore, violent outburst, etc.)	+1
Personal significance (presence of a loved one, etc.)	+1

The standard Horror Threshold modifiers are applied on a case-by-case basis to each PC before comparing the adjusted total to the PC's Charisma score.

In addition to the standard Horror Threshold modifiers, the GM may wish to add or subtract dice for certain creature types in order to reflect the prevailing philosophy of his campaign. For example, in an Archaic setting of barbaric sword-and-sorcery, the GM may decide that Aberrations are no more horrific than any other beast—the people of this campaign espouse a particularly pragmatic, "If it bleeds, I can kill it," philosophy that is uncommon in more civilized ages. However, in such a primitive campaign—indeed, in any humanocentric campaign where the dead are expected to *stay* dead— Undead creatures may very well impose a +1d6 modifier. Similarly, in an apocalyptic setting, the GM may decide that Constructs and mutated Aberrations alike suffer a -1d6 penalty to all Horror Threshold rolls, as the inhabitants of such a world are well-accustomed to berserk killing machines and tentacled mutants.

The guidelines below should suit most campaigns falling into the three main settings of *Grim Tales*:

Table 10-3: Era-specific Horror Threshold Modifiers

Creature Type	*Archaic*	*Modern*	*Apocalyptic*
Aberration	-	+1d6	-1d6
Animal	-[1]	-	-
Construct	-	+1d6	-1d6
Dragon[2]	+1d6	+1d6	+1d6
Elemental	-	-	-
Fey	+1d6	-	-
Giant	-	-	-
Humanoid/ Monstrous Humanoid	-	-	-
Magical Beast	-	+1d6	+1d6[3]
Ooze	+1d6	+1d6	-
Outsider[4]	+1d6	+1d6	+1d6
Plant	-[1]	-	-
Undead[5]	+1d6	+1d6	+1d6
Vermin[6]	-[1]	-	-1d6

1 In some prehistoric Archaic settings, dire animals, dinosaurs, carnivorous plants, and many large vermin, though commonly encountered, may carry a +1d6 modifier: such instinctive fears are not easily shaken, and in some cases primitive man is more frightened of known dangers than of the unknown.
2 Dragons are fearsome creatures in any era. The Horror check is made over and above any check for the dragon's *frightful presence*, which follow the rules as normal.
3 It is important to note the difference between mutant creatures (most of which are Aberrations) and Magical Beasts, which display some clearly magical or supernatural ability. If the viewers reasonably mistake the Magical Beast for an Aberration, do not apply this modifier.
4 Outsiders, both good and evil, are awe-inspiring in any era.
5 Undead apply a +1d6 modifier in any era.
6 Normal-sized Vermin should not normally require a Horror check of any kind, unless appearing in a swarm of significantly horrific size.

Explanation of Horror Check Results

No Effect: The PC may act normally.

Dazed: The PC is *dazed* until the end of his first action, but may act normally thereafter.

Shaken: The PC is *shaken* for the duration of the encounter. A *shaken* character takes a -2 penalty on attack rolls, saving throws, skill checks, and ability checks.

Frightened: The PC is *frightened* for 1d6+1 rounds. A frightened character flees from the source of fear as best he can. If unable to flee, he may fight. A *frightened* character takes a -2 penalty on all attack rolls, saving throws, skill checks, and ability checks. A *frightened* character can use special abilities, including spells, to flee; indeed, he must use such means if they are the only way to escape. When the *frightened* state ends, the character can act normally, but he remains *shaken* for the duration of the encounter.

Berserk: The PC goes *berserk* for 1d6+1 rounds. He fights with wild ferocity, unable to tell friend from foe, using whatever weapon is in hand against the nearest foe.

If there is a target within melee reach of the *berserk* PC, he must use a full attack action against that target. (If there are two or more targets within reach, the PC may choose).

If there are no targets within reach, and the PC has a ranged weapon in hand, he may use that weapon against the nearest target.

If there are no targets within melee reach and the PC does not have a ready ranged weapon, he must move towards the nearest target, charging if possible, and using a double-move if not.

In essence, the only actions a *berserk* PC may take is an attack, a full attack, or a move. They may not perform special attack actions, draw or ready a weapon, use skills, cast spells, etc.

Panicked: The PC is *panicked* for 1d6+1 rounds. A *panicked* character immediately drops anything held in his hands and must flee at top speed from the source of his fear, as well as any other dangers he encounters, along a random path. He can't take any other actions. In addition, the character takes a -2 penalty on all saving throws, skill checks, and ability checks. If cornered, a *panicked* character does not fight, typically using the total defense action in combat. A *panicked* character can use special abilities, including spells, to flee; indeed, he must use such means if they are the only way to escape. When the *panicked* state ends, the character can act normally, but he remains *shaken* for the duration of the encounter.

Cowering: The PC *cowers* for 1d6+1 rounds. The character is frozen in fear and can take no actions. A *cowering* character takes a -2 penalty to Armor Class and loses his Dexterity bonus (if any). When the *cowering* state ends, the character can act normally, but he remains *shaken* for the duration of the encounter.

An ally may use the Aid Another action (shaking, slapping, urging, etc.) to allow a cowering character a second Horror check. He must accept the result of the second check.

Temporary Insanity: Until the end of the current horrific encounter, the PC suffers the effects of one of the psychological disorders below (see *Insanity* in the following section). If the character is already suffering from any form of insanity, his existing condition worsens and he suffers an immediate outburst (if applicable).

Short Term: The PC *cowers* for the duration of the encounter. In addition, once the encounter is over, he suffers the effects of short-term insanity (see *Insanity* in the following section).

Long Term: The PC *cowers* for the duration of the encounter. In addition, once the encounter is over, he suffers the effects of long-term insanity (see *Insanity* in the following section).

Insanity

Characters who spectacularly fail a Horror check often succumb to short-term or long-term insanity. The GM should prepare himself for cries of outrage from his players; many players feel that some of the crippling disorders that follow are too harsh; many players would rather their characters die than succumb to insanity. The GM is encouraged to humor such requests. A failed Horror check is akin to any other failed saving throw, and a player who refuses to explore the roleplaying opportunities presented by an insane character is free to create a new character.

Duration of Insanity

Depending on the Horror check, insanity is either short-term or long-term. There is leeway within these definitions, depending on the threat level of the campaign:

Short-Term

☠ The effects of insanity last until the end of the current session of play. When the GM and the players next meet to continue the campaign, the character may make a Will save to recover fully (see Self-Recovery in the Treatment section below).

☠☠ The effects last until the end of the current adventure, at which time the character may make a Will save to recover fully. If the adventure is of epic-length, the effects last until the next natural break in the adventure.

☠☠☠ The effects last until the character gains a level, at which point he may make a Will save to recover fully. In the process of leveling up, the character is assumed to shake off the effects of the insanity.

Long-Term

Long-term insanity is just short of permanent, lasting until the patient is cured. The character will never recover normally, but he may be able to recover through psychotherapy, surgery, or magical healing (if such is available in the campaign).

Severity

The severity of insanity is equal to the Horror Threshold roll. The player should record the severity of any insanity in addition to its effects.

High-Charisma characters are less likely to succumb to Horror (requiring a higher Horror Threshold) but, conversely, they are more likely to suffer severe psychological disorders. In effect, their own force of personality works against them. The greater a character's force of personality, the greater the depths of insanity to which they can sink.

Even relatively mild disorders can have a high severity— those annoying but persistent peccadilloes of the charismatic elite.

Example:
A character (Charisma 13) is forced to make a Horror check. The GM rolls the Horror Threshold and the result is a 16— enough to affect the character. The character fails his Horror check, and the Horror table shows that he is afflicted with a long-term insanity.

The GM determines the insanity and the player records it on his character sheet. He also lists the severity of the insanity: 16, equal to the Horror Threshold. When this character later tries to recover from insanity, the severity (16) will set the DC for the various treatments available.

Treatment

Depending on the campaign, various forms of treatment are available. If the campaign uses the Horror rules, the GM should ensure that, no matter the flavor or setting of his campaign, some form of treatment is available.

Self-Recovery

Time heals all wounds, and a character with enough time to reflect and recover may make a Will save to shake off the effects of a short-term insanity. The DC for the save is equal to the severity (i.e., the Horror Threshold of the Horrific encounter that pushed him over the brink).

A character with Heal, Diplomacy, or Profession (psychotherapist, psychologist, etc.) can Aid Another with this check. The assisting character's check DC is 10, and it provides the usual +2 bonus to the afflicted character's Will save.

A character who fails this save does not recover. He may check again after the designated duration (the end of the next encounter, adventure, or after gaining a level).

A character who rolls a natural 1 on this save actually worsens his condition, and suffers the effects of Advancing Insanity (see below).

Self-recovery is not possible with long-term insanity.

Psychotherapy

A character with Profession (psychotherapist, psychologist, psychiatrist, etc.) can attempt to treat both short- and long-term insanity. The DC for this check is equal to 10 + severity.

A character with 5 or more ranks of Craft (alchemy) or Craft (pharmaceutical) can prescribe drugs or "herbal remedies" to accompany the therapy, and receives a +2 synergy bonus to his Profession check.

A character with 5 or more ranks of Diplomacy and/or Sense Motive receives a +2 synergy bonus to his Profession check (a total possible synergy bonus of +4 for both skills).

If the check succeeds, the afflicted character's insanity is cured (if mild) or reduced (if moderate or severe).

If the skill check fails, the afflicted character does not recover. If the skill check is a critical failure, the afflicted character's condition worsens (see below).

Surgery and Physical "Therapy"

Lobotomization, electro-shock therapy, experimental drugs, and even, in less advanced societies, trepanation (the drilling of holes in the skull to "let the evil spirits out")— these methods are crude and widely discredited in the real world.

Fortunately, in the world of Grim Tales there is a place for such colorful and characterful "cures."

A character with the Heal skill (and the Surgery feat) can attempt such a physical cure for insanity. The DC for this check is 15 + severity.

A character with 5 or more ranks of Craft (alchemy) or Craft (pharmaceutical) can prescribe herbs or drugs to assist the treatment, gaining a +2 synergy bonus.

- If the skill check succeeds, the afflicted character is cured of his insanity.
- If this skill check fails, the afflicted character must make a save vs. massive damage, or he begins *dying*.
- If the skill check is a critical failure, the afflicted character immediately begins *dying*. If he recovers, his mental condition also worsens (see Advancing Insanity, below).

Magic

If the campaign allows spellcasting, there are spells (such as *heal*) that instantly cure any and all insanity that a character may be suffering from. At the GM's discretion, insane characters may not admit that they are insane, and may be entitled to a saving throw against any magical cure.

Advancing Insanity

As bad as insanity seems, there's always room for it to get worse.

The effects of insanity are categorized as mild, moderate, and severe. Characters suffering from insanity begin with the effects listed in the mild entry within each description.

However, each of the psychological disorders can progress, the effects worsening with each step, and each effect is generally cumulative with the step before.

There are two ways that an afflicted character's insanity can advance:

- If the character fails another Horror check while already afflicted, the GM can advance his existing condition rather than inflict a new one;
- If the character attempts to recover (either through self-recovery or treatment) and fails.

An existing condition can grow so severe that it advances to another form of insanity. In these cases, advance the condition to the mild stage of the next disorder.

Forms of Insanity

The following psychological disorders, herein classified as insanity, are more properly known as psychological disorders. The GM should choose an appropriate disorder for the character, based on the type of horrific encounter that sent him over the edge.

Table 10-4: Insanities	
Short Term	Long Term
Anxiety Disorders	
General Anxiety	Agoraphobia
Acute Stress Disorder	Obsessive-Compuslive
	Panic Disorder
	Phobias
	Post-Traumatic Stress
Dissociative Disorders	
Depersonalization	Dissociative Fugue
Dissociative Amnesia	
Impusle Control Disorders	
Addiction/Dependence	Addiction/Dependence
	Intermittent Explosive
	Kleptomania/Pyromania/ Trichotillomania
Mood Disorders	
Depression (mild)	Manic Depressive
	Depression (moderate or severe)
Psychotic Disorders	
Brief Psychotic	Delusional
	Schizophrenia
Personality Disorders	
Dependent	Antisocial
Histrionic	Borderline
Paranoid	Schizoid
Sleep Disorders	
Dyssomnia	Hypersomnia
Sleep Terrors	Insomnia
Parasomnia	Narcolepsy
	Sleepwalking
Childhood Disorders	
Selective Mutism	
Stuttering/Tics	

Anxiety Disorders

This category includes a number of disorders featuring abnormal or inappropriate anxiety. An increased heart rate, tensed muscles, and an acute sense of focus are all symptoms of anxiety. They are also part of the body's natural 'fight or flight' phenomenon. While a healthy dose of anxiety is good for any hero, these symptoms become a problem when they occur without reason or when the situation does not warrant such a reaction.

Acute Stress Disorder

This disorder is triggered by a traumatic event involving death or serious injury. The afflicted continue to re-experience the event through thoughts, dreams, or flashbacks, and avoid situations that remind them of the initial traumatic event.

- Mild: If any effect causes the character to become shaken, he suffers the effects of fear instead; fear effects cause panic; and panic causes cowering.
- Moderate: Any encounter that includes combat forces the character to make a Horror check.
- Severe: Advance to Post-Traumatic Stress Disorder.

Agoraphobia

Agoraphobia is the fear of being in places where escape might be difficult or help is not available. Those with agoraphobia avoid most places outside of their known and secure environment including open spaces, driving a vehicle, standing in lines, walking through crowds, and going through tunnels. Being forced to endure these situations often results in physical symptoms of distress.

- Mild: Character is shaken while in uncomfortable environments.
- Moderate: -2 penalty to all Horror checks.
- Severe: Additional -2 penalty to all Horror checks.

General Anxiety Disorder

This disorder is marked by constant, exaggerated anxiety, though there is little or nothing to provoke it. The symptoms may be accompanied by fatigue, headaches, muscle tension and aches, trembling and irritability.

- Mild: +2 bonus to initiative, Spot, and Listen checks
- Moderate: Anytime the GM calls for a Horror check, the character must make a Will save (DC = severity) or become sickened.
- Severe: Advance to Panic Disorder.

Obsessive-Compulsive Disorder

Those with this disorder have difficulty showing warm and tender emotions, display perfectionism and an inability to see the larger picture, and have difficulty doing things in any way but their own. Everything must be just right, and nothing can be left to chance.

- Mild: -2 penalty to initiative.
- Moderate: Double the time required for all skill checks.
- Severe: -2 penalty to all Charisma-based skill checks.

Panic Disorder

Those afflicted with this disorder experience unexpected panic attacks, including the sudden onset of chest pain, choking sensations, and dizziness. Those experiencing a panic attack often experiences a crescendo of fear that results in a sudden exit from wherever he may be.

- Mild: Each time any player rolls a 1 on a d20 check during play, the afflicted character is shaken for 3d6 minutes.
- Moderate: As above, but the character is frightened for 1d6 rounds, and is shaken for 3d6 minutes afterwards.

- Severe: As above, but the character is panicked for 1d6 rounds, and is shaken for 3d6 minutes afterwards.

Phobias (Specific)

Traumatic events often trigger a specific phobia. Symptoms include extreme anxiety and fear associated with the object or situation of their phobia. The GM can choose from any number of real-world phobias, though a phobia associated with the initial Horror check is best. For example, a character who fails a Horror check in an encounter with a giant spider might well develop arachnophobia.

- Mild: The character is shaken in the presence of her phobia.
- Moderate: As above, but the character is affected by fear for 1d6 rounds, and is shaken for 3d6 minutes afterwards.
- Severe: As above, but the character is panicked for 1d6 rounds, and is shaken for 3d6 minutes afterwards.

Post Traumatic Stress Disorder

This disorder is the result of a severe and extraordinary trauma, either environmental (a large fire, hurricane) or violent (war, murder, rape, etc.) There may be dramatic outbursts of fear or aggression, triggered by a sudden recollection and/or re-enactment of the original event.

- Mild: +2 bonus to all initiative checks.
- Moderate: At the beginning of any combat, the character must make a Will save (DC = severity) or go berserk until the end of the encounter.
- Severe: Advance to Dissociative Fugue or Psychosis.

Dissociative Disorders

Dissociative disorders are a survival technique that allow individuals enduring "hopeless" circumstances to maintain some ability to function. During a traumatic experience, a person may dissociate the details of the trauma from his ongoing memory, resulting in a temporary mental escape from the trauma. Unfortunately, in some cases, this leads to a memory gap surrounding the experience.

Depersonalization Disorder

Depersonalization disorder is a feeling of detachment from oneself, a sense of "looking at yourself from the outside." The afflicted observes his own physical actions or mental processes as if he were an observer, leading to a feeling that he is not in control of his own actions.

- Mild: -2 to Listen, Spot, and initiative.
- Moderate: The character may make only a single standard action or move action each round.
- Severe: Advance to Dissociative Fugue.

Dissociative Amnesia

A person with dissociative amnesia is unable to remember personal information. They are aware that they have forgotten something, but do not know what it is. While they are able to perform simple tasks, they usually are unable to perform more complex ones.

- Mild: The character receives no XP for the encounter that caused this insanity. At his discretion, the GM may award this XP after the insanity is cured.
- Moderate: The afflicted character may make skill checks only with skills that may be used untrained.
- Severe: Advance to Dissociative Fugue.

Dissociative Fugue

A person in a dissociative fugue adopts a new identity. This disorder is generally caused by a severe stressor and the fugue is usually limited to a few days, but may last up to months. When the fugue ends, the person is unable to recall what occurred during this state.

- Mild: The afflicted character may make skill checks only with skills that may be used untrained.
- Moderate: As above, and the character may not add any skill ranks gained before the dissociative fugue. Until he recovers, the character may add only his base attribute modifier, plus any ranks gained by his "new identity" during the fugue. The GM may allow the character to choose new core skills for the duration of the fugue.
- Severe: As above, and the new identity develops an additional disorder of its own. If the character is cured of the dissociative fugue, he is cured of this additional disorder as well.

Impulse Control Disorders

Disorders in this category include extreme difficulty in controlling impulses despite an awareness of their negative consequences.

General Addiction/Dependence

(Alcohol, Drugs, Food, Gambling, Sex, etc.)

Characters with an addiction or dependence show the following signs: a tolerance for the addictive substance (needing increased amounts to achieve the same effect); withdrawal symptoms; taking larger amounts than are intended for a longer period of time than is intended; spending a great deal of time attempting to acquire the addictive substance; and finally, continuing to abuse the substance even though the person knows there are negative consequences caused by the addiction.

- Mild: The character suffers a -4 penalty to Will saving throws with regard to the addiction, and gains a +4 bonus to applicable Fortitude saves.
- Moderate: The character automatically fails Will saving throws with regard to the addictive substance.
- Severe: The continuing effects of addiction leave the character sickened until cured.

Intermittent Explosive Disorder

The afflicted character suffers from episodes of violence that begin unexpectedly, with little or no provocation, and end just as abruptly. After the violent act, however, they do display remorse and generally assume responsibility.

- Mild: At the beginning of any encounter, the character must make a Will save (DC = severity) or rage until the end of the encounter. At the end of the encounter, the character is fatigued.
- Moderate: As above, but the character goes berserk.
- Severe: As above, and the character gains no XP for any encounter during which he goes berserk.

Kleptomania/Pyromania/Trichotillomania

Kleptomania is the impulse to steal objects even when they are not needed. The afflicted feel a release of tension after stealing an object. Generally, their sole goal is to relieve the mounting tension.

Pyromania, like other impulse control disorders, shows a release of tension when the person sets a fire. They cannot resist setting fires, and get gratification from watching them. They do not feel remorse or regret for the aftermath, from destruction of property to death. Unlike other impulse control disorders, they may plan their arson in advance, which also brings them pleasure.

Trichotillomania is the irresistible urge to pull one's hair. Resisting the impulse builds tension, and pulling the hair relieves the tension. The hair may be rubbed around the mouth, licked or even eaten.

- Mild: Each time any player rolls a 1 on a d20 during play, the character's impulse begins anew. Until the character satisfies her impulse, she suffers a cumulative -1 penalty to all skill checks, saving throws, and attack rolls. Once the impulse is satisfied, all penalties are removed.
- Moderate: As above, but the character can only lessen the penalty by 1 for each time the impulse is satisfied (instead of removing all penalties).
- Severe: As above, but the character suffers a -2 penalty each time the impulse begins. Satisfying the impulse lessens the penalty by only 1 each time. (In effect, the character must satisfy the impulse twice as often.)

Mood Disorders

The primary symptom of these disorders is a disturbance in mood: inappropriate, exaggerated, or limited range of feelings. These feelings are extreme, such as crying, and frequently feeling depressed or suicidal; or, the opposite extreme, such as excessive energy without sleeping for days at a time, during which time the decision making ability is significantly impaired.

Depression

In typical depressive episodes of all three varieties described below (mild, moderate, and severe), the individual usually suffers from depressed mood, loss of interest and enjoyment, reduced energy, and commensurate fatigue and diminished activity. Marked tiredness after only slight effort is common.

- Mild: -2 penalty to Concentration, Listen, Spot, and Sense Motive.
- Moderate: The character is fatigued at all times, and gains only 2/3 of the benefit of sleep (i.e., he requires 12 hours of sleep to gain the benefits of 8 hours).
- Severe: The character begins to feel suicidal. If the character suffers any fear effect, he goes berserk instead, focusing his attention solely on the most dangerous source of fear.

Manic Depressive

Manic depression causes mood swings in which the afflicted character cycles from depression to mania. Depression is described above; mania is characterized by a decreased need for sleep, decreased self-control, irritability, rage, risk-taking behaviors, and in severe cases psychotic states.

- Mild: Each time the afflicted character rolls a 1 on a d20 check during play, his mood switches from depression to mania or vice versa. When the character is in a manic state, he receives +2 to initiative, +2 to all Charisma-based skill checks, and needs only half as much sleep as normal. When the character is depressed, he suffers the effects of mild depression (see below).
- Moderate: As above, but the effects are more pronounced. When the character is manic, he automatically fails any non-combat saving throw or d20 check related to Willpower. When the character is depressed, he suffers the effects of moderate depression (below).
- Severe: Advance to Psychosis.

Psychotic Disorders

Psychosis involves severe delusions and hallucinations that significantly hinder a person's ability to function (for example, believing that the GM is out to get you, when there is no evidence of it). Hallucinations are false perceptions, including visual (seeing things that aren't there), auditory (hearing), olfactory (smelling), tactile (feeling sensations on your skin that aren't really there, such as the feeling of bugs crawling on you), or taste.

Of all of the insanities presented here, psychotic disorders are the most interesting and the most challenging to roleplay.

Brief Psychotic Disorder

This psychosis has a rapid onset following a major trauma. The afflicted shows symptoms such as delusions, hallucinations, grossly disorganized or catatonic behavior, or disorganized speech.

- Mild: -2 penalty to Concentration, Listen, Spot, Sense Motive, and all Charisma-based checks.
- Moderate: Each time any player rolls a 1 on a d20 during play, the afflicted character becomes confused. This state lasts until the end of the current encounter or scene.
- Severe: As above, but instead of confusion, the character falls into a delusional stupor and is helpless for 1d6 hours.

Delusional Disorder
The afflicted character has a "non-bizzare" delusion- that is, a delusion that could actually occur. Examples are erotomania (the belief that a person of higher status is in love with you); grandiose (in which the afflicted has delusions of inflated self-worth or power); persecutory (in which the afflicted believes they are being mistreated); somatic (where the afflicted believes they have a physical problem, defect, or illness); or a mixture of any of the previous types.

- Mild: The character loses a previous allegiance and adds an allegiance appropriate to their disorder: a love interest, personal power, wealth, etc.
- Moderate: As above. Any time the character's delusion is questioned, challenged, or called into question (intentionally or otherwise), he must make a Will save (DC = severity) or go berserk.
- Severe: Advance to Schizophrenia.

Schizophrenia
Schizophrenia is akin to the Delusional Disorder, but is more severe in that the delusions are more bizarre: hallucinatory voices giving a running commentary on the character's actions; persistent, inappropriate or impossible delusions, such as religious or political identity; or superhuman powers and abilities (such as being able to control the weather, or being in communication with aliens from another world). In extreme cases, catatonic behavior, mutism, and stupor may occur.

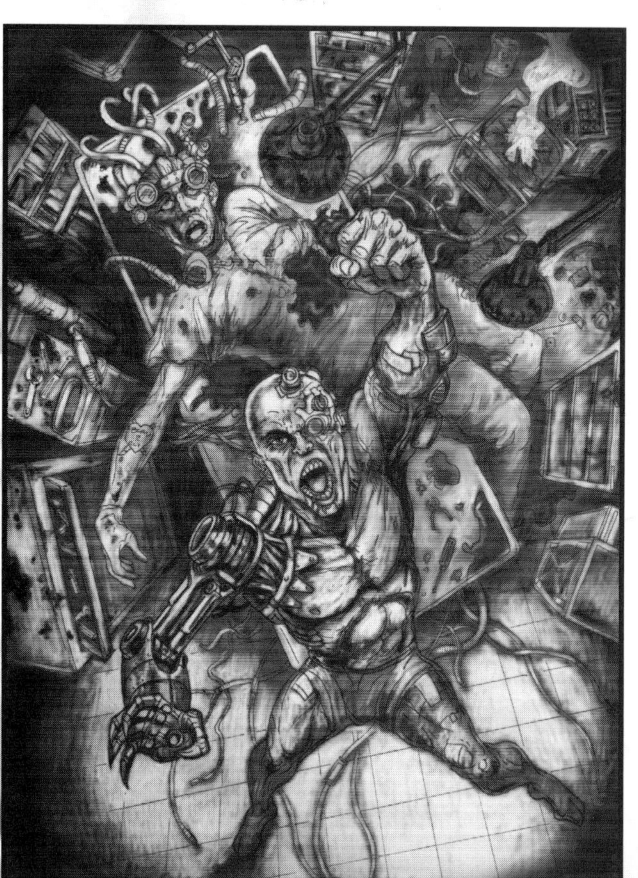

Like other forms of this insanity, the description of game effects are minimal and the burden is upon the player to roleplay the affliction in a genuine and interesting way.

- Mild: -2 penalty to Concentration, Listen, Spot, Sense Motive, and all Charisma-based checks.
- Moderate: Additional -2 penalty to Concentration, Listen, Spot, Sense Motive, and all Charisma-based checks.
- Severe: Each time any player rolls a 1 on a d20 during play, the afflicted character goes into catatonic withdrawal and is helpless for 2d6 hours.

Personality Disorders

Personality Disorders include symptoms that pervade nearly all aspects of the person's life. Although the symptoms vary in intensity, the afflicted shows difficulty with the intensity, appropriateness, and range of their emotions; interpersonal skills and relationships, and impulse control.

Antisocial Personality Disorder (Sociopath)
Antisocial Personality Disorder results in what is commonly known as a Sociopath. The afflicted shows an ongoing disregard for the rights and safety of others, failure to conform to social norms and lawful behaviors, repeated lying or deceit for personal profit or pleasure, and lack of remorse for actions that hurt other people in any way.

- Mild: The character loses any allegiance to law and/or good, and gains an allegiance to self.
- Moderate: -4 penalty to Diplomacy and Gather Information checks, and a +4 bonus to Bluff (only when lying).
- Severe: As above, and if the character fails any Charisma-based skill check, he must succeed at a Will save (DC = severity) or go berserk.

Borderline Personality Disorder
This disorder is characterized by unstable personal relationships, a poor self-image, and poor impulse control. The afflicted fears abandonment and will go to any length to prevent this, including threats of suicide and self harm. When criticized by others, the afflicted is prone to outbursts of intense anger and impulsive acts.

- Mild: The character loses any allegiance to law and gains an allegiance to chaos.
- Moderate: The character suffers a -2 penalty to all Charisma-based skill checks.
- Severe: The character suffers an additional -2 penalty to all Charisma-based skill checks. If the character loses an opposed Charisma-based skill check, she goes berserk.

Dependent Personality Disorder
Those with Dependent Personality Disorder have trouble assuming responsibility for major aspects of their own lives, preferring instead to allow others to make their decisions. The show a lack of self-confidence and in some cases cannot even function independently.

- Mild: During any encounter, the character is unable to take any action (other than delaying an action) until at least one ally has taken an action.
- Moderate: The character may succeed at a Will save (DC = severity) in order to take any action or skill check that provokes an opposed skill check.
- Severe: The character automatically fails any opposed skill check unless the result is a critical success.

Histrionic Personality Disorder

Those afflicted with this disorder are always calling attention to themselves. They are lively and overly dramatic, and even minor situations can cause wild mood swings. They easily become bored and crave new, novel situations and excitement. They form relationships quickly, but the relationships are often shallow, with the afflicted demanding increasing amounts of attention.

- Mild: +2 bonus to Bluff, Diplomacy, and Perform checks.
- Moderate: The above bonus is negated, and the character suffers a -2 penalty to Bluff, Diplomacy, Perform, and Sense Motive checks.
- Severe: As above, and the character suffers an additional -2 penalty to Bluff, Diplomacy, Perform, and Sense Motive checks.

Paranoid Personality Disorder

The afflicted has an ongoing, baseless suspicion and distrust of people, and develops an emotional detachment. He suspects that others are exploiting or deceiving him, that others are not loyal or trustworthy, perceives threats or attacks on his character in innocent statements by others, and bears persistent grudges.

- Mild: +2 bonus to Initiative, Gather Information, and Research skill checks. If the character has reason to feel wronged by someone, he gains an allegiance to revenge against that individual or group.
- Moderate: As above, and a -2 penalty to Diplomacy and Sense Motive checks.
- Severe: Additional +2 bonus to Initiative. The character loses all previous skill modifiers listed above and instead suffers a -4 penalty to Diplomacy, Gather Information, Research, and Sense Motive checks.

Schizoid/Schizotypal Personality Disorder

A person with Schizoid Personality Disorder has minimal social and interpersonal relationships and difficulty expressing emotions. They also have exhibit magical thinking (if I think this, I can make that happen), paranoia, and other strange thoughts. They may talk to themselves, dress inappropriately, and are very sensitive to criticism.

- Mild: -2 penalty to Concentration, Listen, Spot, Sense Motive, and all Charisma-based checks.
- Moderate: Additional -2 penalty to Concentration, Listen, Spot, Sense Motive, and all Charisma-based checks, and a -1 penalty to all other Wisdom-based checks.
- Severe: Additional -2 penalty to Concentration, Listen, Spot, Sense Motive, and all Charisma-based checks, and an additional -1 penalty to all other Wisdom-based checks.

Sleep Disorders

Persons afflicted with sleep disorders have trouble sleeping, waking, and dreaming- either too much or too little in some combination. The specifics of the sleep disorder lead to the various classifications below.

Dyssomnias

Dyssomniacs suffer from changes in the amount, restfulness, timing, and quality of sleep. There are otherwise no physical symptoms (as with Parasomnias).

- Mild: The character suffers a -2 penalty to all Concentration, Search, Spot, and Knowledge checks.
- Moderate: As above, and the character is fatigued at all times.
- Severe: Advance to Hypersomnia.

Hypersomnia

This disorder is characterized by excessive sleepiness lasting for at least a month. The sufferer has long undisturbed sleep periods and difficulty waking up. They may experience "sleep drunkenness" or other disorientation upon waking. They often take long daytime naps, which do little to refresh and recharge them.

- Mild: The character requires an extra 4 hours of sleep per day.
- Moderate: As above, and the character suffers a -2 penalty to Listen, Spot, and Initiative checks for 2d6 rounds after waking.
- Severe: As above, and the character is confused for 2d6 rounds after waking.

Insomnia

Insomnia is the inability to fall asleep or maintain sleep. The afflicted feels tired or irritable the next day, and may be consumed with worry before going to bed, for fear that they won't be able to sleep. During they day they may fall asleep at unexpected times.

- Mild: The character suffers a -2 penalty to all Concentration, Search, Spot, and Knowledge checks.
- Moderate: As above, and the character suffers a -2 penalty to all Bluff, Diplomacy, and Gather Information checks.
- Severe: Advance to Narcolepsy.

Narcolepsy

Narcolepsy is sudden sleepiness, sometimes accompanied by loss of muscle tone (from mild to total collapse). Narcolepsy is generally the result of boredom, but can occur at any time.

- Mild: Each time any player rolls a 1 on a d20 during play, the afflicted character must succeed at a Will save (DC = severity) or fall into a deep sleep for 1d6 minutes. This does not apply during combat or encounters that include interaction with NPCs. If the player is awakened before awakening naturally, he is confused for 1d6 rounds.

- Moderate: As above, though the character may fall asleep even in the midst of interaction with others (though still not during combat). This may cause the character to fail certain skill checks (such as falling asleep in the midst of a diplomatic negotiation).
- Severe: As above, and the character may fall asleep at any time, even during combat.

Parasomnia

A parasomnia is a disruptive physical act that occurs during slumber. These physical acts may disturb the sleep-stage transition. The most common are talking while asleep, starting or jerking, and disorientation upon waking.

- Mild: During each sleep period, the character must succeed at a Will save (DC = severity) or startle himself awake.
- Moderate: As above, and if the character is awakened, he is confused for 2d6 rounds.
- Severe: Advance to Sleepwalking.

Sleepwalking Disorder

Sleepwalking is the act of getting out of bed and wandering around. This normally occurs during the first third part of the sleep cycle. The person is characterized by having a blank stare, is basically unresponsive to others, and will be difficult to wake. They can at times perform complex functions such as unlocking doors. The person will have no memory of the episode.

- Mild: During each sleep period, the character must succeed at a Will save (DC = severity) or begin speaking aloud for 2d6 rounds. In addition to waking those around them, the afflicted may speak things that the conscious mind would prefer to remain unspoken. If the character is awakened during this time, he is confused for 1d6 rounds.
- Moderate: As above, and the character will actually get up and walk around in a confused state for 1d6 minutes. If the character is awakened in this state, he must succeed at a Will save (DC = severity) or go berserk.
- Severe: As above, and the GM is in control of the character's words and actions during the sleepwalking episode. The character will behave in accordance to his subconscious desires, as interpreted by the GM for maximum mischief.

Sleep Terror Disorder

This disorder is characterized by an abrupt awakening from sleep, usually accompanied by a scream. The person cannot be comforted by outside parties, and it must be allowed to run its course. They show signs of intense fear, such as rapid breathing, sweating, and a rapid heartbeat, and they later will have no memories of the incident.

- Mild: During each sleep period, there is a 2 in 6 chance that the character will awaken with a loud scream. The character falls back asleep almost immediately, but those sleeping near the afflicted must fail a Listen check or be awakened themselves.
- Moderate: As above. The character must succeed at a Will save (DC = severity) or be awakened by his terrors. The character will be shaken and confused for 2d6 rounds after waking.
- Severe: As above. The character is automatically awakened by his own terrors, and is shaken and confused for 2d6 rounds.

Special: Childhood Disorders

The following disorders generally manifest only in children. However, in the context of a Horror check, the GM may rule that the afflicted character "regresses" to childhood and adopts one of these disorders. They are applicable as both short- and long-term disorders.

Selective Mutism

Selective Mutism is a disorder in which the afflicted may talk in comfortable surroundings but refuses to talk in social situations.

- Mild: The character must succeed at a Will save (DC = severity) in order to speak in unfamiliar settings. This may have the effect or rendering may skills and talents (such as spellcasting) impossible.
- Moderate: As above. If the Will save is successful, the afflicted character manages to vocalize only with difficulty. All language-dependent skill checks suffer a -2 penalty, and spells with a verbal component have a 20% chance of failure.
- Severe: The character is rendered completely speechless in unfamiliar surroundings, with no Will save allowed.

Stuttering/Tics (Tourette's Syndrome)

A tic is an involuntary, rapid, recurrent movement or vocalization. Tics tend to be irresistible but they can be suppressed for limited periods. Common motor tics include eye-blinking, neck-jerking, facial grimacing, or inappropriate gestures. Common vocal tics include throat-clearing, barking, or the use of obscenities.

- Mild: The character must succeed at a Will save (DC = severity) in order to speak in unfamiliar settings. This may have the effect or rendering may skills and talents (such as spellcasting) impossible.
- Moderate: As above. If the Will save is successful, the afflicted character manages to vocalize only with difficulty. All language-dependent skill checks suffer a -2 penalty, and spells with a verbal component have a 20% chance of failure.
- Severe: The character is rendered completely speechless in unfamiliar surroundings, with no Will save allowed.

Vehicles

Exciting chases and deadly dogfights are an important part of any gritty action adventure. The following rules allow the GM to incorporate vehicles into the campaign.

Vehicle Statblock

In many ways, the vehicle statblock mirrors the creature statblock. You can use vehicles from any d20 source, particularly the d20 Modern Roleplaying game, but to use them in Grim Tales, you will only need the following statistics:

Size

Vehicles have the same size categories as creatures, and take up the same space on the battle grid. Some vehicles are so large that they exceed Colossal size.

A vehicle's size modifier applies to its initiative modifier, maneuver modifier, and AC.

Vehicle Size[1]	Size Modifier	Examples
Colossal	-8	Yacht, semi with trailer
Gargantuan	-4	Tank, limousine
Huge	-2	Luxury car, SUV, armored car
Large	-1	Economy car, Harley
Medium	+0	Racing bike, dirt bike

1 For vehicles smaller than medium size, the GM should use the size modifiers found in Chapter X: Combat.

Move

The vehicle's base move speed. Vehicle speeds are listed in both tactical scale (feet per combat round) and MPH. Vehicles are capable of moving so fast that they will quickly leave the standard battle grid; once a vehicle-to-vehicle chase or dogfight begins, vehicles are only tracked relative to each other, rather than keeping their positions exact on the battle grid.

Like creatures, a vehicle moves in multiples of its base speed.

Multiplier	Speed	Movement Modifier
x1	Tactical	0
x2	Tactical	0
x3	Cruise	2
x4	Chase	4
x5	Daredevil	8

Tactical speed means the vehicle is moving no more than x2 its base move.

Cruise speed (x3) is analogous to a jog or trot for creatures. It is faster than normal, but still sustainable over long distances.

Chase speed (x4) is the normal maximum for both vehicles and creatures. It is the fastest possible movement rate and implies few maneuvers.

Daredevil speed (x5) can be accomplished only with feats. Creatures or characters must have the Run feat to move at x5 speed; a vehicle's driver must have the Daredevil feat to move at this speed.

Multiplier: A faster moving vehicle has a better AC, but it also takes more damage from vehicle crashes and collisions (intentional or not). (See Crash Damage below.)

Movement Modifier: Apply this modifier as a penalty to all attack rolls made from the vehicle, and as a bonus to the vehicle's AC against all incoming attacks.

Converting Move Speed/MPH

Generally speaking, the MPH speed of a vehicle or creature is 1/10 its tactical movement rate. For example, a creature with a 30 move speed is traveling at about 3 MPH.

Remember that this is the vehicle's (or creature's) normal tactical speed (x1); the chase or top speed (x4) of a creature with a 30 move is thus about 12 MPH.

To find the tactical move speed of a vehicle whose top speed is known in MPH (for example, if you wish to import a vehicle from the real world into your game), multiply the top MPH speed by 2.5. For example, a vehicle with a top speed of 80 MPH has a tactical movement rate of 200.

Armor Class

A vehicle's AC is generally equal to 10 + Size modifier + Driver's Dexterity modifier. In the vehicle combat system presented here, a moving vehicle also gains a bonus to its AC equal to the Movement Modifier for its current speed.

Hardness

Most vehicles have a Hardness; like any object, a vehicle's Hardness is deducted from any damage received.

Hit Points

Like creatures, vehicles have hit points. A vehicle reduced to 0 hit points is destroyed.

Maneuverability

Vehicles have a maneuverability rating that determines how well they handle. All Dogfight maneuver checks and some Chase maneuvers (see below) must apply the maneuverability modifier.

The maneuverability modifier is a cumulative penalty. When a driver makes more than one Drive check in a round (either willingly or by necessity, whether acting or reacting), the penalty stacks with each additional check.

Maneuverability	Type	Maneuverability Modifier
A	Perfect	+0
B	Good	-1
C	Average	-2
D	Poor	-4
E	Clumsy	-8
F	Driver may not make Drive checks.	

Perfect maneuverability is rare among vehicles. A vehicle or creature with perfect maneuverability may make any number of turns, climbs, dives, and can accelerate or decelerate without penalty. Examples in this category include alien spacecraft.

Good maneuverability includes vehicles designed for handling, such as sports cars, racing bikes, or police cruisers.

Average maneuverability includes the majority of "standard" vehicles.

Poor maneuverability includes large or heavily laden vehicles such as semi-trucks or buses.

Clumsy vehicles are ponderous and slow to maneuver. Examples include river barges, hovercraft, or zeppelins. (Few ground vehicles fall into this category, as any vehicle with such poor maneuverability is generally considered unsafe for the roads!)

A vehicle with maneuverability class F cannot maneuver. The driver may not make Drive checks and automatically fails any opposed roll. Examples in this category include hot air balloons.

Living creatures on the ground or swimming generally have perfect maneuverability at Tactical speed or less. Running or swimming at x3 speed or higher is generally possible only in a straight line.

Crew Compartment

The protection a vehicle affords to the crew comes in three broad categories:

Open-Topped: Any vehicle whose crew compartment is open to the air falls in this category. Examples include chariots, wagons, motorcycles, convertibles, jet-skis, hot-air balloons, etc.

Closed: Any vehicle whose crew compartment can be completely enclosed (even by such simple means as rolling up the windows) falls into this category. Examples include most modern day automobiles.

Armored: Vehicles in this category are not only closed, they are reinforced and designed for combat. Examples include armored limousines and, of course, modern-day tanks and APCs.

Vehicle Combat

Vehicles that are stationary or moving at tactical speed can be tracked on the battle grid alongside other vehicles or creatures. However, when vehicles become involved in combat or a chase at excessive speeds, the GM should switch to the following rules.

1. Determine Speed Advantage

Divide the base move speed of the faster vehicle by the base move speed of the slowest vehicle (round down).

The result is the speed advantage modifier for the faster vehicle. The speed advantage applies to all Chase maneuvers and some Dogfight maneuvers.

Essentially, this means that a vehicle that is 2 times faster has a +2 speed advantage; 3 times faster has a +3 speed advantage, 4 times faster has a +4 speed advantage, and so on.

However, in close or tight terrain (see below) the slower vehicle can use obstacles to negate the speed advantage.

A driver can voluntarily forego any portion of his speed advantage. Because the speed advantage increases the damage from collisions, a driver may not always want to use his full speed advantage.

2. Determine Terrain

When the combat or chase begins, the GM should determine the predominant terrain. There are three types of terrain:

Open: Open terrain is easy to handle, with few changes in elevation and few dangerous obstacles. In open terrain, the faster vehicle can take full advantage of speed; there is no maximum speed advantage modifier.

Close: Close terrain is more narrow and/or filled with obstacles that must be avoided, requiring more Drive checks. The maximum speed advantage modifier in close terrain is +8; a vehicle more than 8 times faster than the slowest vehicle gains no additional advantage.

Tight: Tight terrain is the most dangerous of all terrain. It requires near-constant vigilance from the driver to avoid numerous obstacles. The maximum speed advantage in tight terrain is +4.

3. Determine Range

The range between vehicles in a high-speed combat or chase situation is relative:

Point-Blank

Generally speaking, point-blank range is from zero (vehicles are touching or ramming each other) out to a distance of one interval. Using this relative scale, the slowest vehicle can still escape point-blank range using only a single move.

During a vehicle combat, character-scale weapons may only be used at Point Blank range.

Short/Medium/Long Range

Once again, the distances are relative, not exact. Vehicle-mounted, vehicle-scale weapons can be used at short range with a -2 range penalty, -4 at medium range, and -8 at long range.

Extreme Range

Extreme range is the farthest two vehicles can be apart and still remain in combat, though extreme range is out of range for even vehicle-scale weapons. A vehicle that moves beyond extreme range has broken off from combat.

Combat Sequence

Determine Initiative

Roll a d20 for initiative as normal. All characters involved in the combat take their actions on their initiative count, as normal. When the driver's action comes up, proceed with the following steps.

1. Choose Speed

On his action, each driver can choose to maintain his current speed or to increase or decrease his speed multiplier by one (x1 to x2, x2 to x3, etc.).

Increasing your speed does not change the range between you and other vehicles (see Close/Lengthen, below), but it does improve your vehicle's AC.

2. Choose Maneuver

As a full-round action, the driver chooses a maneuver and makes a Drive check. While engaged in vehicle combat, a driver may normally only make one Drive check in a round. A Driver who makes more than one Drive check (including reaction rolls, opposed rolls, and Crash checks) must apply the maneuverability modifier as a cumulative penalty to each Drive check beyond the first.

Some maneuvers allow the defending driver to choose to make a Drive check to react to the acting driver in some way. These maneuvers are marked "Reaction Roll: Y." Even when presented with multiple opportunities to respond, a driver can only choose to respond to one other vehicle maneuver per round, unless she has the Driving Reflexes feat.

3. Check for Obstacles

The GM rolls to determine if any obstacles have appeared in the path of the combat. Obstacles do not necessarily imply a physical object; it could include weather effects such as a patch of ice on the road, a sudden glare, or a bank of fog.

An obstacle appears on a random roll: 1 in 10 in Open terrain, 1 in 8 in Close terrain, 1 in 6 in Tight terrain.

When an obstacle appears, all drivers must make a Drive check or risk a Crash (see below).

Maneuvers

Chase Maneuvers

Chase maneuvers are generally used to change the range between vehicles. In chase maneuvers, any speed advantage is key.

Chase Maneuvers	Modifiers Applied:	
	Maneuverability	Speed Advantage
Close/Lengthen	N	Y
Stand Off	Y	Y
Ram	Y	Y
Breakaway	N	Y
Pace	N	Y
Rejoin	Y	Y
Hard Brake	Y	Y
Gun It	N	Y
Escape	N	Y

Close/Lengthen

Range: any
Reaction Roll: Y

Using this maneuver the driver can increase or decrease the range between his vehicle and an opposing vehicle. The opposing driver chooses whether to make an opposed roll against this maneuver; if the maneuver is unopposed, the maneuver check is DC10.

Special: If the opposing driver previously chose the Stand Off maneuver (see below) the DC for the Close/Lengthen maneuver is equal to the result of her Stand Off check (see below).

If the Close/Lengthen maneuver is successful, the acting driver can change the range between himself and the opposing vehicle by one range category, plus one range category per 5 points by which he beats the opposed roll.

Stand Off

Range: any
Reaction Roll: N

Using this maneuver, the driver attempts to stand off from the combat while maintaining his current range from all other vehicles. The driver makes a Drive check; his result is the DC for any vehicle attempting the Close/Lengthen maneuver.

Ram

Range: Point Blank only
Reaction Roll: Y

Using this maneuver, the acting driver rams his vehicle into the opposing vehicle. The DC for this check is the AC of the target vehicle, modified as indicated in the following table.

Type of Ram Attempted	DC Modifier
Rear-End	+0
T-Bone	+5
Head On	+10

After a successful Ram, but before rolling her Crash check, the targeted driver may make a Drive check with a DC equal to the result of the attacker's Ram check. If this check is successful, the targeted driver can reduce the damage to her vehicle, if any, by one-half.

A successful Ram causes a collision. Resolve the damage as detailed below. Following the collision, both vehicles must make a Crash check. The acting driver receives a +4 bonus to his check.

Breakaway

Range: any
Reaction Roll: Y

Using this maneuver, the acting driver attempts to peel away from the combat and change the prevailing terrain. If the GM determines that this is even possible (and given the overall location, it may not be), the check is DC20. If the check succeeds, the acting vehicle moves into a new type of terrain (open, close, or tight). Any vehicle who wishes to follow may react, but they must also make a DC20 Drive check.

If the acting vehicle fails his maneuver, the terrain does not change, the acting vehicle must make a Crash check, and opposing vehicles do not. If the acting vehicle succeeds, any driver that chose to pursue and who also failed her maneuver must make a Crash check.

If the acting vehicle succeeds and no vehicles pursue, the acting vehicle has left combat (but may Rejoin, see below). If any vehicles do pursue, the GM should start tracking a new vehicle combat for the group that has splintered off.

Pace

Range: any
Reaction Roll: Y

The driver attempts to keep his vehicle moving in the same direction and at the same rate of speed as the opponent. If the opposing driver chooses not to react, the maneuver succeeds.

If the opposing driver chooses to react, make opposed Drive checks. If the acting driver wins, the maneuver is successful. If the check is failed, there is no effect.

If the maneuver is successful, the acting driver (and his crew/passengers) take no attack penalty for their own vehicle's movement modifier, and the movement modifier to the opponent's vehicle AC is likewise negated.

Rejoin

Range: up to Long
Reaction Roll: N

Using this maneuver, a driver who has broken off from combat may attempt to reengage. This maneuver may only be attempted in the round immediately following a successful Breakaway (either by the acting vehicle or the opponent).

The Rejoin maneuver is DC15. If the maneuver is successful, the vehicle rejoins the combat one range greater than the previous range (Point Blank becomes Short, Short becomes Medium, etc.).

If the acting vehicle fails to Rejoin, the opposing driver may automatically choose to Escape and end the chase/combat (no check required).

Hard Brake

Range: any
Reaction Roll: N

Using this maneuver, the driver can slow his vehicle by up to two speed multipliers in the same turn. If the driver already decelerated by one multiplier when speed was chosen in Step Two (above) his total deceleration for the round could be up to three multipliers.

The Hard Brake maneuver is DC15. If the check succeeds, the vehicle decelerates as intended. If the check fails, the vehicle does not change speeds, and the driver must make a Crash check or lose control.

Special: If another vehicle is Tailing the acting vehicle when he performs a Hard Brake, the Tailing vehicle has three options:

- Rear-end the braking vehicle (resolve the damage as detailed below)
- React with a Hard Brake of her own
- Move past the braking vehicle and increase range to Short

Gun It
Range: any
Reaction Roll: N

Gun It is the opposite of a Hard Brake: the driver attempts rapid acceleration to increase his speed by an additional multiplier. If the driver already increased his speed in Step Two, his total acceleration for the round could be up to two multipliers.

The Gun It maneuver is DC15. If the check succeeds, the vehicle accelerates as intended. If the check fails, the vehicle does not change speed, and the driver must make a Crash check or lose control.

Escape
Range: Extreme only
Reaction Roll: N

A driver may only attempt this maneuver if all other vehicles are at extreme range. The Escape maneuver is DC20. If the check succeeds, the acting vehicle has escaped the combat. If the check fails, combat continues.

Dogfight Maneuvers
Dogfight maneuvers are generally used to evade, pursue, and line up the opposite vehicle for an attack. In dogfight maneuvers, maneuverability is key.

Dogfight Maneuvers	Modifiers Applied:	
	Maneuverability	Speed Advantage
Evasive Maneuver	Y	Y
Wingman	Y	N
Crowd	Y	N
Sideswipe	Y	Y
Tail	Y	Y
Lock On	Y	N
Blind Spot	Y	N
Shake 'Em	Y	Y

Evasive Maneuver
Range: any
Reaction Roll: N

With this maneuver, the driver turns his concentration to defense.

The Evasive Maneuver is DC15. If the check is successful, the driver may choose to deduct a number (up to his total number of Drive ranks) from any subsequent Drive checks until the start of his next action, and add this number to his vehicle's AC until the start of his next action.

If the Evasive Maneuver check fails, the acting driver must make a Crash check or lose control.

Wingman
Range: Point Blank only
Reaction Roll: N

Using this maneuver, the driver designates one allied vehicle for whom he wishes to act as wingman. The Wingman maneuver is DC15. If the check is successful, the wingman receives a free attack (similar to an attack of opportunity) against any opposing vehicle who attempts to Tail or Lock On to the vehicle he is protecting. This lasts only until the start of the acting driver's next turn (at which point he must select the Wingman maneuver again if he wishes to continue protecting the allied vehicle).

Crowd
Range: Point Blank only
Reaction Roll: Y

The driver maneuvers his vehicle into position to force the opposing vehicle into an obstacle. The opposing vehicle may choose not to react; in this case, the maneuver is resolved as a successful Sideswipe (no check necessary) and the damage is resolved accordingly.

If the opposing driver chooses to react, make opposed Drive checks. If the acting driver wins, the opposing vehicle is forced to avoid an obstacle (see below). If the opposing driver succeeds, there is no effect.

Sideswipe
Range: Point Blank only
Reaction Roll: Y

Using this maneuver, the acting driver sidles up next to the opposing vehicle and slams the vehicles together. The DC for this check is the AC of the target vehicle.

After a successful Sideswipe, but before rolling her Crash check, the targeted driver may make a Drive check with a DC equal to the result of the attacker's Sideswipe check. If this check is successful, the targeted driver can reduce the damage to her vehicle by one-half.

A successful Sideswipe causes a collision, dealing damage as detailed below. After the damage is resolved, both vehicles must make a Crash check. The acting driver receives a +4 bonus to his check.

Tail
Range: Point Blank only
Reaction Roll: Y

The driver moves his vehicle into position behind the opposing vehicle. If the opposing driver chooses not to react, the maneuver succeeds.

If the opposing driver chooses to react, make opposed Drive checks. If the acting driver wins, the maneuver is successful and the tail is established.

If the check is failed, there is no effect.

The acting driver can maintain the tail as long as the range remains at Point Blank (though the opposing driver may try the Shake 'Em maneuver, below).

Lock On
Range: Point Blank only; must be Tailing
Reaction Roll: N

If you are tailing another vehicle, you may attempt to Lock On. The DC for this maneuver is equal to the AC of the opposing vehicle. If the Lock On maneuver is successful, the acting driver receives a +2 bonus to hit the opposing vehicle. (Some weapons require a lock on before firing, but never miss once they have locked on.)

If the check is failed, there is no effect.

Blind Spot
Range: Point Blank only; must be Tailing
Reaction Roll: N

If you are tailing another vehicle, you may veer into their blind spot. The DC for this maneuver is equal to the AC of the opposing vehicle. If the Blind Spot maneuver is successful, all weapons fired from the acting vehicle increase their critical threat range by 1 (20 becomes 19-20, 19-20 becomes 18-20, etc.)

If the check is failed, there is no effect.

Shake 'Em
Range: Point Blank only
Reaction Roll: Y

The acting driver attempts to shake an opposing vehicle who is tailing. If the opposing driver chooses not to react, the Shake 'Em maneuver is successful and the tail is broken.

If the opposing driver chooses to react, make opposed Drive checks. If the acting driver wins, the maneuver is successful and the tail is broken.

Daredevil Maneuvers

The following maneuvers are available only to drivers with the Daredevil feat.

Daredevil Maneuvers	Modifiers Applied:	
	Maneuverability	Speed Advantage
Barnstorm	N	N
Bootleg Reverse	Y	N
Eat This!	Y	N
Redline	N	Y
Push It	special	special

Barnstorm
Range: Point Blank only
Reaction Roll: N

Using this maneuver, the driver intentionally barrels his vehicle through an area full of obstacles: a shopping mall, a sidewalk cafe, or, quite literally, a barn. Your vehicle automatically takes damage as if from a failed Crash check, as does any vehicle that is Tailing you. Any opposing vehicles at Point Blank range, and any vehicles attempting to Close to Point Blank range until the start of your next turn, must make a Crash check.

Bootleg Reverse
Range: any
Reaction Roll: N

The acting driver throws his vehicle into a controlled skid or spin, bringing his speeding vehicle to a halt facing the opposite direction. This maneuver is DC20 + movement modifier. If the check succeeds, the vehicle's speed drops to zero. All opposing vehicles at Point Blank range move to Short range.

If the check is failed, the driver must make a Crash check or lose control.

Eat This!
Range: Point Blank only; opposing vehicle must be Tailing
Reaction Roll: N

The driver throws his vehicle into a flat spin in order to bring all of the vehicle's weapons to bear on his pursuer.

This maneuver is DC20. If the maneuver is successful, the acting driver and/or his crew may fire one shot with each vehicle mounted weapon, regardless of fire arc, at the tailing vehicle. The acting vehicle gains +2 to hit, +1 for every 5 points by which he beats the DC.

This maneuver does not allow the acting driver or his crew to fire more weapons than normal; it only allows the vehicle to bring weapons to bear that are normally out of firing arc.

If the maneuver check fails, the acting driver must make a Crash check or lose control.

Redline

Range: any
Reaction Roll: N

You deliberately push the vehicle past its normal operating specs to squeeze out every ounce of speed. The vehicle increases its speed by two multipliers, up to a total of x5. If the driver already increased his speed in Step Two, his total acceleration for the round could be up to three multipliers.

The Redline maneuver is DC15, +5 for each speed multiplier you increase, plus an additional +5 if you increase your speed multiplier to x5.

The vehicle accelerates to the desired speed regardless of the result of the Drive check. If the check succeeds, there is no other adverse effect. If the check fails, at the beginning of the acting driver's next action, the vehicle suffers an automatic critical to the engine.

Push It

(special)

A driver with the Daredevil feat may spend an action point to Push It. He may choose two maneuvers this round (each as a move action). In addition to the normal penalties for multiple maneuvers, the driver who chooses to Push It suffers an additional -4 penalty to all Drive checks until the beginning of his next action.

Obstacles

Drivers can never be sure when an obstacle is going to pop up; this uncertainty, coupled with the vehicle's maneuver modifier, means that a driver must be at the top of his game at all times.

Every round of vehicle combat, there is a chance that an obstacle appears; the tighter the terrain, the greater the chance of an obstacle. When an obstacle appears, all drivers must make a Drive check to avoid it.

When making a Drive check, the driver (or the GM, at his option) chooses one of the following methods for avoiding the obstacle:

Hard Brake (DC15 + movement modifier)

Similar to the Hard Brake maneuver, the driver attempts to slam on the brakes before striking the obstacle. (If the vehicle is being Tailed, it must be resolved as the Hard Brake maneuver above!).

If the check succeeds, the obstacle is avoided and the vehicle drops two speed categories. If the check is failed, the vehicle does not decelerate and the obstacle is struck. The driver must make a Crash check (see below) for striking the obstacle.

Jump (DC10 + 1 per foot distance)

A jump is usually required by the GM in special circumstances (usually as a special feature of the adventure). The GM determines the distance of the jump (in feet), either consulting his notes or determining randomly (4d10 feet). If the check succeeds, the obstacle is avoided. If the check is failed, the driver must make a Crash check (see below) for losing control.

Swerve (DC15 + movement modifier)

The driver attempts to swerve around the vehicle and continue on his way. If the check succeeds, the obstacle is avoided. If the check fails, the driver must make a Crash check (see below) for losing control.

White Knuckles (DC10 + movement modifier)

The driver grips the controls and plows through the obstacle, gritting his teeth and hoping for the best. Size is an advantage: add the vehicle's size modifier to the Driver check result. If the check succeeds, the vehicle automatically strikes the obstacle, taking damage as normal. Resolve damage to the vehicle as detailed below. Any passenger who succeeds at his Reflex save takes no damage (instead of half damage as normal).

Passenger/Crew Actions

Movement

Passengers and crew may take move actions. In most cases this will require a Balance check (DC10 + movement modifier). If the check succeeds, the character may continue his move action.

If the check is failed, the acting character balks, grabbing onto the vehicle for support, and loses his move action. If the check is a critical failure— and circumstances allow it— the character may fall out or off the vehicle.

When two vehicles are at Point Blank range, a character may use his move action to Jump between vehicles (DC15 + movement modifier of the faster moving vehicle). If the check is failed, the character falls (apply damage as for a Crash, below).

Attacks

Passengers and crew apply the vehicle's movement modifier as a penalty to all attack rolls. Melee attacks may only be made between vehicles at Point Blank range.

Damage to Vehicles

When a vehicle is hit by an attack, subtract the vehicle's hardness from the damage, and apply the remainder to the vehicle's hit points.

As a vehicle's hit points are whittled away, its condition deteriorates in much the same manner as a creature:

- **Crippled:** The vehicle suffers a -4 penalty to all Drive checks. The driver must make an immediate Crash check with a +5 modifier to the DC.
- **Disabled:** The vehicle shuts down completely and comes to a halt. The driver must make an immediate Crash check with a +10 modifier to the DC.

- **Destroyed**: A vehicle that has suffered damage in excess of twice its normal hit point total is spectacularly destroyed– skidding, spinning, rolling, and eventually crashing. Apply damage as from a failed Crash check (see below). The passengers may make Reflex saving throws (DC20 + vehicle's movement modifier prior to the crash) for half damage.

Vehicle Hit Points	Condition
50% or more	no effect
less than 50%	Crippled
0 or less	Disabled
suffered 2x maximum HP	Destroyed

Critical Hits
Although most objects are immune to critical hits, it is possible to score a critical hit on a vehicle during vehicle combat. When a critical threat is scored on a vehicle, you do not need to spend an action point and you do not multiply the damage as with a normal critical hit. Subtract the vehicle's hardness from the damage done as above; if any damage remains, apply it to the vehicle's hit points, then roll a d10 on the table below.

	Hit Location		
d10 roll	Open-Topped	Closed	Armored
1	Engine	Engine	Engine
2-3	Controls	Controls	Controls
4-6	Handling	Handling	Handling
7	Systems	Handling	Handling
8	Crew	Systems	Systems
9	Crew	Crew	Systems
10	Crew	Crew	Crew

- **Engine**: A critical hit to the engine reduces the vehicle's top speed by one multiplier (x4 drops to x3, x3 to x2, etc.).
- **Controls**: This critical hit damages the internal control systems. For each critical hit to the controls, the vehicle's maneuverability drops by one category (A to B, B to C, etc.). A vehicle's maneuverability cannot be reduced below F. Each subsequent critical hit forces an immediate Crash check.
- **Handling**: A critical hit to the handling damage's the vehicle's external steering mechanisms– tires, flaps, rudder, etc. Each hit to this location imposes a cumulative -1 penalty to all Drive checks. A vehicle cannot take more than 4 hits to this location (for a total penalty of -4); each subsequent hit is applied to Controls instead.
- **Systems**: The attack targets one of the vehicle's auxiliary systems: communications, weapons, sensors, etc. If the vehicle has no auxiliary systems, target the Handling instead.
- **Crew**: The attack targets the crew compartment, bypassing the vehicle's body, shattering a window, or striking a soft spot in the vehicle's armor. Apply the attack to a random crew member or passenger and compare the attack roll to his AC. If the attack misses, apply it to the next passenger in line. If this attack also misses, the shot passes through the crew compartment without further damage.

Crash Checks

Drivers must make Crash checks for a variety of reasons, but the end result of a failed Crash check is the same: disaster for the vehicle and its occupants.

A driver should make a Crash check when:

- The driver gets a critical failure on a Drive check;
- A maneuver calls for a Crash check;
- The vehicle collides with another vehicle or obstacle.

The Crash check DC varies according to the terrain:

Terrain	Crash Check DC
Open	10 + movement modifier
Close	15 + movement modifier
Tight	20 + movement modifier

If the Crash check succeeds, the vehicle continues moving at its current speed and position.

If the Crash check is failed, the vehicle takes damage, as detailed below.

Crash Damage

Generally speaking the damage from a crash is based on the size of the vehicle or obstacle involved and the speed at which it is moving. Find the base damage on the table below, add the speed modifier of the vehicle (if applicable), then multiply by the speed multiplier as further detailed in the crash descriptions below.

Vehicle/Object Size	Base Damage
Colossal	4d6
Gargantuan	2d8
Huge	2d6
Large	d8
Medium	d6
Small	d4
Tiny or smaller	d3

Vehicle Strikes an Obstacle
The base damage to the vehicle is based on the size of the obstacle, plus the vehicle's speed advantage, multiplied by the vehicle's speed multiplier. (If damage to the obstacle is relevant, the obstacle takes damage based on the vehicle's size, plus the speed advantage, multiplied by the vehicle's speed multiplier.) After the collision, the vehicle drops one speed category, unless the object struck was two or more

sizes smaller than the vehicle, in which case the vehicle continues moving at the same speed.

Vehicle Strikes another Vehicle

The damage to the vehicle is based on the size of the opposing vehicle striking it, and the damage is multiplied as follows:

- **Head-On Collision:** When two vehicles strike head on (within a 45 degree margin), each vehicle takes base damage based on the size of the opposing vehicle, plus the speed advantage of both vehicles, multiplied by the sum of their speed multipliers. After the crash, both vehicles drop 3 speed categories.
- **T-Bone Collision:** When two vehicles strike at right angles (within a 45 degree margin), each vehicle takes base damage based on the size of the opposing vehicle, plus the speed advantage of the vehicle that strikes head on, times its speed multiplier. After the crash, both vehicles drop 2 speed categories.
- **Rear-End Collision:** In a rear-end collision (within a 45 degree margin), each vehicle takes base damage based on the size of the opposing vehicle, plus the speed advantage of the vehicle striking from the rear. Subtract the speed multiplier of the slower vehicle from the speed multiplier of the faster vehicle before multiplying damage. After the crash, both vehicles continue moving at the speed of the slower vehicle.
- **Sideswipe:** A sideswipe occurs when the vehicles strike nearly parallel to each other. If the sideswipe occurs when the vehicles are moving in the same direction, calculate the damage as for a rear-end collision, then halve all damage. If the vehicles are moving in opposite directions, calculate the damage as for a head-on collision, then halve all damage. After the crash, both vehicles continue at the same speed.

Vehicle Loses Control

The vehicle takes base damage based on its own size, plus its speed advantage, times its current speed multiplier. After the crash, the vehicle continues at the same speed.

Damage To Passengers/Crew

The vehicle's crew compartment offers some protection, but the passengers still take half damage from every Crash. Passengers on the vehicle may choose to jump clear of the vehicle. Make a Reflex save (DC equal to the failed Crash check DC) to cut the damage in half again.

After a Crash

Just because a vehicle fails a crash check does not mean it has stopped moving. Assuming the vehicle still has at least 1 hit point, it can continue moving.

Aerial Combat

When a vehicle combat involves flying vehicles, the GM should track the ground as a separate "combatant." The GM determines the starting range from the vehicles to the ground. Vehicles may Close/Lengthen their distance from the ground (Dive/Climb) as if they were maneuvering against another vehicle.

An aerial vehicle that fails a Crash check, in addition to any other effects, moves one range category closer to the ground. An aerial vehicle that fails a Crash check at Point Blank range with the ground has crashed, and suffers 20d6 falling damage in addition to any Crash damage.

Characters who choose to jump clear of an aerial crash exit the vehicle and immediately suffer the normal effects of gravity.

Special Aerial Maneuvers

Immelman Turn

[Daredevil; Maneuverability: Y; Speed Advantage: N]
Range: any
Reaction: Y

An Immelman Turn allows an aircraft to rapidly change direction. The maneuver is DC20. If the maneuver is successful, all opponents at Point Blank Range move to Short range. Opponents who are Tailing (and who may also perform Daredevil maneuvers) may react by attempting an Immelman Turn of their own. Any driver who fails the check must make a Crash check or lose control.

Land

[Special; Maneuverability: N; Speed Advantage: N]
Range: Point Blank
Reaction: N

An aerial vehicle within Point Blank range of the ground and moving at a speed no greater than x2 may attempt to land. This maneuver is DC15. If the check succeeds, the vehicle lands. It continues moving as a ground vehicle at its current speed. If the check is failed, the driver must make a Crash check or lose control (risking a crash with the ground as detailed above).

Take-Off

[Special; Maneuverability: N; Speed Advantage: N]
Range: Point Blank
Reaction: N

An aerial vehicle moving along the ground at a speed at least x2 may attempt to take off. This maneuver is DC15, but add the vehicle's movement modifier as a bonus to the driver's check. If the check succeeds, the vehicle takes off and continues moving at its current speed. Its distance relative to the ground is Point Blank. If the check is failed, the driver must make a Crash check or nose-dive into the ground.

Web Enhancement

A Vehicle Combat Card that you can use to track multiple vehicles in combat is available for free download at www.badaxegames.com.

Fantastic Technology

In the many worlds of Grim Tales, one constant theme is that supernatural or superhuman abilities are dangerous, and not to be trusted. Whether speaking of the supernatural abilities of spellcasters and other occultists, or speaking of ancient, alien, or otherwise highly advanced technology, players should be aware that such power always comes at a price.

Cyberware

Cyberware (including bioware and genetic manipulation), whenever available in the campaign, is almost guaranteed to lure players with its dark promises of superhuman capability. Grim Tales offsets the advantages of cyberware with a high price tag, not only in terms of actual cost, but also in the toll that cyberware takes on the human body and the human psyche.

"Any sufficiently advanced technology is indistinguishable from magic." The following rules for cyberware embrace that philosophy. The GM will note that the effects and pricing of cyberware mirror the design parameters of magic items. Whereas magic items are limited to a certain number of "slots" on the body (1 hat, 1 vest, 1 pair of gloves, 1 pair of boots, etc.), the amount of cyberware that a body can accept is limited by the host's ability to heal, both in body and mind. Players should be aware that going under the knife carries serious risks, and to entrust themselves only to capable cybersurgeons.

Cyberware Ratings

Cyberware comes in three different "ratings" of increasing power— and increasing "invasiveness" to the host body: Minor, Moderate, and Major. The higher the rating, the more difficult the surgery, the more traumatic the replacement, and the longer the recovery and acclimation period for the patient.

Minor cyberware, sometimes called alpha-grade (α), covers mostly cosmetic operations or enhancements to the body's natural systems. Examples in this area would be enhancements to the eyes, ears, and minor augmentation of muscle and bone, while leaving the underlying natural systems intact.

Minor cyberware is Rating-1, carries no CHA penalty, and generally has a cost under 20,000 ¢ (Purchase DC 28).

Moderate cyberware, sometimes called beta-grade (β), is more extensive, requiring the replacement of non-vital flesh and blood systems with entirely artificial components. Examples in this category might include entire replacement of the eyes, skin, muscle, and bone.

Moderate cyber is rating-2. Each piece of moderate cyberware imposes a -1 penalty to all CHA-based checks. Moderate cyberware generally has a cost between 20,000 and 100,000 ¢ (Purchase DC 28-34).

Major cyberware, sometimes called gamma-grade (γ), is extremely invasive, replacing vital natural systems, such as entire limbs or organs. Examples in this category could include an entire cybernetic leg or arm, or complete artificial replacement of the heart, lungs or other vital organs.

Major cyber is rating-4. Each piece of major cyber imposes a -2 penalty to all CHA-based checks. Major cyber generally costs between 100,000 and 1,000,000 ¢ (Purchase DC 34-42).

Rumors abound of delta-grade (δ) cyberware that not only exceeds the known limitations of most cyberware, the patient suffers minimal side effects. If such cyberware does indeed exist, it lies in the hands of top-secret, high-level military and corporate organizations.

Getting Cybered

Adding cyberware requires surgery. Surgery is based on the Heal skill as well as the Surgery feat.

Minor Cyber: Heal DC15 base + modifier
Moderate Cyber: Heal DC20 base + modifier
Major Cyber: Heal DC25 base + modifier

The modifier for all checks is the sum rating of all cyberware in the body, plus the rating of the new cyber. If you already have rating-12 worth of cyber in you, and you go to add another rating-1 cyber, the DC is +13. Minor surgery, but still DC28.

Limits on Cyberware

Physical Limitations

The total sum of all cyberware ratings can not exceed the unmodified CON of the character. You can only stick so much cyber into the human body. (Creatures without a CON score are not alive, and effectively have no limit to the amount of cyberware they can implant.)

Psychological Limitations

The invasive nature of cyberware has psychological effects, as well. As more and more of the body is carved away and replaced with circuitry and cold steel, the host loses more and more of his connection with his fellow man and starts thinking like a machine. Eventually, this can lead to a state of cyber-psychosis.

To represent this, for each two rating points of the piece of cyberware installed, the host suffers a -1 penalty to all CHA-based checks.

Risks of Cyberware

Physical Risk:

A character who undergoes cyber-surgery must succeed at a Death From Massive Damage save immediately on completion of the surgery. The DC for this save is 10 + the total rating of all cyberware in the body.

If the check is made, the body accepts the cyberware. The character must spend time in recovery and therapy: 1d4 days for minor cyberware, 1d4 weeks for moderate cyberware, and 1d4 months for major cyberware. A healer can provide long-term care (DC15) to reduce the recovery time by half (though never less than one day).

If the check fails, the host's body rejects the cyberware; the host immediately drops to -1 hp and begins *dying*. The surgeon will have to act quickly to save the patient.

Psychological Risk:

At the end of the host's recovery period, he must make a Charisma check against DC5. Remember that the cumulative effects of moderate and major cyberware impose a penalty to all CHA-based checks, and this check is no exception.

If the check passes, the host is mentally acclimated to the cyberware. He suffers a penalty to all Charisma-based checks as normal for all cyberware in his body, but there is no further dangerous effect.

If the check fails, all CHA penalties become more severe: The host permanently loses 1 CHA for every rating point of cyber in his body. If this reduces the host's CHA to 0 or less, he withdraws into a catatonic state of cyber-coma; or, at the DM's discretion, he succumbs to cyber-psychosis and begins a violent spree of death and destruction not unlike a golem gone berserk.

It is possible to rescue a host from cyber-coma or cyber-psychosis by removing all cyberware from the body. This requires surgery (DC20 + total cyber rating) and many weeks of intense physical and psychological therapy: 1 week per total point of cyber removed. The host regains lost CHA at a rate of 1 per week; once the character rises above 0 CHA he regains awareness but must complete his recovery period.

Once the host completes the recovery period and regains all lost CHA, he can, of course, opt to go back under the knife for the latest in wonderful cybertechnology.

Stacking Cyberware

It should be noted that all cyberware provides a named bonus (a cyber bonus) and thus, cyberware *does not stack* with itself. For example, a character with both a +1 cyber bonus to STR and a +2 cyber bonus to STR does not receive a total of +3 STR; only the highest cyber bonus applies (in this case +2 STR).

For this reason, characters may from time to time seek to remove a piece of cyberware to make room for an upgrade. Removing a piece of cyberware requires surgery (DC20 + item's rating) and 1 week of recovery time per point of cyber removed.

Sample Cyberware

Adrenal Booster

This cyberware stimulates the adrenal gland at key moments, providing the host with improved reaction time (virtual Improved Initiative feat).
Moderate cyberware, rating-2, CHA penalty -1, 50,000 ₵.

Cyber Eyes

This piece of cyberware provides the user with low-light vision. The user can specify any natural eye color, or perhaps opt for the trendy "all chrome" look.
Minor cyberware, rating-1, no CHA penalty, 20,000 ₵.

Combat Cyber Eyes

A superior version of standard cyber eyes. This enhancement offers darkvision, optical magnification (+4 Spot bonus) and targeting crosshairs (virtual Far Shot feat). Because the dizzying amounts of information provided by these eyes must be integrated with a neural net, this is a

major piece of cyberware. In addition, it is impossible to disguise the eerie red glow of these eyes.
Major cyberware, rating-5, CHA penalty -3, 106,000 ¢.

Dermal Armor
A weave of bioengineered silksteel is layered just beneath the skin, providing a +2 natural armor bonus to the host. It takes a skilled surgeon to hide the bunching and puckering of the skin that is often a side-effect of this procedure.
Moderate cyberware, rating-2, CHA penalty -1, 80,000 ¢.

Dermal Plating
Unlike dermal armor, which at least attempts to disguise the unnatural enhancements, dermal armor pulls no punches. In this cybernetic enhancement, the surgeon grafts armor plates to the *outside* of the recipients skin. This enhancement grants the user DR 4/-.
Major cyberware, rating-4, CHA penalty -2, 320,000 ¢.

Enhanced Immune System (w/ Renal Filter)
This enhancement to the immune system, kidneys, and liver greatly improves the host's ability to filter out dangerous toxins and to recover from injury or illness. The user is immune to poison and receives a +4 bonus to all Fortitude saves.
Major cyberware, rating-4, -2 CHA penalty, 160,000 ¢.

Muscle Augmentation
Layers of electrostatically-stimulated fibers are layered underneath and through the body's existing musculature. As augmentation is increased, it is often necessary to augment the skeletal system as well, to insure that the bone structure can support the increased lifting capacity of the augmented muscle.

+1 STR: minor cyberware, rating-1, no CHA penalty, 10,000 ¢.

+2 STR: moderate cyberware, rating-2, -1 CHA penalty, 40,000 ¢.

+4 STR: major cyberware, rating-4, -2 CHA penalty, cost 160,000 ¢.

SkillDEX
A microcomputer is added to the cerebral cortex, allowing the user access to preprogrammed skills and motor responses. The user gains a +4 cyber bonus to a skill of his choice.
Minor cyberware, rating-1, no CHA penalty, 16,000 ¢.

Creating New Cyberware

Table 12-1 shows standard cyberware effects and costs. Using the guidelines presented there, you can design new cyberware for your campaign. Like magic items, the design of new cyberware is the exclusive purview of the GM.

It is possible to combine effects into a single piece of cyberware. Add all of the components together and round up to the next highest rating.

It is even possible to exceed rating-4. However, each rating point above 4 imposes a -1 penalty to CHA-based checks. (Normally the CHA penalty is -1 per 2 rating points).

Table 12-1: Standard Cyberware Effects and Costs

Effect	Currency	Wealth
Minor Cyberware (α) (no penalty to CHA-based checks)		
+1 cyber bonus to an ability score[1]	10,000 ¢	DC26
+1 cyber bonus to natural armor[2]	20,000 ¢	DC28
+2 cyber bonus to one saving throw (Will, Reflex, or Fort)[3]	20,000 ¢	DC28
+4 bonus to a skill[4]	16,000 ¢	DC27
Minor special quality (e.g. low-light vision)[5]	20,000 ¢	DC28
Moderate Cyberware (β) (-1 penalty to CHA-based checks)		
+2 cyber bonus to an ability score	40,000 ¢	DC30
+2 cyber bonus to natural armor	80,000 ¢	DC33
Virtual feats (e.g. Combat Reflexes, etc.)[6]	50,000 ¢	DC31
Improved special qualities (e.g. darkvision, scent)[7]	80,000 ¢	DC33
Major Cyberware (γ) (-2 penalty to CHA-based checks)		
+4 cyber bonus to an ability score	160,000 ¢	DC35
Supernatural qualities or talents (e.g. blindsight, evasion, etc.)	1,000,000 ¢	DC42

1 Bonus squared x 10,000 ¢
2 Bonus squared x 20,000 ¢
3 Bonus squared x 5000 ¢
4 Bonus squared x 1000 ¢
5 Or similar design factor valued at 0.1. Cost is valued at (factor x10) squared x 20,000 ¢. See Appendix One for details on design factors.
6 Cost is based on an entry level feat with no prerequisites. If prerequisite feats exist, the cost increases exponentially: (number of feasts + prerequisites) squared x 50,000. For example, to replicate Cleave (1 feat + 1 prerequisite: Power Attack) costs 200,000 ¢. This cost of the prerequisite must be included, even if the character has the prerequisite feats through normal means.
7 Design factors above 0.1 but less than 0.4 generally qualify as moderate cyberware. Design factors 0.4 or greater are invariably major cyberware. See Appendix One for details on design factors.

Combining Cyber and Magic Items
Although cyberware provides its own named bonus, and ordinarily stacks with other bonuses (magical, cyber, or otherwise), the GM is free to rule that magic items will not work on any body location or appendage that contains major cyberware. (Placing a magic ring onto a metallic cyber-hand, for example, does nothing.)

Timeline of Real-World Inventions	
Date	Invention
-400	Catapult (Greece)
1000	Chinese discover gunpowder
1335	Earliest record of a mechanical clock (Italy)
1450	Printing Press (Johannes Gutenberg)
1698	Steam pump (Thomas Savery)
1695	Early steam engine (Thomas Savery)
1717	Diving bell (Edmund Halley)
1760	Bifocal eyeglasses (Benjamin Franklin)
1765	Steam Engine (James Watt)
1769	Motorized carriage (Nicolas Cugnot)
1775	Submarine (David Bushnell)
1783	Hot-air Balloon (Montgolfier brothers)
1784	Shrapnel shell (Henry Shrapnel)
1787	Steamboat (John Fitch)
1793	Cotton gin (Eli Whitney)
1799	Electric battery (Alessandro Volta)
1804	Steam locomotive (James Watt) Screw propeller (John Stevens)
1810	Breech-loading rifle (John H. Hall)
1814	Railway locomotive (George Stephenson)
1816	Bicycle (Karl D. Sauerbronn)
1834	Electric streetcar (Thomas Davenport)
1835	Revolver (Samuel Colt)
1837	Telegraph (Samuel F.B. Morse)
1838	Morse code (Samuel F.B. Morse)
1843	Vulcanized rubber (Charles Goodyear)
1845	Guncotton (Christian Schonbein)
1849	Conical bullet (Claude Minie)
1848	Hydraulic turbine (James B. Francis)
1852	Elevator (Elisha G. Otis) Nonrigid airship (H. Giffard)
1852	Breech-loading cannon (W.G. Armstrong)
1855	Red-phosphorous matches
1855	Bessemer steel furnace (Henry Bessemer)
1857	Sleeping car (George M. Pullman)
1860	Pasteurization (Louis Pasteur) Gas engine (Etienne Lenoir)
1861	Ironclad steamboat (John Ericsson) Gatling gun (R.J. Gatling)
1862	Blasting cap (Alfred Nobel)
1864	Self-propelled torpedo (Robert Whitehead)
1866	Dynamite (Alfred Nobel)
1873	Colt Peacemaker .44-.40
1875	Internal combustion engine (Siegfried Marcus)
1876	Telephone (Alexander Graham Bell) Gas engine (Nikolaus A. Otto)
1879	Electric light bulb (Thomas Edison)
1877	Glider (Otto Lilienthal)
1884	Machine gun (Hiram Maxim)
1884	Steam turbine (C.A. Parsons)
1885	Gasoline-powered automobile (Karl Benz)
1887	Air-inflated rubber tire (J.B. Dunlop)
1888	Kodak camera (rolled film) (George Eastman)
1889	Paper matches (Joshua Pusey)
1889	Bolt-action rifle (P. von Mauser)
1891	Tesla Coil (Nikola Tesla)
1892	Diesel engine (Rudolph Diesel)
1893	Zipper (W.L. Judson)
1898	Electric flashlight (Conrad Hubert)
1900	Dirigible (Ferdinand Zeppelin)
1903	Aeroplane (Wright Brothers)
1908	Model-T automobile (Henry Ford)
1911	Lewis gun (Isaac Lewis)
1911	Gyrocompass (Elmer A. Sperry) Hydroplane (Glenn Curtis)
1914	Tank (E.D. Swinton)
1918	Automatic rifle (John Browning)
1922	Ethyl gasoline (T. Midgley, Jr.)
1923	Traffic Signal (Garrett A. Morgan)
1926	Liquid-fuel rocket (R.H. Goddard)
1927	Television (Philo Farnsworth)
1930	Bathysphere (Charles William Beebe)
1932	Electron microscope (Max Knoll, Ernst Ruska)
1934	Garand rifle (John C. Garand)
1937	Jet propulsion (Frank Whittle)
1939	Helicopter (Igor Sikorsky)
1942	Duct tape (Johnson & Johnson); Nuclear reactor (head of project Enrico Fermi)
1942	Guided missile (Wernher von Braun)
1944	Ballistic missile (Wernher von Braun)
1945	Atomic bomb (head of project J. Robert Oppenheimer)
1952	Hydrogen bomb (head of project Edward Teller)
1954	Solar cell (D.M. Chaplin, C.S. Fuller, G.L. Pearson)
1955	Carbon dating (head of project W.F. Libby)
1956	Hovercraft (Christopher Cockerell)
1958	Neutron bomb - (head of project Samuel Cohen)
1968	Superconducting magnetic levitation (James Powell, Gordon Danby)
1971	Kevlar (Stephanie Kwolek)

Creature Creation

Using the system below, you can tweak monsters from outside sources, or create new monsters from scratch.

There are basically two paths of creature creation. The first is a creature designed to challenge a party of a certain power (for which the GM will already have a target CR in mind). The second is where the GM has an idea for a creature, including all of its abilities, and the CR is not known until after the creation process.

In the second case, a creature can be created in a freeform manner, while in the first case the GM will have to do some forward planning. Essentially, if you have a target CR in mind for a creature you wish to design, a good idea is to take half the proposed CR and convert that to Hit Dice for the appropriate creature type.

List of Challenge Rating Design Factors
Character Levels
Templates
1. Size
2. Traits (Type/Subtype/Race)
3. Hit Dice
4. Speed
5. Armor Class
6. Full Attack
7. Special Abilities/Qualities

 7.01 Ability Score Loss
 7.02 Breath Weapons
 7.03 Create Spawn
 7.04 Damage Reduction
 7.05 Disease
 7.06 Energy Drain
 7.07 Energy Resistance
 7.08 Fast Healing
 7.09 Gaze Weapons
 7.10 Generic Abilities
 7.11 Immunities
 7.12 Insight/Luck/Profane/Sacred Bonus
 7.13 Poison
 7.14 Ray Attacks
 7.15 Regeneration
 7.16 Spell-like Abilities
 7.17 Spell Resistance
 7.18 Spellcasting
 7.19 Summoning
 7.20 Turn Resistance
 7.21 Vulnerabilities

8. Ability Scores
9. Skills
10. Feats
11. Equipment

Challenge Ratings

Challenge Ratings (CRs) are a measurement of raw power. Two groups with equal CR are evenly matched; against such an opponent, the heroes stand roughly a 50% chance of succeeding, and then only by pulling out all the stops and spending every ounce of resources at their fingertips.

Generally speaking, player characters have a CR equal to their character level. This assumes that the characters have wealth and equipment appropriate to their level, and do not have ability scores or additional resources above and beyond the norm. Even if such is the case, the system below allows the GM to easily track the CR of his players as well as his monsters, ensuring that each encounter is appropriately challenging.

Monster Challenge Ratings.

To determine a monster's Challenge Rating:

- Total all factors.
- Apply the *Golden Rule*.
- For monsters, multiply this figure by 2/3 and round the result as indicated below.
- Round down all fractions if the total is 4 or more; if the total is less than 4 apply the result to the fractional CR table below.

Fractional CRs

Original CR Total	Rounded CR
4.01 to 5.00	5
3.51 to 4.00	4
3.01 to 3.50	3.5
2.51 to 3.00	3
2.01 to 2.50	2.5
1.76 to 2.00	2
1.51 to 1.75	1.75
1.26 to 1.50	1.5
1.01 to 1.25	1.25
0.51 to 1.00	1
0.01 to 0.50	2/3
-0.49 to 0	1/2
-0.99 to -0.50	1/3
-1.24 to -1.00	1/4
-1.49 to -1.25	1/5
-1.74 to -1.50	1/6
-1.99 to -1.75	1/7
-2.124 to -2.00	1/8
-2.24 to -2.125	1/9
Up to -2.25	1/10

Design Parameters

Within each of the sections below, you will find ways to increase the CR of a creature by adding certain abilities. However, certain design parameters must be kept in mind. You could, for example, create a very low HD creature with epic, world-destroying powers— but its CR would not accurately predict the creature's capabilities. Each factor has certain design parameters; as long as your design falls within those parameters, you can be confident of the creature's CR to predict its performance in your campaign.

Golden Rule

Class Levels or Hit Dice should always comprise at least 50% of the creatures total CR. Halve all CR beyond double the creature's CR modifier for Class Levels and Hit Dice.

For example, a creature with a +9.8 CR modifier for HD may add up to another 9.8 CR at full value, but all factors above 19.6 are halved.

Final 2/3 Adjustment

Monsters (but not characters) apply a final multiplier of 2/3 to their design factors. Creatures whose total CR before this adjustment is CR1 or less should instead "step down" two rows on the fractional CR table at left (2/3 becomes 1/3, 1/5 becomes 1/7, etc.).

Character Levels

Character levels always add their full CR. Character levels are never subject to the 2/3 multiplier or the Golden Rule.

Class Levels

- Base CR +1.0/Level (with equipment)
- Base CR +0.8/Level (without equipment)

Templates

If the GM uses Templates for his monsters, he should keep a listing of each template, along with all relevant factors. Each template can then be added as a "lump sum" to each creature without recalculating each time. Templates are subject to the Golden Rule, multipliers and rounding as normal.

1. Size

The Size factor accounts for changes to a creatures' AC, base attack and damage, space/reach, and adjustments to Strength, Dexterity, Constitution, and Natural Armor.

Example:
Ogre (Large) = +1.4 with attributes, +0.2 without

A creature's size also determines the base damage of its natural attacks. Creatures generally have either one primary attack (at x1.5 Str mod to damage), two claws or slams (at x1 Str mod to damage), or some combination of two claws and a bite (at x1 Str mod to damage for the primary attack(s) and x1/2 Str mod to damage for the secondary attack(s)).

The creature's base damage is found on Table 13-1 and modified according to the type of attack (see below).

Attacking Appendage	
Bite/Pincer	+1 Size Category
Claw/Slam	Same Size Category
Stomp	+2 Size Categories
Tail Slap	-1 Size Category
Wing Buffet	-1 Size Category
Creature Density	
Dense/Muscled	+1 Size Category
Very Dense/Muscled	+2 Size Categories
Appendage Dominance	
Oversized Appendage	+1 Size Category
Dominant Appendage	+2 Size Categories

Table 13-1: CR Modifiers for Size

Size	base CR	No Att[1]	Size	Space	Reach	AC/ Attack	Grapple/ Hide[2]	STR	DEX	CON	Natural Armor	Base Damage[3]
Fine	+0.55	+1.35	6 inches	6 in x 6 in	0	+8	16	-10	+8	-2	+0	1
Diminutive	-0.3	+0.3	1 foot	1 ft x 1 ft	0	+4	12	-10	+6	-2	+0	1d2
Tiny	-0.55	+0.05	2 feet	2.5 x 2.5	0	+2	8	-8	+4	-2	+0	1d3
Small	-0.4	+/-0	4 feet	5 x 5	5	+1	4	-4	+2	-2	+0	1d4
Medium	+/-0	+/-0	8 feet	5 x 5	5	+0	0	+0	+0	+0	+0	1d6
Large	+1.4	+0.2	16 feet	10 x 10	10	-1	4	+8	-2	+4	+2	1d8
Huge	+2.9	+0.2	32 feet	15 x 15	10	-2	8	+16	-2	+8	+5	2d6
Gargantuan	+4.4	+0.1	64 feet	20 x 20	15	-4	12	+24	-2	+12	+9	2d8
Colossal	+5.6	-0.4	64 feet +	30 x 30	15	-8	16	+32	-2	+16	+14	4d6

1 Use this column if you do not want to include automatic size adjustments for Strength, Dex, Con, and Natural armor. You can apply these factors separately at a later step.
2 Small creatures gain a bonus to Hide and a penalty to Grapple. Larger creatures gain a bonus to Grapple and a penalty to Hide.
3 For creatures whose size and/or base damage increases "off the chart," double the damage for every +2 size increases.

2. Traits (Type/Subtype)

Apply the following bonus or penalty where applicable.

Table 13-2: Challenge Rating Modifiers for Traits

Type/Subtype	Challenge Rating Modifier
Creature Type	
Aberration	+0.2 (from Darkvision)
Animal	-0.75
Construct	+0.7 (+1.4 if Intelligent)
Dragon	+0.5
Elemental	+1.2
Fey	+0.1 (from Low Light Vision)
Giant	+0.2 (from Darkvision)
Humanoid	+/-0
Magical Beast	+0.2 (from Darkvision)
Monstrous Humanoid	+0.2 (from Darkvision)
Ooze	+1.9 (+2.6 if Intelligent)
Outsider	+/-0
Plant	+0.6 (+1.3 if Intelligent)
Undead (Intelligent)	+1.1
Undead (Mindless)	-1.1
Vermin	-0.5
Creature Subtype	
Angel	+3.44
Archon	+2.14
Demon	+1.9 (excludes Summoning)
Devil	+1.8 (excludes Summoning)
Eladrin	+1.9
Energy	+0.5
Guardinal	+2.24
Incorporeal	+1.3 (excludes Summoning)
Swarm (Tiny)	+2.66
Swarm (Diminutive or Fine)	+7.0

Type Traits

Animals (CR -0.75)

Intelligence 1 or 2 CR -0.85
Low Light Vision CR +0.1

Constructs (CR +0.7; Intelligent constructs CR +1.4)

No Constitution Score CR +1.9
Darkvision CR +0.2
Hit Point Bonus CR +0.2
Low-Light Vision CR +0.1
No Natural Healing CR -1.0
No Intelligence Score CR -0.7

Dragons (CR +0.5)

Darkvision CR +0.2
Low-Light Vision CR +0.1
Paralysis/Sleep Immunity CR +0.2

Elementals (CR +1.2)

Cannot be Raised etc. CR -0.2
Cannot be Flanked CR +0.2
Critical Hit Immunity CR +0.5
Darkvision CR +0.2
Poison Immunity CR +0.2
Sleep/Paralysis/Stun Immunity CR +0.3

Oozes (CR +1.9; Intelligent oozes CR +2.6)

Blindsight CR +1.0
Critical Hit Immunity CR +0.5
Cannot be Flanked CR +0.2
Hit Point Bonus CR +0.2
Poison Immunity CR +0.2
Polymorph Immunity CR +0.2
Sleep/Paralysis/Stun Immunity CR +0.3
No Intelligence Score CR -0.7

Outsiders (CR +/-0)

Cannot be raised etc. CR -0.2
Darkvision CR +0.2

Plants (CR +0.6; Intelligent plants +1.3)

Critical Hit Immunity CR +0.5
Low Light Vision CR +0.1
Poison Immunity CR +0.2
Polymorph Immunity CR +0.2
Sleep/Paralysis/Stun Immunity CR +0.3
No Intelligence Score CR -0.7

(Intelligent) Undead (CR +1.1)

Can be Turned etc. CR -1.5
No Constitution Score CR +1.9
Darkvision CR +0.2
Immune to Mind Effects CR +0.5

(Mindless) Undead (CR -1.1)

Can be Turned etc. CR -1.5
No Constitution Score CR +1.9
Darkvision CR +0.2
No Intelligence Score CR -0.7
No Natural Healing CR -1.0

Vermin (CR -0.5; Intelligent vermin CR +0.2)

Darkvision CR +0.2
No Intelligence Score CR -0.7

Subtype Traits

Angel (CR +3.44)

Acid Immunity	CR +1.0
Cold Immunity	CR +1.0
Electricity Resistance 10	CR +0.2
Fire Resistance 10	CR +0.2
Low-Light Vision	CR +0.1
Petrification Immunity	CR +0.2
Poison Save +4	CR +0.04
Protective Aura	CR +0.5
Tongues	CR +0.2

Archon (CR +2.14)

Aura of Menace	CR +0.2
Electricity Immunity	CR +1.0
Low-Light Vision	CR +0.1
Magic Circle vs. Evil	CR +0.2
Petrification Immunity	CR +0.2
Poison save +4	CR +0.04
Teleport	CR +0.2
Tongues	CR +0.2

Demon (CR +1.9)

Acid Resistance 10	CR +0.2
Cold Resistance 10	CR +0.2
Electricity Immunity	CR +1.0
Fire Resistance 10	CR +0.2
Poison Immunity	CR +0.2
Summoning	(Factor Separately)
Telepathy	CR +0.1

Devil (CR +1.8)

Acid Resistance 10	CR +0.2
Cold Resistance 10	CR +0.2
Fire Immunity	CR +1.0
Poison Immunity	CR +0.2
See through Darkness	CR +0.1*
Summoning	(Factor Separately)
Telepathy	CR +0.1

*Already has Darkvision from Outsider Traits.

Eladrin (CR +1.9)

Cold Resistance 10	CR +0.2
Electricity Immunity	CR +1.0
Fire Resistance 10	CR +0.2
Low-Light Vision	CR +0.1
Petrification Immunity	CR +0.2
Tongues	CR +0.2

Energy [cold, fire] Subtype (CR +0.5)

Energy Immunity	CR +1.0
Opposing Energy Vulnerability	CR -0.5

Guardinal (CR +2.24)

Cold Resistance 10	CR +0.2
Electricity Immunity	CR +1.0
Fire Resistance 10	CR +0.2
Lay on Hands	CR +0.2
Low-Light Vision	CR +0.1
Petrification Immunity	CR +0.2
Poison save +4	CR +0.04
Sonic Resistance 10	CR +0.2
Speak with Animals	CR +0.1

Incorporeal (CR +1.3)

Deflection Bonus	(Factor Separately)
Ignore Damage (50% chance)	CR +1.0
Ignore Solid Objects	CR +1.0
Move Silently	CR +0.5
Non-magical Attack Immunity	CR +1.0
No Strength Score	CR -2.2

Swarm (CR +2.66 (Tiny) /+7.0 (Diminutive/Fine))

Always Hit (Single Attack)	CR +1.0
Can't be Bull-Rushed/Tripped/Grappled	CR +0.3
Critical Hit Immunity	CR +0.5
Distraction	CR +0.5
Cannot be Flanked	CR +0.2
Spell Immunity (limited)	CR +1.0
Spell Vulnerability (limited)	CR -1.0
Weapon Resistance (Slashing/Piercing)	CR +0.66 (Tiny)
Weapon Immunity	CR +5.0 (Dim./Fine)
Wind Vulnerability	CR -0.5

3. Hit Dice

Table 13-3: CR rating per HD

Creature Type	CR per HD
Dragon	0.75
Outsider	0.70
Magical Beast	0.65
Monstrous Humanoid	0.60
Aberration, Animal, Elemental, Giant, Humanoid, Ooze (Intelligent), Plant (Intelligent), Vermin (Intelligent)	0.55
Fey	0.50
Construct (Intelligent), Ooze, Plant, Undead (Intelligent), Vermin	0.45
Construct, Undead (Mindless)	0.35

Examples:
Hezrou (10 HD Outsider) = CR +7
Iron Golem (18 HD Construct) = CR +6.3

Design Parameters

For all natural creatures (that is, creatures with a physical body that generally adheres to the science of living things) Hit Dice and size are indelibly linked: the larger the creature, the more HD it should have. Generally speaking, a creatures should have +1 HD for every 2 feet in size:

Size Category	Size	Typical HD
Fine	1/4 ft	1 Hit Point
Diminutive	1/2 ft	1/4 HD
Tiny	1 ft	1/2 HD
Small	2 ft	1 HD
Medium	4 ft	2 HD
Large	8 ft	4 HD
Huge	16 ft	8 HD
Gargantuan	32 ft	16 HD
Colossal	64 ft	32 HD

In addition, a creature's body shape can modify the final HD parameters.

Body Type	*Example*	HD Modifier
Stocky/Bulky	*Dwarf*	x1.5
Thin/Frail	*Skeleton*	x2/3
Very Stocky/Bulky	*Xorn*	x2
Very Thin/Frail	*Snake*	x1/2

Some creatures, such as outsiders, do not have a natural physiology, and so it is not necessary that their HD be tied to their size. However, such creatures should generally have at least as many HD as their size indicates, although they can exceed this amount.

Constructs generally have as many HD as their creator's caster level.

4. Speed/Movement

Apply this factor to each mode of movement. All creatures gain one mode of movement (usually ground movement) based on size for free. Adding additional modes of movement or increasing the speed above norm for the creature's size increases the cost.

Standard Movement Rates (by Creature Size)		
Size	**non-Flight**	**Flight**
Fine	5 ft	10 ft
Diminutive	10 ft	20 ft
Tiny	15 ft	30 ft
Small	20 ft	40 ft
Medium	30 ft	60 ft
Large	40 ft	80 ft
Huge	50 ft	100 ft
Gargantuan	60 ft	120 ft
Colossal	70 ft	140 ft

Table 13-4: Speed/Movement	
Movement Type	**CR increase**
Burrow (soft earth)	CR +0.2
Burrow (stone)	CR +0.5
Climb	CR +0.2
Flight (clumsy)	CR +0.2
Flight (poor)	CR +0.4
Flight (average)	CR +0.6
Flight (good)	CR +0.8
Flight (perfect)	CR +1
Can't Run	CR -0.2
Swim	CR +0.2

- CR +0.2/each doubling of typical speed
- CR -0.2/each halving of typical speed
- Only apply this to the fastest mode of movement.

Example:
Solar = CR +0.8 for movement
Flight (Good Maneuverability) = CR +0.8
Flight Speed 150 ft (70 ft greater than typical for its size) = CR +/-0

5. Armor Class

Armor class that is not derived from equipment is valued as follows:

Type of AC bonus	CR per +1 AC
Deflection	+0.1
Natural Armor	+0.1
Insight, Luck, Profane, Sacred	+0.125

Examples:
Spectre (+2 Deflection) = CR +0.2
Elder Earth Elemental (Natural Armor +15) = CR +1.5

Design Parameters

A creature's armor bonus is generally determined by its HD and its physical appearance (including size). Fey, Outsiders and intelligent Undead typically receive a deflection bonus based on their Charisma modifier.

Table 13-5: Natural Armor		
Description	*Example*	Typical Bonus
Normal Skin	*Orc*	0 / + 1 per 8 HD
Tough Hide/Fur/Bone	*Dire Bear*	1-2 / + 1 per 4 HD
Scales/Exoskeleton	*Lizardfolk*	3-4 / + 1 per 2 HD
Carapace/Shell	*Gorgon*	5-8 / + 1 per HD
Construct	*Iron Golem*	Material Hardness + HD
Large size		+2
Huge size		+5
Gargantuan		+9
Colossal		+14

Example:
A 6 HD Medusa (scaly skin) should have natural armor +6 or +7.

6. Full Attack

Apply this factor to a creature's natural attack sequence. Creatures pay only for their attack dice; do not factor any cost for Strength bonus to damage and do not factor manufactured weapons. The cost is based on the type of damage die for each attack. (A creature's natural attack dice are generally determined by its size.)

Table 13-6: Full Attack	
Base Damage	Cost Per Damage Die
1	0.1
1d2	0.15
1d3	0.2
1d4	0.25
1d6	0.35
1d8	0.45
1d10	0.55
• Secondary attacks (made at -5 from the creatures normal BAB) cost half. • CR -1 if the creature has no effective physical attacks.	

Example:
Marilith (demon)
6 slams @ 1d8 and 1 tail slap (secondary) @ 4d6
(6 x 0.45) + (4 x .35 x 50%) = CR 3.4

7. Special Attacks/Qualities

Nearly all of the special qualities a creature can have are found in this section. For abilities not listed, find a spell that simulates the effect and determine the cost as a spell-like ability.

For creatures that can ply the same special attack more than once per round, multiply the cost by the number of times it can be used only if the effects stack.

Example of Stacking Effects:
Ghoul: 3 attacks/round with Paralysis Touch. Paralysis does not stack with itself so only rate the ability once.

Five-Headed Pyrohydra: 5 possible breath attacks/round dealing 3d6 fire damage. The fire damage stacks with itself so you total the effects; in this case treat as 15d6 energy damage.

Sections 7.01 through 7.21 detail most of the special attacks and qualities a creature can possess.

7.01 Ability Score Damage/Drain

The touch of some creatures can damage or drain ability scores.

Die Type	Ability Damage[1]	Ability Drain[2]
1d3	0.30	0.40
1d4	0.375	0.50
1d6	0.525	0.70
1d8	0.675	0.90
1 CR +0.15/point of average Ability Score Damage 2 CR +0.2/point of average Ability Score Drain		
• Used as Ray Attack = CR x2 • Used as Breath Weapon (1d4 round delay) = CR x2 • Used as Breath Weapon (At Will) = CR x3 • Used as a Gaze weapon = CR x4		

Example:
Wraith: 1d6 Constitution Drain = CR +0.7

Design Parameters

A creature's ability score damage on a single attack should generally not exceed twice its HD. Maximum ability score drain on a single attack should not exceed the creatures HD.

7.02 Breath Weapons

Some creatures can breathe forth a cloud of energy, such as cold or fire, while some creatures have even deadlier breath weapons, such as the petrifying breath of the gorgon.

Damage Dealing Breath Weapons:

- Base CR +0.1/die of damage

Type of Damage	Die Type
Alignment/Allegiance (good, evil, etc.)	d8
Divine (profane/sacred)	d3
Energy (fire, cold, acid, etc.)	d6
Force based damage	d4

Spell Effect Breath Weapons:
- CR +0.2/level of duplicated Spell Effect
- Touch Spell = CR x2
- Ranged Single Target or Ray Spell = CR x1.5

Breath Weapon Range:

- CR +0.2 per additional range increment

Breath Weapon Range by Creature Size		
Creature Size	**Cone**	**Line**
Fine	5 ft	10 ft
Diminutive	10 ft	20 ft
Tiny	15 ft	30 ft
Small	20 ft	40 ft
Medium	30 ft	60 ft
Large	40 ft	80 ft
Huge	50 ft	100 ft
Gargantuan	60 ft	120 ft
Colossal	70 ft	140 ft

Breath Weapon Uses/Day:	
5/day (or more)	CR x1
4/day	CR x0.8
3/day	CR x0.6
2/day	CR x0.4
1/day (or less)	CR x0.2
Delay Between Breaths	
None	CR x1.5
1d4 rounds	CR x1

Examples
Dragon Turtle Breath Weapon = CR +1.2
12d6 Energy based damage = CR +1.2
1d4 round delay = CR x1
Cone +20 ft greater than typical size = CR +0

Gorgon Breath Weapon = CR +1.8
Spell Effect: Flesh to Stone (6th-level spell) = CR +1.2
Ranged single target spell effect = CR x1.5
Range: Cone +20 ft greater than typical size = CR +/-0

Design Parameters

Damage dealing breath weapons should not exceed 1 die of damage per HD of the creature. Spell-effect breath weapons should be limited to a spell level no greater than half the creature's HD (round up). Thus, a creature with 7 Hit Dice should not possess a spell-effect breath weapon greater than a 4th level spell.

7.03 Create Spawn

Some creatures, particularly the undead, are capable of creating additional creatures that rise from the bodies of fallen opponents.

- Base CR +0.1 per CR of spawn creature

"Gestation" 1d4 days = CR ÷2
"Gestation" 1d4 rounds = CR +0

Example:
Wraith: create Wight (CR 5) in 1d4 rounds = CR +0.5

Design Parameters

No creature should be able to create spawn greater than its own CR.

7.04 Damage Reduction

Damage reduction is the ability to subtract, or reduce, a set amount when damage is taken. Most forms of damage reduction have a weakness— some type of damage that bypasses the DR completely.

- Base CR +0.1 per point of DR

Modifiers to Damage Reduction	
Weakness	**Modifier**
Multiple Types/Materials	x1/4
Single Type/Material	x1/3
Rare or Epic Type/Material	x1/2
Combination of Types/Materials	x1/2
Combination of Types/Materials (including any rare material)	x3/4
No Physical Weakness	x1
No Weakness	x2

Types of damage include slashing, bludgeoning, piercing, good, or evil.

Materials include common "alchemical" substances that may bypass DR, including silver, gold, cold iron, or magic weapons. (Depending on the style of campaign, magic weapons may qualify as rare.)

Rare materials include mithral, adamantine, or epic magic.

No Physical Weakness applies to all physical weapons, including magic weapons, but does not apply to energy types (cold, fire, acid) or to most magic spells.

No Weakness applies to all damage, regardless of whether the source is physical, energy, magical, or otherwise.

Examples:
Babau (DR 10/cold iron or good) = CR +0.25 (1 x 1/4)
Zombie (DR 5/slashing) = CR +0.166 (0.5 x 1/3)
Iron Golem (DR 15/adamantine) = CR +0.75 (1.5 x 1/2)
Lich (DR 15/bludgeoning and magic) = CR +0.75 (1.5 x 1/2)
Solar (DR 15/epic and evil) = CR +1.125 (1.5 x 3/4)
Mummy (DR 5/-) = CR +0.5 (0.5 x 1)

Design Parameters

Damage Reduction is typically rated in units of five (5/10/15/20). DR should not exceed 5 + half the creature's HD (round to the nearest unit of 5).

A creature's weaknesses also play an important role. No creature with less than 10 HD should require any rare material, and no creature with less than 20 HD should require an epic material.

Example:
A 12 HD creature could have DR 10/(any factor except epic).

7.05 Disease
Some creatures are able to inflict disease, either through their natural attacks (such as rats) or through some supernatural means (such as mummy rot).

Die Type	Ability Damage[1]	Ability Drain[2]
1d3	0.06	0.08
1d4	0.075	0.10
1d6	0.105	0.14
1d8	0.135	0.18
1 CR +0.03/point of average Ability Score Damage 2 CR +0.04/point of average Ability Score Drain		
Incubation Period		
1 week	CR x½	
1 day	CR x1	
1 hour	CR x2	
1 minute	CR x4	
1 round	CR x8	
• Cannot be healed naturally = CR x2 • Used as Breath Weapon (1d4 round delay) = CR x2 • Used as Breath Weapon (At Will) = CR x3 • Used as a Gaze weapon = CR x4		

Examples:
Mummy Rot = CR +1.68
1d6 CON + 1d6 CHA damage = CR +0.21
Cannot be healed naturally = CR x2
Incubation Period 1 minute = CR x4

Design Parameters
A creature's maximum damage per incubation period is keyed to its Hit Dice.

Incubation Period	Maximum Damage
1 day	Up to 2 x HD
1 hour	Up to 1 x HD
1 minute	Up to ½ HD
1 round	Up to ¼ HD

Thus, a 6 HD creature could deal 2d6 Strength damage per 1 day incubation period, or 1d3 damage per 1 minute incubation period.

7.06 Energy Drain
Energy drain is the ability to drain the life-force and inflict negative levels on the target.

- Base CR +0.4 per energy Level drained

Type of Energy Drain	Modifier
Used as Ray Attack	CR x2
Used as Breath Weapon (1d4 round delay)	CR x2
Used as Breath Weapon (at will)	CR x3
Used as a Gaze weapon	CR x4

Energy drain can be bought either in whole numbers (attack drains 2 levels, cost +0.8) or as the average of a random roll (1d4 level drain = 2.5 average, cost = CR 2.5 x 0.4 = +1).

Example:
Spectre (2 Level Energy Drain) = CR +0.8

Design Parameters
This ability is suggested for creatures with HD 4 or more. No creature should drain more than 1 level per 4 HD.

7.07 Energy Resistance/Immunity
Energy resistance is defined by the type of energy (acid, cold, fire, electricity, and sonic) and the amount.

- Base CR +0.1 per 5 points of Energy Resistance
- Energy immunity +1.0 per type of energy

Example:
Quasit (Fire Resistance 10) = CR +0.2

7.08 Fast Healing
Fast healing allows a creature to regain hit points at the beginning of each of its combat turns. Unlike regeneration, fast healing does not allow a creature to regrow or reattach body parts.

- Base CR +0.075/point of Fast Healing

Example:
Marut (Fast Healing 10) = CR +0.75

Design Parameters
Fast healing should be less than or equal to HD.

7.09 Gaze Attacks

A gaze attack allows a creature to affect every target within range and line of sight with a single attack.

- Base CR +0.2 per level of duplicated spell effect

Modifiers	
Converting effect from a touch spell	CR x4
Converting effect from a ranged single target or ray spell	CR x2
Converting effect from an area spell	CR x1.5
Range 30 ft.	CR +0.0
Each additional 30 ft. range	CR +0.2

Example:
Medusas Gaze = CR +2.4
Spell Effect: Flesh to Stone (6th-level spell) = CR +1.2
Converted from ranged single target spell effect = CR x2
Range: Typical = CR x1

Design Parameters
Spell-effects should be limited to a spell level no greater than half the creature's HD (round up).

7.10 Miscellaneous Abilities

Many creatures have additional miscellaneous abilities that can increase their combat effectiveness and CR.

Ability	CR Increase
Alternate Form	CR +0.2
Blindsense	CR +0.2
Blindsight	CR +1
Change Shape	CR +0.5
Constrict	CR +0.2 per die of damage
Crush	CR +0.2 per die of damage
Darkvision	CR +0.2
Fear Aura	CR +0.5
Frightful Presence	CR +0.5
Improved Grab	CR +0.2
Low-Light Vision	CR +0.1
Pounce	CR +0.2
Powerful Charge	CR +0.2 per die of damage
Rake	CR +0.2 per die of damage
Rend	CR +0.2 per die of damage
Scent	CR +0.2
Swallow Whole	CR +0.2 per die of damage
Tail Sweep	CR +0.2 per die of damage
Telepathy	CR +0.2
Trample	CR +0.2 per die of damage
Tremorsense	CR +0.1

Example:
Mariliths Constrict Ability (4d6) = CR +0.8

7.11 Immunities

Some creatures are immune to specific attack forms or spell effects. Many of these factors are included in the type or subtype; remember not to count them twice.

Immunity	CR Increase
Ability Score Loss	CR +0.5
Critical Hits	CR +0.5
Disease	CR +0.2
Energy Drain	CR +0.5
Magic (as Golem)	CR +10
Mind Affecting Effects	CR +0.5
Petrification	CR +0.2
Poison	CR +0.2
Polymorph	CR +0.2
Sleep/Paralysis/Stunning	CR +0.3 (+0.1 each)
Spell Level Immunity (each)*	CR +0.5*

*Spell Immunity (from 0th to 9th-level) is treated as CR +5, whereas Magic Immunity is treated as CR +10. Spell immunity applies only to spells and spell-like effects; magic immunity protects against both spells and all supernatural effects and abilities.

7.12 Insight, Luck, Profane, and/or Sacred Bonuses

Some creatures receive bonuses to attack rolls, saving throws, damage, and so forth that are not otherwise tied to any other factor.

- Base CR +0.125 per point of bonus

Example:
Paragon Creature (+25 Luck bonus to Attacks) = CR +3.125

7.13 Poison

Creatures with poison attacks are rated by the type (ability damage or ability drain) as well as whether the damage occurs after the initial or the secondary saving throw.

Die Type/ Damage	Initial Effect		Secondary Effect	
	Damage[1]	Drain[2]	Damage[1]	Drain[2]
1d3	0.12	0.16	0.06	0.08
1d4	0.15	0.20	0.075	0.10
1d6	0.21	0.28	0.105	0.14
1d8	0.27	0.36	0.135	0.18
Alternate Effects				
"Half"	0.6		0.3	
Death	1.2		0.6	

1 CR +0.06/0.03 per point of average Ability Score Damage
2 CR +0.08/0.04 per point of average Ability Score Drain

- Used as Breath Weapon (1d4 round delay) = CR x2
- Used as Breath Weapon (At Will) = CR x3

Example:
Pit Fiend's Poison Bite = total CR +0.46
Initial Effect: 1d6 Constitution damage = CR +0.21
Secondary Effect: 'Death' = CR +0.25

Design Parameters

The maximum initial damage should not exceed the creature's HD, and the maximum secondary damage should not exceed 2 x HD.

7.14 Touch and Ray Attacks

Damage Dealing Attacks	
Per die of damage: d8 Alignment d12 Bane d3 Divine d6 Energy d4 Force	CR +0.05
Per point of permanent damage	CR +0.1
Ray Attack	CR x2

Attacks with Spell-Like Effects	
Touch spells	CR +0.1 per spell level
Convert Area of Effect Spell to Ray	CR +0.2 per spell level
Convert Touch Spell to Ray	CR +0.4 per spell level
Per additional increment of typical range (see below)	CR +0.2

Uses/Day	
5/day (or more)	CR x1
4/day	CR x0.8
3/day	CR x0.6
2/day	CR x0.4
1/day (or less)	CR x0.2

Typical Ray Ranges by Creature Size	
Size	Typical Range
Fine	20 ft
Diminutive	40 ft
Tiny	60 ft
Small	80 ft
Medium	120 ft
Large	160 ft
Huge	200 ft
Gargantuan	240 ft
Colossal	280 ft

Example:
Yrthaks Sonic Lance (ray) = CR +0.6
Sonic Lance: 6d6 Energy (sonic) damage = CR +0.3
Ray effect = CR x2
Range: (60 ft., standard or less) = CR x1

Design Parameters

As with breath weapons and gaze attacks, damage dealing attacks should not exceed 1 die of damage (or ½ hit point of permanent damage) per HD of the creature. Spell-effects should be limited to a spell level no greater than half the creature's HD (round up).

7.15 Regeneration

- CR +0.2/point of Regeneration with no vulnerabilities
- CR +0.1.5/point of Regeneration with a single vulnerability (acid, fire, holy, etc.)
- CR +0.1/point of Regeneration with two or more vulnerabilities

Example:
Troll (Regeneration 5) = CR +0.5

Design Parameters

As with fast healing, the amount of regeneration should be less than or equal to HD.

7.16 Spell-Like Abilities
Many creatures have spell-like abilities to aid them in combat. Although spell-like abilities have a caster level and a spell level, they do not cause spell burn or require a caster level check.

Spell-Like Abilities	
Use	Challenge Rating Factor
Always Active	Caster Level x Spell Level x 0.005
At Will	Caster Level x Spell Level x 0.005
5/day (or more)	Caster Level x Spell Level x 0.005
4/day	Caster Level x Spell Level x 0.004
3/day	Caster Level x Spell Level x 0.003
2/day	Caster Level x Spell Level x 0.002
1/day (or less)	Caster Level x Spell Level x 0.001

Example:
Pit Fiend's Spell-like Abilities = total CR +6.102
At Will abilities: 18 (Caster Level) x 64 (Spell Levels) x 0.005 (At Will) = CR +5.76
1/day Abilities: 18 (Caster Level) x 9 (Spell Levels) x 0.001 (1/day) = CR +0.162
1/year abilities: 20 (Caster Level) x 9 (Spell Levels) x 0.001 (1/year) = CR +0.18

Succubus Spell-like Abilities = total CR +1.64
At Will Abilities: 12 (Caster Level) x 28 (Spell Levels) x 0.005 (At Will) = CR +1.64

Design Parameters
No creature should have a spell-like ability of a level greater than half its HD, and no creature should have more than two abilities at each given spell level.

Example:
A 10 HD creature could have two spell-like abilities at each spell level from 1st to 5th.

7.17 Spell Resistance
Spell resistance enables creatures to ignore the effects of spells and spell-like abilities. Spell resistance is purchased first as a "base" amount equal to 11 + the creature's CR (which you can calculate when the creation process is complete). You can then purchase SR above or below the base amount for an incremental cost.

- Base CR +2.0 for SR = CR + 11
- CR +/- 0.2 per point above/below base

Some creatures' spell resistance is based on their class level; the cost remains the same, but the creature's base SR is calculated on its class level instead of its total CR.

Example:
Pit Fiend (SR32) = CR +2.2
Base SR = 11 + 20 = 31
Increase SR + 1 for +0.2 CR

Design Parameters:
A creature's total spell resistance should not exceed its HD + 12.

7.18. Spellcasting
Some creatures cast spells using the normal spellcasting rules. In this case the CR factor is based on the type of caster, their caster level, and the type of spells known.

Casts Spells As	Adept Type	Spells Known	CR per caster level
Wizard/Sorcerer	Arcane or Wild	Arcane	+0.44
Cleric	Divine	Divine	+0.38
Druid	Divine or Wild	Druid	+0.28
Bard	Wild	Bard	+0.15

Example:
Planetar (17th-level Cleric) = CR +6.46

7.19 Summoning
Some creatures, particularly demons and devils, have the ability to summon additional creatures during combat. The cost of this ability is based on the CR of the creature summoned.

- Base CR = (Summoned CR)^2 x (Uses Factor) x (Success)

Uses	CR Factor
5/day (or more)	x0.005
4/day	x0.004
3/day	x0.003
2/day	x0.002
1/day	x0.001

Chance of Success: Multiply the final total by the chance of success (i.e. 80% chance of success = x.80).

There is no extra charge for the ability to summon multiple creatures, either singly as a choice from a list, or even in groups. The cost is based on the highest CR of either a single creature or group.

Examples:
Pit Fiend Summoning = CR +0.462
Highest Summoning (Gelugon) = CR 21
Uses: 2/day
(1/2) x (21)^2 x (.002)

Succubus Summons = CR +0.036
Highest Summoning (Vrock) = CR 15
Uses: 1/day
30% chance of success
(1/2) x (15)^2 x (.001) x (.30)

Design Parameters
The total CR of summoned creatures should not exceed the CR of the summoning creature.

7.20 Turn Resistance
- Base CR +0.1 per +2 points of Turn Resistance

Example:
Allip (Turn Resistance +2) = CR +0.1

7.21 Vulnerabilities
Apply a reduction for standard vulnerabilities using the examples below as guidelines, or use the creature weaknesses section (below).

Light Sensitivity (Kobold) CR -0.1

Vulnerability to [Energy] (Treant) CR -0.5

Vulnerability to Sunlight (Bodak) CR -0.2

8. Ability Scores
Ability scores are calculated only when they are inherent; that is, not gained as a result of size, type, magic items, etc..

Unless increased, ability scores follow the standard array: 11, 11, 11, 10, 10, 10 (arranged as the GM wishes).

- Base CR +/- 0.1 per point above/below 10

Unrated Ability Scores
No Strength Score = CR -2.2
Always fail Strength checks CR -0.2
Can't interact with surroundings CR -2

No Dexterity Score = CR -2.2
Always fail Dexterity checks CR -0.2
Can't move CR -2

No Constitution Score = CR +1.9 (and special*)
Always fail Constitution checks CR -0.2
Cannot be Raised etc. CR -0.2
Destroyed at 0 hp (Never *disabled* or *dying*) CR -0.2
Immune to Ability Score Damage CR +0.5
Immune to Critical Hits CR +0.5
Immune to Energy Drain CR +0.5
Immune to Fortitude saves CR +1
(including Disease; Paralysis; Poison; Sleep; Stun etc.)
No possible Hit Point Bonuses CR -0.1/Hit Dice*

**Already factored into Construct and Undead Hit Dice CR factors.*

No Intelligence Score = CR -0.7
Always fail Intelligence checks CR -0.2
Immune to Mind Affecting Effects CR +0.5
Mindless CR -1

No Wisdom or Charisma = special
No Wisdom or Charisma means the means the 'creature' is not self aware, and is therefore an object. As such it has no CR score.

Design Parameters
Use the standard array for most creatures. Use the elite array for group leaders, as well as all constructs, dragons, outsiders, fey, and free-willed undead.

- Standard Array: 13, 12, 11, 10, 9, 8 (average 10.5)
- Elite Array: 15, 14, 13, 12, 10, 8 (average 12)

If you wish to increase the ability scores above the starting array, plus all intrinsic modifiers for size, etc., keep bonuses within +1 per HD for creatures using the standard array and +2 per HD for creatures using the elite array.

Example:
Sample Large 18 HD Outsider
Starting array (elite): 15, 14, 13, 12, 10, 8
Modifiers: Size (Large): +8 Str, +4 Con, -2 Dex
Acceptable increases allowed: up to +36 (+2 per HD)
Sample ability scores (within design parameters):
Str 31, Dex 18, Con 23, Int 18, Wis 16, Cha 14

9. Racial Skill Bonuses
Some creatures have racial skill bonuses that increase their total skill point expenditures above the norm for their level or HD.

- Base CR +0.02/bonus skill point

Example:
Lich (+48 points racial skill bonuses) = CR +0.96

10. Bonus Feats
Some creatures have bonus feats above and beyond the normal number of feats for a creature of their class or level (normally one feat per 3 HD).

- Base CR +0.2/bonus feat

Example:
Vampire (5 bonus Feats) = CR +1

11. Wealth/Equipment
Creatures or characters are more effective when they are properly equipped.

- Base CR +/- 0.2 per level of PC Equipment
- Base CR +/- 0.125 per level of NPC Equipment

The GM determines the appropriate level of PC Wealth/ Equipment for his campaign. The exact totals are not important provided that the GM is consistent. If a monster has equipment appropriate to a 10th level PC in the campaign, the CR should be adjusted accordingly.

Notice that combining Factor #1 (+0.8 per character level) with Factor #13 (+0.2 per level of PC wealth) results in the 1 Character Level = 1 CR design parameter.

You can also use this factor to increase the CR of a creature who comes standard with certain items (for example, the *vorpal sword* and *flaming whip* of a balor). In such cases, find the total value of all of the creature's equipment and compare it against the minimum PC level needed to purchase that equipment.

Examples:
10th-level Hero (with no equipment) = CR +8
10th-level Hero (with NPC equipment) = CR +9.125
10th-level Hero (with PC equipment) = CR +10
10th-level Hero (with 20th-level PC equipment) = CR +12

Reduction Factors

There are a few ways you can "buy back" some of the design factors:

- Fewer skill points: The creature receives 1 less skill point per HD or level. -0.1 CR.
- Lost feat: The creature has one less feat than normal. -0.2 CR.
- Weakness: The creature has one of the weaknesses listed below. The value of a weakness is based on the strength of the weakness and the effect.

Creature Weaknesses

Although a creature's type and species determine many of its traits and abilities, GMs are encouraged to alter a creature's physiology, behavior, abilities, tactics, and defenses when it serves the story or to confound players who think they know everything about their opponents.

The rules provided allow GMs to build custom monsters and ascribe special qualities to them. When designing a creature, the GM should also think of ways the creature can be defeated. From the heroes' point of view, a creature's weaknesses are more important than its abilities. Assigning weaknesses to creatures gives under-powered or poorly equipped heroes a fighting chance.

The Sources of Weakness table below lists many sources to which a creature may be vulnerable. A source can be a specific object, location, substance, sound, sensation, or activity. How the creature interacts with a source of weakness is left up to the GM, although most sources must be in close proximity to the creature (if not touching the creature) to affect it. GMs may roll randomly on the table, choose a source that suits the creature, or devise their own.

Source Strength

A creature gets either a Fortitude or Will saving throw to overcome or resist the source of weakness; the DC of the save varies depending on the source's strength:

Strength of Source	Save DC	CR[1]
Easily resistible	10	-0.0
Moderate	15	-0.05
Strong	20	-0.10
Overpowering	25	-0.20
Irresistible	No Save	x2

1 The CR reduction values (listed below for each type of reaction) is increased as the source becomes harder to resist.

Source Effects

After determining a creature's source of weakness, the GM needs to decide how the creature reacts when confronted by the source. Pick an effect that seems appropriate for the creature and the source.

Sources of Weakness

d%	Result
01-02	Alcohol (moonshine, whisky, vodka, etc.)
03-04	Ale, wine, or beer
05-06	Archways
07-08	Bells or chimes
09-11	Blood
12-13	Books
14-16	Bright light
17-18	Cats / Dogs
19-20	Children
21-22	Clocks / Timepieces
23-24	Cracks
25-27	Crossroads / Corners
28-30	Crosses or crucifixes
31-32	Crows
33-34	Drugs, natural (opium, hemp, mushrooms, etc.)
35-37	Element, pure (fire, water, earth, or air)
38-40	Flesh (including raw meat)
41-43	Flower (rose, poppy, tulip, garlic, lavender, etc.)
44-45	Gambling
46-48	Gemstone (diamond, pearl, amber, etc.)
49-51	Geometric shape (circle, triangle, square)
52-54	Gold, silver, or iron
55-57	Grave dirt / grave stones / graveyards
58-60	Holy symbols / holy water / consecrated ground
61-62	Unholy symbols / unholy water / desecrated ground
63-64	Keys
65-66	Laughter
67-69	Ley lines or power nexuses
70-72	Magic Circle (pentagram, crop circle, etc.)
73-75	Magical substance (mithril, adamantine, etc.)
76-77	Moonlight
78-79	Music (or specific song)
80-81	Neatness / Order
82-83	Numbers (specific number: 3, 6, 7, 8, 666, etc.)
84-85	Salt (or other common spice)
86-87	Shadow or fog
88-89	Specific phrase or word
90-92	Spoken spellcasting or archaic language
93-95	Sunlight, starlight, or moonlight
96-97	Virgins
98-00	Wood (oak, ash, pine, cherry, dogwood)

Creatures usually react to a source of weakness in one of six ways:

Attraction (CR -0.05)

The creature is compelled to move as fast as it can toward the source. On a successful Will save, the creature resists the compulsion. On a failed save, the creature moves toward the source at its maximum speed, taking the safest and most direct route. Once it reaches the source, the compelled creature seeks to possess it. If the source isn't something the creature can easily possess, it gets a new save every round to break the compulsion.

Even creatures immune to mind-affecting effects are susceptible to a source-induced attraction.

Strategy: Attraction is the least useful weakness for PCs to exploit; indeed, being near or possessing the source of the attraction can place a PC in even more danger.

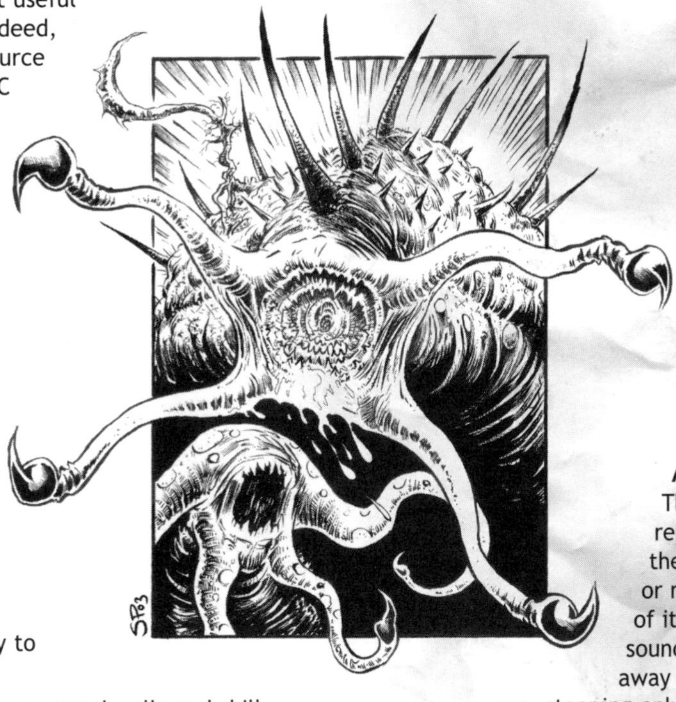

Addiction (CR -0.10)

The creature is compelled to ingest, imbibe, or inhale the source. The source must be within 5 feet of the creature to affect it. On a successful Will save, the creature negates the compulsion. On a failed save, the creature spends a full-round action indulging its addiction, then may resume normal actions while suffering one or more of the following effects (GM's choice):

- Creature takes a -2 penalty to Dexterity and Wisdom.
- Creature takes a -2 penalty on attack rolls and skill checks.
- Creature loses 10% of its current hit points.
- Blindness: The creature has a 50% miss chance in combat, loses any Dexterity bonus to AC, moves at half speed, takes a -4 penalty on Strength and Dexterity-based skills, and cannot make Spot checks. Foes gain a +2 bonus on attack rolls to hit the creature.
- Deafness: The creature takes a -4 penalty to initiative checks and has a 20% chance of spell failure when casting spells with verbal components. The creature cannot make Listen checks.
- Creature loses one of its extraordinary, supernatural, or spell-like special qualities. For example, if the creature has Damage Reduction, it may temporarily lose this quality, allowing the PCs a chance to harm it.

Each effect lasts 1d4 hours. Even creatures immune to mind-affecting effects are susceptible to a source-induced addiction.

Strategy: An addiction weakness is not easily exploited by the PCs. Once the creature has satisfied its addiction (and suffered some minor side effect) it is able to go about its business as usual.

Fascination (CR -0.15)

The creature finds the source fascinating and ceases all attacks and movement upon seeing, hearing, smelling, or otherwise perceiving it. On a successful Will save, the creature negates the fascination and can act normally. On a failed Will save, the creature can take no actions, and foes gain a +2 bonus on attack rolls against the creature. Any time the creature is attacked or takes damage, it gets a new save to negate the fascination. Otherwise, the fascination lasts as long as the creature can see, hear, smell, or otherwise perceive the source.

Even creatures immune to mind-affecting effects are susceptible to a source-induced fascination.

Strategy: Clever PCs can exploit a fascination weakness to effect an escape, or to herd the creature in a desired direction, but it is otherwise of little defensive or offensive use.

Aversion (CR -0.20)

The creature finds the source repellent. On a failed save, the creature cannot approach or remain within 1d4 x10 feet of it. In the case of traveling sounds, the creature moves away from the source as fast as it can, stopping only when it can no longer hear it. On a successful Will save, the creature overcomes its aversion and may approach the source freely.

A repelled creature that cannot move the requisite distance from the source suffers one or more of the following effects (GM's choice):

- Creature takes a -2 morale penalty to Strength and Dexterity.
- Creature takes a -2 morale penalty on attack rolls, damage rolls, and skill checks.
- Creature takes a -2 penalty to AC.
- Blindness: See Addiction, above.
- Deafness: See Addiction, above.
- Creature loses one of its extraordinary, supernatural or spell-like special qualities.

Each effect lasts until the creature leaves the affected area and for 1d4 rounds afterward. Even creatures immune to mind-affecting effects are susceptible to a source-induced aversion.

Example: Kobolds and orcs who are sensitive to sunlight (-2 penalty); dark elves who lose their spell resistance in sunlight; a demons who loses its fast healing on holy ground.

Strategy: An aversion weakness can be exploited by the PCs, and though a creature with an aversion is free to act within the boundaries of its weakness, most will simply choose to retreat. The creature must have a compelling reason to stay, or have well-laid plans for removing the source of its aversion.

Fear (CR -0.30)

The creature is frightened by the source. If it fails its Will save, the creature flees from the source as fast as it can. If unable to flee, the creature takes a -2 morale penalty on attack rolls, weapon damage rolls, and saving throws. On a successful save, the creature overcomes the fear and can approach the source or otherwise act without penalty.

Even creatures immune to mind-affecting effects are susceptible to a source-induced fear.

Strategy: Fear is more easily exploited by the PCs than aversion, as the affected creature has no option other than to flee.

Harm (CR -0.50 or more)

Contact with the source or proximity to the source harms the creature in some fashion. On a successful Fortitude save, the creature negates the effect or, in the case of instant death or disintegration, takes damage instead. GMs may choose one of the following effects or invent their own:

- Blindness and deafness: See Addiction, above. The blindness and deafness last 1d4 hours.
- Creature loses all of its supernatural and spell-like special qualities.
- Creature loses 50% of its current hit points.
- Creature is turned to stone instantly.
- Creature drops dead. On a successful save, the creature takes 3d6+15 points of damage instead.
- Creature is disintegrated. On a successful save, the creature takes 5d6 points of damage instead.

Even creatures immune to effects that require Fortitude saves are susceptible to source-induced harm.

Strategy: A harm weakness is crippling and can be easily exploited by the PCs. Creatures with such weaknesses go to great lengths to conceal their weaknesses or to mislead their foes as to the true nature of their weakness.

Player Characters and Design Factors

You can use the creature creation rules to create new races or to give PCs unusual abilities or enhancements, from magical abilities to mutations.

The creature creation rules work in concert with the EL experience point system (see Chapter Thirteen). When calculating party EL, add all of the PC's character levels *and* any additional CR granted to any of the characters by unusual abilities.

This will have the effect of increasing the total party CR and thus, the total party EL; experience points earned for a given encounter will be correspondingly reduced.

When calculating XP, find the XP multiplier for the party's relative EL. When awarding experience points, the XP is multiplied by each PC's character level— additional CR for unusual abilities does not result in additional XP.

Using this method, there is no need for the GM to determine "Level Adjustment" for players who wish to roleplay as monsters; in fact, the GM may add "monstrous" abilities piecemeal, allowing a character to develop more slowly without outpacing the rest of the PCs or the power level the GM prefers.

Example:

After a horrifying encounter in a dark alley, the GM decides that one of the PCs (currently a 3rd level character) is being slowly turned into a vampire. First the GM adds to the PCs ability scores (+2 to Strength and +4 to Charisma) and gives the PC a bit of natural armor (+2). Using the design factors so far, the PC has a CR increase of +0.8. The GM bumps this to an even +1.0 by adding an Alternate Form (wolf, +0.2) to the character.

This character's total CR is now 4.0: +3.0 for character levels and +1.0 for her budding vampirism. Using Table 14-1 the GM determines that the character is EL9.

Acting alone, the character adventures on. Her next encounter (against a group of the original vampire's human thugs, as it turns out) is EL5. Now that she is enjoying the benefits of early vampirism, this encounter is of moderate difficulty (EL5 - EL9 = EL -4). The XP multiplier for a moderate encounter is 75; as always, the character earns XP based on her character level (3rd) for a total XP gain of 225.

Without the increased CR, this character would have been CR3, and thus only EL7. The encounter would have been difficult, with an XP multiplier of 150. If she'd survived, the character would have earned 450 XP.

This method, rather than artificially inflating the character's level (so that she has to gain more experience to gain a level), instead gives an accurate assessment of the character's CR and decreases the amount of XP earned, while keeping the character on the same target path for level advancement.

The results are not as dramatic in a party of PCs, but all players should be aware that when the enhanced abilities of one character begin to make every encounter easier for the group, the group as a whole earns fewer XP.

Characters and the Golden Rule

You should strive never to add more CR factors to a character than double his levels or hit dice.

If you do so, you should apply the Golden Rule to all additional CR factors, otherwise there is a risk that the character will not be able to overcome challenges designed for his increased CR. Each time the character gains a level or HD, adjust his CR accordingly.

Designing New Races

When using the creature creation rules to design new races for the campaign, the GM may opt to allow a certain increase (for example, up to +0.4 or less) without actually changing or tracking this additional CR.

A list of standard fantasy races (including a breakdown of CR factors) follows:

Dwarf Racial Traits [CR +0.21]

Ability Scores (Total +/-0)	CR +/-0
Attack Bonus (orcs/goblins)	CR +0.04
Darkvision	CR +0.2
Dodge Bonus (giants)	CR +0.04
Movement (-10 ft Speed)	CR -0.1
Movement Unrestricted by Armor	CR +0.05
Poison Save (+2)	CR +0.02
Save Bonus vs. Magic (+2)	CR +0.1
Skill Bonuses (+6)	CR +0.12
Stability	CR +0.04
-1 Feat	CR -0.2
-1 Skill Point per level	CR -0.1

Elf Racial Traits [CR +0.06]

Ability Scores (Total +/-0)	CR +/-0
Low-Light Vision	CR +0.1
Save Bonus vs. Enchantment (+2)	CR +0.04
Sleep Immunity	CR +0.1
Skill Bonuses (+6)	CR +0.12
-1 Feat	CR -0.2
-1 Skill Point per level	CR -0.1

Gnome Racial Traits [CR +0.0625]

Ability Scores (Total +/-0)	CR +/-0
Attack Bonus (kobolds)	CR +0.04
Dodge Bonus (giants)	CR +0.04
Difficulty Class Bonus (to Illusions)	CR +0.05
Low-Light Vision	CR +0.1
Save Bonus vs. Illusions (+2)	CR +0.04
Skill Bonuses (+4)	CR +0.08
Small Size (Modified)	CR +/-0
Spell-like Abilities	CR +0.0125
-1 Feat	CR -0.2
-1 Skill Point per level	CR -0.1

Half-Elf Racial Traits [CR +0.08]

Low-Light Vision	CR +0.1
Save Bonus vs. Enchantment (+2)	CR +0.04
Sleep Immunity	CR +0.1
Skill Bonuses (+7)	CR +0.14
-1 Feat	CR -0.2
-1 Skill Point per level	CR -0.1

Halfling Racial Traits [CR +0.18]

Ability Scores (Total +/-0)	CR +/-0
Attack Bonus (thrown weapons)	CR +0.1
Morale Bonus (+2) (fear)	CR +0.02
Save Bonus (+1)	CR +0.2
Skill Bonuses (+8)	CR +0.16
Small Size (Modified)	CR +/-0
-1 Feat	CR -0.2
-1 Skill Point per level	CR -0.1

Half-Orc Racial Traits [CR -0.3]

Ability Scores (Total -2)	CR -0.2
Darkvision	CR +0.2
-1 Feat	CR -0.2
-1 Skill Point per level	CR -0.1

Human Racial Traits [CR +0.0]

Grim Tales is humanocentric; all characters start with the bonus feat and +1 skill point per level. They are costed out below for reference.

Bonus Feat	CR +0.2
Skill Bonuses (x5+)	CR +0.1

GAMEMASTERING

In the many worlds of Grim Tales, the heroes are beset from all sides. Most foes are mundane, such as the vast numbers of ordinary human henchmen who serve some greater power. Those greater powers, however, acting behind the scenes to thwart the heroes, may have supernatural powers, and some may even hail from other worlds or dimensions.

Regardless of origin, the various foes with which the heroes must contend are called threats. By and large, heroes gain experience by overcoming these threats.

This section enables the GM to design encounters for the players that are matched to their abilities, and to group multiple encounters into a longer session without overwhelming the players. At a glance, the GM will be able to outline each encounter and well as design natural breaks in the action that allow the players to rest and recover, to be challenged without being overwhelmed.

Using Creatures From Other Sources

There is a vast and growing library of "monster books" from which you may draw creatures to threaten your heroes. In addition to the monsters available in the core rulebooks published by Wizards of the Coast, you can use monsters from any other compatible d20 source.

Encounter Level

Challenge Rating (CR) is a measure of absolute power, while Encounter Level (EL) is a measure of relative power. All of a creature's various CR factors indicate its total combat repertoire; however, EL measures what a creature is capable of doing in a single encounter. During an encounter, one side or the other is likely to prevail before a creature has time to bring all of its abilities to bear; thus, even as CR increases, its impact upon EL diminishes: EL does not increase 1-to-1 with CR.

EL measures the difficulty of an encounter. If the difficulty of an encounter is doubled, EL increases by +2; thus, EL14 is twice as difficult as EL12; EL16 is four times as difficult as EL12; EL18 is eight times as difficult as EL12, etc.

The relationship between CR and EL is shown on Table 14-1 below.

Determining EL for Multiple Opponents

Unlike CR, which is an individual rating, Encounter Level is determined for groups of combatants.

To determine the EL of a group, total the CR of each creature in the group. Apply the total CR to Table 14-1 to determine the base EL.

Once the base EL is determined, apply an adjustment based on the total number of allied creatures, using table 14-2 below.

Table 14-1: CR to EL Conversion

CR	EL	CR	EL	CR	EL
1/10	1/10	6	11	192-223	31
1/9	1/9	7	12	224-255	32
1/8	1/8	8-9	13	256-319	33
1/7	1/7	10-11	14	320-383	34
1/6	1/6	12-13	15	384-447	35
1/5	1/5	14-15	16	448-511	36
1/4	1/4	16-19	17	512-639	37
1/3	1/3	20-23	18	640-767	38
1/2	1/2	24-27	19	768-895	39
2/3	2/3	28-31	20	896-1023	40
1	1	32-39	21	1024-1279	41
1.25	2	40-47	22	1280-1535	42
1.5	3	48-55	23	1536-1791	43
1.75	4	56-63	24	1792-2047	44
2	5	64-79	25	2048-2559	45
2.5	6	80-95	26	2560-3071	46
3	7	96-111	27	3072-3583	47
3.5	8	112-127	28	3584-4095	48
4	9	128-159	29	4096-5119	49
5	10	160-191	30	5120-6143	50

Table 14-2: EL Adjustment for Multiple Combatants

# Combatants	EL Adjustment
1	EL +/-0
2	EL -2
3	EL -3
4-5	EL -4
6-7	EL -5
8-11	EL -6
12-15	EL -7
16-23	EL -8
24-31	EL -9
32-47	EL -10
Each subsequent doubling of combatants = -2 EL.	

Fractional CRs

The above method does not work with creatures with a fractional CR (less than CR1). For such creatures, total the CR as normal, but before applying the adjustment on Table 14-2, arrange the creatures into groups equal to the fractional portion of the CR (CR 1/2 is two creatures, CR 1/4 is four creatures, etc.). Each group then counts as a single combatant.

For example, a group of CR 2/3 creatures requires 3 creatures to count as a single combatant. Three such creatures are CR 2 (2/3 x 3 = 2), EL5. Since 3 such creatures count as a single combatant on Table 14-2, there is no further adjustment. Six such creatures would be CR4, EL9; six creatures count as two combatants in this case, so the adjusted EL is 7 (EL9, 2 combatants = EL -2, or EL7).

Generally speaking, the GM should avoid mixing very powerful creatures with weaker creatures, no matter how numerous. When dealing with groups of very powerful creatures mixed with (relatively) very weak creatures, the weaker creatures may be insignificant to the overall EL— in fact, in some cases, the presence of numerous weaker creatures could erroneously *lower* the EL below that of the base creature!

To avoid this, find the EL of the single creature with the highest CR. Any other single creature type (no matter how numerous) whose EL is less than 18 below the toughest creature has no effect on the EL of the combined group.

Examples:
Party of six 10th level characters = EL 19
6 x CR 10 = 60
CR 60 = base EL 24
six creatures = EL -5

1 Hill Giant, 4 Trolls, and an Ogre = EL 17
Hill Giant CR10
4 Trolls CR28
Ogre CR4
CR42 = base EL 22
six creatures = EL -5

Using Encounter Levels

Using Table 14-3 below, compare the party EL with the opponents' EL. The table shows the chance that the party will survive the encounter, as well as what resources they can be expected to expend to survive the encounter.

As a quick reminder, the GM should consider that with evenly matched groups (equal EL), the party has only a 50/50 chance of survival, and that only by expending 100% of their resources.

Obviously, the GM will want to throw weaker encounters at the party, so as not to overwhelm them. Multiple weaker encounters can be used to whittle down the party. The GM should use Table 14-3 as an overview of multiple encounters to determine how often the party will need to rest.

Thus, a party of PCs could handle four PEL -6 encounters (12.5% resources each) and one PEL -2 encounter (50% resources) before requiring rest to recover their resources.

The GM can also use the table above to plan larger, mixed encounters by breaking the groups up into smaller units. Instead of assailing the PCs with consecutive threats as shown above, the GM could throw them a final encounter including a Henchman (50%), a group of Elite Footsoldiers (25%), and twice again as many easy Footsoldiers (12.5% x 2). Overall, this encounter becomes Very Difficult (100% resources).

- Background Only: Irrelevant and Impossible Encounters are referred to as 'Background only'; meaning that they should not be considered 'legitimate' encounters, but may be included to add flavor to an encounter, whether they are insignificant peasants or a rampaging monster of godlike proportions.
- Fodder: Very Easy encounters could be equated to mere Fodder, in that they will almost never tax the PCs abilities, acting as mere diversions or delays to impede their progress, even when encountered in large numbers.

Table 14-3: Using Encounter Levels

Opponent EL	Party Victory	Resources Used	Description
Party EL -12	99.3%	1.5%	Irrelevant (Background Only)
Party -10	98.4%	3.1%	Inconsequential (Cannon Fodder)
Party -8	96.8%	6.2%	Very Easy (Footsoldiers)
Party -6	93.7%	12.5%	Easy (Footsoldiers)
Party -4	87.5%	25%	Moderate (Elite Footsoldiers)
Party -2	75%	50%	Difficult (Henchman)
Party +0	50%	100%	Very Difficult (Nemesis)
Party +2	25%	100%+	Pyrrhic (Major Nemesis)
Party +4	12.5%	100%+	Impossible (Background Only)

- Footsoldier: Easy encounters often represent typical grunts who should only ever pose a significant threat to the PCs progress in sufficient numbers.
- Elite Footsoldier: Encounters of Moderate difficulty are dangerous enough to cause the PCs problems should they act in a churlish or overconfident manner.
- Henchman: Difficult encounters are epitomised by Henchman types. It should be noted that these opponents are virtually equal to the PCs in power. As such, PC casualties are a definite possibility.
- Nemesis: A Very Difficult encounter often represents a party Nemesis: an adversary that is actually more powerful than the PCs themselves. It may well be in the PCs best interests to run from such encounters unless they feel they have an advantage of some kind.
- Major Nemesis: The PCs may be able to win a Pyrrhic encounter such as this, if they are properly prepared,

but even so, they are likely to suffer such heavy casualties as to invalidate the effort. As the finale to a campaign, where the PCs are not expected to survive, such encounters may be legitimate.

Sample Encounter Design

Using the system presented here, the GM can quickly design encounters that are balanced against the party.

1. Calculate the Party EL

Add all of the characters' class levels, plus any CR from additional abilities, cohorts, animals, etc. to determine the party's total CR. Find the base EL on Table 14-1, find the adjusted EL for the number of combatants on Table 14-2.

The party consists of four heroes (each 5th level) and their loyal dog, a CR2 great dane of unusual character. The total party CR is 22 (5x4, +2); the base EL is 18. The adjusted EL (for a party of 6 combatants, EL -5) is EL13.

2. Determine the desired difficulty (EL) of the encounter

Use Table 14-3 to find the appropriate EL for an encounter designed to challenge the party to the GM's specs.

The GM decides he wants an encounter of moderate difficulty (EL -4). The desired encounter is EL9.

3. Determine the "scale" of the encounter (number of opponents involved) and adjust EL

The GM should decide how the encounter will appear "on stage" in terms of the number of opponents involved. The chosen EL is the adjusted EL and the GM must work backwards to determine the base EL. Determine the number of opponents and adjust the EL *upwards* using Table 14-2 to find the base EL.

The GM wants his encounter to feature a horde of punks (posing as flesh-eating zombies trying to scare the heroes away). He decides that 8 opponents is about right. Checking Table 14-2, he finds that 8 opponents is EL -6. His desired, adjusted EL9 translates back to a base EL15.

4. Convert EL to CR

Use the base EL found above to find the total CR of the opposition, using Table 14-1.

A base EL of 15 converts back to CR 12-13.

5. Purchase individual combatants from the CR total

Choose a CR value within the range listed and "buy" each combatant from the CR total. Remember not to overspend or underspend, saving enough CR to purchase all of the opponents allotted. The EL is based on the number of opponents, so you must use a number of opponents that falls within your predetermined range of opponents.

The GM has 12-13 CR to spend on 8 punks. He doesn't have quite enough for each punk to be CR2 (as that would bring the total to CR16). He could make some of the punks a bit tougher, and divide the remainder out— for example, 5 punks at CR2 and 3 punks at CR1 for a total of 8 combatants, CR13.

He doesn't quite like that option, as it seems like too many chiefs and not enough indians, so he checks back to table 14-2. According to the table, there's no EL difference between 8 combatants and 11. He decides to increase the number of combatants to 11. He goes with 10 punks at CR1 each, and one leader at CR2, for a total of 11 punks, CR12.

Just to double check his work, he works forwards using these figures. Total CR12 is base EL15. Checking Table 14-2 again, 11 combatants is EL -6, for an adjusted EL9. That was the target EL for the encounter— perfect!

Awarding Experience Points

The amount of Experience Points (xp) awarded depends firstly on the difference between the opponents' EL and the EL of the Party. Refer to the table below to determine the base XP for a given encounter, then multiply the result shown by each individual character's level. (Using this method, each character requires 13 1/3 encounters of moderate difficulty in order to gain an experience level.)

Table 14-4: Individual Experience Point Awards per Encounter

EL Difference (Opponent EL - Party EL)		Experience Points Awarded (per Character Level)
-12	Irrelevant	4.6875
-11		6.25
-10	Inconsequential	9.375
-9		12.5
-8	Very Easy	18.75
-7		25
-6	Easy	37.5
-5		50
-4	Moderate	75
-3		100
-2	Difficult	150
-1		200
+/-0	Very Difficult	300
+1		400
+2	Pyrrhic	600
+3		800
+4	Impossible	1200

Individual Experience Awards

Using individual experience awards gives the GM and the players much greater flexibility:

- Each character is awarded according to his character level, keeping character advancement regular;
- The party can include animals, monsters, cohorts and henchmen, which will increase the party's EL and chances of victory, without awarding undue experience points for encounters made easier through the use of such resources;
- Using the Design Factors found in Chapter Thirteen: Creature Creation, the GM can design new races or special abilities for the PCs that increase their CR (and their survivability) without having to calculate "effective character level" and other book-keeping annoyances.

Experience points are always *calculated* according to the actual difficulty of the encounter, including all factors; and always *awarded* according to each character's relative contribution, as reflected by his actual character level.

Example:
20th-level Fast hero; 20th-level Smart hero; 15th-level Dedicated hero (a werewolf!) (total CR 18) and an 18th-level Strong Hero = party EL 21

Opponent: one Vrock demon (CR 13) = EL 15
EL Difference -6 = 37.5 XP/Level

The two 20th level heroes each receive 750 XP; the 18th level Strong hero receives 675 XP; and the 15th level Dedicated hero receives 562 XP. Note that although the Dedicated hero's status as a werewolf added to his CR (and thus, made the encounter easier) he does not receive additional XP. XP are awarded by character level only.

Group Experience Awards

If you do not want to award XP individually, simply total all character levels in the party, calculate a lump sum XP award based on Table 14-4, and divide the total evenly among all PCs

Skill Checks and Story XP Awards

The XP awards listed above are centered around combat, but there are other dangers the PCs must face and other ways to overcome them. The GM can award experience points for vital skill checks and story awards.

Skill Checks

Experience points are awarded for skill checks only for checks with a DC15 or higher and only when the success or failure of the skill carries serious consequences. A DC15 skill check is CR1; add +1 to the CR for each +1 increase to the DC. The GM may integrate the skill check CR into a combat encounter or award XP for the skill check as its own encounter (converting CR to EL as normal).

Skill Check DC	CR[1]
15	1
+1 DC	+1 CR
1 Add +1 to the CR if the skill cannot be used untrained.	

Story Awards

The GM can assign non-combat, non-skill related encounters a difficulty using Table 14-4. For example, the GM may devise a "difficult" riddle that the players must solve in order to advance their cause, awarding experience as for a Difficult encounter. Or, he may present them with a moral or ethical dilemma, awarding experience points according to the challenge of the dilemma and his own satisfaction with each character's roleplaying choices.

Designing Serial Adventures

Most GMs are capable of designing a "site based" adventure, such as the typical dungeon crawl. Grim Tales favors a different style of adventure, the Serial Adventure, where the focus is not so much on the slaying of enemies and the accumulation of wealth, as it is on roleplaying, story-telling, and problem-solving.

Serial Adventures are designed to allow the GM and the players to live out the best scenes, stories, and plots of their favorite books and movies.

Every game session (and, in the larger sense, every adventure) draws from the same basic conflicts and methods of conflict resolution. Not all of these "cinematic elements" are always present, but the best adventures, stories, and movies have a good number of them.

Call To Action

At the beginning of the adventure or the evening's session of play, the GM sets the scene. This is where the players receive some call to action; or, "the hook." A problem is presented and the PCs are encouraged to follow up.

Task: The GM must prepare adequate hooks to insure that the players will move into his adventure. He can always force the players into the adventure by springing an extra Chase or Minor Combat on them and forcing them to act; plan such proactive measures ahead.

Research

In this phase, the players seek out additional information on their problem. This covers a wide array of "research" from rumors in the bar, consulting a sage, or even going online (hacking and decking) in a more modern "cyberpunk" campaign.

The key difference between Research and Exploration (see below) is that Research is a fairly safe endeavor; the PCs are not expected to encounter any resistance at this stage.

Task: First, determine what information you want the PCs to have to move further into the adventure, making sure to set locations where this info can be found and the methods (including skill DCs) to obtain it.

Next, the GM must anticipate what other kinds of information the players will try to discover. This is a great way to throw a few juicy red herrings at the players. Have an answer (or red herring) ready for every question you can anticipate. If you don't have an answer handy, the players will know that they are barking up the wrong tree.

Exploration

In this phase, the PCs seek out some exotic or dangerous locale and scout it for further clues. It may be a dungeon crawl; it may be a trip to an old mansion or the graveyard. Exploration is, in essence, "field research." It may lead to a Minor Combat (see below).

Task: The GM needs to prepare a map for the location, even just a rough sketch. Mark where any major adversaries are located (prepare statblocks ahead of time) and where any additional clues are located. Your PCs should move through this locale fairly quickly. Not every area must have an encounter, nor even a full description.

Chase

This optional phase involves a chase of some kind: either the players are pursued, or the players are pursuing. A chase can end in a combat, but a chase is best used to add action when the GM doesn't think combat is appropriate—though a chase scene can be violent and dangerous without involving combat per se. Remember that the Chase *is* the scene, not merely a means to set up another scene.

Task: Familiarize yourself with the chase rules ahead of time and jot down any notes you'll need for improvisation. Know the terrain and any likely obstacles. Make sure that both the PCs and their adversary have the necessary means to make the chase cinematic and exciting.

Minor Combat

This phase is used to inject some action into the session. It is usually a minor combat, easily won by the PCs. A henchman fits nicely into this phase— though, if the henchman is the major villain at this time (as when the major villain has yet to reveal himself), this phase calls for a correspondingly minor adversary. This phase can provide the final clue (taken by force) to propel the action forward.

Task: Prepare a statblock ahead of time, and be ready for the usual ways that such scenes derail. Be prepared for the PCs to flee, to capture their adversary, to negotiate, and even for the PCs to surrender or die.

Preparation/Insulation

The PCs retire or retreat to prepare themselves for the climax. Because this phase is mostly planning, this is a good time in which to showcase roleplaying— a return to the scene for NPCs who rely on the heroes, NPCs who offer aid to the heroes, the resolution or extension of love interests, and so on.

Climax

The final phase of the adventure. Here the PCs will come to grips with the "final villain." However, the best serials should end with a Cliffhanger: a scene that leads from the Climax of adventure A to the Setup of adventure B.

Campaign Planner

Campaign Model

☐ Archaic ☐ Modern ☐ Apocalyptic

Economic Model

☐ Currency ☐ Wealth

Combat

Flat-Footed

☠ ☐ Lose Shield Bonus
☠ ☐ Lose Defense Bonus

Death

☠ ☐ Dead at -CON
☠☠ ☐ Dead at -(10 + CON modifier)
☠☠☠ ☐ Dead at -10

Massive Damage Threshold

☠ ☐ CON + Armor + Natural Armor
☠☠ ☐ CON only
☠☠☠ ☐ 10 only

Fallout

☐ Mutations Allowed

Horror

Horror Check

☠ ☐ Will save ☠☠ ☐ Wis mod ☠☠☠ ☐ No mod

☐ Fight or Flight allowed

Short Term Insanity Duration

☠ ☐ end of current session
☠☠ ☐ end of current adventure
☠☠☠ ☐ until next character level

Spellcasting and Magic

Spell Burn Die

☠ ☐ d4 ☠☠ ☐ d6 ☠☠☠ ☐ d8

Firearms

Era

☠ ☐ Muzzle-loaders
☠☠ ☐ Cartridge
☠☠☠ ☐ Automatic

Other Campaign Options

☐ Cyberware
☐ Undead/Turn Undead
☐ Vehicles

Character Name:		Player:	
Character Level:		XP	

Class Levels

Strong	Smart
Fast	Dedicated
Tough	Charismatic
Other	Other

Reputation
Action Points
Speed
Initiative

Ability Scores

	Ability Score	Ability Mod	Temp Score	Temp Mod
STR				
DEX				
CON				
INT				
WIS				
CHR				

Hit Points

Lethal Damage	Non-Lethal Damage
Massive Damage Threshold	

Saving Throws

Fortitude	CON	Class	Race	Resistance	Other
Reflex	DEX	Class	Race	Resistance	Other
Will	WIS	Class	Race	Resistance	Other

Armor Class

Armor	Shield	Defense	Natural Armor	Deflection	Dex	Other	TOTAL
Armor	Shield	Defense	Natural Armor	Deflection		Other	Flat Footed
		Defense		Deflection	Dex	Other	Touch

Combat

Melee	Base Attack Bonus	Ranged
+ STR	+0 / -5 / -10 / -15	+DEX

Weapon				Total BAB	Damage	Critical
Range	Wt.	Type	Size	Notes		
Weapon				Total BAB	Damage	Critical
Range	Wt.	Type	Size	Notes		
Weapon				Total BAB	Damage	Critical
Range	Wt.	Type	Size	Notes		

Feats and Talents

Feat			
Feat			
Talent			

Skills

Core Skill Name	TOTAL	Modifier	Ranks	Misc
☐ Appraise •		INT		
☐ Balance •		DEX		Armor
☐ Bluff •		CHA		
☐ Climb •		STR		Armor
☐ Concentration •		CON		
☐ Craft (________) •		INT		
☐ Decipher Script		INT		
☐ Diplomacy •		CHA		
☐ Disable Device		INT		
☐ Disguise •		CHA		
☐ Drive (________) •		DEX		
☐ Escape Artist •		DEX		Armor
☐ Forgery •		INT		
☐ Gather Information •		CHA		
☐ Handle Animal		CHA		
☐ Heal •		WIS		
☐ Hide •		DEX		Armor
☐ Intimidate •		CHA		
☐ Jump •		STR		Armor
☐ Knowledge (_______)		INT		
☐ Listen •		WIS		
☐ Move Silently •		DEX		Armor
☐ Perform (________) •		CHA		
☐ Profession (_______)		WIS		
☐ Research •		INT		
☐ Ride (________) •		DEX		
☐ Search •		INT		
☐ Sense Motive •		WIS		
☐ Sleight of Hand		DEX		Armor
☐ Spot •		WIS		
☐ Survival •		WIS		
☐ Swim •		STR		Armor
☐ Tumble		DEX		Armor
☐ Use Unknown Device		CHA		
☐ Use Rope •		DEX		
☐ (______________)				
☐ (______________)				
☐ (______________)				
☐ (______________)				

APPENDIX

The Undead Campaign

The Palelands suffer, oh, and they hate

For every flower that blooms, the Palelands wither

For every babe's first drawn breath, the Palelands grow darker

But for every murder, there is some relief

For every death, an opportunity

To come, in darkness, and destroy

The undead are a universal threat. As old as life itself, the undead are the animated remains of once living creatures or incorporeal remnants of corrupted souls. The undead draw their existence from the Palelands, the plane of unlife, and hence possess a limitless hated for living creatures and an indomitable will for destruction.

Archaic Era

The rise of civilization brings new power to the undead. Society replaces the tribal prophets and shamans with the temple priests. The human population swells and divides into nations and empires. Forever unable to maintain peace, humanity wars with itself on a heretofore-unimagined scale. Inevitably, death and suffering attracts the creatures of the night. Vampires hide and feed in cities, dark cults experiment with the rituals of undeath, the savage innocence of tribalism is lost to the indifference of civilization. And as humanity grows to new heights, it casts a longer, deeper shadow. Can any among the living face the evil that begins at the borders of death?

Lord Tauratep

In an ancient city, the crown prince, Tauratep, paid a dear price for his treachery and love for his brother's wife. Unable to possess her or win her love in return, Tauratep secretly slew his brother and took his wife as his queen upon inheriting the throne. But his two younger bothers, high priests and powerful in their own right, learned what Tauratep had done and sought to avenge their murdered brother. After a protracted and bloody civil war, Tauratep was eventually captured, cursed, and entombed.

Now, somehow, millennia later, Tauratep is free. He sees the burgeoning civilizations of man as corrupt descendents of his usurped throne. He seeks revenge against all mankind for his suffering and for taking from him the only thing he ever loved.

Tauratep is passionate and cruel, but also highly intelligent. He formulates intricate plans and carries them out in exacting detail. Although he sometimes displays the personality of a childish thug, he has the will and power to destroy nations.

Possible Adventures

The following adventure hooks pit the PCs against Lord Tauratep and his forces:

- The PCs inadvertently free Tauratep while exploring ancient ruins. Instead of trying to destroy them, the mummy lord attempts to manipulate the PCs into aiding him in establishing a power base.
- Lord Tauratep is free and beginning to amass an army of undead. He is sending out raiding parties of ghouls and wights to bolster his forces with undead spawn. The PCs are attacked by one such party and must attempt to save a local community from the ravages of Tauratep's army.
- Lord Tauratep and his undead forces have stumbled upon a lethid enclave controlling a small town (the lethid are described later in this chapter). Lord Tauratep wishes to destroy the town and enslave its inhabitants as undead minions. The lethid have dark machinations of their own which involve keeping the townsfolk relatively intact for the time being. The PCs, who may be in the town, must discover the source of the escalating horror and carnage and find a way to move the townsfolk (and themselves) out of danger.

Lord Tauratep

(2nd-level Fast/6th-level Dedicated Human Mummy Lord)
Medium Undead (Augmented Humanoid)

Hit Dice:	8d12 (55 hp)
Initiative:	+6
Speed:	35 ft. (7 squares)
Armor Class:	37 (+2 Dex, +6 Wis, +7 class, +12 natural) Touch 25, flat-footed 29
Base Attack/ Grapple:	+5/+14
Attack:	+2 heavy mace +17 melee (1d6+15) or slam +14 melee (1d8+13 plus mummy rot)
Full Attack:	+2 heavy mace +17 melee (1d6+15) or slam +14 melee (1d8+13 plus mummy rot) or javelin +7 ranged (1d6+9)
Space/Reach:	5 ft./5 ft.
Special Attacks:	Breath of the tomb, despair, mummy rot
Special Qualities:	+4 turn resistance, damage reduction 10/—, darkvision 90 ft., undead traits, vulnerable to fire
Saves:	Fort +8, Ref +9, Will +14
Abilities:	Str 29, Dex 14, Con —, Int 10, Wis 23, Cha 17
Skills:	Bluff +8, Climb +14, Diplomacy +10, Hide +11, Intimidate +14, Jump +14, Listen +15, Move Silently +9, Search +11, Spot +15
Feats:	Alertness[B], Armor Proficiency (light and medium), Blind Fight, Great Fortitude[B], Heroic Surge, Improved Initiative[B], Iron Will, Quickdraw, Toughness, Weapon Focus (heavy mace)
Talents:	Divine Grace, Increased Speed, Smite, Zen Defense
Challenge Rating:	14
Treasure:	Standard, including +2 heavy mace
Allegiance:	Evil, Revenge, Power

The save vs. Lord Tauratep's despair and mummy rot are DC17.

Breath of the Tomb (Su): Three times per day, a mummy lord may enshroud an area in absolute darkness. This ability affects the entire volume of air in a radius of 60 feet from the mummy lord. The area of effect is evacuated of all light and air. Living creatures will suffocate (as per the drowning rules), all flames are immediately extinguished and fire effects in the area are automatically countered, and no light source can penetrate the darkness unless it is a 7th-level or higher magical effect. Any creature with darkvision can see normally. The effect lasts for 10 rounds or until the mummy lord dispels it. This ability is equivalent to a 7th-level darkness negative energy effect.

Despair (Ex): The sight of a mummy forces viewers to succeed on a Will save (DC 10 + 1/2 HD + Cha modifier) of be paralyzed with fear for 1d4 rounds. Whether or not the save is successful, the creature cannot be affected by the same mummy's despair ability for 24 hours.

Mummy Rot (Su): Supernatural disease—natural weapon, Fortitude (DC 10 + 1/2 HD + Cha modifier), incubation period 1 minute; damage 1d6 Con and 1d6 Cha. A character attempting to cast a conjuration (healing) spell on a creature with mummy rot must succeed at a DC 20 caster level check to affect the afflicted character. Unlike normal diseases, mummy rot continues until the victim dies (and shrivels away into sand and dust) or it is magically cured. Mummy rot is actually a curse, not a natural disease, and this curse must first be broken with a successful *break enchantment* or *remove curse* (both require a DC 20 caster level check). After the curse is broken, the character can be affected by healing spells normally and magically cured.

Modern Era

Man is enamored with his great industrial journey. Science and the principles of reason have brought untold wonders to the world: railroads, the telegraph, the electric light. And now that man can vanquish many shadows, he fears the remaining ones all the more. Anxious to deny the inexplicable horrors that lie at boundary between death and life, many seek to forget the undead, while others work to disprove their presence with the light of science. But the undead are surely as powerful as ever before: their essences haunt the slums, paupers' graveyards, terrible mills, and decadent mansions that are the loci of Victorian evil. The powerful night creatures revel in this new secular mindset, and exploit its blindness to renew and invigorate their attack on humanity. Only a few exceptional men and women, those with little to lose or who know too much, are willing to face the darkness and defend humanity from its depredations.

Lord Braunkolbiger

Lord Braunkolbiger is an Austrian duke and the head of one of Europe's five outer-caste vampire clans. At just over 200 years old, he is the youngest vampire lord in Europe and the most reckless. He considers himself "modern" and is anxious to expand his influence in both human and vampire affairs. As such, he is a growing threat in Europe, both as a vampire lord and political puppetmaster.

Possible Adventures

Use the following adventure hooks to draw the PCs into Lord Braunkolbiger's world:

- Lord Braunkolbiger is using a gang of wights to attack border communities and ethnic minorities in an attempt to create hostilities and increase political tension in the region.

- Lord Braunkolbiger's clan has come into a territorial conflict with another outer-caste clan. In the guise of the duke, he employs the PCs to aid him against his enemies.

• One of Lord Braunkolbiger's wights is a wolf that can somehow transmit its evil essence to other animals, thus creating an ever-expanding army of wight animals. The PCs track the wight(s) back to Lord Braunkolbiger's duchy and uncover the greater threat of the vampire duke himself.

Lord Braunkolbiger

(4th-level Charismatic/4th-level Strong Human Vampire Lord)
Medium Undead (Augmented Humanoid)

Hit Dice:	8d12 (52 hp)
Initiative:	+9
Speed:	30 ft. (6 squares), fly 40 ft. (excellent)
Armor Class:	28 (+5 Dex, +5 class, +8 natural) Touch 15, flat-footed 23
Base Attack/ Grapple:	+6/+10
Attack:	+2 *keen* rapier +14 melee (1d6+9/15-20) or slam +12 melee (1d6+10 plus energy drain)
Full Attack:	+2 *keen* rapier +14/+9 melee (1d6+9/15-20) or slam +12 melee (1d6+10 plus energy drain) and +2 *keen* rapier +9 (1d6+9/15-20) or .45 derringer +10/+5 (2d6)
Space/Reach:	5 ft./5 ft.
Special Attacks:	Blood drain, children of the night, create spawn, dark seduction, dominate, energy drain
Special Qualities:	+6 turn resistance, alternate form, dark allure, darkvision 90 ft., damage reduction 10/silver and magic, fast healing 5, gaseous form, resistance to cold 10 and electricity 10, spider climb, +6 turn resistance, undead traits, vampire weaknesses
Saves:	Fort +4, Ref +10, Will +6
Abilities:	Str 22, Dex 19, Con –, Int 13, Wis 14, Cha 23
Skills:	Appraise +4, Bluff +22, Climb +9, Diplomacy +26, Hide +14, Intimidate +17, Jump +9, Knowledge (history) +4, Listen +14, Move Silently +18, Search +15, Sense Motive +22, Spot +16, Survival +2 (+4 following tracks)
Feats:	Agile Riposte, Alertness[B], Armor Proficiency (light), Blind Fight, Cleave, Combat Reflexes[B], Dodge, Frightful Presence, Improved Initiative[B], Iron Will, Lightning Reflexes[B], Personal Firearms Proficiency, Power Attack
Talents:	Coordinate, Ignore Hardness, Inspiration, Melee Smash
Challenge Rating:	15
Allegiance:	Evil, Caste, Vampires

• **Blood drain (Ex):** A vampire lord can drain its victim's blood with its fangs. On a grapple check that leads to a pin for the vampire lord, it can deal 1d6 points of Constitution drain that round and every round it maintains the pin. Each time a vampire lord deals Constitution drain in this way, it gains 5 temporary hit points.

• **Children of the Night (Su):** A vampire lord can command legions of lesser night creatures. Once per day, it can call forth 1d6+3 rat swarms, 1d6+3 bat swarms, a pack of 3d6+4 wolves, or a number of similar appropriate creatures. The creatures arrive in 2d4 rounds and remain under the vampire lord's complete control for 3 hours.

• **Create Spawn (Su):** Any living, native, intelligent creature with an organic physiology of at least size Small slain by a vampire lord rises as a vampire spawn controlled by the vampire lord 1d4 days after burial.

If a victim's Constitution score is reduced to zero by a vampire lord's blood drain and that creature has 5 or more Hit Dice, it will rise as a vampire under command of the vampire lord. It remains so enslaved until the vampire lord releases it or is slain. At any given time, a vampire lord can command up to 4 times its HD in spawn. Its spawn may also have spawn of their own. Freed spawn cannot be re-enslaved by the vampire lord.

• **Dark Seduction (Sp):** A vampire lord has an enthralling presence on free-willed, intelligent creatures. All creatures within 100 feet who can understand the vampire lord must make a Will save (DC equal to 10 + 1/2 vampire lord's HD + vampire lord's Cha modifier) or suffer a -4 to all saves against the vampire lord's mind-affecting powers and opposed rolls against Charisma-based checks employed by the vampire lord for the next 10 minutes. Creatures who successfully save cannot be affected by the same vampire's dark seduction ability for the next 10 minutes. A vampire lord can deactivate this ability as a free action. In addition, once per day, a vampire lord who has activated its dark seduction ability may cause its speech to affect all intelligent creatures exactly as a *mass suggestion* spell (this ability is a free action that cannot disrupted, caster level 15th).

• **Dominate (Su):** A vampire lord can dominate a creature just by looking at it. If a vampire uses a standard action to lock eyes with a creature, that creature must immediate succeed at a Will save (DC equal to 10 + 1/2 vampire lord's HD + vampire lord's Cha modifier) or fall under the vampire's influence as though affected by a *dominate monster* spell (caster level 15th). This ability has a range of 50 feet.

• **Energy Drain (Su):** Any living creature struck by a vampire lord's slam attack (or other natural weapon a vampire lord might possess) gains three negative levels. For each such negative level bestowed, the vampire lord gains 5 temporary hit points. A vampire lord may only use this ability once per round.

• **Alternate Form (Su):** A vampire lord may temporarily adopt the form of a bat, dire bat, dire wolf, or wolf (or another appropriate creature at the GM's discretion) as a standard action. This effect is similar to a *polymorph* spell as though cast by a 15th level caster, except the vampire lord does not regain hit points for changing form. While in this form, a vampire lord cannot use its dark seduction, dominate, or dark allure abilities. The vampire lord gains proficiency with all the natural attacks of the form it assumes. It can maintain the form as long as it wishes, or until the next sunrise.

- **Dark Allure (Su):** A vampire lord is a leader of vampires. In its presence, all vampires and vampire spawn within 1,000 feet gain the following bonuses: turn resistance +3 (as opposed to the normal rule, this turn resistance bonus stacks with other turn resistance bonuses); +2 profane bonus to Charisma; +2 profane bonus to Will saves; +2 temporary hit points per Hit Die. The affected creatures need not be able to see or otherwise sense the vampire lord.
- **Gaseous Form (Su):** A vampire lord reduced to 0 hit points immediately becomes a cloud of vapor. A vampire lord with 1 or more hit points can assume its gaseous form at will once per day. Treat this effect as a *gaseous form* spell as though cast by a 15th-level caster, except that the vampire lord may maintain the form indefinitely. The vampire lord retains its fly speed but gains perfect maneuverability. In this state, the vampire lord must reach its coffin before dawn or be destroyed utterly. Any additional damage the vampire lord receives in this form is ignored. Once in its coffin, it regains 1 hit point in one hour, after which its fast healing is restored.
- **Spider Climb (Ex):** A vampire lord can climb as though with a permanent *spider climb* spell.

Apocalyptic Era

From the blood and dust of the apocalypse emerges a new renaissance for the undead. Untold anguish, billions dead, and global strife have multiplied the undead's numbers to new heights. Legions of radioactive zombies scour the deserts under the command of a twisted cyborg lich. Rumors spread of vampires breeding humans as livestock. Unquiet spirits haunt the ruins of cities, rising night after night in a terrifying horde to recreate the final moments before the cataclysm. The dead rest uneasily, as do the living, who quail in the darkness, haunted by what they have seen and what they fear they have not. But some do not falter; they see the horror and know what they must do: if man is to survive on this broken world, he must find the strength face both the darkness without and within.

Tyrannius, the Lord of the Wastes

Lord Tyrannius was already a necromancer with a terrible command of the powers of magic and technology before the apocalypse. Part of his power stemmed from his willingness to cut all ties to his humanity and subject himself to dangerous cybernetic and necromantic experimentation for the sake of his ambitions. By replacing most of his major organ systems with steel and fiber optic circuitry, Tyrannius was able to withstand magical forces and mishaps that would have killed any normal man and could conduct research at an incredible rate. He had either the great fortune or the prescience to attain lichdom on the eve of the great destruction. Unlike every other living being on the planet, this destruction was a great boon to Tyrannius. He quickly moved to marshal a force of undead from the thousands of people who had succumbed to the apocalypse, carving out a small protectorate by laying waste to a cluster of towns in Texas and enslaving their populace. With servants sufficient to protect him and support his magical research, it was not long before he had the power to smash a neighboring cabal of free-willed undead and take over the army base they had controlled. Here, he had the resources to dominate the region, bringing slavery and ineffable horror to all of the people in his domain, and gaining the knowledge and resources to elevate himself to lordship. Now Tyrannius seeks to unleash his armies upon the entire world and claim the entire blasted planet as his eternal empire of waste.

Possible Adventures

Use the following ideas to bring your PCs under Lord Tyrannius' baleful influence:

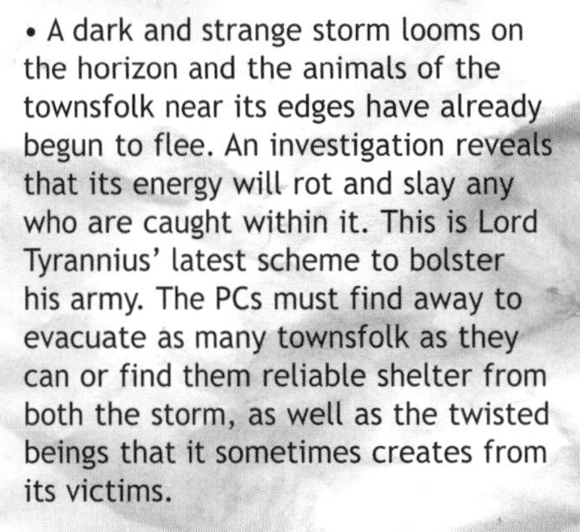

- A dark and strange storm looms on the horizon and the animals of the townsfolk near its edges have already begun to flee. An investigation reveals that its energy will rot and slay any who are caught within it. This is Lord Tyrannius' latest scheme to bolster his army. The PCs must find away to evacuate as many townsfolk as they can or find them reliable shelter from both the storm, as well as the twisted beings that it sometimes creates from its victims.
- The leaders of the PCs' well-armed settlement have recently signed a truce with their strange neighbor, the self-styled Lord of the Wastes, who seems occupied in a conflict with other peoples far to the East. But there is something very odd about this Lord Tyrannius, and his taciturn and pungent armor clad servants who never show their faces nor request food or drink. As rumors of spying and kidnapping by Tyrannius' soldiers surface, someone is going to need to investigate the trustworthiness of this bizarre ally.
- Lord Tyrannius' forces have run into surprising resistance from a group of survivors who managed to reach a mountain fortress containing a small detachment of highly trained soldiers and their arsenal of powerful military hardware. The PCs are among this group. Although they have seen unprecedented success, the leaders of the group realize that it will be impossible to hold out for much longer against Lord Tyrannius' siege. The group's only hope is for a small group to use the network of underground tunnels running beneath the fortress to emerge behind the army of undead, and then find some way to deal enough of a blow to Tyrannius that his army is forced to retreat.

Tyrannius, Lord of the Wastes

Lich, Cyborg Smart 11/Dedicated 5
Medium Undead (Augmented Humanoid)

Hit Dice:	16d12+12 (136 hp)
Initiative:	+10*
Speed:	30 ft. (6 squares)
Armor Class:	28 (+3 Dex, +7 class, +8* natural), touch 20, flat-footed 25
Base Attack/ Grapple:	+8/+10
Attack:	Touch +13 melee touch (1d10+10 plus paralyzing touch) or cybernetically integrated mastercraft pulse laser cannon** +15 ranged (3d8)
Full Attack:	Touch +13 melee touch (1d10+10 paralyzing touch) or cybernetically integrated mastercraft pulse laser cannon** +14/+14/+9 ranged (3d8)
Space/Reach:	5 ft./10 ft.*
Special Attacks:	Aura of horror, lord of the dead, paralyzing touch, spells, spell-like abilities
Special Qualities:	+8 turn resistance, damage reduction 17/ bludgeoning and magic, darkvision 90 ft., evasion*, immunity to cold, electricity, polymorph, and mind-effecting effects, lordly presence, spell resistance 16, undead traits
Saves:	Fort +8, Ref +9, Will +10
Abilities:	Str 19*, Dex 16*, Con –, Int 29*, Wis 14, Cha 20
Skills:	Computer Use +26, Craft (Chemical) +30, Craft (Electronic) +30, Craft (Mechanical) +30, Craft (Pharmaceutical) +30, Disable Device +23, Intimidate +16, Knowledge (Arcana) +32, Knowledge (Earth and Life Sciences) +30, Knowledge (Religion) +31, Knowledge (Tactics) +31, Knowledge (Technology) +32, Listen +23, Research +25, Search +32, Spellcraft +28, Spot +23
Feats:	Alertness*, Dodge, Frightful Presence, Great Fortitude, Heroic Surge, Improved Initiative, Lightning Reflexes, Skill Focus [Computer Use +3, Craft (Chemical) +2, Craft (Electronic) +2, Craft (Mechanical) +2, Craft (Pharmaceutical) +2, Intimidate +3, Knowledge (Arcana) +3, Knowledge (Religion) +2, Knowledge (Tactics) +2, Knowledge (Technology) +3, Spellcraft +3], Toughness x4*, Weapon Focus (ray*, touch attack*)
Talents:	Improved Caster Level [Arcane] x7***, Insight (Spellcraft), Magical Adept (Arcane), Master Arcane Flow
Challenge Rating:	26
Allegiance:	Evil, Knowledge

*Cybernetically provided ability or value. 44 points of cyberware.

** Cybernetically integrated pulse laser grants a +2 circumstance bonus to hit and an extra attack when its user employs the full attack option.

*** Extra talent provided from ascension to lich-lord.

- **Aura of Horror (Su):** A lich lord is surrounded by an aura of ineffable evil. Encountering a lich lord always triggers a Horror check unless the lich lord chooses to suppress its aura. An encounter involving a lich lord adds +4 to the Horror Threshold roll.

- **Lord of the Dead (Su):** A lich lord can Turn, Command, and Destroy mindless and fettered undead as though it had those talents. It affects mindless and fettered undead as a Dedicated hero of a level equal to its HD plus any levels of Dedicated hero it has. A lich lord can command or destroy any mindless or fettered undead creature, regardless of its allegiance. When attempting to command or destroy undead that would normally be unaffected by these abilities because of their allegiances, the lich lord affects these undead as though it were a Dedicated hero of 4 levels lower than its HD plus its Dedicate hero levels. There is no limit to the number of times per day a lich lord can use its ability to affect mindless and fettered undead.

- **Paralyzing Touch (Su):** Any living creature struck by a lich lord's touch attack or natural weapons must succeed at a Fortitude save or be permanently paralyzed. *Removed paralysis* or any spell that could negate a curse created by *bestow curse* can free the victim. The effect cannot be dispelled. Anyone paralyzed by a lich seems dead, though a DC 25 Spot check or a DC 20 Heal check reveals that the victim is still alive.

- **Spells:** A lich lord is a spellcaster of awesome power. A lich lord casts spells as the base creature, but gains a bonus caster level in any one magical tradition and a +1 bonus to its spell drain resistance (exactly as though it gained Improved Caster Level as a bonus talent). It gains an additional +4 bonus to all caster level checks. Whenever a lich lord casts a spell, it rolls a bonus spell drain die. After rolling, the lich lord may discard the result of any one of its spell drain dice. A lich lord always applies spell burn to its Strength score, as it has no Constitution score.

- **Spells Known:** Lord Tyrannius knows every arcane spell in the Player's Handbook and/or the d20 Modern Roleplaying Game from 0th–4th level, as well as every necromancy spell from 5th–8th level. Tailor the remainder of his high level spells as you see fit, with an emphasis on evocation and transmutation spells.

- **Spell-like abilities:** In addition to its formidable spellcasting abilities, a lich lord can employ the following spell-like abilities at will: *animate dead, darkbolt, deeper darkness, dispel magic, hold monster, slay living.*

- **Lordly presence (Su):** All undead controlled by the lich lord within 1 mile gain the following bonuses: turn resistance +4 (as opposed to the normal rule, this turn resistance bonus stacks with other turn resistance bonuses); +2 profane bonus to Will saves, +2 to the DC of all its supernatural and spell-like abilities; +1 temporary hit point per Hit Die. The affected creatures need not be able to see or otherwise sense the lich lord.

The Dragon Lords Campaign

The primal dragons are a universal myth, stories of which are found in nearly every culture in every age of man. They are the most powerful and mysterious force on the planet. Little is known of them beyond myth and legend; their origins and motivations—and their very existence—are clouded in mystery.

A dragon's life force is bound to its earthly talisman, a unique focus hidden deep in the earth. A dragon talisman can take a variety of forms, from a gigantic natural crystal, to a huge intricately wrought sculpture, to a deep pool of liquid mercury. A dragon can only be permanently destroyed if its talisman is also destroyed.

Archaic Era

Townsfolk spread rumors of great flying beasts. Tales of terrible destructive forces cross the lands. Occasionally, cities vanish in the pitched battles between these great creatures. As civilization advances, so grows the dragons' interest in humanity. Ambitious and political, they see humans as playing pieces to further their own influence and power, and to exploit against the other dragons.

Tehlitocan

In its true form, the dragon of the Americas, Tehlitocan, is a 350-foot long lizard-like creature. Instead of scales, however, Tehlitocan has smooth, slate-like skin and is festooned with great rainbow patterned feather-like adornments at the base of its head, behind its claws, and at the end of its tail.

When the dragons awoke after their great slumber, Tehlitocan was one of the first to establish territory and recognize the tiny industrious creatures scattered across the globe as a potential source of power. It is likely during this age, when the primal dragons were more numerous and not averse to appearing in the skies, that the dragon mythos was first established in the human consciousness.

Tehlitocan is a trickster, preferring traps and misdirection to open conflict. It is a powerful illusionist capable of altering perceived reality on a massive scale.

Possible Adventures

- Tehlitocan has recently awoken from a long slumber to find the Earth overrun with hairless monkeys. It will test the PCs, using illusions, summoned creatures, and threats, to asses their capabilities.
- The PCs stumble across an enormous impact crater, at the bottom of which lies the broken body of a primal dragon recently defeated by Tehlitocan . The dragon bargains with the PCs to return to the nearby town, its base of operations, to root out the traitors in its own organization and return with its talisman so that it may recover from its wounds. The PCs will be opposed, not only by the injured dragon's traitorous forces, but by assassins sent by Tehlitocan to recover the talisman.

Tehlitocan

Colossal Primal Dragon

Hit Dice:	60d12+1020 (1410 hp)
Initiative:	+4
Speed:	80 ft. (16 squares), fly 250 ft. (good), swim 80 ft.
Armor Class:	45 (-8 size, +43 natural) Touch 2, flat-footed 45
Base Attack/ Grapple:	+60/+100
Attack:	Bite +74 melee (4d8+27/19–20)
Full Attack:	Bite +74 melee (4d8+27/19–20), two claws +69 melee (4d6+13), tail slap +69 melee (4d6+40), two wings +69 melee (2d8+13)
Space/ Reach:	40 ft./30 ft.
Special Attacks:	Awesome presence, crush, energy blast, prismatic storm, rend, spells, sweep
Special Qualities:	Blindsight 60 ft., damage reduction 15/epic, darkvision 120 ft., earth glide, immunity to: cold, compulsion, fire, lightning, magic sleep, paralysis, and petrification; low light vision, primal dragon traits, spell resistance 42
Saves:	Fort +49, Ref +32, Will +49
Abilities:	Str 64, Dex 10, Con 44, Int 44, Wis 45, Cha 45
Skills:	Appraise +80, Bluff +82, Climb +89, Concentration +80, Decipher Script +80, Diplomacy +86, Disguise +80, Gather Information +80, Hide +47, Intimidate +84, Knowledge (arcana) +83, Knowledge (geography) +83, Knowledge (history) +83, Knowledge (the planes) +83, Listen +82, Move Silently +63, Research +80, Search +80, Sense Motive +82, Spellcraft +82, Spot +82, Survival +80, Use Unknown Device+80
Feats:	Ability Focus (awesome presence), Ability Focus (prismatic storm), Alertness, Cleave, Flyby Attack, Frightful Presence, Great Cleave, Greater Spell Penetration, Greater Spell Focus (illusion), Hover, Improved Critical (bite), Improved Initiative, Leadership, Power Attack, Quicken Spell-Like Ability (disintegrate), Quicken Spell-Like Ability (dominate person), Skill Focus (Bluff, Intimidate), Skill Focus (Diplomacy, Sense Motive), Spell Focus (illusion), Spell Penetration, Wingover
Challenge Rating:	70

Combat

Though awesomely powerful, Tehlitocan often employs tactics based on subterfuge and misdirection. Using its illusions, Tehlitocan will sow fear and confusion and then use its rock glide ability to strike from an ambush. Tehlitocan is also known to prolong a conflict just for the joy of toying with its opponents.

- **Awesome Presence (Su):** Tehlitocan's presence is so powerful that it weakens creatures that come near it. If the dragon chooses, any creature within 100 feet takes 6 Strength and 6 Charisma damage. A DC 59 Fortitude save negates this effect.
- **Crush (Ex):** As a full round action, a primal dragon can crush any number of opponents 2 or more size categories smaller. This requires a full-round action. A creature that fails its Reflex save is pinned until it succeeds in an opposed grapple check or Escape Artist roll. Tehlitocan's crush deals 4d8+40 points of damage (save DC56).
- **Earth Glide (Ex):** Tehlitocan may meld and move through the earth as if swimming through water. As it moves through stone or soil—not metal or living matter—it causes no ripple or disturbance and leaves no tunnel or hole.
- **Energy Blast (Su):** Tehlitocan's energy blast is an 80-foot cone that deals 30 dice of damage (DC 57) of any energy type.

- **Prismatic Storm (Sp):** Once per day, Tehlitocan may summon a powerful magical storm. The storm lasts for 2d6 rounds and has a radius of 100 feet, centered on the dragon's head. Each round, every creature within the area of effect suffers as though struck by a prismatic spray. Tehlitocan is immune to these effects. The save DCs for these effects are Charisma-based.
- **Rend (Ex):** If a primal dragon makes a successful grapple check, it may attempt a grapple check to rend. This attack deals twice the dragon's normal claw damage + 1-1/2 times the dragon's Str modifier. Tehlitocan's rend deals 8d6+40 points of damage.
- **Spell-Like Abilities:**

  At will—*detect thoughts, suggestion, tongues*

  5/day—*confusion, disintegrate, dominate person,*

  3/day—*permanent image, reverse gravity, scintillating pattern*

  1/day—*dominate monster, mage's disjunction*
- **Spells:** Tehlitocan casts spells as a 30th-level caster (wild adept). The save DCs are Charisma-based.
- **Spells Known:** 0—*detect magic, read magic, dancing lights, flare, ghost sound, light, mage hand, message, open/close*; 1st—*alarm, charm person, color spray, disguise self, ventriloquism*; 2nd—*blur, hypnotic pattern, minor image, misdirection, spectral hand*; 3rd—*dispel magic, haste, hold person, major image*; 4th—*confusion, greater invisibility, hallucinatory terrain, lesser geas*; 5th—*dream, false vision, mirage arcana, permanency*; 6th—*geas/quest, permanent image, shadow walk*; 7th—*insanity, limited wish, statue*; 8th—*mind blank, screen, temporal stasis*; 9th—*shades, time stop, wish.*
- **Sweep (Ex):** Tehlitocan can use its long body to sweep opponents from the field. The sweep affects a semi-circle 50 feet in diameter centered on any square of the dragon's body. This attack deals 3d6+40 points of damage. Targets of this effect may make a DC 57 Reflex save to halve the damage.

Modern Era

Modern communications, weaponry, and finance have altered the geopolitical landscape to favor small groups of inordinately influential people. Whoever controls those groups can control the world. Improbable political and economic alliances are formed as monarchs and transportation magnates play a great game of diplomatic intrigue and imperialistic expansion. But even a few manipulators sense that their webs are but a small part of something greater. Someone or something is stirring dissent in Europe. The shadow of a massive military build-up stretches across the world. Crackpots and scholars alike expound wild theories. But are they crazy? And who has the courage and wits to find out?

Xiaotan

Xiaotan is the Asiatic dragon. In its natural form, Xiaotan is a 500-foot-long snake-like creature with sinuous limbs and gleaming iridescent scales. Its likeness is seen in many ancient oriental mythological creatures, a legacy of the last time it is known to have surfaced in its true form.

Xiaotan is subtle beyond measure, possessing intelligence and cunning greater than humans can even conceive. Like the other dragons, Xiaotan has patience that spans millennia and is willing to wait hundreds or thousands of years for a plan to come to fruition. Xiaotan is also the most malicious of the dragons, often acting with cruel vengeance over any slight infringement on its territory or domains of influence.

Xiaotan regards every opponent (other than another primal dragon) with contempt, often times utterly ignoring creatures that cannot harm it. However, it does not tolerate intruders to its home. Any living creature that comes within a dozen miles its lair, even if completely unaware of its significance, is immediately killed and all evidence of its existence utterly destroyed.

Possible Adventures

- Jotanhor's network controls most of Europe's financial institutions, and hence its governments. Europe's industrial power at the turn of the century, however, is extremely appealing to the other dragons. The annual European Banking Federation meeting is coming up in Brussels, and Xiaotan intends to wipe out as many of the major bankers in attendance as it can through a mass assassination, executed by a puppet paramilitary army of Balkan Marxists. In the aftermath, Xiaotan will begin a series of carefully planned takeovers that will leave his agents in control of much of Europe's manufacturing capacity. The PCs are hired by the bankers to provide security, and they must stop Xiaotan's agents, with or without the help of Jotanhor's agents. The PCs may find that Jotanhor's aid comes at its own price, notwithstanding the dangers of opposing Xiaotan!
- In a petty, politically loaded move, the Czar has demanded the return of a collection of Russian crown jewels that were ransomed to Austro-Hungary after a brief altercation in the last century. The jewels, a collection of rare colored diamonds worth millions, are being secretly transported by rail from Vienna to St. Petersburg. The GM may assign the PCs as guards on the train or have them as bystanders.

  No less than four other organizations— each working at the behest of a dragon lord— have agents on the train. The diamonds are guarded by the Czar's mysterious Turkish monk; also on the train are several Japanese Black Agents intent on stealing the diamonds. The Austrian count who has until recently been holding the diamonds has sent a jewel thief to covertly recover "his" jewels. And yet another agent, the Man from Minsk, has been sent to switch the real gems for fakes that would surely discredit the Austrian regime and perhaps catalyze a power shift in the entire region.

Xiaotan

Colossal Primal Dragon

Hit Dice:	59d12+1003 (1387 hp)
Initiative:	+6
Speed:	60 ft. (12 squares), fly 300 ft. (perfect), swim 120 ft.
Armor Class:	48 (+2 Dex, -8 size, +44 natural), touch 4, flat-footed 46
Base Attack/ Grapple:	+59/+99
Attack:	Bite +75 melee (4d8+24/19-20)
Full Attack:	Bite +75 melee (4d8+24/19-20), two claws +70 melee (4d6+12), tail slap +70 melee (4d6+36)
Space/Reach:	40 ft./30 ft.
Special Attacks:	Awesome presence, constrict, crush, energy blast, improved grab, rend, spells, sweep
Special Qualities:	Blindsight 60 ft., damage reduction 15/ epic, darkvision 120 ft., immunity to: cold, compulsion, fire, lightning, magic sleep, paralysis, and petrification; low light vision, primal dragon traits, spell resistance 42
Saves:	Fort +49, Ref +34, Will +49
Abilities:	Str 59, Dex 15, Con 45, Int 44, Wis 45, Cha 44
Skills:	Appraise +79, Bluff +81, Climb +86, Concentration +79, Decipher Script +79, Diplomacy +85, Disguise +79, Gather Information +79, Hide +48, Intimidate +83, Knowledge (arcana) +82, Knowledge (geography) +82, Knowledge (history) +82, Knowledge (the planes) +82, Listen +81, Move Silently +64, Research +79, Search +79, Sense Motive +81, Spellcraft +81, Spot +81, Survival +79 (+81 when following tracks), Use Artefact +79
Feats:	Ability Focus (awesome presence), Ability Focus (dominate), Alertness, Cleave, Flyby Attack, Frightful Presence, Great Cleave, Greater Spell Penetration, Greater Spell Focus (enchantment), Improved Critical (bite), Improved Initiative, Leadership, Power Attack, Quicken Spell-Like Ability (chain lightning), Quicken Spell-Like Ability (dominate person), Skill Focus (Bluff, Intimidate), Skill Focus (Diplomacy, Sense Motive), Spell Focus (enchantment), Spell Penetration, Track
Environment:	Subterranean (Asia)
Challenge Rating:	70

Combat

If bent on destruction or faced with a serious danger, Xiaotan will employ a maximal threat reduction strategy, eliminating the most hazardous elements first with whatever attacks are appropriate.

Though Xiaotan is subtle and conniving, it wastes no time or effort in battle. Its tactics are efficient and lethal. The dragon rarely stops to speak, especially not to a barely evolved monkey or other lesser creatures.

- **Awesome Presence (Su):** Xiaotan's presence is so powerful that it weakens creatures that come near it. If the dragon chooses, any creature within 100 feet takes 6 Strength and 6 Charisma damage. A DC 60 Fortitude save negates this effect.
- **Constrict (Ex):** On a successful grapple check, Xiaotan deals 4d6+36 points of bludgeoning damage.
- **Crush (Ex):** As a full round action, a primal dragon can crush any number of opponents 2 or more size categories smaller. This requires a full-round action. A creature that fails its Reflex save is pinned until it succeeds in an opposed grapple check or Escape Artist roll. Xiaotan's crush deals 4d8+36 points of damage (save DC 56).
- **Energy Blast (Su):** Xiaotan's energy blast is an 80-foot cone that deals 29 dice of damage (DC 56) of any energy type.
- **Improved grab (Ex):** With a successful melee attack, Xiaotan can attempt to grapple its opponent as a free action. This attack only affects creatures and objects size Huge and larger. If the grapple check is successful, Xiaotan wraps around its opponent and can deal constriction damage in addition to the normal damage for the attack. The dragon can continue to constrict each round until the hold is broken.

  If the dragon wishes, it may take a -20 penalty to its grapple check and simply hold the opponent. When the dragon holds the opponent in this way, it is not considered grappled and may continue to act normally; it retains its Dex bonus to AC, can cast spells, still threatens an area, and can continue to use its remaining attacks. Xiaotan can only hold one opponent at a time in this manner.

  A creature or object held by Xiaotan's improved grab moves into the dragon's squares without provoking an attack of opportunity. Xiaotan may then move freely with the creature or object as long as the dragon is strong enough to drag it.
- **Rend (Ex):** If a primal dragon makes a successful grapple check, it may attempt a grapple check to tear the creature's flesh. Xiaotan's rend deals 8d6+36 points of damage.
- **Spell-Like Abilities:**

  At will—*detect thoughts, fog cloud, suggestion, tongues*

  5/day—*confusion, dominate person, greater invisibility*

  3/day—*chain lightning, control weather, ethereal jaunt*

  1/day—*dominate monster, return, storm of vengeance, whirlwind*
- **Spells:** Xiaotan casts spells as a 29th-level caster (wild adept). The save DCs are Charisma-based.
- Spells Known: 0—*detect magic, read magic, daze, cure minor wounds, flare, light, mage hand, message, open/close;* 1st—*alarm, command, disguise self, identify, ventriloquism;* 2nd—*daze monster, locate object, misdirection, spectral hand, hideous laughter;* 3rd—*dispel magic, hold person, protection from energy, wind wall;* 4th—*charm monster, confusion, lesser geas, scrying;* 5th—*feeblemind, hold monster, permanency, teleport;* 6th—*geas/quest, greater dispel magic, heal;* 7th—*greater scrying, limited wish, mass hold person;* 8th—*antipathy, mind blank, screen;* 9th—*foresight, mass hold monster, wish.*
- **Sweep (Ex):** Xiaotan can use its long body to sweep opponents from the field. The sweep affects a semicircle 50 feet in diameter centered on any square of the dragon's body. This attack deals 3d6+36 points of damage. Targets of this effect may make a DC 56 Reflex save to halve the damage.

Apocalyptic Era

Like everyone else, the dragons are rebuilding. They rise above the earth in their true forms for the first time in millennia. They are eager to rebuild their empires and to directly battle the others.

Jotanhor

The most "dragon"-like of the three active dragons is Jotanhor, the master of Europe, Scandinavia, and Northern Africa. Covered in black, diamond-hard plates, Jotanhor has a thick body, broad wings, and a comparatively short tail and neck. Although Jotanhor measures only 250 feet in length, it weighs more than either Xiaotan or Tehlitocan.

When the dragons first emerged on earth, they sought to discover more about themselves and each other. They also battled each other, testing their strength and fortitude. Jotanhor is perhaps the most physically powerful of all the primal dragons. Despite this advantage, Jotanhor was unable to gain the upper hand in the dragons' early struggles, for they all quickly learned to fight through subterfuge and alliance. Eventually the earth cooled, as did Jotanhor's passions, and he has since learned to move with more cunning.

Still, Jotanhor is the least subtle of the remaining dragons, preferring a direct approach to solving problems, both in combat and politics. This quality makes Jotanhor and his human organizations a little less difficult to deal with compared to the other dragons.

Possible Adventures

- An aggressive militaristic cult is operating in the same region as the PCs. The *Gatekeepers of Asgaard* is a small cult who prophesize that a great dragon-like god, Jottentor, will soon wake from its slumber to rule the earth. When the PCs investigate, they realize that the cultists are searching for Jotanhor's sleeping place. If the cultists succeed in finding the lair, they will wake Jotanhor and trigger a final destruction of the entire region (for Jotanhor will ensure that no knowledge of its lair remains anywhere in its vicinity).

- Long ago, a primal dragon constructed a labyrinth to test the character of man. The traps, illusions, and guardian beasts are so potent that all who have stumbled across it have met their demise. Rumors come to the PCs of the labyrinth and the valuables that must surely lie within. If the PCs successfully overcome all challenges, the dragon lord will invite them to become its agents, pitting them against the forces of the remaining dragon lords.

Jotanhor

Colossal Primal Dragon

Hit Dice:	58d12+1102 (1479 hp)
Initiative:	+4
Speed:	80 ft. (16 squares), fly 300 ft. (good), swim 80 ft.
Armor Class:	47 (-8 size, +45 natural), touch 2, flat-footed 47
Base Attack/ Grapple:	+58/+103
Attack:	Bite +79 melee (4d8+29/19-20)
Full Attack:	Bite +79 melee (4d8+29/19-20), two claws +74 melee (4d6+14/19-20), tail slap +74 melee (4d6+43), two wings +74 melee (2d8+14)
Space/Reach:	40 ft./30 ft.
Special Attacks:	Awesome presence, crush, energy blast, rend, spells, sweep
Special Qualities:	Blindsight 60 ft., damage reduction 15/ epic, darkvision 120 ft., immunity to: cold, compulsion, fire, lightning, magic sleep, paralysis, and petrification; low light vision, primal dragon traits, spell resistance 42
Saves:	Fort +50, Ref +31, Will +48
Abilities:	Str 69, Dex 10, Con 49, Int 44, Wis 45, Cha 41
Skills:	Appraise +78, Bluff +78, Climb +89, Concentration +90, Decipher Script +78, Diplomacy +82, Disguise +78, Gather Information +76, Hide +45, Intimidate +80, Knowledge (arcana) +81, Knowledge (geography) +81, Knowledge (history) +81, Knowledge (the planes) +81, Listen +80, Move Silently +61, Research +78, Search +78, Sense Motive +78, Spellcraft +80, Spot +80, Survival +78, Use Artifact +78
Feats:	Ability Focus (awesome presence), Ability Focus (energy blast), Alertness, Cleave, Flyby Attack, Frightful Presence, Great Cleave, Greater Spell Focus (evocation), Improved Critical (bite), Improved Critical (claw), Improved Initiative, Leadership, Power Attack, Quicken Spell-Like Ability (acid fog), Quicken Spell-Like Ability (hold monster), Skill Focus (Bluff, Intimidate), Skill Focus (Diplomacy, Sense Motive), Spell Focus (evocation), Spell Penetration, Wingover
Challenge Rating:	70

Combat

In combat, Jotanhor is direct and deadly. It will identify the greatest threats and systematically eliminate them, usually leading with its devastating charge, shockwave, and energy blast. Jotanhor is not averse to injury and will not hesitate to incur some damage in order to maximize the punishment it inflicts. Although Jotanhor prefers direct physical confrontation, it also possesses a wide variety of spells and will employ them if they would be of greater effect than its physical attacks.

- **Awesome Presence (Su):** Jotanhor's presence is so powerful that it weakens creatures that come near it. If the dragon chooses, any creature within 100 feet takes 6 Strength and 6 Charisma damage. A DC 61 Fortitude save negates this effect.

- **Crush (Ex):** As a full round action, a primal dragon can crush any number of opponents 2 or more size categories smaller. This requires a full-round action. A creature that fails its Reflex save is pinned until it succeeds in an opposed grapple check or Escape Artist roll. Jotanhor's crush deals 4d8+43 points of damage (DC68).

- **Devastating Charge (Ex):** Jotanhor can deliver an earth shaking charge by slamming head first into an opponent or structure. Jotanhor may target a 10-foot by 10-foot square in lieu of a single target if it wishes. Creatures in the area may make a DC 56 Reflex save to avoid taking damage. The devastating charge deals 8d8+58 damage.

- **Energy Blast (Su):** Jotanhor's energy blast is an 80-foot cone that deals 29 dice of damage (DC 60) of any energy type.

- **Shockwave (Ex):** Once every 6 rounds, Jotanhor may emit a massive wave of force that expands 200 feet in all directions centered on its centre of mass. This wave is powerful enough to uproot trees and topple buildings. The shockwave deals 29d8 force damage to all creatures and fixed objects within the area of effect. A DC 58 Fortitude save halves the damage. Standing creatures must make a DC 58 Fortitude save or be knocked prone and stunned for 6d6 rounds. The shockwave ignores hardness when damaging objects or structures if those objects are rooted to the earth or otherwise immovable.

- **Rend (Ex):** If a primal dragon makes a successful grapple check, it may attempt a grapple check to tear the creature's flesh. Jotanhor's rend deals 8d6+43 points of damage.

- **Spell-Like Abilities:**

  At will—*detect thoughts, haste, tongues*

  5/day— *dominate person, hold monster, wind wall*

  3/day—*acid fog, statue, true seeing*

  1/day—*maze, power word kill, return*

- **Spells:** Jotanhor casts spells as a 29th-level caster (wild adept). The save DCs are Charisma-based.

- **Spells Known:** 0—*detect magic, read magic, dancing lights, flare, light, mage hand, message, open/close,* *ray of frost;* 1st—*alarm, charm person, color spray, magic missile, Tenser's floating disk;* 2nd—*blur, continual flame, gust of wind, misdirection, spectral hand;* 3rd—*dispel magic, fireball, lightning bolt, wind wall;* 4th—*confusion, lesser geas, shout, wall of fire;* 5th—*feeblemind, permanency, telekinesis, wall of force;* 6th—*chain lightning, geas/quest, contingency;* 7th—*control weather, forcecage, limited wish;* 8th—*antipathy, greater shout, sunburst;* 9th—*foresight, meteor swarm, wish.*

- **Sweep (Ex):** Jotanhor can use its long body to sweep opponents from the field. The sweep affects a semi-circle 50 feet in diameter centered on any square of the dragon's body. This attack deals 3d6+43 points of damage. Targets of this effect may make a DC 58 Reflex save to halve the damage.

The Lethid Campaign

Little is known—or will likely ever be known—of the lethid. No more than a rumor in history, the lethid have not made an overt move since their devastating war with Atlantis in the shadows of pre-archaic history.

The lethid are the twisted children of a great darkness, an extra-dimensional evil beyond imagining and a power beyond reckoning. This darkness is a force from beyond the stars, an evil so vast and transcendent that even its shadow was powerful enough to corrupt this plane.

The lethid are powerful mentalists that can control men and beasts as puppets and make one's greatest fears a horrific reality. They spread hate, fear, and pain all across the world, expanding virus-like through all nations and cultures. Though the lethid's ultimate designs are unfathomable and their actions often inhumanly bizarre, they are very skilled at inflicting death and suffering.

As all lethid are material manifestations of a singular malevolent entity, each individual lethid shares the same unfathomably evil motivations, yet remain independent entities on this dimension. As such, the lethid form a perfectly harmonized society that organizes itself in natural hierarchy of task specialization.

Individual lethid know intuitively to arrange themselves according to power and abilities. The *true aboleth* are the undisputed overlords of all lethid: their intelligence, psionic powers, and strength are without equal.

The *nihileth* serve as lieutenants to the aboleth. Powerful in their own right, especially when in control of a particularly intelligent host, each may direct hundreds or thousands of lesser lethid who orchestrate their activities across the globe. The nihileth can act with arrogance, sometimes chafing under the orders of the aboleth, but they will not hesitate to collaborate with each other to surmount obstacles, solve problems, or spread horror on a larger scale.

The *shibboleth*, although nominally subservient to the nihileth, are extremely powerful and strong-willed, and prone to acting independently. These huge creatures are the lethid's spymasters. They can control vast numbers of animals and vermin, which can then penetrate deep into human cities to gather vast amounts of knowledge about their prey for their masters in the deeps.

The *rgleth* provide the lethid with brute force and far outnumber the nihileth and shibboleth. Though seemingly unable to control more intelligent creatures, the rgleth are capable of dominating large animals to serve as powerful combatants and laborers. These are the lethid a human will most likely survive seeing.

Unlike the Undead and Dragon villains that have come before, the lethid are not individual creatures, but an entire race of evil beings on which you can base an entire campaign.

Lethid Abilities

Implant

The lethid are parasitic creatures that devour the brains (and thoughts) of intelligent creatures. Two subraces of lethid in particular, the nihileth and rgleth, similar in appearance and physiology, are physically adapted to this purpose.

Both nihileth and rgleth are squid-like in appearance, with six tentacles: four grasping tentacles, and two implantation tentacles. The nihileth is more advanced mentally, with a larger brain and weaker tentacles; while the rgleth is more physically robust, with a smaller brain and longer, more powerful grasping tentacles.

The nihileth prefer to prey on the major humanoid races, while rgleth tend to control combat capable animals and powerful beasts of burden. Both of these lethid can also implant themselves into aberrations, dragons, giants, humanoids, magical beasts, and monstrous humanoids of the proper size and intelligence level (see table below). Each possesses a special attack that allows it to *implant* itself into a target creature's nervous system, and a corollary ability, *unhost*.

Lethid Subrace	Size Threshold	Int Threshold
Nihileth	1 - 3 sizes larger (Medium - Huge)	6 or more
Rgleth	1 - 4 sizes larger (Medium - Gargantuan)	2 or less

- Implant (Ex): To use this ability, a nihileth or rgleth must first establish a hold by successfully grappling a creature with one of its grasping tentacles. If the lethid begins its turn with a hold on the creature, it can try to attach its two implantation tentacles with a single grapple check. The lethid gets a +2 circumstance bonus to this check for every grasping tentacle that it has attached beyond the first.

  If the lethid begins a round with its two implantation tentacles attached to a creature, it can attempt to graft itself to its victim's nervous system. The victim must succeed at a DC 25 Will save.

Creatures failing their Will save who fall within the size and Intelligence thresholds of the attacking lethid are transformed into a *hosted* nihileth or rgleth (see the template below)—the implanted lethid now has complete control of the victim's mind and body.

Creatures outside the attacking lethid's control thresholds suffer 1d4 damage and 2d4 Wisdom damage (Fortitude save DC 18 halves Wis damage) when a nihileth or rgleth uses its implantation tentacles to attack.

Nihileth prefer hosts from the major humanoid races and rgleth prefer predatory animals, but each can implant themselves into aberrations, dragons, giants, humanoids, magical beasts, and monstrous humanoids. Nihileth can only implant themselves into creatures with a single head and brain and a permanent Intelligence score of at least 6. Rgleth can only dominate creatures with an Intelligence score of 2 or less.

A hosted lethid intertwines itself so closely to the host creature's vital organs that the two are effectively a single creature with a single hit point total. Consequently, it is impossible to simply cut a hosted nihileth or rgleth free from its host without killing the host, or even to damage the lethid parasite without damaging the host. If a nihileth or rgleth separates from its host, divide the total damage dealt to the templated creature equally between the lethid and its host; this may leave one or both of the creatures dead or *dying*.

- Unhost (Ex): A nihileth or rgleth can unhost itself from the creature to whom it is attached as a full-round action, which does not provoke attacks of opportunity. A lethid that is feeling particularly malevolent (as is usually the case) can attempt to kill its host by destroying its nervous system as it departs (see below).

Removing a Lethid

Removing a hosted lethid without killing the host is difficult although not impossible. A nihileth or rgleth may voluntarily decide to unhost (see above). A *heal, limited wish*, or *remove disease* spell will force the lethid to make a Fortitude save (DC 5 + caster level) or be ejected from the host's body; a wish or *miracle* will automatically eject it. Note that all of these effects must first overcome the lethid's spell resistance.

It is also possible to remove a lethid through mundane means (such as pulling or cutting the lethid from the host) but at significant risk to the host. A hosted lethid can only be removed through mundane means if it is unconscious or dead. Removal of a dead lethid requires a DC 25 Heal check (and the Surgery feat).

For a hosted lethid that is merely unconscious, any amount of continuous electrical shock will automatically disrupt its hold on the host and allow a Surgery check (DC27) to remove and kill it. A conscious lethid may be removed through surgery if it is somehow incapacitated for the entire duration of the surgery, such as by a *hold monster* spell.

If a living or dead lethid is forcefully removed from a creature, even by delicate surgery, there is a chance of catastrophic brain damage. The host must make a Death From Massive Damage Fortitude save (DC20); allow a +1 bonus to this check for each point by which surgeon's skill check exceeded the Surgery DC. Failing this save leaves the host forever comatose; the brain stem is damaged or destroyed. Success means that the host survived, but may still suffer from long-term physical or psychological effects at the GM's discretion.

Freed hosts are rarely the creatures they were previous to their infestation. Though victims often recall very little, they usually suffer dark and terrifying nightmares for the remainder of their days. Some hosts retain a strange insight into the world of their former captors, but they are not eager to speak about their visions.

Psionics

The lethid are powerful mentalists. Each subrace possesses one or more of the following spell-like or supernatural abilities, as noted in its stat block. The DC for these abilities are based on the attacking lethid's Charisma modifier, and the effects are resolved at a caster level equal to the lethid's HD. Lethid do not have to roll caster level checks to activate these abilities, nor do they suffer spell burn.

Aphasic Hammer [Sp]
Range: Medium
Will save (DC13 + Cha modifier) negates

The lethid can project a 30 ft. radius burst of psionic energy that renders all creatures within it unable to speak or form coherent vocal utterances for 1d10 minutes. A creature afflicted in this way can be cured by *dispel magic*, *heal*, or any magical effect that can cure insanity or aphasia. This is a mind-affecting effect. This ability is equivalent to a 3rd-level spell effect.

Blast of Discord [Sp]
Range: 0
Will save (DC13 + Cha modifier) negates

Some lethid can emit a powerful blast of mental energy which leaves all creatures within a 30 ft. radius *confused* for 2d4 rounds. Lethid (and creatures hosting or under the mental control of a lethid) are immune to this effect. This is a mind-affecting effect. This ability is equivalent to a 3rd-level spell effect, but it may not be dispelled once a creature has been affected.

Greater Blast of Discord [Sp]
Range: 0
Will save (DC14 + Cha modifier) negates

All intelligent creatures within a 30 ft. radius of the lethid must make a Will save or be *confused* for 3d4 rounds. This is a mind-affecting effect. This ability is equivalent to a 4th-level spell effect, but it may not be dispelled once a creature has been affected.

Phase Mastery [Su]
This lethid has mastered the ability to shift between dimensions, as if it were under the effect of a *blink* spell. It can begin or end this effect as a move-equivalent action, which does not provoke an attack of opportunity. Once every 3 rounds, a lethid with phase mastery can also use *plane shift* as a spell-like ability, effective caster level 9th. The lethid may only use this ability to shift itself (or its willing or unwilling targets) between the Prime Material Plane and the lethid dimension.

Presence Leech [Sp]
Range: 60 feet (Sp):
Will save (DC 14 + Cha modifier) negates.

Some lethid can attempt to siphon the psychic energy from one creature with an Intelligence score of 6 or greater within 60 feet. The target must succeed at a Will save (DC equal to 14 + Cha modifier) or suffer 2d4 points of temporary Charisma damage. This temporary Charisma damage lasts 1 hour. If the attack succeeds, the lethid gains an enhancement bonus to its Charisma equal to the damage dealt for 1 hour. This is a mind-affecting effect. This attack is equivalent to a 4th-level spell.

Ray of Disruption [Sp]
Range: Medium
Fortitude save (DC16 + Cha modifier) for half

The lethid can launch a focused wave of matter-disrupting psionic energy at a single target within range. The lethid must make a successful ranged touch attack to affect a creature with this ability, which deals (HD+2) d6 points of disruption damage. This attack has a critical threat range of 19-20. If used against an object, the wave ignores its hardness. Any creature or object reduced to 0 or fewer hit points by this attack is completely dissolved into an incoherent jumble of dust and ooze. This ability is equivalent to a 6th-level spell effect.

Synaptic Avalanche [Sp]
Range: 60-foot cone
Will save (DC15 + Cha modifier) negates (see below)

This psionic attack is an overwhelming flood of mental stimulus that affects all intelligent creatures within a 60 ft. cone. Creatures caught in its path must succeed at a Will save or suffer 1d6 points of Wisdom damage and become *stunned* for 3d6 rounds. Creatures must *subtract* their Intelligence modifier from their saving throw roll against this attack (e.g. a character with an Intelligence score of 16 suffers a -3 penalty, whereas a character with an Intelligence score of 8 gets a +1 bonus). A successful save halves the Wisdom damage and negates the *stunning* effect. This is a mind-affecting effect. This ability is equivalent to a 5th-level spell, but it may not be dispelled once a creature has been affected.

Lethid Subtype Template/Traits
For GMs who wish to expand their campaign with their own lethid creatures, the lethid subtype definition is as follows:

Traits: A lethid possesses the following traits (unless otherwise noted in the creature's description).

- Amphibious—lethid can breathe both air and water; they can take 10 with Swim checks (even in stressful conditions) and can use the run action when swimming in a straight line.
- +4 racial bonus to Climb checks and a +2 racial bonus to Concentration, Listen, and Spot checks.
- +2 racial bonus to Will saves.
- +4 skill points per Hit Die.
- Lethid are *vulnerable* to electricity.
- Immune to disease and poison.
- Resistance to acid 5 and cold 5.
- Spell-like ability: At will—*detect thoughts* (DC equal to 12 + Cha modifier). Effective caster level equal to HD.
- *Telepathy* 100 ft.
- Lethid almost always also have the *extraplanar*, *evil*, and *native* subtypes.
- CR adjustment: +1.4

Archaic Era

Ten thousand years ago, Atlantis vanished beneath the ocean, sacrificing itself to save the Earth. No one remembers. Yet, humanoid civilization rises again. Great empires abound, wars are fought under the banners of great religions, and the humanoids' ambitions yet grow. But shadows also stalk the land: tales of ghastly horrors spread, dark cults emerge and infect the souls of nations, and politics have taken a grim turn. Who has the skill and guile to find and face this dark threat? And if there are heroes who can answer this call, can their wills withstand the terrible truths they might uncover?

Rgleth

The grizzly was wary. She could smell the dank, rotting wetness of the intruder. With a low growl, she shuffled a little deeper into her den. Near the back, hovering and pulsing with a sickening green light, was a tentacled beast. The bear did not hesitate to attack. With a vicious swipe of her claws she tore into one of the creature's spiked tentacles, but not before another had wrapped around her foreleg. Despite her fury, it was not long before the strange creature was around her neck. Within moments, the bear ceased her struggle and growled triumphantly. With a green flash in her eye and the great spiked tentacles waving about her head, she turned toward the opening of the den. And then, with a slight rush of air and without touching the intervening space, she displaced herself out into the darkness. To hunt. To kill.

A rgleth resembles a large hovering squid, but instead of the nihileth's many relatively thin tentacles, a rgleth has 6 thick spined tentacles used for grappling and combat and two smaller ones that hold it fast to its host's spinal column.

A rgleth attaches to the spinal column and enhances its host's animalistic lower-brain responses, while feeding on the host's neural energy to enhance its own psionic abilities. The result is a fearsome lethid combatant. Rgleth are similar to the nihileth but without large brains or developed feeding tentacles, or the varied psionic abilities of their more developed kin.

Possible Encounters

- This adventure can take place in almost any wilderness area where the PCs are traveling. During their journeys, they meet a badly injured scholar who tells them of an enormous black monolith he and his fellow archeologists uncovered. The stone seemed to pulse with evil. He claims that soon after the group began studying the stone, it began to bleed. Frightened, the scholar ran to a nearby hilltop, leaving the other less timid diggers to continue the investigation. He watched in horror as two bull elephants and a lion, each with tentacles growing from its neck, appeared out of nowhere and attacked his companions. None of the other archeologists survived. The scholar implores the PCs to chase down these creatures and stop their transport of the evil artifact.

If they accept, the PCs face the daunting task of taking on three hosted rgleth. But the PCs have two advantages: surprise and mobility, as the two elephants are carrying the stone on a sling between them and will have a difficult time participating in combat without loosing the stone. The rgleth are under strict orders to fetch the stone and bring it back immediately and the elephants do not deviate from their task unless directly attacked. Even if they are directly attacked, one rgleth elephant maintains contact with the stone at all times. The lion is the party's primary adversary, as it begins hunting them when the rgleth realize they are being followed. The lion's dimensional fetish allows it to continually ambush the party from the shadows.

If the PCs can defeat, avoid, or outsmart the lion, they have four days to figure out how to stop the elephants before they reach their destination. If the PCs cannot stop them during that time, they may see the elephants pass through a magically warded illusory wall and forever beyond their reach.

The monolithic black stone could serve as a central focus for a lethid campaign or series of adventures.

Rgleth

Small Aberration (*Evil, Extraplanar, Lethid, Native*)

Hit Dice:	4d8+8 (26 hp)
Initiative:	+9
Speed:	10 ft. (2 squares), swim 30 ft., fly 10 ft. (good)
Armor Class:	18 (+1 size, +3 Dex, +4 natural) Touch 14, flat-footed 15
Base Attack/ Grapple:	+3/+8
Attack:	Tentacle +7 melee (1d3+1 plus paralysis)
Full Attack:	6 Tentacles +7 melee (1d3+1 plus paralysis) and bite +4 melee (1d6+1)
Space/Reach:	5 ft./5 ft.
Special Attacks:	Burst of speed, constrict (1d3+1 plus paralysis), implant, improved grab, poison, psionics
Special Qualities:	Amphibious, darkvision 60 ft., damage resistance 5/magic, dimensional fetish, immunity to disease and poison, lethid traits, resistance to fire 5 and acid 5, telepathy 100 ft., vulnerability to electricity
Saves:	Fort +2, Ref +4, Will +7
Abilities:	Str 12, Dex 17, Con 12, Int 5, Wis 12, Cha 14
Skills:	Concentration +4, Climb +7, Hide +16, Jump +8, Listen +7, Move Silently +12, Spot +7, Swim +10, Tumble +10
Feats:	Improved Grab[B], Improved Initiative, Mobility[B], Weapon Finesse
Environment:	Aquatic, underground
Organization:	Solitary or group (5-10)
Challenge Rating:	5
Treasure:	None
Allegiances:	Always Leth-Thol'Zad, evil, lethid
Advancement:	5-6 HD (Small), 7-9 HD (Medium)

Combat

When not in their lair, rgleth are almost always out hunting for hosts. They typically stalk their prey, using cover to hide to the best effect, before surprising their victims and attempting to implant themselves as quickly as possible.

Rgleth avoid combat while unhosted. When confronted by a concerted attack, rgleth will either retreat or attempt to find the largest, fiercest animal available to use as a host.

* Rgleth have a +4 racial bonus to grapple checks.

- Burst of speed (Ex): Once every three rounds, a rgleth can move with phenomenal quickness, increasing its speed by 30 ft. during that round.
- Constrict (Ex): A rgleth deals 1d3+1 damage plus its poison with a successful grapple check.
- Dimensional fetish (Su): A rgleth with this ability is linked to a specific physical feature of the Prime Material Plane that it can use as a conduit for slightly longer forays to the lethid dimension. Roll 1d8 or choose from the following table to determine the rgleth's fetish:

1. Flat mirrored surfaces	5. Knots
2. Shadows	6. Book pages
3. Standing water	7. Smoke
4. Corners (inside vertices)	8. Circles

For a physical feature to count as a dimensional fetish, it must be a significant part of an object or area no smaller than 2 sizes smaller than the rgleth (or hosted creature). When within 5 feet of an object that matches its dimensional fetish, a rgleth can jump to the lethid dimension as a free action. This ability is identical to *ethereal jaunt* cast at 9th level, except it transports the rgleth to the lethid dimension and the rgleth must, at some point during the action, return through a location within 5 feet of an instance of its dimensional fetish, anywhere in this plane, no matter what the distance. This ability can only be employed as part of a move action.

- Implant (Ex): See description above.
- Improved grab (Ex): To use this ability, a rgleth must hit with a tentacle attack. It can then attempt to start a grapple as a free action. If it wins the grapple check, it establishes a hold and can constrict.
- Paralysis (Ex): A rgleth's tentacles are coated with a contact sedative that slows its prey's reflexes. A creature hit or grappled by a rgleth's tentacles must make a DC 14 Fortitude save or be paralyzed for 2d4 rounds. A rgleth that has implanted itself into a creature can inject an antidote into its nervous system, which immediately removes all penalties dealt by the rgleth's sedative. The save DC is Constitution-based.
- Psionics (Sp): A rgleth can employ several psionic abilities. At will—clairaudience, daze (DC 12), detect thoughts (DC 14). The save DCs are Charisma-based. Effective caster level 7th.
- Unhost (Ex): See description above.
- Vulnerability to electricity (Ex): Electricity attacks deal an additional 50% damage to rgleth. In addition, an electricity attack that deals damage in excess of the rgleth's Constitution forces it to make a Fortitude save (DC equal to the damage dealt) or be stunned for 1d4 rounds.
- Skills: Rgleth have a +2 racial bonus on Concentration, Listen, Move Silently, and Spot checks. An unhosted rgleth's chameleon-like skin gives it a +4 racial bonus to Hide checks.
- A rgleth has a +8 racial bonus to Swim checks. It can always take 10 on Swim checks, even in dangerous or distracting conditions. It can also use the run action when swimming in a straight line.

Sample Hosted Rgleth

This example uses a 5 HD black bear as the base creature and a 4 HD rgleth as the base rgleth.

When not under control of another lethid, a hosted rgleth creature will fight aggressively if confronted. For example, this leopard will immediately attack if it feels threatened. If grossly outnumbered, it will resort to its blast of discord or flee with dimensional fetish.

Solitary, uncontrolled hosted rgleth are rare because the immediate instinct of a rgleth once it gains a host is to return to the nearest known lethid enclave.

Sample Hosted Rgleth

Hosted Rgleth Black Bear
Medium Aberration (Augmented Animal)

Hit Dice:	5d8+10 (32 hp)
Initiative:	+6
Speed:	40 ft. (8 squares)
Armor Class:	15 (+2 Dex, +3 natural), touch 12, flat-footed 13
Base Attack/ Grapple:	+6/+10
Attack:	Claw +11 melee (1d4+5)
Full Attack:	2 claws +11 melee (1d4+5) and bite +6 melee (1d6+2) and 2 tentacles +6 melee (1d3+2 plus paralysis)
Space/Reach:	5 ft./5 ft.
Special Attacks:	Blast of discord, improved grab, paralysis, psionics
Special Qualities:	Darkvision 60 ft., dimensional fetish, overstimulation, telepathy 100 ft., sensitivity to electricity, unhost
Saves:	Fort +6, Ref +6, Will +8
Abilities:	Str 21, Dex 15, Con 15, Int 5, Wis 15, Cha 15
Skills:	Climb +5, Concentration +4, Listen +12, Spot +12, Swim +9
Feats:	Alertness, Endurance, Improved Initiative[B], Run
Challenge Rating:	4
Treasure:	None
Advancement:	—

Creating a Hosted Rgleth

Any creature that falls victim to a rgleth's implant attack immediately becomes a hosted rgleth. The creature's voluntary brain functions are supplanted by those of the rgleth.

A hosted rgleth uses all the base creature's statistics and special abilities, except as noted here:

- Size and Type: The creature's type becomes aberration. Do not recalculate its Hit Dice, base attack bonus, saves, or skill points. It loses any alignment or allegiance subtypes. Size is unchanged.
- Hit Dice and Hit Points: Current and future Hit Dice remain those of the base creature.
- Armor Class: Increase the base creature's natural armor bonus by +1.
- Base Attack/Grapple: Add the rgleth's base attack bonus to the base creature's base attack bonus, and include the rgleth's +4 racial bonus to grapple to the hosted creature's grapple bonus.
- Attack: The hosted rgleth retains the base creature's primary attacks.
- Full Attack: The hosted creature retains the base creature's primary and secondary attacks and gains two tentacle attacks as secondary attacks.
- Damage: The hosted rgleth's tentacles do damage equal to the base rgleth's tentacle damage plus 1/2 the hosted rgleth's Strength modifier plus paralysis.
- Special Attacks: A hosted rgleth retains all the special attacks of the base creature except for spells and spell-like abilities. It also gains a number of psionic and extradimensional abilities. The save DC for these abilities is 10 + 1/2 hosted rgleth's HD + Cha modifier, unless otherwise noted.
- Blast of discord (Sp): See description above. It can use this ability 3 times per day.
- Paralysis (Ex): A hosted rgleth retains its paralysis attack.
- Psionics (Sp): A hosted rgleth can employ several psionic abilities. At will—clairaudience, daze, detect thoughts. Effective caster level 9th.
- Special Qualities: The hosted rgleth retains all of the base creature's special qualities and gains the following:
  - Darkvision 60 ft.
  - Dimensional fetish (Su): A hosted rgleth retains the rgleth's dimensional fetish ability (see rgleth entry).
  - Overstimulation (Ex): A hosted rgleth can push its body beyond normal natural limits for short bursts of time. The hosted rgleth gains +4 to Strength, +4 to Constitution, and +5 ft. to speed for a number of rounds equal to its Hit Dice. A hosted rgleth is dazed for the next round after its overstimulation ends. A hosted rgleth can begin or end overstimulation as a free action on its turn. It can overstimulate a number of times per day equal to its Con modifier.
  - Sensitivity to electricity (Ex): A hosted rgleth that suffers an electricity attack that deals damage in excess of the hosted rgleth's Constitution must make a Fortitude save (DC equal to damage dealt) or be stunned for 1d4 rounds.
  - Telepathy 100 ft.
  - Unhost (Ex): See description above.
- Saves: The hosted creature retains the base creature's Fortitude and Reflex saves. Substitute the base rgleth's

base Will save. Hosted rgleth have a +2 racial bonus on Will saves.

- Abilities: Increase the base creature's Strength by +2 and Dexterity by +2. Replace the base creature's Intelligence, Wisdom, and Charisma scores with the base rgleth's scores.
- Skills: The base creature retains all of its skills and racial skill bonuses and gains the base rgleth's ranks in the latter's Intelligence, Wisdom, and Charisma-based skills. Hosted rgleth have a +2 racial bonus to Concentration, Listen, and Spot checks.
- Feats: The hosted rgleth gains Alertness and Improved Initiative.
- Challenge Rating: Same as base creature +2.
- Advancement: Same as base creature and base rgleth.
- Allegiances: Always Leth-Thol'Zad, evil, lethid.

Modern Era

Factories produce a constant rain of soot in London. The gears of industry grind the faith of millions. Never before have so many people suffered so badly. And never have the shadows had such power. Is there respite for those exceptional souls who battle madhouses full of white-eyed puppets, track fearsome tentacled beasts to their gruesome masters, or come to understand—at the price of their sanity—some small part of the world's peril?

Shibboleth

Nearly blind from the stench of sewage and decay, the group neared the last corner, around which lay the city's central sewer pit. O'Reilly paused to reload his Winchester and revolver with shaking hands. Meredith, still bleeding from the gash on her neck, sagged against the slime-covered wall and prayed feverishly that they had seen their last pack of rats. Having bandaged the cuts on his arm, Morgan wiped away the ribbon of white ichor coating his blade and resolutely squared his shoulders. With a silent consensus, the three charged around the corner, throwing phosphorus flares into the vast room. Behind a pack of snarling white-eyed dogs was a gelatinous beast of a thousand tentacles. Meredith moaned and sank to her knees; O'Reilly's Winchester flashed twice; Morgan lit and threw his last stick of dynamite. Then the dogs attacked...

Shibboleth are huge intelligent amorphous creatures covered with a mass of strong, octopus-like tentacles. Shibboleth are powerful psionicists that can control large groups of animals and vermin (packs of rats, swarms of insects, packs of dogs, etc). Their oozing bodies secrete a psionically infused slime, which rots its victims' brains, eventually killing them and leaving their bodies as puppets under the shibboleth's control. Most creatures under this effect have dead white eyes and may act unnaturally, depending on the skill and knowledge of the shibboleth. These creatures often live underneath large cities and form vast spy networks.

Possible Encounters

- One of the PCs' friends or relatives—or perhaps one of the PCs after a particularly traumatic experience—has succumbed to mental illness and has been temporarily committed to the local asylum. The first time the PCs visit the asylum, whether on admitting the patient or at a later time, they notice that the asylum is in terrible upkeep. The inmates are locked in small, dirty rooms and manacled to their beds. The walls are dank and an alert PC may notice some sort of slime or mold growing on it. Roaches scurry across floors strewn with mouse droppings. The staff appear either harried or uncaring, and far too few for the 120 beds they must administer. Alerting a magistrate will do little in the short term; the city only has a few overworked inspectors who must work very hard to visit each asylum twice a year.

  When the PCs' speak to their contact in the asylum, their reports are hair-raising. The asylum is overrun with vermin who get into all of the inmates' food and clothing. They have also noticed that there seem to be many patients who exhibit a mysterious set of symptoms. They possess completely blank, nearly catatonic gazes and they stumble with jerky movements when the attendants take them to the overgrown courtyard for their brief weekly exercise. If the PCs examine some of the patients on their own, they find that they are utterly unresponsive and a strange, foul-smelling fluid leaks from their skin. They are also covered with rat and vermin bites. PCs who are astute enough to track the vermin discover that many of them originate from an abandoned mansion at the city's outskirts.

  As time passes, the disorder in the asylum grows as more inmates succumb to the strange catatonia. Inmates report hearing and seeing strange and horrifying noises, lights, and phantoms in the hallways, driving some of them past the final edge of sanity. Some staff members quit, swearing that the asylum is haunted. Soon, staff members and inmates begin disappearing. If the PCs thoroughly investigate the disappearances, they may discover that the victims are being murdered or abducted and taken to the same mansion from which the vermin originate.

  The cause of this trouble is a rogue shibboleth who lurks in that mansion (after being recently summoned by the eschatological cult that was using the mansion as a base). The shibboleth ate the cultists, but could not figure out how to get home. The creature developed a fascination with the insane when it discovered the nearby asylum and realized that the inmates' diminished mental state leaves them vulnerable to the shibboleths's mind rot disease, spread through its vermin puppets. The shibboleth began casually destroying the minds of some of the inmates and possessing their bodies, using its psychic conduit ability to torment others with illusions and mind-reading spells. The shibboleth found the latter especially fascinating: intrigued by the darkest psychopathic fantasies of some of the inmates, the shibboleth decided that it would try to act on some of these dark images by abducting people to its lair and visiting these images upon other people with its illusions.

Fortunately for the local people (although perhaps not necessarily for the PCs), the shibboleth is not allowed to continue its depredations unabated. A few weeks after the disappearances start (perhaps while the PCs are trying to figure out what to do about the beast), high-ranking lethid notice this unsupervised shibboleth. Consequently, a pair of powerful nihileth lieutenants is dispatched to eliminate the rogue shibboleth. If the PCs are present, the battle is astounding and ends in a huge conflagration, which consumes the mansion.

Shibboleth

Huge Aberration (*Evil, Extraplanar, Lethid, Native*)

Hit Dice:	16d8+32 (104 hp)
Initiative:	+4
Speed:	15 ft. (3 squares), swim 40 ft.
Armor Class:	21 (-2 size, +2 Dex, +11 natural) Touch 10, flat-footed 19
Base Attack/ Grapple:	+12/+35
Attack:	Slam +17 melee (2d6+7 plus 2d4 acid plus disease)
Full Attack:	5 slams +17 melee (2d6+7 plus 2d4 acid)
Space/Reach:	15 ft./10 ft.
Special Attacks:	Acid, constrict 2d6+7 plus 2d4 acid, disease, greater blast of discord, improved grab, psionics, spray
Special Qualities:	Damage reduction 10/magic, darkvision 60 ft., frightful presence, immunity to poison and disease, lethid traits, psychic puppets, resistance to fire 5 and acid 10, spell resistance 24, telepathy 100 ft., vulnerability to electricity
Saves:	Fort +9, Ref +7, Will +19
Abilities:	Str 25, Dex 14, Con 15, Int 19, Wis 24, Cha 20
Skills:	Bluff +19, Climb +17, Concentration +26, Gather Information +24, Intimidate +16, Knowledge (history) +20, Knowledge (local) +22, Knowledge (the planes) +18, Listen +25, Move Silently +17, Sense Motive +21, Spot +25, Swim +17
Feats:	Alertness, Combat Casting, Combat Reflexes, Great Fortitude, Improved Grapple[B], Improved Initiative, Psionic Focus (illusion)
Environment:	Aquatic, underground
Organization:	Solitary
Challenge Rating:	14
Allegiances:	Always Leth-Thol'Zad, evil, lethid
Advancement:	17-20 HD (Huge), 21-30 HD (Gargantuan)

Combat

A single shibboleth can control hundreds of creatures, usually of the one or two species with which the shibboleth is most familiar. Any living creature with a nervous system and an Intelligence score of 2 or lower that comes into contact with a shibboleth's ooze is affected as by a disease (DC 20 Fort save). Once infected, a creature suffers from Shibboleth Mind Rot until its Intelligence reaches 0, at which point the creature dies and its body becomes a psychic puppet under the control of the shibboleth.

Vermin are immediately affected by the shibboleth's ooze because of their simple brain structure. A vermin exposed to the ooze must make a DC 27 Fort save or become a psychic puppet instantly.

A vermin that failed its Fortitude save, or an infected creature whose Intelligence score reaches 0, may become a psychic puppet if it dies is within 20 miles of a willing shibboleth. The shibboleth can keep an animated body "alive" for months by nourishing it with its ichor before it rots away. Shibboleth will often use swarms of vermin to defend itself and its lair.

A shibboleth's diseased ooze only affects creatures with Intelligence scores of 2 or less—although it can affect higher animals whose Intelligence score has temporarily fallen to 2 or less (as a result of the shibboleth's *feeblemind* ability, for example).

A shibboleth can control up to 10 times its HD in psychic puppets.

- Acid (Ex): A shibboleth's body secretes acid that dissolves only flesh. Any melee hit or constrict attack inflicts 2d4 points of acid damage.
- Constrict (Ex): A shibboleth inflicts 2d6+7 slam damage and 2d4 acid damage with a successful grapple check.

- Disease (Ex): Any time a creature comes into physical contact with a shibboleth, its secretions, or one of its minions, it must make a Fortitude save (DC 20) or contract shibboleth mind rot. Creatures with an Intelligence score of 3 or more are immune to the shibboleth's disease.

Shibboleth Mind Rot

Disease:
A psionic brain-wasting disease spread by shibboleth.

Infection:
Contact with a shibboleth's ooze by touching an infected creature or through a shibboleth's Spray attack. This disease only affects creatures whose Intelligence score is 2 or less at the time of exposure, as well as living creatures lacking an Intelligence score, such as vermin. Successful successive saving throws do not allow creatures to recover normally from the disease unless their Intelligence is greater than 2 (but does prevent damage). An infected creature with an Intelligence score less than 2 can only recover normally if it is farther than 20 miles of the infecting shibboleth.

Fortitude DC:
DC20 (Infected creatures with an intelligence score greater than 2 receive a +7 bonus to their saving throws. Vermin must save against DC 27). A creature that successfully saves is immune to shibboleth mind rot for the next 24 hours.

Incubation Period:
12 hours.

Damage:
1d6 Intelligence plus a second saving throw or 1 point of the damage is permanent. When an infected creature's Intelligence reaches 0, that creature is dead (its brain is now ooze) and its body subject to use as a psychic puppet for a willing shibboleth within 20 miles.

A sentient creature converted to a psychic puppet often shows outward signs, such as a jerkiness or stiffness of motion, slurring of speech, etc. It can be detected by making an opposed Sense Motive check against the shibboleth's Bluff. The shibboleth suffers a -1 penalty to its check for every mile that separates it from its puppet.

- Improved Grab (Ex): To use this ability, a shibboleth must hit with a tentacle attack. As a free action, it can then start a grapple without provoking an attack of opportunity. If it wins the grapple check, it establishes a hold and can constrict.

- Psionics (Sp): A shibboleth is a powerful psionicist. Shibboleth have the following psionic abilities, usable at will: detect thoughts (DC 17), hypnotic pattern (DC 18), illusory wall (DC 20), mirage arcana (DC 21), misdirection (DC 18), programmed image (DC 22), project image (DC 23). It can psionically crush its opponents' minds, as per feeblemind (DC 20), 3 times per day.

  In addition, a shibboleth can employ the lethid psionic ability greater blast of discord (DC 19) 3 times per day.

  The save DCs for its psionics are Charisma-based. Effective caster level 12th.

- Psychic Puppets (Su): A shibboleth can control up to 10 times its Hit Dice worth of creatures that have succumbed to its mind rot. This ability has a 20-mile range.

  Taking control of or giving a command to such a creature is a free action for the shibboleth.

  A shibboleth has a telepathic link with its psychic puppets that allows it to use the puppets' senses as though they were its own. The shibboleth's complex alien intelligence allows it to process information through any number of puppets simultaneously without difficulty. The controlling shibboleth can treat a single psychic puppet it designates as its psionic conduit as an extension of its body for the purpose of determining the range of its psionic abilities, as long as it is within 1 mile. It may only designate a new psionic conduit once per hour, even if the current psionic conduit is incapacitated, dies, or leaves the shibboleth's range.

  A shibboleth will often control hundreds of creatures simultaneously, usually vermin, and have several vermin swarms guarding its lair at all times. Shibboleth have been known to control packs of dogs, dire animals, and humanoids they have afflicted with feeblemind.

- Spray (Ex): Once every 3 rounds, a shibboleth can spray a 30 ft. cone of diseased, acidic ooze. The ooze inflicts 8d6 acid damage and exposes all creatures who take damage from this attack to shibboleth mind rot disease. Creatures caught in the attack make a DC 20 Reflex save to take half damage. The save DC is Constitution-based.

- Vulnerability to Electricity (Ex): Electricity attacks deal an additional 50% damage to shibboleth. In addition, an electricity attack that deals damage in excess of the shibboleth's Constitution forces it to make a Fort save (DC equal to damage dealt) or be stunned for 1d4 rounds.

- Skills: Shibboleth have a +2 racial bonus on Concentration, Spot, Listen, and Move Silently checks.

  A shibboleth has a +8 racial bonus to Swim checks. It can always take 10 on Swim checks, even in dangerous or distracting conditions. It can also use the run action when swimming in a straight line.

  Shibboleth have a +4 racial bonus to grapple checks.

Sample Psychic Puppet

This sample uses a 4 HD rat swarm as the base creature.

Psychic Puppet Rat Swarm

Tiny Aberration (Augmented Animal Swarm)

Hit Dice:	4d8 (18 hp)
Initiative:	+2
Speed:	15 ft. (3 squares), climb 15 ft.
Armor Class:	14 (+2 size, +2 Dex) Touch 14, flat-footed 12
Base Attack/ Grapple:	+3/—
Attack:	Swarm (1d6 plus disease)
Full Attack:	Swarm (1d6 plus disease)
Space/Reach:	10 ft./0 ft.
Special Attacks:	Disease, distraction
Special Qualities:	Darkvision 60 ft., half damage from slashing and piercing, immunity to poison and disease, psionic conduit, resistance to acid 5, scent, sensitivity to electricity, shibboleth dependency, swarm traits
Saves:	Fort +4, Ref +6, Will +16
Abilities:	Str 2, Dex 15, Con 10, Int —, Wis 12, Cha 2
Skills:	Balance +10, Climb +10, Hide +14, Listen +6, Spot +7, Swim +10
Feats:	Alertness, Weapon Finesse
Environment:	Within 20 miles of controlling shibboleth
Organization:	Solitary, group (5-10 swarms), plague (11-20 swarms)
Challenge Rating:	2
Allegiances:	—
Advancement:	None

Creating a Shibboleth Psychic Puppet

Once a creature has succumbed to shibboleth mind rot, it becomes a psychic puppet that is completely under the shibboleth's control. If that shibboleth dies, so too do all its puppets.

A sentient creature converted to a psychic puppet often shows outward signs, such as a stiffness of motion, slurring of speech, etc. It can be detected by making an opposed Sense Motive check against the shibboleth's Bluff check. The shibboleth suffers a -1 penalty to its check for every mile that separates it from its puppet.

- Size and Type: The creature's type becomes aberration. Do not recalculate Hit Dice, base attack bonus, saves, or skill points. It loses any allegiance subtypes. Size is unchanged.
- Special Attacks: A psychic puppet retains all of the special attacks of the base creature except for class abilities, spells, spell-like abilities, psionics, and abilities that require an Intelligence score.
- Disease (Ex): A psychic puppet is a carrier of shibboleth mind rot. Creatures who make any physical contact with this creature or its carcass must make an immediate Fortitude saving throw or contract the disease. A creature need only make one successful save per 24 hours no matter how many times it is exposed to the disease. This disease ability applies in addition to any other disease ability the base creature normally possesses.
- Special Qualities: The psychic puppet retains all of the base creature's special qualities that do not require an Intelligence score. Psychic puppets gain the following special qualities:
  - Darkvision 60 ft.
  - Immunity to poison and disease
  - Psionic conduit (Su): The controlling shibboleth can treat a psychic puppet within 1 mile as an extension of its body for the purpose of determining the range of the shibboleth's psionic abilities. A shibboleth can only select a new psionic conduit once per hour, even if the existing one is killed or incapacitated.
  - Resistance to acid 5
  - Sensitivity to electricity (Ex): A psychic puppet that suffers electricity attack that deals damage in excess of its Constitution must make a Fort save (DC equal to damage dealt) or be stunned for 1d4 rounds.
  - Shibboleth dependency (Ex): The psychic puppet dies if its controlling shibboleth dies or if the shibboleth is more than 20 miles away.
- Saves: The puppet retains the base creature's Fortitude and Reflex saves. Substitute the controlling shibboleth's total Will save.
- Abilities: A psychic puppet retains the base creature's ability scores, except that it has no Intelligence score. Psychic puppets are immune to all mind-affecting effects.
- Skills: Psychic puppets cannot use skills with Intelligence as their key ability. It retains all of the base creature's other skill ranks.
- Feats: The puppet retains all feats except those related to Intelligence-based skills or abilities.
- Environment: Same as the controlling shibboleth.
- Organization: Solitary (shibboleth often use single spies), group (5-10), or plague (11-50, when gathered by the controlling shibboleth and depending on creature type).
- Challenge Rating: Same as base creature.
- Allegiances: —
- Advancement: Same as base creature.

Apocalyptic Era

Civilization lies in ruins and the human race, keenly aware of its diminished and vulnerable state, concentrates on survival. Humanity is fractured, frightened, and tribal. But there are whispers that man is not the only survivor. Other, greater powers are rebuilding and their reborn ambitions hold nothing but fear, pain, and a final ending for the human race. Firepower and sheer guts are humanity's best defense—but only if it can relearn the skills of peace and brotherhood burned away when the sky rained fire.

Nihileth

Her squad had hunted this creature for three days. It had cost her Jorryn, her lover and second in command. Finally, it was cornered in the great hall. Then, out it came, calmly striding to the middle of an open area. It had a grotesquely glistening ovoid head, and its humanoid body was adorned with shiny black armor and long sword not unlike Jorryn's. The first four men rushed it, two a side. In a whirling flash the creature struck each of the men a wicked blow, felling two of them. She recognized that devastating technique. It was Jorryn's. She let out a shriek of horror and dropped her own sword. The creature laughed in a horrid imitation of her former lover.

A nihileth without a sentient host resembles a flying octopus, but they are rarely seen in this vulnerable state. The nihileth are the lieutenants to the aboleth, and they command all lesser lethid. Devious strategists and ruthless taskmasters, a single nihileth can be trusted to control a large group of lesser lethid.

Possible Adventures

The Councilor calls the PCs into his office. He shows them a photograph of a cement wall on the side of a hill. Near the top, covered in vines, is a name: Paradise Bunker. He tells the PCs that the photo was found on the body of a drifter who died the day before from a bad case of tremors. The Councilor asks the PCs to backtrack along the drifter's path to find where he came from.

Paradise Bunker is in the hills only a couple hundred miles away. The PCs are welcomed into a spacious, brightly lit complex filled with healthy children and adults. The group is invited to stay for dinner, where all their questions will be answered. They are served fresh vegetables and remarkably tasty meat-like chunks from the bunker's nutrient vats. Their hostess, one of the administrators, explains that their bunker has a working reactor and enough space to grow hydroponic vegetables and livestock. The PCs are invited to stay and are given free reign of the facility, except for the lower reactor levels.

An astute observer may notice a lack of elderly people in the Bunker, and even some of the healthy adults try hard to hide a slight tremor of the hands.

The bunker is home to two nihileth who reside in the dark maintenance levels and control Paradise's access to power and water. The residents do not know what is down in the maintenance levels but have learned to do as they are instructed and have accepted the price for peace and protection. They will fiercely protect their way of life.

Periodically all the lights in the bunker go out. At this time, the residents are trained to kneel face down, hold out their hands in front of them, and remain motionless. When the lights return, one or two bunker residents are gone. The 'taken' are usually adults who developed the tremors; the sick, disabled, or disgruntled; or the strongest adult if one of the nihileth needs a new host.

In a sealed utility room in the lowest maintenance level, the nihileth have constructed a horrific temple-nursery. The nihileth carefully extract the brains of their victims, adding them to a large vat in their lair, in which tiny larval lethid squirm and compete for the fresh nutrients. The unused human remains are dumped in the nutrient vats from which the humans are fed. This chronic semi-cannibalism causes a degenerative neurological disease in the residents and is the source of their tremors.

Nihileth (Unhosted)

Small Aberration (*Evil, Extraplanar, Lethid, Native*)

Hit Dice:	6d8+6 (33 hp)
Initiative:	+2
Speed:	10 ft. (2 squares), swim 30 ft., fly 15 ft. (average)
Armor Class:	17 (+1 size, +2 Dex, +4 natural) Touch 13, flat-footed 15
Base Attack/ Grapple:	+4/+8
Attack:	Tentacle +7 melee (1d3 plus poison)
Full Attack:	4 tentacles +7 melee (1d3 plus poison)
Space/Reach:	5 ft./5 ft.
Special Attacks:	Implant, unhost, poison, psionics
Special Qualities:	Amphibious, damage reduction 5/magic, darkvision 60 ft., immunity to poison and disease, lethid traits, resistance to acid 5 and fire 5, spell resistance 18, telepathy 100 ft., vulnerability to electricity
Saves:	Fort +3, Ref +4, Will +10
Abilities:	Str 10, Dex 14, Con 12, Int 18, Wis 16, Cha 17
Skills:	Climb +5, Concentration +12, Hide +15, Intimidate +12, Knowledge (the planes) +13, Knowledge (arcana) +13, Listen +14, Sense Motive +8, Move Silently +13, Spellcraft +9 (+11 scrolls), Spot +14, Swim +9
Feats:	Ability Focus (ray of disruption), Combat Casting, Improved Grapple[B], Weapon Finesse
Environment:	Aquatic, Urban
Organization:	Solitary, pair, cadre (3-15)
Challenge Rating:	7
Allegiances:	Always Leth-Thol'Zad, evil, lethid
Advancement:	7-8 HD (Small); 9-12 HD (Medium); 13-18 HD (Large)

Combat

An unhosted nihileth employs different tactics depending on whether it is actively hunting a host. If it is searching for a host, it will attempt to stun the most mentally powerful or charismatic member of its opponents with its psionics and then attempt to implant itself as quickly as possible. If it only wants to neutralize its opponents, then it will attempt to attack its opponents with its powerful psionic abilities from a distance, only using its tentacles and devastating implant/unhost combination if it is forced into close combat or if it has incapacitated all of its opponents with its psionics.

* Unhosted nihileth get a +4 racial bonus to grapple checks.

- Implant (Ex): See description above.
- Unhost (Ex): See description above.
- Poison (Ex): Contact, Fortitude DC 16, initial and secondary damage 1d6 Wis. The save is Wisdom-based.
- Psionics (Sp): All nihileth have following abilities, usable at will—charm monster (DC 17), detect thoughts (DC 15), dimension door, hypnotism (DC 14), levitate.

  In addition, a nihileth has the phase mastery ability (DC 18) and can also employ each of the following lethid psionic abilities once every 3 rounds: ray of disruption (8d6 damage, DC 21 Fort halves), presence leech (DC 17), synaptic avalanche (DC18).

  A nihileth uses all of its psionic abilities at effective caster level 9th. All of the save DCs are Charisma-based.

  Note: There are rumors of variant nihileth which possess slightly different psionic powers akin to those of the aboleth, shibboleth, or rgleth, including aphasic flare, greater blast of discord, and overstimulation. The GM may add these abilities or replace existing ones at his discretion.
- Vulnerability to Electricity (Ex): Electricity attacks deal an additional 50% damage to nihileth. In addition, an electricity attack that deals damage in excess of the nihileth's Constitution (12, unless hosted) forces it to make a Fort save (DC equal to damage dealt) or be stunned for 1d4 rounds.
- Skills: A nihileth has a +2 racial bonus on Concentration, Listen, Move Silently, and Spot checks, as well as a +8 racial bonus to Swim checks. It can always take 10 on Swim checks, even in dangerous or distracting conditions. It can also use the run action when swimming in a straight line.

Sample Hosted Nihileth

This example uses a 9th-level Smart Hero (and magical adept) as the base creature and a 6 Hit Die nihileth as the base nihileth.

Hosted Nihileth

(9th-Level Human Smart Hero)
Medium Aberration (Augmented Humanoid, Extraplanar, Evil, Lethid, Native)

Hit Dice:	9d4+9 + 6d8+6 (66 hp)
Initiative:	+6
Speed:	30 ft. (6 squares), swim 20 ft.
Armor Class:	21 (+2 Dex, +2 natural, +5 bracers of armor +5, +2 ring of protection +2) Touch 19, flat-footed 19
Base Attack/ Grapple:	+7/+6
Attack:	Tentacle +9 melee (1d3 plus poison); or masterwork staff +7 melee (1d6-1)
Full Attack:	4 tentacles +9 melee (1d3 plus poison); or masterwork staff +7 melee (1d6-1)
Space/Reach:	5 ft./5 ft.
Special Attacks:	Poison, psionics, ray of disruption, presence leech, spells
Special Qualities:	Amphibious, damage reduction 5/magic, darkvision 60 ft., familiar, immunity to poison and disease, lethid traits, phase mastery, resistance to acid 5 and fire 5, spell resistance 18, telepathy 100 ft., unhost, sensitivity to electricity
Saves:	Fort +6, Ref +7, Will +17
Abilities:	Str 8, Dex 14, Con 13, Int 20, Wis 18, Cha 23
Skills:	Bluff +17, Concentration +24, Craft (alchemy) +10, Diplomacy +12, Intimidate +17, Knowledge (the planes) +14, Knowledge (arcana) +26, Listen +17, Sense Motive +9, Spellcraft +22 (+24 scrolls), Spot +17
Feats:	Ability Focus (ray of disruption)[B], Alertness, Combat Casting[B], Greater Spell Focus (evocation), Improved Grapple*, Improved Counterspell, Improved Initiative, Spell Focus (evocation), Weapon Finesse*
Environment:	Aquatic, Urban
Organization:	Solitary, pair
Challenge Rating:	15
Allegiances:	Always Leth-Thol'Zad, evil, lethid
Advancement:	By character class

- Typical Spells Known (save DC 16 + spell level or DC 18 + spell level, evocation]): 0—*daze, detect magic;* 1st—*expeditious retreat, magic missile, obscuring mist, ray of enfeeblement;* 2nd—*minor image, touch of idiocy;* 3rd—*dispel magic, fireball,* 4th—*greater invisibility, stoneskin.*
- Possessions: bracers of armor +5, cloak of Charisma +4, ring of protection +2, rod of metamagic (lesser empower))

Creating a Hosted Nihileth

"Hosted nihileth" is an acquired template that can be added to any aberration, dragon, giant, humanoid, magical beast, or monstrous humanoid of size Gargantuan or smaller that has a head and a single brain and an Intelligence score of at least 6.

A hosted nihileth uses all of a creature's base statistics and abilities except as noted here.

- Size and Type: The creature's type changes to aberration. Do not recalculate the creature's base attack bonus, Hit Dice, saves, or skill points. It gains the extraplanar, evil, lethid, and native subtypes. Size is unchanged.
- Speed: If the base creature does not have a swim speed, it gains a swim speed equal to 2/3 its base land speed.
- Hit Dice: Same as the base creature plus those of the base nihileth. All other HD are unchanged.
- Armor Class: The base creature's natural armor bonus improves by +2.
- Base Attack/Grapple: Add the BAB attack bonus for the base nihileth to the base attack bonus for the base creature. Hosted nihileth make all tentacle attacks as if they had Improved Grapple and Weapon Finesse.
- Attack: A hosted nihileth retains all the attacks of the base creature. It also gains four tentacle melee attacks (1d3 plus poison) that it can use as a primary attack.
- Full Attack: A hosted nihileth retains all the attacks of the base creature. It also gains 4 tentacle melee attacks (1d3 plus poison) that it can use at its primary attacks.
- Damage: The hosted nihileth's tentacle attacks do 1d3 points of damage plus poison (no Str modifier).
- Special Attacks: A hosted nihileth retains all the special attacks of the base creature, and the special attacks and psionics of the nihileth. Hosted nihileth employ all of their psionic abilities at effective caster level 12th.
- Special qualities: A hosted nihileth has all the special qualities of the base creature, plus the following:

— Damage reduction 5/magic.

— Darkvision 60 ft.

— Immunity to poison and disease

— Resistance to acid 5 and fire 5

— Spell resistance 18

— Telepathy 200 ft.

— Sensitivity to Electricity (Ex): An electricity attack that deals damage in excess of the nihileth's Constitution forces it to make a Fort save (DC equal to damage dealt) or the hosted nihileth is stunned for 1d4 rounds.

—Unhost (Ex): see description above.

- Saves: Add the base save bonuses of the base nihileth to the base save bonuses of the base creature. Hosted nihileth have a +2 racial bonus to Will saves.

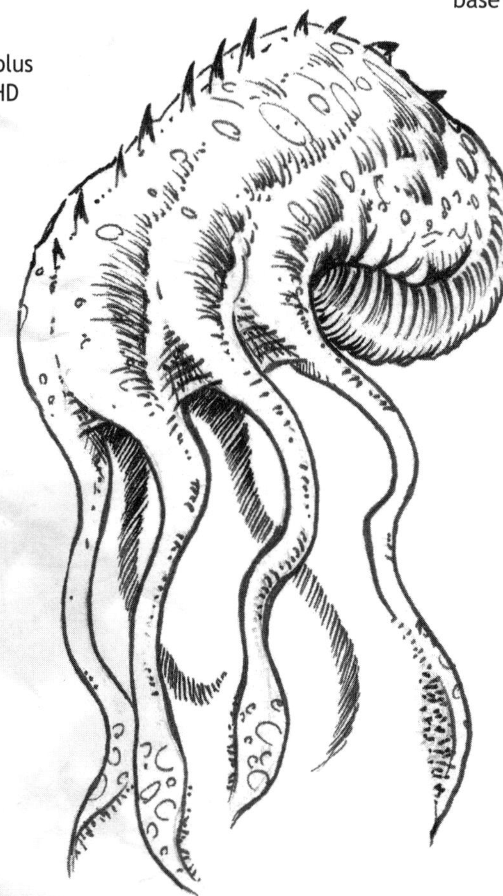

- Abilities: A hosted nihileth retains the base creature's original Strength, Dexterity, and Constitution scores. The hosted nihileth's Intelligence, Wisdom, and Charisma scores become that of the base nihileth's score +2, or that of the base creature, whichever is higher.
- Skills: A hosted nihileth retains all of the base creature's skills, or the base nihileth's ranks in Intelligence, Wisdom, or Charisma-based skills (whichever is higher). Hosted nihileth have a +2 racial bonus on Concentration, Listen, and Spot checks.
- Feats: Hosted nihileth attack with their tentacles as if they had the Improved Grab and Weapon Finesse feats. They also gain Combat Casting and Ability Focus in one of its psionic abilities (usually ray of disruption or presence leech).
- Environment: Same as the base creature and aquatic.
- Organization: Solitary, pair, cadre (3-15).
- Challenge Rating: Same as the base creature's, modified by base nihileth's HD: 6 HD to 8HD, +6; 9 HD to 11 HD, +8; 12-14 HD, +10; 15-18 HD, +12.
- Allegiances: Always Leth-Thol'Zad, evil, lethid.

INDEX

Open Game License Version 1.0a

blown away is knocked down and rolls 1d4 x 10 feet, taking 1d4 points of nonlethal damage per 10 feet. A flying creature that is blown away is blown back 2d6 x 10 feet and takes 2d6 points of nonlethal damage due to battering and buffering.

Checked
Prevented from achieving forward motion by an applied force, such as wind. Checked creatures on the ground merely stop. Checked flying creatures move back a distance specified in the description of the effect.

Confused
A confused character's actions are determined by rolling d10 at the beginning of his turn:

1	Attack last perceived threat with melee or ranged weapons (or close with target if attacking is not possible)
2	Act normally
3-5	Do nothing but babble incoherently
6-7	Flee away from last perceived target at top possible speed
8-10	Attack nearest creature

A confused character who can't carry out the indicated action does nothing but babble incoherently. Attackers are not at any special advantage when attacking a confused character. Any confused character who is attacked automatically attacks its attackers on its next turn, as long as it is still confused when its turn comes. A confused character does not make attacks of opportunity against any creature that it is not already devoted to attacking (either because of its most recent action or because it has just been attacked).

Cowering
The character is frozen in fear and can take no actions. A cowering character takes a –2 penalty to Armor Class and loses her Dexterity bonus (if any).

Crippled
A crippled creature's movement is impaired. The creature's movement rate is reduced to one-half and the creature cannot charge or run. A creature can be crippled in one form of movement (for example, flight) while maintaining full mobility in another form of movement (e.g. ground).

Dazed
The creature is unable to act normally. A dazed creature can take no actions, but has no penalty to AC.

A dazed condition typically lasts 1 round.

Dazzled
The creature is unable to see well because of overstimulation of the eyes. A dazzled creature takes a -1 penalty on attack rolls, Search checks, and Spot checks.

Dead
The character's hit points are reduced to –10 or less, his Constitution drops to 0, or he is killed outright by some effect. The character's soul leaves his body. Dead characters cannot benefit from healing. A dead body decays normally unless preserved.

Deafened
A deafened character cannot hear. She takes a –4 penalty on initiative checks, automatically fails Listen checks, and has a 20% chance of spell failure when casting spells with verbal components. Characters who remain deafened for a long time grow accustomed to these drawbacks and can overcome some of them.

Disabled
A character with 0 hit points, with negative hit points that do not yet exceed his Constitution modifier, or one who has negative hit points but has become stable and conscious, is *disabled*. A *disabled* character may take a single move action or standard action each round (but not both, nor can she take full-round actions). She moves at half speed. Taking move actions doesn't risk further injury, but performing any standard action (or any other action the DM deems strenuous, including some free actions such as casting a quickened spell) deals 1 point of damage after the completion of the act. Unless the action increased the *disabled* character's hit points, she is now in negative hit points and *dying*.

A *disabled* character with negative hit points recovers hit points naturally if she is being helped. Otherwise, each day she must make a Fortitude save (DC20) to start recovering hit points naturally (starting with that day); otherwise, she loses 1 hit point. Once an unaided character starts recovering hit points naturally, she is no longer in danger of losing hit points (even if her current hit points are negative).

Dying
A *dying* character is unconscious and near death. A *dying* character can take no actions and is unconscious. At the end of each round (starting with the round in which the character was *disabled*), he must make a Fortitude save (DC20) to see whether he becomes stable. If he does not, he loses 1 hit point.

Energy Drained
The character gains one or more negative levels, which might permanently drain the character's levels. If the subject has at least as many negative levels as Hit Dice, he dies. Each negative level gives a creature the following penalties: –1 penalty on attack rolls, saving throws, skill checks, ability checks; loss of 5 hit points; and –1 to effective level (for determining the power, duration, DC, and other details of spells or special abilities).

Entangled
The character is ensnared. Being entangled impedes movement, but does not entirely prevent it unless the bonds are anchored to an immobile object or tethered by an opposing force. An entangled creature moves at half speed, cannot run or charge, and takes a -2 penalty on all attack rolls and a -4 penalty to Dexterity. An entangled character who attempts to cast a spell must make a Concentration check (DC 15 + the spell's level) or lose the spell.

Exhausted
An exhausted character moves at half speed and takes a -6 penalty to Strength and Dexterity. After 1 hour of complete rest, an exhausted character becomes fatigued. A fatigued character becomes exhausted by doing something else that would normally cause fatigue.

Fascinated
A fascinated creature is entranced by a supernatural or spell effect. The creature stands or sits quietly, taking no actions other than to pay attention to the fascinating effect, for as long as the effect lasts. It takes a -4 penalty on skill checks made as reactions, such as Listen and Spot checks. Any potential threat, such as a hostile creature approaching, allows the fascinated creature a new saving throw against the fascinating effect. Any obvious threat, such as someone drawing a weapon, casting a spell, or aiming a ranged weapon at the fascinated creature, automatically breaks the effect. A fascinated creature's ally may shake it free of the spell as a standard action.

Fatigued:
A fatigued character can neither run nor charge and takes a -2 penalty to Strength and Dexterity. Doing anything that would normally cause fatigue causes the fatigued character to become exhausted. After 8 hours of complete rest, fatigued characters are no longer fatigued.

Flat-Footed
A character who has not yet acted during a combat is flat-footed, not yet reacting normally to the situation. A flat-footed character loses his Dexterity bonus to AC (if any) and cannot make attacks of opportunity.

Frightened
A frightened creature flees from the source of its fear as best it can. If unable to flee, it may fight. A frightened creature takes a -2 penalty on all attack rolls, saving throws, skill checks, and ability checks. A frightened creature can use special abilities, including spells, to flee; indeed, the creature must use such means if they are the only way to escape.

Frightened is like shaken, except that the creature must flee if possible. Panicked is a more extreme state of fear. A character who is frightened and suffers a shaken or frightened result again is panicked.

Grappling
Engaged in wrestling or some other form of hand-to-hand struggle with one or more attackers. A grappling character can undertake only a limited number of actions. He does not threaten any squares, and loses his Dexterity bonus to AC (if any) against opponents he isn't grappling.

Helpless
A helpless character is paralyzed, held, bound, sleeping, unconscious, or otherwise completely at an opponent's mercy. A helpless target is treated as having a Dexterity of 0 (-5 modifier). Melee attacks against a helpless target get an additional +4 bonus (equivalent to attacking a prone target). Ranged attacks gets no special bonus against helpless targets. You can use the sneak attack talent against helpless targets.

As a full-round action, an enemy can use a melee weapon to deliver a coup de grace to a helpless foe. An enemy can also use a ranged weapon, provided he is adjacent to the target. The attacker automatically hits and scores a critical hit. If the defender survives, he must make a Fortitude save (DC 10 + damage dealt) or die.

Delivering a coup de grace provokes attacks of opportunity.

Creatures that are immune to critical hits do not take critical damage, nor do they need to make Fortitude saves to avoid being killed by a coup de grace.

Incorporeal
Having no physical body. Incorporeal creatures are immune to all non-magical attack forms. They can be harmed only by other incorporeal creatures, +1 or better magic weapons, spells, spell-like effects, or supernatural effects.

Invisible
Visually undetectable. An invisible creature gains a +2 bonus on attack rolls against sighted opponents, and ignores its opponents' Dexterity bonuses to AC (if any).

Knocked Down
Depending on their size, creatures can be knocked down by winds of high velocity. Creatures on the ground are knocked prone by the force of the wind. Flying creatures are instead blown back 1d6 x 10 feet.

Nauseated
Experiencing stomach distress. Nauseated creatures are unable to attack, cast spells, concentrate on spells, or do anything else requiring attention. The only action such a character can take is a single move action per turn.

Panicked
A panicked creature must drop anything it holds and flee at top speed from the source of its fear, as well as any other dangers it encounters, along a random path. It can't take any other actions. In addition, the creature takes a -2 penalty on all saving throws, skill checks, and ability checks. If cornered, a panicked creature cowers and does not attack, typically using the total defense action in combat. A panicked creature can use special abilities, including spells, to flee; indeed, the creature must use such means if they are the only way to escape.

Panicked is a more extreme state of fear than shaken or frightened.

Paralyzed
A paralyzed character is frozen in place and unable to move or act. A paralyzed character has effective Dexterity and Strength scores of 0 and is helpless, but can take purely mental actions. A winged creature flying in the air at the time that it becomes paralyzed cannot flap its wings and falls. A paralyzed swimmer can't swim and may drown. A creature can move through a space occupied by a paralyzed creature—ally or not. Each square occupied by a paralyzed creature, however, counts as 2 squares.

Petrified
A petrified character has been literally turned to stone and is considered unconscious. If a petrified character cracks or breaks, but the broken pieces are joined with the body as he returns to flesh, he is unharmed. If the character's petrified body is incomplete when it returns to flesh, the body is likewise incomplete and there is some amount of permanent hit point loss and/or debilitation.

Pinned
Held immobile (but not helpless) in a grapple.

Prone
The character is on the ground. An attacker who is prone has a -4 penalty on melee attack rolls and cannot use a ranged weapon (except for a crossbow or firearm). A defender who is prone gains a +4 bonus to Armor Class against ranged attacks, but takes a -4 penalty to AC against melee attacks.

Standing up is a move-equivalent action that provokes an attack of opportunity.

Shaken
A shaken character takes a -2 penalty on attack rolls, saving throws, skill checks, and ability checks.

Shaken is a less severe state of fear than frightened or panicked. A character who is already shaken and becomes shaken again is frightened. A character who is shaken and becomes frightened is panicked.

Sickened
The character takes a -2 penalty on all attack rolls, weapon damage rolls, saving throws, skill checks, and ability checks.

Stable
A character who was *dying* but who has stopped losing hit points and still has negative hit points is stable. The character is no longer *dying*, but is still unconscious. If the character has become stable because of aid from another character (such as a Heal check or magical healing), then the character no longer loses hit points. He has a chance each hour of becoming conscious and *disabled* (even though his hit points are still negative).

If the character became stable on his own and hasn't had help, he is still at risk of losing hit points. Each hour, he has a 10% chance of becoming conscious and *disabled*. Otherwise he loses 1 hit point.

Staggered
A character whose nonlethal damage exactly equals his current hit points is staggered. A staggered character may take a single move action or standard action each round (but not both, nor can she take full-round actions).

A character whose current hit points exceed his nonlethal damage is no longer staggered; a character whose nonlethal damage exceeds his hit points becomes unconscious.

Stunned
A stunned creature drops everything held, can't take actions, takes a -2 penalty to AC, and loses his Dexterity bonus to AC (if any).

Turned
Affected by a turn undead attempt. Turned undead cower, flee, or are shaken.

Unconscious
Knocked out and helpless. Unconsciousness can result from having current hit points between -1 and -9, or from nonlethal damage in excess of current hit points.

Hazardous Environments

Acid

Corrosive acid deals 1d6 points of damage per round of exposure except in the case of total immersion (such as into a vat of acid), which deals 10d6 points of damage per round. An attack with acid, such as from a hurled vial or a monster's spittle, counts as a round of exposure.

The fumes from most acids are inhaled poisons. Those who come close enough to a large body of acid to dunk a creature in it must make a DC 13 Fortitude save or take 1 point of Constitution damage. All such characters must make a second save 1 minute later or take another 1d4 points of Constitution damage.

Creatures immune to acid's caustic properties might still drown in it if they are totally immersed (see Drowning).

Cold

Cold and exposure deal nonlethal damage to the victim. This nonlethal damage cannot be recovered until the character gets out of the cold and warms up again.

Once rendered unconscious through the accumulation of nonlethal damage, the cold and exposure begins to deal lethal damage at the same rate.

A character with the Survival skill may receive a bonus to the saving throw for cold exposure, and may be able to apply this bonus to other characters as well (see the skill description).

An unprotected character in cold weather (below 40° F) must make a Fortitude save each hour (DC 15, + 1 per previous check) or take 1d6 points of nonlethal damage.

In conditions of severe cold or exposure (below 0° F), an unprotected character must make a Fortitude save once every 10 minutes (DC 15, +1 per previous check), taking 1d6 points of nonlethal damage on each failed save.

Extreme cold (below -20° F) deals 1d6 points of lethal damage per minute (no save), and 1d4 points of nonlethal damage (Fortitude save DC15 + 1 per previous check negates).

A character who takes any nonlethal damage from cold or exposure is beset by frostbite or hypothermia (treat as fatigued). These penalties end when the character recovers the nonlethal damage taken from the cold and exposure.

Those wearing metal armor or coming into contact with very cold metal take 1d4 points of lethal damage per round of contact.

Snow

Falling snow has the same effects on visibility, ranged weapon attacks, and skill checks as rain, and it costs 2 squares of movement to enter a snow-covered square. A day of snowfall leaves 1d6 inches of snow on the ground.

Heavy Snow

Heavy snow has the same effects as normal snowfall, but also restricts visibility as fog does (see Fog, below). A day of heavy snow leaves 1d4 feet of snow on the ground, and it costs 4 squares of movement to enter a square covered with heavy snow. Heavy snow accompanied by strong or severe winds may result in snowdrifts 1d4×5 feet deep, especially in and around objects big enough to deflect the wind—a cabin or a large tent, for instance. There is a 10% chance that a heavy snowfall is accompanied by lightning (see Thunderstorm, below). Snow has the same effect on flames as moderate wind.

Sleet

Essentially frozen rain, sleet has the same effect as rain while falling (except that its chance to extinguish protected flames is 75%) and the same effect as snow once on the ground.

Hail

Hail does not reduce visibility, but the sound of falling hail makes Listen checks more difficult (-4 penalty). Sometimes (5% chance) hail can become large enough to deal 1 point of lethal damage (per storm) to anything in the open. Once on the ground, hail has the same effect on movement as snow.

Ice

Characters walking on ice must spend 2 squares of movement to enter a square covered by ice, and the DC for Balance and Tumble checks increases by +5. Characters in prolonged contact with ice may run the risk of taking damage from severe cold (see above).

Avalanches

Avalanches are a deadly peril in many mountainous areas. While avalanches of snow and ice are common, it's also possible to have an avalanche of rock and soil.

An avalanche can be spotted from as far away as 1d10×500 feet downslope by a character who makes a DC 20 Spot check, treating the avalanche as a Colossal creature. If all characters fail their Spot checks to determine the encounter distance, the avalanche moves closer to them, and they automatically become aware of it when it closes to half the original distance. It's possible to hear an avalanche coming even if you can't see it. Under optimum conditions (no other loud noises occurring), a character